Charles D. Fletcher holds a Ph.D. in Islamic Studies from McGill University. He specializes in Islamic thought, comparative religion and interfaith relations.

ISMAI'L AL-FARUQI
(1921-1986)

MUSLIM-CHRISTIAN ENGAGEMENT IN THE TWENTIETH CENTURY

The Principles of Interfaith Dialogue
and the Work of Isma'il al-Faruqi

CHARLES D. FLETCHER

I.B. TAURIS

LONDON · NEW YORK

Published in 2015 by I.B.Tauris & Co
Ltd 6 Salem Road, London W2 4BU
175 Fifth Avenue, New York NY 10010
www.ibtauris.com

Distributed in the United States and Canada
Exclusively by Palgrave Macmillan
175 Fifth Avenue, New York NY 10010

Library of Middle East History 59

ISBN 978 1 84885 509 0

A full CIP record for this book is available from the British Library
A full CIP record for this book is available from the Library of Congress

Library of Congress catalog card: available

Printed and bound by CPI Group (UK) Ltd, Croydon, CR0 4YY
from camera-ready copy edited and supplied by the author

For my Mother and Father

CONTENTS

CONTENTS

ABBREVIATIONS

AAR	American Academy of Religion
ADC	American-Arab Anti-Discrimination Committee
AJISS	*American Journal of Islamic Social Sciences*
AMSS	American Muslim Social Scientists (now known as NAAIMS)
CIIR	Central Institute of Islamic Research (Karachi, Pakistan)
EI²	*Encyclopaedia of Islam* (2nd edition)
GCWR	Global Congress of the World's Religions
ICMR	*Islam and Christian Muslim Relations*
IHAS	Institute of Higher Arabic Studies (Cairo University)
IIFSO	International Islamic Federation of Student Organizations
IIIT	International Institute of Islamic Thought
IIU	International Islamic University
IMA	Islamic Medical Association
IRPC	Inter-Religious Peace Colloquium
ISNA	Islamic Society of North America
JDL	Jewish Defence League
MJCC	Muslim-Jewish-Christian Conference
MSA	Muslim Students Association
NAAIMS	North American Association of Islamic and Muslim Studies
NAIT	North American Islamic Trust
NCC	National Council of Churches
NCCC	National Council of Churches of Christ
NIV	*New International Version of the Bible*
PPBox	Personal papers of al-Faruqi housed at IIIT and itemized by year in file boxes
WCC	World Council of Churches

ACKNOWLEDGEMENTS

Every academic work reflects the contributions of many people. A special thanks to my Professors at the Institute of Islamic Studies at McGill University, Robert Wisnovsky, Donald P. Little, Eric Ormsby, Issa Boullata, Wael Hallaq, Üner Turgay and Sajida Alvi. McGill University and the Institute of Islamic Studies also offered fellowships, travel grants, research funding and teaching opportunities all of which made this work possible. The course of research was greatly assisted by Hisham Altalib and Iqbal Yunus at the International Institute of Islamic Thought in Herndon, VA. Not only did they make available Isma'il al-Faruqi's personal papers, but they also offered insights from their own recollections. Special thanks also to John L. Esposito and Hasan Hanafi who offered their time for interviews and for their willingness to share their memories of al-Faruqi. Other colleagues offered insights or read various chapters, including Md Salleh Yaapar, Ibrahim Mohamed Zein, Yushau Sodiq, Seth Ward, Maurice Boutin and Fady Shehata. I am particularly appreciative of John L. Esposito, Imtiyaz Yusuf and Steve Millier who read and commented on the final manuscript. Lastly, I want to thank and honour my parents for their encouragement and support over the years.

INTRODUCTION

Within the last century, much has been written about Christian-Muslim dialogue and interaction.[1] In an effort to supersede the history of polemic and debate between the two faiths various thinkers and institutions have initiated projects of interfaith dialogue and study. The vast majority of these participants have been Christian, whether as individual authors or as institutions, such as the Vatican or the World Council of Churches (WCC). Indeed, Christians, reflecting a growing sense of pluralism and secularism in the West, have initiated much of the post-World War II interactions. Of the contemporary Muslim writers who have entered into the stream of dialogue only a few are well-known to both Muslims and Christians in the West. These include Seyyed Hossein Nasr, Tariq Ramadan, Mahmoud Ayoub, Hasan Askari, Khurshid Ahmad, Mohammed Talbi, Hasan Hanafi, Akbar Ahmed and Isma'il al-Faruqi.[2] Of these, the most systematic attempt to articulate a theoretical basis for dialogue was made by al-Faruqi, primarily through his various publications and his willingness to apply his theories in active dialogue and debate.[3]

Isma'il al-Faruqi[4] (1921-1986) was an Arab Palestinian exile who contextualised his faith in the West and emerged as a passionate activist-scholar intent on preparing the Muslim *ummah* (community) to engage the western world. He spent most of his long academic career engaging in various forms of interfaith study and dialogue from a Muslim perspective until he and his wife Lois were murdered in 1986.

The importance and role of al-Faruqi in the field of religious dialogue is sometimes overshadowed by his reputation as a tenacious and unyielding interlocutor.[5] However, the significance of his place in Muslim study and engagement of Christianity is recognised, but as yet not studied in detail. Anyone setting out to write on the contemporary environment of Muslim-Christian dialogue will inevitably wind their way toward al-Faruqi. Kate Zebiri, in her book *Muslims and Christians*

Face to Face, comments on the dearth of contemporary Muslim specialists in the study of Christianity and notes that al-Faruqi has thus far produced the most exhaustive Islamic treatment of Christianity by a Western Muslim.[6] Jane I. Smith agrees, recognising that he was one of the most active Muslims in interfaith work and a major contributor to its development, even a kind of "Muslim father of the dialogue."[7] Kenneth Cragg (1913-2012) who knew and engaged him in dialogue, writes: "It will be fair to say that there are few Muslims in the realm of Muslim, Jewish, Christian dialogue who, from mid-to-late twentieth-century, have served and stirred it more spiritedly than Isma'il al-Faruqi."[8] Zafar Ishaq Ansari goes even further, citing al-Faruqi as the dominant Muslim figure in comparative religion in the last (twentieth) century.[9] John L. Esposito reflecting upon al-Faruqi's career adds that: "He was a major force in Islam's dialogue with other world religions"; and "His writings, speeches and participation and leadership role in interreligious meetings and organizations ... made him the most visible and prolific Muslim contributor to the dialogue of world religions."[10] Finally, Jacques Waardenburg, in a discussion about Muslims who study religion, notes: "... a scholarly monograph on al-Faruqi's work in its context is needed."[11] Our intention is not only to contribute to fulfilling this need, that is, to study the contextual development of one prominent Muslim intellectual's methodological approach to non-Muslims, but also to assess its usefulness.

To this end we will critically examine al-Faruqi's methodology of engagement with non-Muslims, investigate its practical applications, and explore reasons why he spent a lifetime involved in religious dialogue. In essence the heart of our investigation revolves around the contextual development of the man, the scholar and the participant in dialogue. As Kenneth Cragg wisely observes: "... it will always be important to seek the text of life as well as the text of the writing."[12] Thus, attention is particularly focused on al-Faruqi's life in relation to his thought.

We are approaching al-Faruqi's thought from a comparative religious studies perspective. This seems entirely appropriate as al-Faruqi himself during his three-year research fellowship at McGill University (1958-1961), under the partial direction of Wilfred Cantwell Smith (1916-2000) and the School of Divinity, completed his study of Judaism and Christianity within an atmosphere of comparative religious study. Al-Faruqi will be allowed to present his ideas through carefully documenting his writings and development of thought as he matured and tested his ideas. To accomplish this, *epoché* (suspension of judgment) will be practised to allow as much as possible his voice to be heard before any attempt is made to analyse his ideas. This is not a new approach, but something practised during centuries of Islamic philosophy, *kalām* (speculative theology) and various kinds of Islamic works on refutation. One first seeks to accurately summarise and understand another's thought before embarking on a critique. For example, al-Ghazālī's (1058-1111) sympathetic summation of philosophy in his *Maqāṣid al-falāsifah* (The Aims of the Philosophers) led to his later critical work entitled, *Tahāfut al-falāsifah* (The Inconsistency of the Philosophers).

This book is divided into three parts. Since his academic career spanned almost thirty years, the contextual factors that shaped and informed his thought such as his own identity issues as an Arab, a Palestinian and a Muslim in the West and his willingness to engage in dialogue and ecumenical meetings are explored first. Thus in Part One, his biography (Chapter 1) and the development of his life and thought (Chapter 2) are presented. The latter chapter provides a detailed examination of the person of al-Faruqi using the identity theory of Marya Schechtman to uncover some of the reasons why interfaith study and dialogue were important to him and to provide a context for his work.[13] Part Two traces the contextual development of his thought by systematically working through his writings and the opportunities he had to engage non-Muslims. This section (chapters 3-5) charts his early work leading to his theoretical model for interfaith dialogue including the reception of his ideas by non-Muslim. In Part Three, we present a critical assessment of his ideas (Chapter 6) where an analysis is offered not only of his presuppositions and method, but also of the overall theoretical and practical viability of his approach for Christians and Muslims. The first assesses the theoretical feasibility of his ideas in terms of the conceptual elements including internal coherence, his presuppositions and the overall cogency of his method. The second examines the practical aspects of the application of his ideas as he presented these in his writings and in his various interfaith discussions. Here attention is focused on the application of his method and its observed usefulness in promoting and sustaining such dialogue. The final chapter examines al-Faruqi's contributions to the future of interfaith dialogue between Muslims and primarily Christians.

PART ONE

THE LIFE AND THOUGHT OF ISMAʿIL AL-FARUQI

1

A BIOGRAPHY OF ISMAʿIL AL-FARUQI

In order to understand the thought of al-Faruqi, the first task is to study his life. Since our broader objective is to grasp the development of his approach to non-Muslims and not just the approach itself, some effort needs to be spent to determine who al-Faruqi was as a man and a scholar. This is approached from two directions. First, in this chapter, his biography is presented in descriptive form summarizing what can be termed the 'facts' of his life. This entails a chronological account. It is not exhaustive, but is sufficiently detailed to allow for the necessary contextual background in which to situate his thought. Second, in the following chapter, we will try to answer who he thought he was and how he projected his identity to others. This is a difficult task, but the insights it can potentially provide will allow us to peer into his life in order to better understand his choices as a scholar, including the development of his ideas toward engaging non-Muslims. For example, during his life it was relatively rare to find a Muslim scholar who was so interested and devoted academically to the comparative study of Christianity and Judaism and who also sought to actively participate in various forms of dialogue. There must be reasons why this was so important to him. The answer begins with his biography.

Life in Palestine

Ismaʿil Raji Abu l-Huda al-Faruqi, born January 1ˢᵗ 1921 in Jaffa, Palestine, was the son of ʿAbd al-Huda al-Faruqi, a *qāḍī* of the Sharīʿah court during the British Mandate.[1] The family was well-known and influential, with roots in the Ramleh region.[2] Ismaʿil al-Faruqi received his early education from his father and the local mosque school.[3] In 1926, he entered the French Dominican College des Frères (St. Joseph) and received his high school diploma in 1936.[4] By the time he was fifteen years old he was fluent in Arabic and French and had received his first exposure to Christianity.[5] The following year he was admitted to the College of Arts and Sciences at the American University in Beirut (AUB), where he studied English and went on thereafter to complete a B.A. with a major in Philosophy.[6] Stanley Brice Frost (1913-2013), in his foreword to al-Faruqi's *Christian Ethics*, notes that Isma'il's first year at university was unsuccessful. Frost writes:

> Nothing is more indicative of his future career than the way in which he sat down to analyze his failure and to discover that his former method of learning – by rote – was of little use to him in the new strange world of the western university.[7]

Having completed his undergraduate degree in 1941, al-Faruqi received an appointment as Assistant to the Registrar of Arab Cooperative Societies under the British Mandate government in Jerusalem in 1942.[8] Then he became an administrative officer and in 1945, at twenty-four years of age, he was promoted to the post of district magistrate (*ḥākim*) for the Galilee district.[9] This came to an abrupt end with the creation of Israel in 1948 rendering him, according to Braibanti, the final Palestinian governor of the region.[10] His family fled to Beirut and in due course al-Faruqi decided to pursue graduate studies in the United States.[11] Al-Faruqi himself, in a letter dated just prior to his death in 1986, writes of this time:

> When the Rescue Army (*Jaysh al-Inqādh*) was set up, I was working as an administrative magistrate (*ḥākim*) in the northern regions which were occupied by the army until they fell into the enemy's hands. By then I had gone to the U.S. for studies.[12]

Shafiq comments that when Israel was created in 1948, al-Faruqi joined the armed struggle against Israel:

> Consumed with a desire for revenge, al Faruqi took up arms against the Israeli occupation and saw action in the field. Disappointed by Muslim disunity and internal division, he gradually made his way to the United States.[13]

This was a highly significant moment in his life and Hisham Altalib largely confirms the comments made by Shafiq.[14] Al-Faruqi seems to indicate that he was present when the Rescue Army was set up, but by the time the region fell into enemy hands (the Israeli forces), he had left the area. Any armed involvement on his part must have preceded the establishment of the Rescue Army.

Life in North America and academia

In the fall semester of 1948, al-Faruqi entered the Graduate School of Arts and Sciences at Indiana University.[15] Here he worked on a Master's degree in Philosophy and also met and later married Lois Ibsen who was working on a Master's degree in Music.[16] In 1949, he graduated with a thesis entitled, *The ethics of reason and the ethics of life (Kantian and Nietzchean ethics)*. Desiring further studies, he was accepted into Harvard in 1950 and after passing the preliminary written examination, the special topical exam in ethics and value theory and fulfilling the residence requirements, was forced to withdraw due to a lack of finances.[17] For his efforts he was awarded an M.A. degree in Philosophy in 1951. Needing to support himself he managed to work as a translator for the American Council of Learned Societies where he received $1000 USD to translate three books from Arabic into English.[18] He then turned to contract building where he prospered in his specialty of providing fully decorated and furnished homes for sale.[19] Once he decided that he had earned sufficient funds, he left this potentially lucrative career in order to re-enter academia.[20] Enrolling in the Ph.D. programme at Indiana University he graduated in 1952 with a dissertation entitled, *On Justifying the Good: Metaphysics and Epistemology of Value*. John Esposito noted that during al-Faruqi's academic years in the U.S., he struggled to support himself[21] and there is some indication that even during his Ph.D. studies at Indiana he continued to work as a carpenter.[22]

Once finished, like many recently graduated doctoral students, he found there was a scarcity of employment in his field.[23] So, he sought out opportunities for post-doctoral studies. He went to the Middle East with Lois in 1953 and received a Rockefeller Foundation fellowship to study Islam and Islamic intellectual history at al-Azhar University in Cairo from 1954-1958.[24] Lois studied Arabic.[25] With the completion of this fellowship, he was invited by W. C. Smith to study at McGill University's Institute of Islamic Studies (1958-1959). Fazlur Rahman, who was teaching at the Institute and met al-Faruqi for the first time in 1958, writes: "Professor W. C. Smith invited him [al-Faruqi] to McGill on a senior Fellowship hoping that he would apply his training in philosophic thought to Islamic materials."[26] However, it appears that al-Faruqi demonstrated little interest in applying his intellectual training to classical Islamic texts.[27] He spent the year as a Research Associate involved in lecturing, studying and working on his theory of Arabism.[28] There is no support for the speculation offered by Quraishi that the reason W. C. Smith invited al-Faruqi to study at McGill was to persuade him to become a Christian.[29] This would certainly have been out character for either Smith or the Institute of Islamic Studies itself, which was founded to foster mutual understanding between Muslims and Christians.[30]

Toward the end of his one-year fellowship, W. C. Smith thought to offer him "some kind of an indefinite job" such as "some sort of Associate Professorship".[31] In the end, a two-year Rockefeller Foundation Fellowship was arranged for him to become a fellow of the Faculty of Divinity at McGill.[32] The Dean of Divinity at the time, Stanley Frost, who readily welcomed the idea, recollects:

> It was while he [al-Faruqi] was in the Institute as a Research Associate that his breadth of understanding for western culture and his innate sympathy for Islamic thought, as well as his evident sincerity of religious concern, suggested to Professor Wilfred Cantwell Smith, then Director of the Institute, that Dr. Fārūqī should be attached for two years to the faculty of Divinity as a Research Associate, to have the experience of living in a Christian environment and of bringing a critical if friendly Muslim mind to bear upon current theological trends.[33]

He spent these two years attending lectures, seminars, reading widely, and researching his book *Christian Ethics*.[34]

During his time at McGill, he became close friends with Fazlur Rahman.[35] He would on many occasions drive Rahman to McGill University.[36] When the latter accepted a position at the Central Institute of Islamic Research (CIIR), newly created by the Pakistani government, he asked then director Dr. I. H. Qureshi to offer a two-year appointment to Dr. al-Faruqi.[37] Thus, from 1961-1963 al-Faruqi served as Professor of Islamic Studies in Karachi, Pakistan and was involved in the development of the Institute's journal, *Islamic Studies*. Rahman commented that his motive in recruiting al-Faruqi was to allow him to see a large body of Muslims who were not Arabs.[38] However, al-Faruqi's theory of Arabism drew strong criticism from inside and outside of the

Institute.[39] For example, when he was invited to Egypt to deliver a series of lectures and perhaps in anticipation of the potentially negative response to his theory of Arabism, he encouraged Rahman to join him in Cairo. He writes: "Personally, I would not like at all to go without you, since your presence will give me a great support in advocating the thesis of Arabism to people whose thinking must needs be re-islamized."[40] During this period, he represented his department through a number of lectures at Cairo's Institute of Higher Arabic Studies (IHAS) (1962), al-Azhar (1962), and the University of Cairo (1963).[41] It is interesting to note the types of lectures he was asked to present revolved around Islam and its place within the wider political and religious world. At the Institute of Higher Arabic Studies he was invited to give ten lectures on the relation of Islam to Nationalism, at al-Azhar twenty lectures on the history of religion in the Near East and ten lectures at the University of Cairo on comparative religion.[42] He also joined Rahman in a lecture series on the relation of Islam to Nationalism at IHAS in 1963 and likewise presented on Zionism and universalism in the Old Testament.[43]

By 1963, growing disillusioned with the direction of the CIIR, al-Faruqi tendered his resignation and sought a position back in the United States.[44] He was offered and accepted a one-year appointment for the academic year 1963-1964 as visiting Professor of History of Religion at the University of Chicago's Divinity school.[45] The following year (1964) he secured an Associate Professorship at Syracuse University's department of Religion where he taught Islamic Studies and the History of Religion until 1968.[46] In that same year, Temple University obtained his services as Professor in the department of Religion.[47] There he founded the Islamic Studies programme and demonstrated an intense commitment to his students. In fact, students became a central focus for him - whether his own graduate students or the wider Muslim student community in the form of the Muslim Students Association (MSA).

During his tenure at Temple, al-Faruqi recruited numerous Muslim students, found them scholarships, and undertook to care for and mentor them. John Esposito, who became al-Faruqi's first doctoral student in 1968, recalled that he went well beyond the usual professor-student relationship. He would meet them at the airport, find housing, funding and help in numerous ways, and even hosted an annual picnic. Esposito writes: "Ismaʿil seemed tireless in his recruitment of students and he and Lamya' spent many an afternoon or evening entertaining them at his home."[48] Others including Quraishi, Braibanti, Shafiq, and Dr. Wright, a colleague at Temple, echo this sentiment.[49] He especially enjoyed securing scholarships for students. Braibanti comments that: "He would ask the universities abroad to send him a good Muslim student, and he would take care of their intellectual growth."[50] He also attracted numerous graduate students from the U.S., as Dr. Esposito readily attests from his own personal experience.[51]

Aside from his own students, he became involved in the Muslim Students Association (MSA).[52] There is some question as to when he first came in contact with MSA, but it seems clear that by 1965 he knew of and had become involved in providing leadership to the organisation.[53] An active chapter existed at Temple and his involvement was deeply appreciated and important.[54] Since this experience proved foundational for him it will be revisited in the next chapter.

Academic interests and pursuits

Al-Faruqi displayed a wide and vibrant interest in numerous projects. Once settled at Temple University, he began to undertake a number of activities, from lecturing and consulting to initiating, founding and participating in various organisations. His commitment to reviving and reforming the Muslim *ummah* first took shape during his days at McGill, continued at the Central Institute for Islamic Research in Pakistan and then blossomed at Temple where he implemented the Islamic Studies programme in the Department of Religion. His involvement and leadership in MSA was a natural outcome and led him into a wider Muslim student population beyond those who were studying under him.

The concept of the Islamization of knowledge, first presented by 'AbdulHamid AbuSulayman in his work on reforming Muslim thought and methodology in the late 1960s and early 1970s, provided al-Faruqi with the idea of an institutional means through which to effect Muslim reform.[55] Ba-Yunus writes: "This concept became a driving force in Ismāʿīl's activist career, particularly in the formation of the AMSS."[56] Now known as the North American Association of Islamic and Muslim Studies (NAAIMS), the American Muslim Social Scientists (AMSS) was founded in 1972 with al-Faruqi as its first President (1972-1978, 1980-1982) and was created partially in response to the changing demographics of the MSA.[57] A number of Muslim students who graduated remained in the USA and Canada to pursue professional careers and there was a growing need for some forum beyond the MSA. Prior to the AMSS, the Islamic Medical Association (IMA) was founded in 1967 and the Association of Muslim Scientists and Engineers also came into existence in 1969.[58] In the 1980s the AMSS was joined by the Islamic Society of North America (ISNA). Again Ba-Yunus writes that for al-Faruqi the AMSS was an organisation whose aim was to introduce "a new strain of social science in the world of modern academia."[59] This led directly into the founding of one of al-Faruqi's most enduring projects.

In 1981, ten years after the creation of the AMSS, he helped to create the International Institute of Islamic Thought (IIIT) at Herndon, Virginia, which moved beyond the social science objectives of the AMSS as well as the borders of North America.[60] He worked to outline, articulate and promote Islamic methodologies and appropriation of knowledge in order to address the epistemological dilemma confronting Islam, using criteria "internally generated by an Islamic value system."[61] Al-Faruqi's vision also included establishing an Islamic university in the USA, but this project was never completely fulfilled. In its stead the American Islamic College was founded in Chicago, where he acted as its first president and advisor. His commitment to education extended also to other levels of education when he assisted in the founding of the Sister Clara Muhammad School in Philadelphia. Even here, al-Faruqi found time to lead Friday prayers. According to Braibanti, he went on to help establish the American Institute of Pakistan Studies and the American Council for the Study of Islamic Societies.[62] Somehow he also found time to chair the boards of the North American Islamic Trust (NAIT) and the Editors of American Trust Publications as well as join the board of advisors for the Islamic Foundation in Leicester, UK.[63]

During this busy period, time was set aside to visit many Muslim countries to lecture, consult and promote his Islamization project and Islamic curricula. He helped design and advise Islamic studies programmes in Pakistan, South Africa, India, Malaysia, Libya, Saudi Arabia and Egypt.[64] He served as chairman of the International Scholar Committee advising the Malaysian government in 1982.[65] He lectured widely at universities in the Philippines, Malaysia and Indonesia, among others.[66] Esposito humorously comments that whenever he sought to contact al-Faruqi, he was either on his way out of the country or just arriving back from somewhere.[67]

Although the Islamization of knowledge project consumed much of his time, he remained committed to active involvement in inter-religious relations. This was demonstrated early in his career with the publication of *Christian Ethics* and numerous articles.[68] His interest in comparative religious studies and Islam led him to spearhead the creation of the Islamic Studies Group of the American Academy of Religion (AAR) in 1976.[69] This fit well with his desire to see Islam take a more central place within the wider academic community. As Esposito comments, in the late 1960s and through much of the 1970s, Islam was not a high priority in American academic circles.[70] This changed dramatically with the 1979 Iranian revolution. It is not surprising then that it took a few years to convince the AAR to sanction a full section for Islamic studies.

Following the 1972 AAR meetings, around the time that the AMSS was launched, a Temple colleague of al-Faruqi, Franklin Littell, who was then chairman of the History of Christianity Section, suggested the possibility of setting up a sub-section on Muslim-Christian Encounter.[71] Welcoming the idea, al-Faruqi organised a programme for the 1973 and 1974 annual meetings. With the term of Littell coming to an end after the meetings in 1974, he encouraged the establishment of an independent Islamics programme unit, which was duly applied for but turned down. Fortunately, in 1975 the Islamics programme was able to continue under the History of Christianity section. It was not until 1976 that independent status was received. Al-Faruqi chaired the Islamic Studies Group until 1982, having by that point been involved for ten years. A quick glance at the discussions from 1973 until 1981 shows that the early panels focused on Muslim-Christian encounter (1973, 1974), then moved onto Islam and modernism, thought and education (1975-1978, 1980), and then turned to Muslim-Christian-Jewish relations, such as the Abrahamic Trialogue (1979) and interaction between Islam and Christianity and Islam and Judaism (1981).[72] Interestingly, much of these discussions mirrored to some extent his interests in interfaith relations and Islamic intellectual thought and education.

Concurrent with these projects, he was invited to participate in a number of symposia, conferences and organisations dealing with various forms of interfaith dialogue. The details of these will be left for later discussion,[73] but for now mention should be made of two organisations in which he was involved. These were the Inter-Religious Peace Colloquium (IRPC) and the Global Congress of the World's Religions (GCWR).

Begun in 1975, the IRPC, which later became known as the Muslim-Jewish-Christian Conference (MJCC), remained active until 1980.[74] Al-Faruqi became involved in 1976 and then joined the board of directors the following year.[75] In 1978 he became Vice-President of the organisation and co-wrote the foreword to one of its publications.[76] When the 1979 AAR meeting of the Islamic Studies Committee sought to initiate a Jewish-Christian-Muslim discussion, assistance came from the MJCC, uniting two of his organisational commitments.[77]

Seemingly not content with these opportunities, he responded to an invitation to present a paper at the 1979 Global Congress of the World's Religions in Los Angeles.[78] He ended up the next year on its board of trustees, a position he held until 1982 at which time the IIIT was demanding more of his attention.[79]

Throughout his academic career, he published and lectured widely. Often these lectures were presented in the context of conferences and meetings and were subsequently published. His commitment to publishing included at various times involvement on the editorial boards of seven journals.[80] He also managed to secure a number of awards and grants as well as a Fulbright Research Fellowship in 1974.[81]

By now it should be obvious that al-Faruqi was not an idle scholar but one who was engaged in an impressive array of activities, ranging from mentoring students to implementing programmes as diverse as Islamic studies curricula, Islamization of knowledge projects, and interfaith dialogues and organisations. Thus, when at the age of sixty-five he met his death; it left a visible gap in many lives and organisations.

The deaths of the Isma'il and Lois (Lamya') al-Faruqi

The deaths of Isma'il and Lois on May 27, 1986 came as a shock to both the local Muslim community and to the wider Muslim world with which they were so familiar. However, as the Toronto Star reported a few months later on August 17, 1986:

The May 27 slayings went largely unnoticed in the major U.S. news media. But the possibility - as yet unsupported by firm evidence - that the killings may have been motivated by racism or politics sent shock waves through the U.S. Arab community and elsewhere.[82]

In what follows below we will provide only a short account of the details surrounding these events beginning with the events themselves followed by reactions to their deaths including their funeral, memorial service and the eventual arrest and conviction of the perpetrator.

The following account of the events of May 27th is drawn from newspaper articles and various other sources. Associated Press reported that on May 27, 1986, Isma'il (65) and Lamya' (59) were stabbed to death in their suburban Wyncote, Philadelphia home at 2:48 AM. Isma'il was found in the second floor den while Lamya' was on the floor in the shed adjacent to the kitchen. Their 27-year-old, eight months pregnant daughter, Anmar el-Zien survived wounds to her chest and arms requiring 200 stitches. Her 18-month-old son was hidden by her sister Tayma (21 years old), who were upstairs out of harm's way.[83]

The previous Monday evening (May 26, 1987) Isma'il al-Faruqi had attended the *iftar* meal with the local chapter of the MSA and returned home around 11:00 PM.[84] Early Tuesday morning Lamya' came downstairs into the kitchen, heard a noise and then met her attacker. Her scream awoke Anmar who confronted the person and after being stabbed managed to phone the police.[85] Subsequently Isma'il came down and faced the attacker on the second floor. The perpetrator was described at the time as a tall, large Afro-American man about 5 feet 10 wearing a black scarf below his eyes. The weapon recovered near Isma'il was a 15 inch serrated 'survival type' knife.[86] In a garbage container a few houses away a leather knife sheath and a screwdriver were recovered.[87]

The reaction of the authorities was quick, with police searching the area, but finding no suspect. Initially the FBI was called because Isma'il was known to have connections with the Arab world, but the Cheltenham Police department believed the assailant was a local man.[88] The police were unsure whether the crime was a bungled burglary or premeditated murder.[89] Lt. Detective Robert Krauser noted the sloppiness of the incident, leading police to believe it was not a professional assassination.[90] The Montgomery County Coroner, Dr. Theodore Garcia, surmised it was not a burglary but premeditated murder due to the number of knife wounds (13 for Ismaʿil and 8 for Lamya'). Garcia was quoted as saying:

> No one hacks away with a jungle type knife so deliberately, intent on killing, and then leaves, taking nothing. Anybody who saw those terrible, penetrating wounds on the bodies – 13 on the husband and 8 on the wife – would reach that conclusion. A burglar doesn't commit that kind of damage on two innocent people.[91]

Garcia further comments that: "He is going to try to convince the district attorney that this is first degree premeditated murder – and that if and when a suspect is caught it should be prosecuted as such."[92] About two dozen local, county and FBI investigators were involved in the case.[93] Fortunately fingerprints were recovered on the window broken to gain access to the Faruqi's home.[94]

Some within the local Muslim community immediately speculated that the murders were the work of the Jewish Defence League (JDL).[95] The Jordanian ministry of Islamic Affairs also claimed that extremist Zionist groups in the USA carried out the act.[96] However, no credible evidence was found to support these assertions. Meir Halevi, National Director of the JDL in Canada, denied any possibility of involvement in these crimes.[97] Hafez Malek, a Political Science Professor at Villanova University, told reporters that Dr. al-Faruqi often spoke of death threats in the 1970s and early 1980s due to his outspoken support of the Palestinians, but that there were no recent threats.[98] Dr. Gerald Sloyan, a colleague at Temple, noted Dr. al-Faruqi was a great partisan of Islam who did not make his political views the subject of discussion at the Department of Religion and he felt it highly unlikely there was any connection between their deaths and Middle East violence.[99] Faris Bouhafa of the American-Arab Anti-Discrimination Committee (ADC) in Washington also commented: "While he (al-Faruqi) was not politically active or visible, he was a prominent member of the Arab community."[100] However, to balance these sentiments, Judaism Professor at Temple University Norbert Samuelson said that Faruqi's views were "uniquely his own and would make everyone unhappy. So there is no end of possible political opponents."[101] Quraishi, who viewed al-Faruqi as non-political, does mention that al-Faruqi would at times express his pain over the situation facing the Palestinians. Quraishi then quotes an uncited New York Times article in which al-Faruqi is quoted as saying:

> The injustice perpetrated by Zionism, is so complex, so compounded and so grave that there is practically no means of stopping or undoing it without a violent war in which the Zionist army, state and all its public institutions would have to be destroyed.[102]

To be sure, this was something al-Faruqi had written before, and it is a strong political statement.[103] It seems slightly odd that Quraishi would cite this as an example of not being political. In any case, such a statement could have fueled some of the speculations that the JDL had a hand in the murders.

Funeral prayers were held May 30th at the Sister Clara Muhammad School and Masjid Muhammad. Estimates were that between 2000 - 4000 people attended.[104] Later in the day the Faruqis were buried at the Forrest Hills cemetery in lower Moreland Township, a suburb of Philadelphia.[105] A memorial committee was struck by ISNA in cooperation with IIIT and AMSS.[106] A lawyer named Jawad George was engaged as attorney to pursue the murder investigation on behalf of the local Muslim community.[107] A reward of $50,000 was offered for information leading to the arrest and conviction of those involved in the murders.[108] The committee also organised a large memorial service to be held September 26, 1986.[109]

Immediately following news of the tragedy, numerous messages of condolences were received from around the world. Telegrams arrived from some fifty embassies and Muslim dignitaries, particularly from Kuwait, Egypt, Malaysia, Pakistan, the Philippines, Jordan, and South Africa.[110] The journal *Islamic Horizons* published a special issue devoted to the Faruqis in August that included several pages of messages.[111] Notable among these messages were the Bishop's Committee for Ecumenical and Interreligious Affairs of the National Conference of Catholic Bishops which states in part: "Dr. Fārūqī was an honoured and esteemed participant in numerous interreligious dialogues, both nationally and internationally. The community of dialogue will miss him sorely."[112] The Committee on Christian-Muslim Relations of the National Council of Churches of Christ (NCCC) in the USA along with the Canadian Christian-Muslim National Liaison Committee sent their thoughts.[113] Another respondent was the Macdonald Centre of Hartford Seminary which writes: "The human community has lost two persons who contributed significantly to it by their lives and work, and the circle of those concerned with interfaith relations has lost two of its most valuable participants."[114] Finally, the General Secretary of the National Conference of Catholic Bishops writes: "He was also a leading contributor to dialogue between the Catholic and Muslim communities, not only in the United States, but internationally as well."[115]

The memorial service held September 26 at the Ritz Carlton Hotel in Washington drew numerous speakers such as Dr. Abdullah Omar Nasseef, secretary-general of the Muslim World League, Rev. Jesse Jackson (at the time a Presidential candidate), Dr. Yvonne Haddad (History Professor at Massachusetts University), John Esposito (Religious Studies Professor at Holy Cross College), Marsten Speight (NCC and Director of the Office on Christian-Muslim Relations), and Ralph Braibanti of Duke University, who moderated the programme.[116] In the aftermath, the International Islamic University (IIU) in Indonesia set up a bi-annual Isma'il al-Faruqi award for its own promising and outstanding scholars[117] and the AMSS inaugurated the annual Isma'il al-Faruqi Memorial lecture.[118]

On January 17, 1987 police announced they had arrested a suspect in the murders of the Faruqis based upon information received from the Philadelphia Muslim community.[119] Joseph Louis Young, a 41-year-old Afro-American Muslim, was being held on an aggravated assault charge when police charged him with the murders.[120] According to Jawad George, the tip was a result of the $50,000 reward offered by the Faruqi Memorial Committee.[121] Young, also known as Yusuf Ali, had become loosely involved with the local MSA chapter and knew the Faruqis, even visiting their home on occasion.[122] He later confessed to the killings.

On January 27, 1987, Young was formally charged with first-degree murder, among other charges, and was held without bail.[123] Within six months, Young was convicted on two counts of first-degree murder and the jury recommended the death penalty.[124] Young said before hearing the death sentence recommendation: "I regret the incident. It was a vicious crime. I did it, but I'm sorry. I wasn't in my right mind when I did this."[125] His defence attorney Stephen G. Heckman announced he would appeal the verdict citing the mental illness of his client. Young apparently believed he received instructions from the

Prophet Muhammad to kill the Faruqis who, as distasteful as this claim was, were allegedly forcing Muslim Malaysians to perform homosexual acts in exchange for scholarships to Temple University.[126] Young believed it was his mission to exact retribution. He also claimed that he felt used and betrayed by his fellow Muslims, whom he accused of using a form of psychiatry to try and manipulate him.[127] Prosecutors contended that Young's mental problems emerged after his January 16th arrest and were therefore a ploy.[128]

The U.S. Supreme Court, on March 29, 1994 upheld the death sentence of Joseph Young by refusing to hear the appeal without comment.[129] On February 28, 1996, at age 50, Young died of natural causes in Greene County Memorial Hospital,[130] but this was not entirely the end of the matter. In the post 9/11 atmosphere, a review of the 1986 murders was conducted by the Montgomery County authorities at the request of the U.S. Attorney's office in Philadelphia looking for any information about possible terrorist cells in Philadelphia. District attorney Bruce L. Castor Jr. is quoted as saying: "Joseph Young was part of a group of Muslim extremists. He was an outsider and he thought he could gain more acceptance in the group if he killed (the al-Faruqis) who were perceived as the enemies of Islam."[131] As yet, no evidence to support this claim has become available.

2

THE DEVELOPMENT OF HIS LIFE AND THOUGHT

The preceding account, as interesting as it may be as a narrative of his life, does not offer a complete picture of al-Faruqi nor does it explain the factors and influences that shaped his thought. This is more difficult to discover because it deals with motivation, personal goals, various influences and issues of identity. Essentially, the question is: Why was al-Faruqi interested in and committed to interfaith study and dialogue? A narrative of his life can only tell us what he did and not necessarily why. To begin the process of answering this question, we turn to analytical philosophy, specifically, identity theory.

Using Marya Schechtman's theory of personal identity, as discussed in her work *The Constitution of Selves*, al-Faruqi's life will be analysed as a form of self-narrative. This will include his writings and the views of others who knew him in order to try and draft a portrait of his self-perception in terms of how he wanted the world to view him. This changed, as it does for all of us, over the course of time. As his self-narrative is explored, we will further understand how his thought developed in relation to the different periods of his life. We will begin first by laying out identity theory and its theoretical models and then, later, apply this to al-Faruqi.

Simply stated, the overall objective of the following is to explore and support the premise that al-Faruqi's interest and participation in interfaith dialogue was a result of his self-understanding. One may argue that this is somewhat obvious because we know this intuitively. If a person takes time out in a busy schedule to pursue gardening, we correctly conclude that this activity is important to the person. If this interest continues over many years, including learning more about gardening, attending meetings and being invited to give talks, then we identify this person as an avid gardener who loves to be involved in all levels of gardening. Furthermore, if asked to describe herself, this person would include 'gardening' as part of her self-identity. What the above does not tell us is why or how such a passion became central to this identity. One way to deepen such exploration, in an attempt to move beyond intuitive insight, is to use Personal Identity Theory to begin to try and uncover the reasons why certain characteristics become foundational to identity.

Over the course of the last number of years, there has been considerable academic interest in exploring identity issues within Muslim communities in North America. Yvonne Yazbeck Haddad and M. A. Muqtedar Khan, among others, have produced studies examining various factors such as politics, values, education, immigrant ethnicity and issues of assimilation.[1] Yet, although mention is made of individuals such as al-Faruqi, the focus remains generally upon the wider community's self-perception. Studying an entire community is different than the study of one individual, but there is a certain overlap since communities can behave like individuals, such as by voting as a single block or holding in common certain values or beliefs. One attempt at linking an individual's experiences to the wider community's is Ghamari-Tabrizi's unique study of al-Faruqi and the Muslim Diaspora.[2] Here the intention was to demonstrate that 'diasporic *displacement*'[3] does not need to create hybridity (being at home in two places at the same time), but can result in a balance between the two as seen in the life of al-Faruqi.[4] To these studies we will return later, for they provide insight from the perspective of a community's view and appropriation of an individual. In this case, the wider Muslim community perceived al-Faruqi in certain ways, but this does not necessarily provide us with any insight into his life. If anything, it shows the impact of his person upon a larger group, which, while valuable, is insufficient to our purposes.

What is proposed here requires a slightly different approach precisely because the interest is in an individual's identity. The main way to understand a person's motives is to understand the person. The application of personal identity theories allow for a more rigorous analysis by providing a framework through which to examine not only the life of al-Faruqi, but more specifically the relation between his person and his interfaith work. This as yet has not been done, as far as I know, for al-Faruqi. Often identity theorists pose thought experiments to test their ideas or draw examples from literary characters, but here the subject is real. This will not be a complete biographical analysis, but will nonetheless examine general trends in his life to account for the longevity of his interfaith interest.

Now before introducing, in general, the discipline of personal identity theory, it should be noted that the main focus of identity research is theoretical. It is not a finely honed methodology replete with a clear set of applications. This has required some careful thought as to how to best make use of the theory within the context of this study. This is not a disclaimer, but rather the reality of the nature of studying people. Who you are and why you do what you do are profound questions that are not easily answered. Fortunately some answers, even if incomplete, can be discovered.

Personal Identity Theory

The question of personal identity is of interest to a variety of disciplines and sub-disciplines. Analytical philosophy, moral psychology, sociology, anthropology and of course personal identity theorists, who may count any of the above disciplines as their own, are all seeking to understand what makes a person a person.[5] For example, the main concern of contemporary analytical philosophers of personal identity is in the metaphysical question of how a single entity persists through change.[6] In other words, how can a person change physically and psychologically through time and yet retain the same identity. This applies both within the person who identifies himself as the same person as yesterday as it does to other persons who make the same assessment about that person. The goal then of contemporary personal identity theorists is to provide criteria for personal identity over time. One criterion can be how we can know whether something is identical or consonant with its past. The question is metaphysical and not epistemological because the concern is not just how we *know*, but also what makes the person the same at two different times.[7] This question includes the wider issue of whether we consider identity associated with the body (physical elements) or with the mind (psychological elements).

The argument for identity of consciousness (psychological) and not of substance (body) was provided in the seventeenth-century by John Locke in his seminal work, *An Essay Concerning Human Understanding.*[8] His was the first systematic attempt in the West to present personal identity in psychological terms and subsequent theorists have needed to address Locke's ideas.[9] This is not the place to discuss Locke's theories or to delve too deeply into the field. It is sufficient to recognise that Marya Schechtman's theory of personal identity is in response to Locke's ideas and those of others.[10] Her work moved the field in a different direction than previous metaphysical discussions about personal identity and forms the basis for our exploration of al-Faruqi.[11] Therefore, a more in depth discussion of her ideas is required before moving on to their application.

According to Schechtman, Personal Identity Theory is concerned with two main questions.[12] The reidentification question asks what makes a person at some period in the past (t_1) the same person at some later time (t_2). The interest is in discovering the logical relation of identity over time, such as physical features. On the other hand, the characterisation question deals with the features or characteristics that make a person who they are. Beliefs, values, desires and other psychological features unique to each person form what is considered to be a person's identity. Schechtman argues that identity theorists have confused or overlapped these two questions when they should be separated.[13] In other words, trying to determine what makes a person the same last year as she is today does not necessarily determine who she is.

Generally, there are two sets of intuitions concerning persons.[14] One set views persons as identifiable with their bodies and the other as identifiable with their psyches (mind, personality). These conceptions tend to recognise people as objects (bodies) and as subjects (inner lives, autonomy, agency). Persons as objects are identified in reference to their bodies, such as physical characteristics, DNA and fingerprints. Persons as subjects are identified by considering issues such as their beliefs, values, motivations and desires. Normally, we use both ways to identify people and it is not an either/or question. However, each way provides distinct answers to different questions. Schechtman writes: "According to this approach, our inclination to identify persons with their bodies arises primarily within the context of the reidentification question and the inclination to identify them with their psyche arises primarily in response to questions of characterization."[15] For example, if the police need to identify a body their interest is in physical characteristics such as fingerprints, dental records, DNA and the testimony of those who personally know the appearance of the deceased. These are all within the province of reidentification questions. For identification purposes the police will not care about the deceased's beliefs or values. For those who knew the person, they may identify the body as belonging to their friend, but they would view their friend as more than his body. Identity, therefore, includes psychological features that are distinct from the body. We know this intuitively. For example, if the police are seeking a suspect in a crime, they will be equally interested in physical identity (appearance and other physical evidence) as well as issues of motivation (characterisation questions).

Schechtman proposes four features of personal existence. These are survival, moral responsibility, self-interested concern and compensation (hereafter referred to as the four features).[16] A person's identity is linked to these four features on the psychological level (characterisation) and not on the physical level (reidentification). One may argue that survival is intimately linked with the body, but in fact the body is valuable primarily because it hosts the psychological identity.[17] People without brain activity and yet whose body can be kept functioning artificially are nonetheless considered "dead". Regarding this distinction, Noonan comments that: "The reason why .... brain identity should be preferred to bodily identity as a criterion of personal identity is that it is the brain and not the rest of the body that carries with it psychological identity – identity of memory, personality and character."[18] As was mentioned previously, contemporary identity theorists are generally interested in the maintenance and recognition of identity over the course of time, which basically addresses only the reidentification question. The characterisation question explains the intuitive link between identity and the four features. Of course these two questions are not completely independent, but interconnected, providing different perspectives on what comprises identity.[19]

For us our main concern rests with issues of characterisation and not reidentification. For example, there is no need to study al-Faruqi's physical appearance. This would be important if the concern was to distinguish him from anyone wanting to impersonate him.[20] The emphasis remains instead upon studying his beliefs, motivations and desires in relation to how he defined himself. Therefore, Schechtman's analysis of the deficiencies of the psychological continuity theory introduced by Locke and supported by others will not be discussed beyond her own brief summation:

There are, then, many different versions of the psychological continuity theory; they all however, share two features. First, they start with the goal of offering a reidentification criteria for persons. Second, they accept the basic intuition that personal identity is constituted by psychological continuity. The goal of psychological continuity theorists is thus to provide a theory that defines the identity of persons over time in terms of psychological connections between person-stages at different times.[21] ... The notion of psychological continuity to which reidentification theorists are driven by the structure of their view does not seem to bear any relation to the practical importance of identity or to provide a plausible basis for survival, responsibility, self-interested concern, or compensation. By putting their intuitions into the form of a reidentification criterion, psychological continuity theorists thus undermine the original support for their view.[22]

At issue here is the concept of the characterisation question, its relation to the four features and the subsequent theory of narrative self-constitution. This will provide the framework to study al-Faruqi. In what immediately follows, we will quickly define in more detail the characterisation question along with the four features, and then provide an explanation of the narrative theory before examining the life of al-Faruqi.

Essentially, the characterisation question asks which actions, beliefs, values, motivations, desires, experiences, character traits, and so on are to be attributed to a given person.[23] When taken in total these characteristics make a person who he is. It is these features that answer the question: Who are you? If a person becomes unsure of these defining characteristics which constitute and inform his identity, then one can speak of an 'identity crisis'.[24] This need not be the result of a mental illness or physical injury influencing the brain, but simply of a midlife crisis or immigration or any other situation that requires a person to define themselves in new ways. For example, a person may discover that much of her identity was a construct of the expectations and definitions of others which, when realised, requires her to find out what she *really* believes and values apart from the demands of others. The characterisation question seeks to discover which characteristics are part of a person's life and what role they play. Certainly some are more central than others and that can change with time. The issue is not only what characteristics are present, but also the degree to which they are held.[25] Someone may have various beliefs with some held more strongly than others.

Our intuitive conviction that identity is linked with survival, moral responsibility, self-interest and compensation requires some explanation. It is obvious by now that identity can be defined, in part, as survival.[26] If you do not exist, you have no identity. This applies biologically and psychologically. Generally, people value biological survival because it is required for psychological existence. Further, a healthy body without psychological continuation is not the kind of survival people really want. Some would consider keeping the body artificially functioning without brain activity as not being alive, but merely existing. However, if the brain could function without the body, then you could still be considered alive. Our psychological selves seem more important. This is borne out by the bitter experience of prisoners of war, hostages and those who suffer from dementia, which can affect deeply the psychological self to such an extent that we speak of people as 'no longer the same person,' or 'the person we knew is gone'.

Identity and moral responsibility are also intuitively linked.[27] We hold a person responsible for his own actions. If someone accidentally trips and pushes you, this is judged differently than if you are deliberately pushed. Thus, what one chooses to do, informs the associated moral judgment and identity. We speak of a person who feels no sense of moral obligation as selfish or in extreme cases a sociopath. We judge a hired killer more culpable than someone who kills in self-defence or accidentally. The degree to which moral actions are evident helps indicate whether it is something incidental in one's life, something that is held loosely perhaps enforced by culture or society, or something foundational to one's character and identity. A person may believe killing seal pups is not something they would do for a living, but is fine for others. Another may believe more strongly and advocate that someone should stop this activity and still others may become directly involved by protesting and physically trying to stop this practice. Each case informs about identity.

Schechtman's third feature of personal identity, self-interested concern, is the concern a person has with being in a position to fulfil desires and pursue personal goals.[28] One way to determine the level of interest is that generally people prefer pleasure to pain, but in certain circumstances are willing to endure pain in order to achieve their goal (pleasure) later. People make sacrifices for religious convictions, relationships and their principles and for numerous other reasons. The point is, by examining what one is willing to make a priority, we are better able to discern values and desires and thereby determine which interests are most central to identity.

This is closely related to the last feature, the characteristic of compensation.[29] If the compensation is considered sufficiently valuable then present desires can be denied in order to realise other desires considered more important. For example, a student may forgo attending a party in order to study and obtain better grades such that at some future time he may enter medical school. Here the immediate desire to have fun is sacrificed for a more important desire: a medical career.

These four features form the basis of the concept of personal identity and are related to the characterisation question because they provide insight into the values, desires, beliefs, and so on, that together constitute the life story of each person. These features change over the course of time, but when a person continuously sustains certain beliefs or desires over an extended period, then we conclude these are central to the identity of that person.

Having moved away from the reidentification question, which focuses on the body or substance as the feature of identification, and having posited the characterisation question as the best means through which to address the intuitive aspects of identity as comprised by the four features, we are now in a position to examine the theory of self-narrative. Theorists have argued persons are either self-creating or their lives are narrative in form.[30] The former holds that people create themselves over time based on their desires including the way they wish people to see them. The latter views people's lives as a narrative, often constructed chronologically within the context of a logical life story. This is seen in biographical accounts. Schechtman offers her theory in which a person creates identity by forming an autobiographical narrative to account for who they are (narrative self-constitution theory) and this becomes a person's life story.[31]

There are two elements implicit in this theory.[32] First, individuals represent themselves as persons by creating a self-narrative. Second, there are cultural limitations that impose a form of identity-constituting narrative. Personhood is a concept connected to society.

In general, it is embedded in the interaction between people and includes accepted behaviours, customs and culture. This is learned naturally as we grow in our families and into wider society. Thus an individual's self-identity, expressed as narrative, must generally conform to the narratives others tell about this individual. In Schechtman's words:

> These then, are the two basic sets of intuition that lead to the narrative self-constitution view as I meant it: first, that in order to be a person one needs a particular kind of subjectivity and orientation towards one's life, and second, that in order to be a person one's self-conception must cohere with what might be called the 'objective' account of her life – roughly the story that those around her would tell.[33]

The narrative self-constitution view asserts that a person's identity is created by a self-conception that is narrative in form. Thus, a person organises experiences, beliefs and values around a coherent and intelligible self-conception.[34] This implies that people selectively choose to emphasize certain aspects of life that conform to how they see and want to see themselves, and how they are seen by others. There is the expectation that a person's beliefs, values, emotions, actions and experiences fit together in such a way that make what he says, does and feels psychologically intelligible. If someone is supposed to be your friend yet treats you badly, we ask them: Why, if she is your best friend, do you treat her in this way? Thus the components of narrative derive meaning from the wider context of society and are interpreted to fit our self-conception. Jerome Brunner adds:

> A narrative is composed of a unique sequence of events, mental states, happenings involving human beings as characters or actors. These are its constituents. But these constituents do not, as it were, have a life or meaning on their own. Their meaning is given by their place in the overall configuration of the sequence as a whole - its plot - *tabula*.[35]

Without belabouring this any further, for the objective here is application rather than an extended theoretical discussion, the narrative self-constitution view means a person experiences events in life as interpreted through a sense of one's own story. This proceeds from one's past whence self-conception emerges to the present in which one reinforces and adjusts this self-conception, leading to the future where one expects the self-conception to continue.[36] Again Schechtman: "... creating an autobiographical narrative is not simply composing a story of one's life – it is organising and processing one's experiences in a way that presupposes an implicit understanding of oneself as an evolving protagonist."[37] The aspects of articulation and reality act as restraints or boundaries for this narrative such that a person should be able to answer questions about themselves, including explaining why they act the way they do, and a person's narrative should conform to the reality of facts whether empirical or interpretative.[38] A person whose narrative includes believing he is Napoleon Bonaparte would see that portion of the narrative rejected because the facts deny the claim.

Having introduced Personal Identity Theory and Schechtman's narrative self-constitution view, we can move on to the life of al-Faruqi.

Al-Faruqi and narrative self-constitution

Our application of identity theory will be twofold. First, there will be a general examination of al-Faruqi's life noting the chronological development of his interest in interfaith subjects and the role (or roles) this played in his own self-narrative. Second, a more specific analysis based closely on Schechtman's four features (survival, moral responsibility, self-interested concern and compensation) will be offered to discover his values, beliefs, motivations and desires regarding interfaith ideas. These are not the only ways in which to study the development of al-Faruqi's ideas, but they provide a more rigorous framework than applying simple intuition or observation.

There are always some limitations in discovering the life story or narrative of a person.[39] In this case the obvious restriction is that al-Faruqi is no longer present to communicate his self-narrative. It must be reconstructed from primary sources, which were not written to address issues of his identity, but rather issues that were important to him and thereby reflect his identity. The challenge, then, is to sift through his writings to learn what we can about his values, motivations and desires. The other sources available are the recollections and opinions about him held by those who knew him. Many of these are available in written form and while they are important because they tell us what others thought about him, they also are necessarily interpretive. Al-Faruqi influenced many lives and as such he has become part of other peoples' self-narratives. Thus these self-narratives interpret the memories and the impact of al-Faruqi's life upon their own. John Esposito, for example, has spoken of the role al-Faruqi played in influencing his own decision to pursue Islamic studies during a time when such study was relatively marginal in academia.[40] In essence, al-Faruqi has become part of Esposito's own self-narrative – albeit a small part, but present nonetheless. The point is that such testimony and memories of al-Faruqi are already interpreted and appropriated by those who knew him. The fact that they inform us about their authors as much as about al-Faruqi cannot be avoided. Hence, these recollections are primarily useful to confirm his self-narrative.

The development of al-Faruqi's self narrative

In May 1986, some days before his death, al-Faruqi wrote a very short biographical summary of his curriculum vitae at the request of a friend who was writing a book. It reads:

After I graduated from the American University in Beirut, I worked as a registrar in the Arab Cooperative Societies in Palestine, then as an administrative officer and as magistrate (ḥākim) in the province of Galilee.

When the Rescue Army (Jaysh al-Inqādh) was set up, I was working as an administrative magistrate (ḥākim) in the northern regions which were occupied by the army until they fell into the enemy's hands. By then I had gone to the U.S. for studies.

After I obtained my doctorate in western philosophy, I became aware of the state of my ignorance and remoteness from the Islamic legacy. So I retreated and entered al-Azhar University to learn anew, but with a very fast intensive special programme as if I was doing another doctorate in the three years that I was spending at the quarters of al-Azhar.

Thereafter I worked as a Professor of Islamic Studies at various universities. My involvement in the Islamic students' movement in the US had helped create the development of a new outlook, that is, to cultivate and develop Islam in the U.S. apart from training the Muslim youth in Islamic activities and deepening their Islamic vision.

This the activity in which I am still engaged.
Ismāʿīl Rājī al-Fārūqī
1 May 1986.[41]

From this letter it is clear that he divided his life into various stages roughly comprised of four overlapping sections: Palestine (1926-1948), US academic experiences (1948-1954), Arabism/Islamic legacy (1954-1968) and Islam and activism (1968-1986).[42] These will be used to ascertain the development of his self-narrative and in particular the place of inter-religious interest.

Palestine (1926-1948)

There is a relative paucity of information regarding his upbringing and the early influences that shaped his life. Beyond the information already presented, there appears little else to draw upon. It was during these early years that al-Faruqi was first introduced to Christianity as the result of ten years (1926-1936) at the French Dominican College des Frères. Not only did he learn French there, but he also absorbed a great deal about Catholic Church tradition, doctrine, and practice. Altalib noted that the College was a boarding school where the brothers helped the young al-Faruqi to further develop his life-long intense work ethic. In fact later in life, al-Faruqi believed long weekends should be used not just for rest, but also for other kinds of work.[43] Since his father was a *qāḍī*, then Ismaʿil would have learned something about Islamic jurisprudence and Muslim practice. This would have been re-emphasized during his few years at the local Mosque school. That he went on to study philosophy at University indicates he was a thinker interested in rational ideas and the fact that it was an English programme further shows his willingness to learn.[44] Obviously his family valued education and had the means to send him to the French Dominican school and later to university.

After graduation, his career in the civil service, administration and later as magistrate (*ḥākim*) of the district of Galilee, all under the British Mandate, shows his acumen for organisation, leadership, politics and administration. These talents expressed themselves throughout his later career. However, arguably the creation of Israel and the subsequent loss of his homeland, Palestine, had the largest impact upon his self-conception. Fazlur Rahman, Kenneth Cragg and others comment that he was deeply affected by these events. During al-Faruqi's years at McGill, Rahman saw him as an angry young Muslim Palestinian and Cragg reflects that "... his share in this ongoing tragedy of Palestinian displacement immersed him, and his thinking, in the mystery of pain, resentment, privation, and distress. That prevailing circumstance of his mind and story shadowed all his work."[45] When, in 1948, he went to the USA to pursue graduate studies, he arrived as a young man in search of knowledge, his future and along the way, his identity.

US academic experience (1948-1954)
It was in the USA that al-Faruqi was forced to examine his life and through a mixture of discovery and decision began to determine who he would be. These early years, fuelled by the trauma of exile and the struggle to survive and support himself, led him to recount: "There was a time in my life when all I cared about was proving to myself that I could win my physical and intellectual existence from the West, that I could succeed as a man. But, when I won it, it became meaningless."[46] Like all immigrants, al-Faruqi sought to establish himself and build a new life in his new home. It appears from the above quote that his early identity partially revolved around the need to "succeed as a man" both in terms of physical needs and intellectual pursuits. These were the ambitions he was beginning to achieve when he left Palestine – a career, a homeland and success as defined by his culture. Now in the USA, he naturally sought the same goals, but in a different, predominantly Christian, culture. The path he chose was scholarship, but this would not ultimately provide him with answers to the deeper questions of identity.

Maysam al-Faruqi, a niece of Isma'il, notes in a short essay, that there was a driving force within him that was "always present in his life and his work, and that remained the same throughout the different phases of his life."[47] She identifies this force as the search for truth as an all-encompassing ideology including the 'moral ought' under which all humanity must live. Maysam writes:

> He left Palestine an angry youth, whose heart had bled over the destruction of his homeland – yet never turning bitter or sterile. He had seen his country torn apart, himself thrown out, his

people unjustly killed and dispossessed, and all the basic rights of human beings violated with contempt. So he set out to restore the dignity of the individual in the universe, because he could not stand to lose his own *raison d'etre*. But the violence he witnessed brought, as a first reaction, a rebellion in al-Faruqi. A rebellion which was directed, in the beginning, against his own religion and culture, because he thought these were the causes behind his people's inability to defend themselves. Thus he sailed to the West, hoping to find answers to the multiple questions which motivated his search for an all encompassing system that would satisfy his philosophical inclinations. He began by adopting theories and ideologies which came close to his aspirations for truth and justice. His early espousal of Nietzsche's philosophy, for instance, betrayed at once his rebellion against a reified interpretation of his religion, and yet he was willing to give morality a solid foundation within humanity itself – if no transcendent realm was to exist.[48]

In his Master's thesis, al-Faruqi explored the ethics of Kant and Nietzsche and in his doctoral studies, value theory, but he soon found the absence of the transcendent leads to moral chaos since all human morality is relative and not absolute. This began for him the process of re-assessing his Islamic heritage. Within six years of his arrival in the USA, he determined the need to study Islam in a more in-depth fashion, which led him to Egypt's al-Azhar University. However, he left the USA different than when he first arrived. Not only were there new questions regarding moral 'oughtness' and a new found drive to 'win his physical and intellectual existence from the West', but he was now married. Lois, who chose the name Lamya', became a partner in his search for himself. According to Hasan Hanafi, who worked with al-Faruqi at Temple (1971-1975), Lois became a Muslim after marrying Isma'il.[49] As she discovered her own Muslimness in American culture as an individual and as a wife, Isma'il probably shaped her ideas. It is at least equally possible that Lois also influenced him. The unfolding of their mutual self-conceptions is thus intertwined, although it is difficult to determine to what degree.

Of interest to this study is that major developments in the formation of his self-identity occurred in a largely Christian culture. Using his philosophical interests and training he turned to western philosophers for ideological answers to his questions. As these were found wanting, he began to more energetically study and integrate his Islamic faith and heritage into life as a Muslim in the West. In his curriculum vitae he writes: "After I obtained my doctorate in western philosophy, I became aware of the state of my ignorance and remoteness from the Islamic legacy. So I retreated and entered al-Azhar University to learn anew ..."[50] This is a reflection on his past in which he interprets and identifies this point in his life with the Islamic conception of 'ignorance' (*jāhiliyya*). His identity creation led him through western philosophy back to a fuller appreciation and understanding of Islam. However, the impact of the West still was present.

Arabism/Islamic legacy (1954-1968)

It was during this period that al-Faruqi's self conception began to take fuller shape as it was narrated within the contexts of the West and Islam. It saw him roam through his Islamic heritage (1954-1958), study in depth and propound his Arabism theory, go on to research Christianity and Judaism (1958-1961), work in Pakistan with Fazlur Rahman (1961-1963), and then at Chicago's Divinity School (1964), and start his time at Syracuse University (1964-1968). The reason why this period ends at 1968 is due to the influence the Muslim Student's Association began to play in his life.

Of his time in Egypt, Ghamari-Tabrizi comments that al-Faruqi was influenced by "revivalist ideas of early Muslim reformers who emphasized the Islamic roots of all modern sciences and rationality."[51] This 'fits' with his rational philosophical perspective and indicates an attempt to bridge the divide between the West and Islam. Esposito adds that from the 1950s to the early 1960s, al-Faruqi sounded like an Arab heir to Islamic modernism and Western empiricism emphasizing Islam as the best of religions.[52] During the years of study at al-Azhar and the Institute of Higher Arabic Studies at Cairo University, he developed his ideas of Arabism.[53]

His concept of Arabism ('*Urūbah*) reflects something of al-Faruqi's own search for identity. As constructed, he postulated that Arab consciousness was the spirit and best expression of Islamic values. Further, it was central to the history of religion, particularly since this Arab spirit was the common strand of identity present in each of the three monotheistic faiths. This was not to be equated with Arab nationalism or non-Arab Islamic revivalism despite Islam's close association with Arabism. Al-Faruqi defined Arabism in archetypal categories of consciousness, which were not necessarily possessed by Arabs alone; nevertheless, it found its fullest expression under Arabs who were Muslims, such as al-Faruqi himself. Regarding Arabism, Esposito has written:

> Arabism is not simply an idea but a reality, and identity, and a set of values integral to and inseparable from the identity of all Muslims and all non-Muslim Arabs. Arabism is the very spirit of the umma; it incorporates not only the Arabic-speaking members of the Arab world, but also the entire world community of Muslims since Arab language, consciousness, and values are at the core of their common Islamic faith.[54]

This theory was generally rejected by both Muslim and western scholars.[55] One example is Fazlur Rahman's assessment: "Where did I stand in regard to this doctrine [Arabism], rejected by both Muslim and Western scholars? I did not, of course, espouse it."[56] Rahman further added that during lecture trips to Egypt, al-Faruqi's theory of Arabism received a polite but sceptical hearing.[57] Rahman recalled questioning al-Faruqi on his Arabism theory, asking why he spoke of Arab and not Islam. The reply was instructive and not what one would expect. Al-Faruqi comments: "You see, we have a large Christian minority and the moment we speak of Islam these people are liable to turn into fifth columnists for Western powers."[58] Obviously al-Faruqi was conscious of the wider implications of his ideas, including political issues. More than that, it seems curious that he would choose to be so concerned with Christian opinion, but this is clarified somewhat when one considers his distaste for colonial imperialism and its negative impact upon Muslims and Islam. Despite the rejection of Arabism at various turns, he held firm to his theory. It can be hard to say in fact where Arabism ends and he begins, for in Arabism one sees the desire to find common ground between Judaism, Christianity and Islam, with Islam as the capstone. Al-Faruqi's life parallels the development of Arabism itself, as he sought to maintain his Muslim identity in a non-Muslim culture whose learning and achievements he was trying to integrate, in much the same way as the Muslim modernists and reformers he studied at al-Azhar. It is no wonder, then, that some twenty years later he sought to promote the Islamization of knowledge project, reflecting again this spirit of gleaning the best and placing it under the rubric of Islam just as he had personally done in his life. He carried these Arabism ideas with him as he entered his years of study and teaching at McGill University.

Between the years 1958-1961, the concept of Arab consciousness met the scholastic study of Judaism and Christianity as mediated through his philosophical perspective on morality and ethics. The history of religion was not a new topic to him because he needed to have some grasp of Judaism and Christianity in order to support his Arabism theory. This may be seen clearly in his book *On Arabism*. We also know that he presented a few lectures on the history of religion during his time at the Institute of Higher Arabic Studies at Cairo University in 1959.[59] It appears that it was during the development of his theory of Arabism that he also developed his interest in the history of religions. It was therefore not surprising that he accepted the offer to study at McGill. Stanley Brice Frost, Dean of Divinity at the time, writes in the preface to al-Faruqi's *Christian Ethics*: "Looking back on those two years, it seems they were one long, continuous provocative discussion, in which my colleagues and I learned to appreciate Dr. Faruqi as a tenacious disputant, a stimulating colleague, and a warm-hearted friend."[60] Rahman echoed this sentiment finding al-Faruqi to be always smiling, personally charming, intellectually lively and never quarrelsome.[61]

After al-Faruqi's first year with the Institute of Islamic studies, W. C. Smith spoke to Rahman about al-Faruqi's future. In the following exchange we are offered another perspective into al-Faruqi's life. Smith begins:

"You know, he frightens me." Then he asked, "What do you [Rahman] think if we could give him some kind of an indefinite job – say, some sort of Associate Professorship? What could be the objection to that?" "Nothing," I said, "provided he is free to write whatever he thinks best."[62]

In the end arrangements were made for al-Faruqi to spend two years as a Fellow of the Divinity School where he studied Judaism and Christianity. As for what 'frightened' Smith, Rahman writes:

He saw a young Muslim Palestinian with high and sophisticated modern intellectual equipment, who, with all his smiles, refused then to play only the scholar, but rather turned his energy and intellectual tools to attack the West in general and Zionism in particular – with the full and painful awareness that it was the West that had created and was wilfully sustaining Israel, which had robbed him and millions of other Palestinians of their hopes and lands. He was an activist by heart, a man dead set on *changing things*.[63]

This desire to change things remained a constant feature in his life. His colleagues at McGill saw him as a warm person who would argue and debate, not content to remain a detached 'objective' scholar, but insisting that scholarship touch the problems of life. In this way, he demonstrated that his scholarship would be a tool at the disposal of his own agenda for change. Esposito noted that the academic religious environment that met al-Faruqi was liberal, with the Death of God Theology and movement away from traditional beliefs among liberal Christian scholars. Al-Faruqi struggled with liberalism and perhaps this is one reason he was so intent on holding firm to his positions to the point of perceived intransigence.[64] Interestingly, when Rahman joined the faculty at the University of Chicago in 1969, "a prominent member of [the] Divinity School, where Isma'il taught for a year, described him as a 'guerrilla scholar'".[65] It had been five years since al-Faruqi had taught at the Divinity School and yet his style lingered on in the memory of at least one faculty member. Rahman makes one final telling comment about the course of his activist-academic life: "This choice he [al-Faruqi] made at the threshold of his career."[66]

During his time in Pakistan (1961-1963), al-Faruqi's Arab-centric views of Islam persisted despite working and living among predominately non-Arab Muslims.[67] One of Rahman's motives in arranging this position for al-Faruqi at the Central Institute of Islamic Research was to allow him to see first-hand a large body of Muslims who were not Arabs.[68] Instead, his Arabism ideas drew strong criticism. If we have learned anything about al-Faruqi up to this point, we should not be surprised that he vigorously defended his theory. Rahman's desire for al-Faruqi to broaden his understanding of Muslims would not be realised until al-Faruqi's return to the USA and his encounter with the Muslim Students Association.

Before turning to this identity-defining moment, a summary of his self-conception up to this point would be helpful. Roughly fifteen years had elapsed since his departure from Palestine. During this time, he studied and then moved away from western philosophy, choosing instead a combination of Islamic thought and Western ideas. In doing so he postulated Arabism as a link between all monotheistic faiths while attempting to remain faithful to the Qur'ān. He began formal study of Judaism and Christianity in support of his Arabism ideas, but did not limit himself to this one dimension of inquiry focusing also on morality and ethics, (the actual development of his methodological ideas will be left for later). His combative style of debate and his intense defence of Arabism left similar impressions upon his colleagues. He was seen as personable, but not easily swayed from his ideas. The influence and impact of Palestine did not diminish; rather, it became channelled into his activist academic pursuit to demonstrate that Islam through Arabism was the heir of all ideals. Esposito noted that Arabism, Islam and western Christian culture were al-Faruqi's religious, historical and cultural baggage.[69] As for his motives in studying Christianity and other non-Muslim faiths, at this point, these appear to have been closely associated with Arabism. However, since he was growing into a scholar-activist, the separation between his beliefs or desires and his scholarship had narrowed to the point at which one can claim that part of his identity and self-understanding was contained in the theory of Arabism. The fact that many did not accept Arabism and hence part of who he was may be one reason he held so tightly to and defended it so strongly, even when confronted by the experience of living among non-Arab Muslims. It was not until he was ready and secure enough in his identity that he was willing to alter or de-emphasize his theory. In his 1982 book *Al-Tawḥīd*, he writes: "They [Judaism and Christianity] and it [Islam] constitute successive moments of *Semitic* consciousness in its [Islam's] long march as the carrier of a divine mission on earth and hence the vortex of human history."[70] (Italics and insertions mine.) Here one can see that Arab consciousness has been replaced with Semitic consciousness, a word that al-Faruqi in his early years opposed.[71] However, it seems that over the course of time Arabism with its Arab consciousness became less emphasized in his thinking, although he still retained the general concept.

A momentous shift in al-Faruqi's thinking occurred upon his return to the USA in the fall of 1963 to take up a one-year post at the University of Chicago's Divinity School. Aside from the telling fact that his return brought him into a Christian environment teaching the history of religions and, as was noted, at least one professor felt he was a guerrilla scholar, his acceptance indicates his willingness and ability to teach Islam as part of wider religious considerations. It also shows that his frustration over the lack of implementation of his vision of Islamic curriculum led him back to the USA and not into a Muslim environment. There is a sense that the USA would provide more freedom and opportunity to set up the kind of Islamic studies programme he envisioned.[72] Originally this desire to establish a curriculum for Muslim students in the traditional Islamic sciences and in western methodologies was the reason he left McGill for Pakistan. Now, he found himself back in North America with the same desire, albeit to be realised in a non-Muslim and secularised environment.

In January 1963, the Muslim Students Association (MSA) was founded on the campus of the University of Illinois at Urbana-Champaign and it was this collection of diverse Muslim students drawn from various parts of the Muslim world that eventually would lead al-Faruqi to shift his thinking from Arabism to Islam as the primary referent in his thought.[73] By 1965, al-Faruqi had been introduced to and become involved in the MSA. According to Quraishi, al-Faruqi was impressed by the *iman* (faith) of the students and became actively involved, particularly at Temple University.[74] In 1968, Ilyas Ba-Yunus visited him while he was a patient at the John Hopkins Ophthalmological centre and was told: "Until a few months ago, I was a Palestinian, an Arab and a Muslim. Now I am a Muslim who happens to be an Arab from Palestine."[75] Quraishi reported a similar conversation a few years later in which al-Faruqi said: "I asked myself: Who am I? A Palestinian, a philosopher, a liberal humanist? My answer was: I am a Muslim."[76]

Having achieved academic success and with his career on a surer footing at Temple, his involvement with the students of the MSA altered his outlook on how to realise the goal of training and equipping Muslims in the West. Ghulam Nabi Fai, reflecting on al-Faruqi's involvement with the MSA, writes: "For him the MSA, as a varied and potent representation of the *ummah*, was an important component of the process of Islamization both in its intellectual and practical aspects."[77] He became one of the MSA's most efficacious advocates and played a major role in the realization of its stated mission as the organisation for "preventing the disintegration of Muslims in the country".[78] Minimising his idea of Arabism, he began to lay the foundation for a universal, homogenous corporate identity, which would globally unify the diverse community of Muslims as one *ummah*.[79] Ba-Yunus writes:

> With his training in philosophy, his experience as a professor, and with his newly acquired commitment to Islam, Ismāʿīl was almost irresistible. He spoke with poise, confidence, knowledge and with a mastery of rhetoric. He could articulate the principles of Islam in terms of western thought and western vocabulary so that his audience could see the relevance and the applicability of Islam to modern time as a universal ideology.[80]

Al-Faruqi no longer needed to be a lone Palestinian Arab Muslim seeking his way in the West trying to effect change, but now saw himself as a Muslim and as part of a large international community of fellow Muslims. He had discovered his identity and with it his direction for activism. Throughout this process he maintained an interest in the study of other religions, publishing and accepting opportunities to address inter-religious gatherings.

Islam and activism (1968-1986)

During the 1960s through to the 1970s, al-Faruqi progressively resolved his identity, emerging into what Esposito has labelled an 'Islamic scholar-activist'.[81] Esposito further comments: "Ismaʿil's concern for Islam and Muslims began with his personal commitment to Islam, and thus, his activities extended far beyond academia."[82] His self-conception included being a part of the wider international *ummah* in which he was a dynamic force for change; hence his role as an activist. According to Esposito, the war of 1967 deeply affected Ismaʿil as a failure of Arab unity.[83] He wanted to see Muslims united and strong and this was to be accomplished through the medium of education at all levels.

When one looks at all his activity from teaching at Temple, recruiting and mentoring students, involvement and leadership in the MSA, consulting with international Muslim universities to Islamize their curriculum, and the many organisations in which he participated, along with his realised dream of the International Institute of Islamic Thought (IIIT), one sees these were means to effect change through altering how Muslims think. This is evident in the numerous extant accounts of his care and concern in guiding his students.[84] The experience of international students coming to the USA was something with which al-Faruqi was well acquainted. Ghamari-Tabrizi writes:

> Most of his efforts were concentrated on Muslim students coming to the United States for higher education. He believed that living as a minority in the West afforded the best opportunity for these students to realize that they are part of one global community of Muslims (the *ummah*). This was a place in which they could transcend their ethnic and national loyalties for the sake of a universal commitment to Muslimhood. His vision was to a large extent autobiographical, for he was a Palestinian refugee who discovered the world of Islam in the West.[85]

This summarises nicely the relationship between his self-conception and his activism. In essence, who he believed himself to be (identity) informed how he viewed his fellow Muslims and the way in which to help them was to shape them from his own experience. Al-Faruqi found a measure of peace with himself as a Muslim living in the West. Intellectually he managed to find the balance between western philosophy and his faith. He tended to present Islam in western categories emphasizing reason, science, progress, and the work ethic. It is even reported that he was often critical of those Muslim students who prolonged their PhDs.[86] Spiritually he saw his own struggles as a parallel for the situations faced by Muslims, whether as a diasporic community or those who suffered in their homeland from Western colonialism. In all his experience he constructed a self-narrative, which became a model for a solution for the ills of the *ummah*. This was not necessarily a dogmatic position; rather, his activism naturally emerged from his identity.

Identity and interfaith relations

The transition from Arabism to Islam as a primary referent in al-Faruqi's life and thought is clearly recognised and mentioned by numerous writers. The fact that this accounted for his activist focus on educating and preparing the wider *ummah* to engage and ultimately supersede and lead the West is also well attested. However, this transition in identity does not so easily account for his continued, even increased efforts in dialogue with and study of non-Muslims, particularly Christians. Since this interest was present before and after this shift, there must have been something consistently present in his life to account for his motivation.[87] Simply stated: Why did he bother to engage non-Muslims when his primary goal was to strengthen the Muslim communities in the West and the Muslim world?

To begin to answer this question we first noted how his identity emerged chronologically, and now are in a position to apply Schechtman's four features of characterisation (survival, moral responsibility, self-interested concern and compensation) to his life to learn of his motivations, beliefs, and values in order to account for his persistent interest and involvement in inter-religious affairs. These features are not independent and overlap does occur. These are merely a means of looking into his life categorised as features for ease of application when in reality life is an integrated whole.

Survival

The feature of survival as presented by Schechtman revolves around primarily psychological rather than biological elements.[88] Al-Faruqi's immigration to the USA may well have felt like a forced exile from his homeland in which the psychological effects endured throughout his life. As was mentioned previously, he was faced with the challenge of re-defining himself in a new culture and in effect finding ways in which he could exist and survive intellectually, as a Muslim, as a man, and as one who could contribute significantly to society and lead a fulfilling life. When he arrived in the USA in 1948 to pursue graduate studies, he entered post-war America as a young, Arab man who in the words of his niece "... sailed to the West, hoping to find answers to the multiple questions that motivated his search for an all encompassing system that would satisfy his philosophical inclinations."[89] He was starting over again. In order to survive in a new culture, he began to re-evaluate his life and his heritage. That it took some years for him to arrive at this re-evaluation is by now obvious and he did in the end re-create himself, blending his use of reason to view and evaluate both the world and religion with his personal faith.

With his marriage to Lamya', the demands of life grew beyond his own personal needs and ambitions. The questions of 'who am I' became questions of 'who are we'? The psychological survival of Isma'il al-Faruqi also included to a large degree the re-discovery of his Islamic heritage as a Muslim. At first this was confined to his self-definition of being an Arab, but later expanded to his being a Muslim. It is important to note his use of the term *jāhiliyya* (ignorance) to describe his past up to and including his doctorate in Western philosophy in 1952. This concept of *jāhiliyya* carries the wider meaning in Islam of the condition of Arab society before the revelations were given to Muhammad. Arabs were 'ignorant' of the ways, laws and demands of the one God. When they received the message of the Qur'ān, they moved from ignorance to knowledge and thus were able to obey the laws of God. Al-Faruqi was equating such a transition with his own life, even though he arrived in the USA as a Muslim. Survival became defined as living and being a Muslim. That this realisation occurred as he moved from a Muslim to a non-Muslim culture is significant because it was in the process of learning and deciding who to be in a new culture that he found himself to be first an Arab (ethnic definition) and then a Muslim (religious definition).

In his self-narrative, he chose to define the experiences of his journey to the West with the Islamic concept of *hijrah* or emigration and not immigration.[90] In an article written in 1981 entitled "Da'wah in the West: Promise and trial," al-Faruqi reveals his thoughts about Muslim *hijrah*.[91] As the article is read, one can see that he reflects the experiences of an émigré (*muhājir*). The article offers some insight as to how he viewed himself and other Muslim émigrés, particularly in relation with other religions. He was not only a Muslim who lived in the West, but a Muslim who lived with a purpose, which can be summarized in one single word: *da'wah* (call, invitation). Since this is quite revealing and significant to this study, a more extensive exploration is needed.

Already we have seen his progress of self-definition from Arab to Muslim, but we have yet to fully touch upon the development of his interfaith interests. In "Da'wah in the West," we begin to see some connections. Al-Faruqi is quite harsh and critical of émigrés who are un-Islamic in mentality,[92] unskilled[93] or mercenary in spirit.[94] He laments the cost of emigration to the *ummah* that the émigrés abandoned and bitterly counters those who speak of such a drain as a great blessing for the international effort.[95] He writes:

> There is no doubt that the 'brainy' émigré is the best recruit for da'wah work overseas, that he is a God-sent blessing to the host country; but only if he undergoes the identity crisis and transforms himself radically into a caller. From the standpoint of the ummah, however, he is a permanent and tragic loss.[96]

The only reason he would advocate emigration is for the express purpose of da'wah.[97] This would be the only justification for a Muslim to leave his homeland for places such as the United States. He discusses the hardships, challenges and choices a Muslim émigré faces as one with first-hand knowledge. He writes:

> Certainly, the estrangement of the muhājir on the emotional, cultural, social and religious fronts and his suffering of separation from home and kin, are the worst degradation, the greatest hardship to which he could be subjected. Without a doubt, the Hijrah is the hardest fate to befall anyone. ...Yet in its darkest hour of tribulation and anguish, Allah injects the Light of Islam which fills the muhājir with optimism, confidence and strength. The muhājir may have come as an immigrant in search of Western knowledge, professional advancement, or well-being. However, in the process, he undergoes an 'identity crisis', a shattering of his self image due to the radical changes his immigrant status in the alien world has brought upon him.[98]

This vivid account speaks of experience, and although he does not state that this was his experience one can conceive of the similarities with his own knowledge and those of his Muslim students whom he likely counselled as they adjusted to a new culture. Significantly he speaks of the need for an 'identity crisis' through which the émigré is broken and then is left with two choices that he himself faced during his own period of 'identity crisis'. One choice is to focus on his past in the old country and opt for isolation or, in contrast, fully embrace the new culture, leaving his old one completely behind. The second choice is to awaken "to a fuller recognition of Islam, of his religion and cultural tradition."[99] He must become not just a new person in a new environment, but a person with a cause and this is supplied by the 'vision of Islam'. He goes on to list several elements of this vision achieved through an Islamic consciousness.[100] This applies equally to temporary émigrés who are students and those who become permanent residents.[101]

The details of his ideas are less important here than the spirit in which they are presented. Reflecting a long search for identity, al-Faruqi concludes that the purpose of da'wah is the most important justification for the émigré. Here is a plausible underlying motivation for his involvement in interfaith dialogue and a component in Schechtman's concept of survival. Survival is more than existence. It includes elements of purpose and hope, that is, something for which to live. Aside from the purpose of living in obedience to God and His ethical laws, exemplified in His Oneness, al-Faruqi found purpose in da'wah and hope in participating in the revival of Islam. Although he came to this conclusion in the midst of his discovery and creation of identity over a period of time, he saw this purpose as something to maintain, build upon and perfect even after settling his self-conception questions. Yes, he was a Muslim, but a Muslim émigré whose purpose was da'wah.

Here there are two applications of da'wah. There is the calling of Muslims to learn how to be Muslims in the wider world and there is the idea of calling non-Muslims to understand and appreciate Islam. Thus we come full circle. Although he did not leave Palestine as a dā'ī (caller), through his search for identity, he discovered this purpose and narrated his life to include da'wah as a value, belief and motivation. This purpose guided many of his efforts be they teaching, mentoring, interfaith dialogue or the Islamization of knowledge, all of which fit under the umbrella of performing da'wah. Jane I. Smith confirms this assessment as she reflected upon al-Faruqi's role in interfaith dialogue. She writes:

> Anyone who heard al-Faruqi speak, or read his writings, would recognize that his essential aim was to promote da'wa or the call to Islam. On more than one occasion I heard him declare that his primary purpose as a scholar of Islam in America was to foster da'wa in the university education system.[102]

Moral responsibility

The leap from Schechtman's concept of survival to moral responsibility is not far in this case. To whom did al-Faruqi feel morally responsible? In al-Faruqi's book *Al-Tawḥīd*, God's Oneness stands at the heart of both Islam and Muslims. As Maysam al-Faruqi, his niece, comments, "*Tawhid* had been, in his work and his aspirations, the measure of al-Faruqi's life." His sense of responsibility was shaped and directed by his understanding of God, reflected in the doctrines and expressions of Islam. He was a Muslim and he expressed his sense of responsibility through *daʿwah*. If the only reason for emigration is *daʿwah*, then it imposes a moral responsibility upon the émigré. Since he was an émigré to the West, then it would follow that his moral responsibility would also be *daʿwah*. If this seems an unwarranted assertion one need only look as far as his writings. In his oft quoted article "Islam and Christianity: Diatribe or dialogue," written in 1968, he writes:

> The man of religion, however, is moral; and in Christianity and Islam, he is so par excellence. He must therefore go out into the world, teach the truth which his religious experience has taught him and in the process refute the contrary claims. ... Hence, both Muslim and Christian are intellectually and morally bound to concern themselves with the religious view of the other, indeed of all other men.[103]

In short, he believed it was his moral responsibility to learn about and engage all religions. Further, he believed this to be binding also upon Christians. Thus for him to perform *daʿwah* adequately, he was obliged to become knowledgeable of both Islam and non-Islamic religions, such as Christianity. This is reflected in many stages of his life, from his early support for the theory of Arabism and the study of Christianity and Judaism at McGill through to the end of his days when, a month prior to his death, he is found involved in academic interfaith dialogue.[104]

Not only was this his personal responsibility, but also something he expected of his students at Temple. Muhammad Shafiq recounts his first week at Temple with this story:

> ... I attended a congregational worship service in a room on the campus of Temple University. Altogether there were eleven of us.

The leader of the service was to be Dr. Isma'il al-Faruqi. His sermon energized us with the spirit of Islam and outlined the purpose of our stay at Temple University. After the service, I and two other new students were welcomed over a cup of tea. I enquired from a student near me: "Are we to spread the teachings of Islam along while we are students here?" He answered simply: "Yes, brother, for this is what al-Faruqi demands of his students."[105]

Perhaps this is one reason why he expected his Muslim students to take courses on other religions during their studies. Such responsibility also predictably extended into all his projects. Ghamari-Tabrizi noted that initially al-Faruqi's concern was mainly "changing things through his individual scholarship and by participating in ecumenical dialogue," but later he sought institutional connections with *da'wah*.[106]

Self-interested concern

As defined by Schechtman self-interested concern is the concern a person has with being in a position to fulfil his desires and pursue his goals, even if that means making sacrifices.[107] It need not be viewed as selfishness because, for example, one's goal may be to help people and realising that goal means the interests of others become the interest of the helper. Early in al-Faruqi's academic career, he made a choice between pursuing a scholarly career and a life driven by financial gain.[108] When he left the Ph.D. programme at Harvard due to a lack of resources, he achieved success in the home construction business, but once there were sufficient funds he chose to return to academia, despite the lure of a possibly lucrative career. In this case, for him, scholarship was more important than making money. This decision was made during his self-defined period of *jāhiliyya*. However, his commitment to education as a vehicle for change continued. For example, given his background in political and administrative work in Palestine, he could have chosen this path to influence and reform the Muslim *ummah* or he could have returned to the Middle East in an attempt to bring reform from within various Muslim cultures. However, he chose to remain among non-Muslims and pursue scholarship as a professor, using this position as the platform from which to perform his *da'wah*. By reviewing his interests, desires and the priorities he set for himself, one can further determine aspects of his identity, and in this case, more completely understand his commitment to interfaith issues.

His self-interest manifested itself in many ways, and can be discovered by examining the themes and subjects that occupied his attention. Of the few topics that appear to dominate his work, based upon sheer volume one stands out: that of inter-religious study.[109] Seyyed Hossein Nasr, who was his colleague for a time at Temple University, provides some insight into the desires and concerns of al-Faruqi, when he writes:

> Without ever losing his attachment for the land he had lost, nor forgetting the lessons he had learned from Western philosophy, he turned away from secularism in all its forms and devoted himself to religious concern – at the heart of which stood Islam, in its relation with both other religions and the secularised modern world. ... The most significant writings of al-Faruqi belong precisely to this central concern of his intellectual life and include a number of works on comparative religion, religious dialogue and non-Islamic religions, including his well-known books *Christian Ethics* and *Trialogue of Abrahamic Faiths*.[110]

A quick perusal of a bibliography of al-Faruqi's writings confirms Nasr's observations.

Another focus of this concern and interest was on dialogue. He chose not only to study and write about other religions, but also to engage them in various forms of interaction, such as in symposia and institutions. This will be more deeply explored later, but for now we will allow Esposito to summarise:

> From the publication of his *Christian Ethics* in 1967 until his death, he was a major force in Islam's dialogue with other world religions. During the 1970s, al-Faruqi established himself as a leading Muslim spokesperson for Islam. It would not be an exaggeration to say that al-Faruqi became one of a handful of Muslim scholars known and respected in both western academia and ecumenical circles. His writings, speeches, participation, and leadership role in interreligious meetings and organizations sponsored by the WCC, the NCC, the Vatican, and the Inter-Religious Peace Colloquium, of which he was vice president from

1977-1982, made him, the most visible and prolific Muslim contributor to the dialogue of world religions.[111]

These observations inform us of his interest, and combined with the preceding discussions about survival and moral responsibility, a picture begins to emerge showing a strong connection between his self-interested concern for inter-religious involvement and his self-conception.

Compensation

The last of Schechtman's four features of characterization, compensation, explores what can crudely be called 'the payoff' or 'what is in it for me'. It is one thing to believe you are an émigré with the moral responsibility for da'wah, but it is quite another to actualise these beliefs. That he did so is seen in his writings and involvement in dialogue, but people often do not continue with activities they do not like or for which they do not receive acceptable compensation. So, what exactly did al-Faruqi receive from all his efforts? While these are normally not stated directly by a person, they can be deduced.

One can surmise that al-Faruqi received some degree of enjoyment and pleasure in providing leadership in Islam's relations with other religions. In his involvement with the Inter-Religious Peace Colloquium he expressed sorrow over the demise of the organisation due to a lack of finances.[112] To be one of a handful of Muslim scholars recognised, invited and honoured for their knowledge of Islam and other religions would appeal to someone who was a scholar.[113] Most academic scholars want recognition from their peers and in al-Faruqi's case he received this inside and outside the Muslim world. At the AAR conference in 1980, a participant notes:

> I observed that while the Muslim members of the panel kept themselves at a respected distance from Dr. Isma'il, they never hesitated to turn to Lamya' with their questions, nor to look to her for answers.[114]

This was written to demonstrate Lois' approachability, but it does show that people held al-Faruqi in high esteem. However, it would be incorrect to speak of academic recognition as the only compensation he received.

A greater level of reward can be seen when his overall vision for Islam and his role within that vision are considered. Certainly, he desired to be a change agent among Muslims as his own self-narrative developed and brought him into a leadership role. Indeed, his prominence amongst Muslims prompted a close friend of the Saudi Ministry of Higher Education to seek al-Faruqi's advice on how to 'plant chairs for Islamic studies at various American universities'. The decision taken by the Saudi cabinet was at the time known only to a privileged few. In a letter dated 31 October 1978, al-Faruqi writes to Dr. Ron Rendel at Cornell University asking for his thoughts, cautioning, "This is still a secret which hardly anyone in the United States knows."[115] Among North American Muslims he also held a distinct place of honour; according to Ghamari-Tabrizi:

> For a large number of American Muslim immigrants, Isma'il al-Faruqi symbolised how an emerging Muslim diaspora community's attempt to construct a Muslimhood which remains in perpetual tension between displacement and settlement, between rupture and community.[116]

Lastly, his high profile within the USA led to numerous inquiries after the Iranian revolution and hostage taking in 1979. He even received a number of threatening phone calls. Lamya' writes of this time:

> During the first months or so of the hostage affair, Isma'il was besieged with requests for information, interviews, T.V. and radio tapings; and all the while, we were feeling great anguish and concern for the results of the moves that were being made on both sides. We feel so involved that every move on both sides become our responsibility. some (sic) how and we want to direct it. Of course, this creates great frustrations![117]

So, whether in the local Muslim community of Philadelphia,[118] on campus, speaking at international conferences both for dialogue and for other Muslim concerns or advising Muslim universities on their curriculum, al-Faruqi obviously believed himself to be making a significant contribution to the development of Islam and the world *ummah*.

There is a great deal more that can be said about al-Faruqi, such as including additional testimonies from people who knew him or by pursuing a fuller examination into all of his interests beyond the immediate interfaith interest, but this is not primarily a biographical study. The purpose here has been to try to understand him in his own context in order to learn about his self-conception and identity for the more specific task of comprehending his motivations for inter-religious involvement. To this end, we conclude with a summary of his self conception, identity and dialogue before moving on to the next chapter to study his methodological approach to non-Muslims.

Al-Faruqi, like all people, was a summation of past experiences, present desires and future hopes mediated through his own self-narrative and the perspectives of others. To accurately understand a person's identity is a fairly difficult task and there are always caveats and areas missed or misunderstood. For these reasons identity theory was introduced as a means to provide some structure and guideline to this study. To the question, who was Isma'il al-Faruqi, opinions abound. For example, Esposito believed al-Faruqi saw himself as a *mujāhid*, one who struggles in the path of Islam,[119] whereas Nasr saw him as a "religious warrior out to defend the citadel of Islam."[120] Ghamari-Tabrizi felt that the Muslim community raised al-Faruqi "to the level of a martyr for Muslim da'wa in the West."[121] For Maysam, al-Faruqi's niece, his life was measured by *Tawḥīd* (God's Oneness), which he viewed as the all-encompassing ideology of life.[122] However, what did he think of himself according to the narrative he used to support his self-conception?[123]

He was a Muslim émigré who carried the pain and memory of exile and whose purpose became *da'wah* within and without the Muslim community. He defined himself as a Muslim who happened to be an Arab Palestinian and who belonged to a world Islamic *ummah*. His passion was to change the way Muslims thought and approached their world using the modernist Muslim reformer approach of education blending Islamic traditional sciences with modern western concepts. He writes:

As social scientists, we have to look back at our training and reshape it in the light of the Qur'an and the *Sunnah*. This is how our forefathers made their own original contribution to the study of history, law and culture. The West borrowed their heritage and put it in a secular mold [sic]. Is it asking too much that we take this knowledge and Islamize it?[124]

He saw himself as a leader, an activist and a proponent engaging his faith and that of all Islam in the arena of interaction with the world beyond Islam, through involvement with the knowledge and religions of the world.

The identity of al-Faruqi was shaped and defined in the context of the West with an early exposure to Christianity in Palestine, the painful creation of Israel, and his move to the USA, leading to an investigation into who he was and who he wanted to be. Arabism led him to the study of Christianity and Judaism and he began to construct his self-narrative with the West as a strong referent. As his identity included being an émigré performing da'wah, he needed to intellectually understand Islam and other faiths. It was out of this identity development that interfaith study and relations emerged. It simply became part of the way he defined himself and sought to interact with the world as a Muslim and on behalf of Islam. Dialogue became more than an exercise of duty; for al-Faruqi it constituted an essential quality of living as a Muslim minority.

PART TWO

THE DEVELOPMENT AND
APPLICATION OF METHODOLOGY

3

PHILOSOPHICAL FOUNDATIONS AND EARLY METHODOLOGY (1948-1962)

Although this and the following chapters specifically examine the methodological thought of al-Faruqi, it is not presented in isolation from his life. To do so would entail an artificial presentation that separated his life from his works. Therefore, it was first necessary in the previous chapters to discuss his life as a narrative of events, experiences and circumstances along with his own self-perceptions as they emerged and were shaped by time and experience. This information must be kept in mind as we move to a discussion about his methodology of engagement with non-Muslims.

As seen previously, al-Faruqi's self-identity influenced his academic choices, particularly as he sought to wed his personal faith with his scholarship. His early years in Palestine and his subsequent move to the United States soon after the creation of the state of Israel left an indelible impression upon his life and thought that was ever present in his work.[1] Even as he pursued an academic life, the search for his identity in a new country led him to define himself first as an Arab and then as a Muslim. With time he shifted his primary self-conception from that of an Arab-Muslim to a Muslim-Arab. His growth as a scholar paralleled his experiences as an immigrant, as a student and then as a Muslim living in a world *ummah*. These various avenues came together and set him on his unique path into the world of comparative religious studies and inter-religious dialogue.

Covering a span of over thirty years, al-Faruqi's work on interfaith engagement gathered around three broad conceptual themes: comparative religion, meta-religion and dialogue. Each of these are examined in the order that they emerged in his writings. As mentioned, these ideas developed over time, but they are not independently discrete and this will be reflected in the chronological examination presented below. This examination follows three phases in the development of his thought and covers the relevant stages in the expression of his self-conception discussed in the previous chapter, which were his U.S. academic experience (1948-1954), the Arabism/Islamic legacy (1954-1968), and Islam and Activism (1968-1986). In order to better reflect his writings and for the purpose of examining his thought, these stages are relabelled as philosophical foundations and early methodological developments (1948-1962), later methodological developments (1963-1968), and refinement and application (1969-1986). His later thought on methodology and it's applications will be addressed in Chapters Four and Five, whereas this chapter focuses on philosophical foundations and the early development of his ideas. The place to begin is with two important developments during his early academic career.

In the course of his post-graduate work in Egypt in the mid-1950s, two major developments were unfolding and these were to influence and shape his career. The first was the rise of the academic discipline of *Religionswissenschaft* (study of religion). The second was the gradual movement within the Christian church towards ecumenism and dialogue. Each of these developments provides important contextual contributions as we study al-Faruqi's methodology.

Al-Faruqi and *Religionswissenschaft*

From the late 1950s through to the 1970s, the period in which al-Faruqi was developing his own models for the study of religion, the field of religious studies was coinciding with a broader ecumenical agenda of dialogue and inter-religious contact. Both interfaith dialogue and al-Faruqi benefited from the ongoing work of *Religionswissenschaft* (study of religion).[2] It was in this atmosphere that he began his work as an historian of religion. By drawing upon a few of his writings we can briefly identify some of the ideas in the field of *Religionswissenschaft* that he adopted and adapted.

In his dissertation, the concept of philosophical phenomenology, particularly as proposed by Max Scheler and Edmond Husserl, was used to guide his thesis on the epistemological conditions for the apprehension of value.[3] Along with Nicolai Hartmann's writings on the phenomenology of values and value-theory, al-Faruqi was introduced quite early to the theory and application of phenomenology from a philosophical perspective.[4] When he entered into the study of religion, he continued to draw upon his earlier training and added insights from the various available approaches for the study of religion. Thus, he writes about the history of religions in 1965 focusing on the need to contextualise, systematise and evaluate the data.[5] He strongly advocates the need to evaluate and judge the content of a religion in order to determine its truth claims.[6] Here al-Faruqi departs somewhat from the general field of *Religionswissenschaft*, which sought objectivity without imposing any kind of value judgment.

In his book *Christian Ethics* (1967), al-Faruqi begins with a long, detailed introduction to his methodological approach.[7] The ideas he presents there guided his subsequent writings on the history of religion. He approached religion rationalistically and objectively, affirming that people can rationally understand the teachings and structures of religious belief and practice. However, this did not preclude the idea of emotional or intuitive apprehension as proposed by Hartmann and presupposed by al-Faruqi. The main difference between mystical and intuitive understanding rests with the source. Intuition and emotions emerge from the person and in this way al-Faruqi could include these under the rubric of rational thought. Mystical ideas emerge from an external source, often supernatural, and are transmitted to and apprehended by human agents, such as the prophets. A mystical understanding or approach was of no methodological use to al-Faruqi in his study of religion. This sentiment was echoed by Ibn Hazm (994-1064) and Ibn Taymiyya (1263-1328), the former of whom deeply impressed al-Faruqi as a seminal thinker in the field of comparative religious studies.[8]

As for his preferred method of religious study, Kraemer in the preface to *Christian Ethics* writes, "... he [al-Faruqi] presents his book as a phenomenological study based on metareligious principles derived from the philosophy of values of Scheler and Nicolai Hartmann."[9] From phenomenology al-Faruqi adopted *epoché* (suspension of judgment) and eidetic vision (the search for the essence and core of religion), which he defined in terms of values and ethics, and he continued with the need to be descriptive and to systematise phenomena in order to compare religions.[10] Aside from his elaboration of meta-religious principles,[11] he added the requirement to evaluate.[12] Thus, in his explanation of *epoché*, one sees the commonly accepted definition of suspended judgment, but he goes further and describes *epoché* as only a tool to understand phenomena and not a permanent condition.[13] This allows the historian or the comparativist of religion to engage in evaluation.

Over the course of the next twenty years, al-Faruqi maintained a commitment to these elements in his study and evaluation of religion. In 1982, he wrote, "Without a doubt, the phenomenological study of religion is the highest point the academic study of religion has reached in the West."[14] Finally, in his last major work, published just prior to his murder, he again re-affirmed the priority of phenomenology, noting that Husserl introduced it to Western philosophy and Scheler to the study of ethics and religion.[15]

In summation, al-Faruqi made use of the general field of *Religionswissenschaft*, preferring as his primary model phenomenology, particularly the use of rational and empirical descriptions, *epoché* and the search for essences. Where he parted from the field was in his adamant call for the use of value judgments and his derivation of meta-religious principles to guide comparative analysis.

The rise of the ecumenical and dialogical movement

The second contextual element that influenced al-Faruqi was the rise and development of the ecumenical movement, including its outgrowth into inter-religious dialogue.[16] The important point to be made is that these developments would eventually include al-Faruqi and become one of the avenues for his attempts at engagement and dialogue.

The religious spirit in various branches of the Christian church during the twentieth-century was marked by a greater openness and willingness to actively engage other religions.[17] While this may have been a by-product of a desire to foster unity and communication among its own diverse congregations throughout the world, it did in the end lead to concrete steps toward dialogue beyond the church. It is significant that these events were taking shape in the late 1950s through to the 1980s, a period in which al-Faruqi was making his own professional and vocational choices. The context of this greater openness and the presence of al-Faruqi as one of the very few western academically trained Muslim scholars in the field of comparative religion, along with his willingness to participate in dialogue, created the environment for him to become fully part of this new stream of dialogue between Muslims and Christians.

Philosophical foundations (1948-1954)

Al-Faruqi's journey into the study of religions, and his eventual articulation and use of a methodology of engagement with non-Muslims, started not with religion, but with philosophy. His doctoral research into the metaphysics and epistemology of value became an essential component of his later evaluation of non-Muslim faiths. It is unlikely that he anticipated the direction in which his philosophical studies would lead him, but with hindsight one can clearly see the role philosophical concepts and certain philosophical thinkers played in his own methodological development.

In his study of the epistemological conditions of the apprehension of value, he derived inspiration from the works of Max Scheler and Nicolai Hartmann.[18] Both introduced al-Faruqi to the use of philosophical phenomenology, which in turn became a reference point in his later study of the history of religions. However, at this juncture in his thought his intention was to demonstrate certain philosophical misconceptions surrounding the understanding of value.[19] He labelled these the "naturalistic fallacy" (the identification of value with its object) and the "dislocative fallacy" (the deduction of a pluralistic ethic from a monistic axiology).[20]

The naturalistic fallacy is discussed at length by the British philosopher G. E. Moore (1873-1958), who argues that one cannot attempt to prove a claim about ethics by appealing to a definition of good based upon a natural property, such as pleasure or desire.[21] He maintained that good is indefinable and that, "It is one of those innumerable objects of thought which are themselves incapable of definition, because they are the ultimate terms by reference to which whatever is capable of definition must be defined."[22] For example, according to Moore, the naturalistic fallacy is committed when the statement 'pleasure is good' is confused with the meaning of good.[23] He cited the example of colour to illustrate that a dictionary definition of yellow is insufficient to understand what yellow is.[24] To comprehend yellow one must be shown examples. Statements about yellow do not provide the meaning of yellow. In the same way statements about good or goodness do not give us the meaning of good. However, in Moore's preface to the second edition of his *Principia Ethica*, which was published after his death, he made two important clarifications. First, he recognised that his use of the term good was ambiguous and that the indefinability of good was only one possible predicate.[25] Second, in answer to the question: "What is the naturalistic fallacy?" he noted that there is no simple answer.[26] In fact, he recognised three different aspects of this fallacy.[27] Despite the deeper nuances of his arguments, Moore's primary concern was that intrinsic value or 'good in itself' is unanalyzable. What is important in our discussion is that al-Faruqi accepted Moore's concept of intrinsic goodness.[28] It should also be noted that Moore's preface to the second edition was published after al-Faruqi's, so that he could not benefit from Moore's reassessment of his arguments.

The naturalistic fallacy is also related to the *is-ought* problem discussed by David Hume (1711-1766) in his *A Treatise of Human Nature*. He pointed out the discrepancies between making *ought* claims or inferences based upon statements about what *is*.[29] To derive prescriptive statements (what ought to be) from descriptive statements (what is) needs to be carefully explained because knowledge of the world does not necessarily inform us of how the world ought to be. Al-Faruqi's understanding of the naturalistic fallacy contains elements of the ideas of both Moore and Hume and his use of the fallacy can be summarised as drawing ethical conclusions from natural facts or deriving an ethical *ought* based upon a metaphysical *is*.[30]

The other misconception surrounding the understanding of value that al-Faruqi identified was the dislocative fallacy. This fallacy is the attempt to derive a pluralistic ethic (an ethic with many values) from a theory of values based upon one ultimate value (monistic axiology).[31] According to Jeffery Brand-Ballard, proponents are known as either principle monists or principle pluralists.[32] Principle monists (those who accept monistic axiology) believe that "... our moral duties, such as fidelity and non-maleficence, can be justified in terms of one basic moral principle."[33] On the other hand principle pluralists see this as a form of simplicity. In Brand-Ballard's account, al-Faruqi would have been a principle pluralist.

Al-Faruqi argued that the use of phenomenology by Scheler and Hartmann provided a means for value theory to move beyond these two fallacies. In the abstract of his dissertation, he wrote:

> The view that value is an ideally self-existent essence known through an a priori emotional intuition saves it from the naturalistic fallacy, and the view that value constitutes a pluralistic realm saves it from the dislocative fallacy.[34]

According to al-Faruqi, Scheler's theory of the ethics of value made two important claims: Value is the "content object" of an *a priori* emotional intuition and good is a pluralistic realm of individually discerned value-essences each constituting its own 'oughtness'.[35] Thus, humanity has an *a priori* intuitive comprehension of value and goodness. Such comprehension does not require discursive knowledge, but is instead recognised in experience.[36]

This led al-Faruqi into a study of axiology (theory of values) where he reasoned that since moral obligations imply moral good, then axiology must precede ethics. In other words: How can a person do good if they do not know what good is and from where does this knowledge or awareness originate? Axiology begins to address this by asking two related questions: What is the good or value?; and, What things are good and valuable? From here al-Faruqi sought to use axiological methodology to determine what kind of thing is goodness and to use phenomenology of values to "co-ordinate, classify, order out in a system and reveal the relations, the inner and outer structure of what is valuable."[37] Thus, his research into values developed into a two-fold study involving a determination of what is goodness followed by the systematic classification of what is considered valuable along with a means to rank or grade values. He divided axiological methodology into two components: axiological ontology and axiological epistemology. The former would discuss what kind of being does the good and the latter how this good can be known.

Al-Faruqi then turned to Nicolai Hartmann's *Ethics* and attempted to demonstrate that values are *a priori*, that is, belonging to an order of experience other than that of any valuable object.[38] Values then become absolute and not relative and they are considered genuine "prime movers".[39] Man, through his consciousness, identifies, defines and apprehends these values. Al-Faruqi wrote:

> Naturally, not everyone is conscious of every value, just as not everyone has insight into every mathematical problem. But where anyone does have genuine valuational consciousness, he is not free to feel anything at random, but only what is itself a value; and this is, in him, a direct witness to the value itself. The value itself, therefore, can be discerned by its presence in consciousness.[40]

With Hartmann, al-Faruqi argued against the tendency to reduce value consciousness into a relativist subjectivism which would only render one opinion 'as good as' another. Instead he postulated that primary consciousness was as secure as logic or mathematics because everyone must judge in the same way – using the same feelings and intuitions. Al-Faruqi again: "We may of course be incapable of experiencing what is really valuable; but if we are capable of it, we can experience the valuable thing only as it is in itself."[41] He contended that value, of which the good or goodness is a component, is a measurable quantity found in conscious experience. However, this is not as straightforward as it appears for he notes:

> The problem of justifying the good boils down, in the final analysis, to that of providing criteria by means of which a genuine consciousness of value and its order of rank could be distinguished from one that is spurious. However, before we are able to consider how a genuine consciousness of value could be distinguished at all, we must know what a consciousness of value, as well as a consciousness or order of rank of value, simply are; we must determine by which cognitive faculty and through which use thereof can value and its order of rank be cognised and how these findings can be established for knowledge.[42]

There is little need at this point to further elaborate his arguments, for it is not the process of argument that is of interest, but rather the results. That he carried his conclusions into the study of religion, as seen particularly in his books *On Arabism* and *Christian Ethics*, is of importance precisely because it demonstrates that he maintained these early ideas toward rational philosophical thought and then wed these to select aspects of *Religionswissenschaft*. For example, he adapted the concept of eidetic vision (the search for the essence and core of religion) as found in the phenomenological method of the study of religion, and narrowed the definition to values and ethics as the criteria to discover essence. However, this was not yet a concern during his doctoral research. He simply concluded his dissertation by writing:

> We have seen that values are absolute; that they are Ideally self-existent essences which become known through an a priori

emotional intuition; that the universality and certainty of their discernment is no less than that of the theoretical a priori principle.[43] ... Values in their Ideal Being do not depend upon man, only their entrance into the actual realm is so dependent.[44]

If, as al-Faruqi asserted, values are absolute and independent of man in their Ideal Being or essence, then from where did these values originate? This question is not new. In Plato's *Euthyphro* Socrates and Euthyphro discuss the nature of holiness.[45] In their dialogue, the question is raised how holiness is to be defined. Euthyphro defines holiness as whatever the gods decide. Socrates then introduces the dilemma by asking, "Do the gods love holiness because it is holy, or is it holy because they love it?" Socrates and Euthyphro come to agree that the gods love holiness because it is holy. It was reasoned that the latter option would make holiness something potentially arbitrary, as if a god could simply define *anything* as holy.

This dilemma reappeared in the medieval Islamic debates between the Mu'tazilites and the Hanbalites. The former were a rationalist religious movement in the first half of the eighth-century and for a short period were the dominant theological school in the ninth and tenth-centuries.[46] The Hanbalites were a traditionalist school of law and differed with the Mu'tazilites over such matters as to whether the Qur'ān was or was not created. One of the basic differences was that the Mu'tazilites started from reason and the Hanbalites started from revelation.[47] Their discussions are similar to the *Euthyphro* dilemma and demonstrate the presence of such questions in Islamic thought. Martin summarises this nicely:

> The Hanbali traditionalists (as well as the Ash'ariya and other groups within the orthodox center) differed sharply with the Mu'tazila on whether the Law (Shari'a) that God revealed through His prophet Muhammad was good because God had revealed it, or whether God revealed it because it was inherently good.[48]

The Hanbalite position was similar to Euthyphro's initial argument. Framed in a different way, the Hanbalites argued that there is no good or bad beyond what God has commanded and forbidden in the Qur'ān. Thus God decides what is good and bad, or in other words good is good because God loves it. Conversely the Mu'tazilites, reminiscent of the conclusion reached by Socrates and Euthyphro, saw that God loves the good because it is good. This implies there is a good that transcends scripture.[49] Given the previous discussion about Moore's concept and al-Faruqi's acceptance of intrinsic goodness, one can see the parallel with the Muʿtazilite position.

In his dissertation al-Faruqi first approached the question of what is goodness and how can it be known from the perspectives and work of Western philosophy. His conclusion that values are absolute, ideally self-existent essences independent from but intuitively recognised by humanity led him to the position that God loves the good because it is good. However, once al-Faruqi came to believe that the absence of the transcendent led to moral chaos because all human morality is relative and not absolute in practice, he could view Allah as both the author and definer of ultimate value in its Ideal Being or essence.[50] In al-Faruqi's account, this explains the universality of value and its absoluteness, rather than a whim left up to the relative discretion of humankind. Al-Faruqi seemed to blend the Muʿtazilite and the Hanbalite positions by viewing the good as self-existent, but also found most perfectly within God, such that all of God's attributes are righteous and therefore normative. So the statement becomes: God loves the good not because it (the good) is good, but because He is good. This is not necessarily circular reasoning. According to al-Faruqi, God is not being *defined* as good because it is impossible to *know* God since He is transcendent.[51] However, humanity can *perceive* God's will, which is given to us as values, such as goodness. Values tell us about God's will and not His nature. Accordingly, values are not God *in esse* but *in percipi*.[52] Al-Faruqi goes on to equate such values with the attributes of God.[53] Out of a perception of these *a priori* values or attributes of God, comes a realisation of the ought-to-be of value. By revealing value God reveals His will. As humanity realizes the will of God, they begin to realize His values and attributes. Therefore God cannot but command the good. All that is left for man is the intuitive realisation and actualisation of those values God has already determined.

In this we can begin to see the connection between al-Faruqi's philosophical research and his personal religious perspective as it was developing during this point in his life. It is from this standpoint that we can perceive al-Faruqi's use of morality, ethics, and value as a means to qualitatively measure non-Muslim faiths against Islamic faith and practice. Although his concept of the good sounds quite similar to conclusions reached by neo-Mu'tazilite thinkers such as the Egyptian thinker Ahmad Amin (1886-1954)[54] and Mu'tazilites of the ninth and tenth-centuries, al-Faruqi's doctoral research was based upon pre-Islamic and later western philosophical thinkers, such as Plato, Aristotle, Aquinas, Kant, Schopenhauer, Nietzsche, Hartmann, C. I. Lewis and Scheler. It was after his doctoral research, when he studied at al-Azhar, that he began to assimilate works written by Muhammad 'Abduh (1849-1905), Ahmad Amin and early Mu'tazilite thinkers.[55] The point here is that it is difficult to support the idea that during his doctoral period he could be identified as a neo-Mu'tazilite. This definition is more plausible only after his time in Egypt. Indeed, in his first major post-doctoral publication, *On Arabism*, he includes the works of Muslim intellectuals, such as Amin and 'Abduh.[56] Thus one can conclude that he came to Islamic intellectual traditions through western philosophy and then married the two in his own thought. As will be discussed, even his theory of Arabism drew upon this ideal sense of consciousness or spirit pervading humanity, including the actualisation of the ideal existence of values in the reality of living. That religion is a prime component of this consciousness becomes more obvious when one considers man's need to understand the 'why' of things.

During these early years of academic study in the U.S. and his search for himself in a new culture, al-Faruqi's philosophical inclinations witnessed an early rebellion against his own religion and culture only to see him return to his Islamic heritage, particularly as western philosophy was found wanting.[57] It was at this point that he went to al-Azhar in Cairo (1954-1958) to study in some detail Islamic thought. However, the impact and presence of his western philosophical studies remained.

Early development of methodology (1954-1962)

Building upon his philosophical ideas and his renewed desire to find their application within Islam, al-Faruqi entered into the study of religion ultimately resulting in his 1962 publication: *On Arabism: 'Urubah and Religion: A Study of the Fundamental Ideals of Arabism and of Islam at Its Highest Moment of Consciousness*. The earliest published evidence of his ideas is found in a series of summaries of six lectures he presented in May 1959 at the University of Cairo.[58] These may reflect ideas he developed over the four years at al-Azhar, but without any source material from these years it is difficult to say anything concrete. However, the content of these lectures indicate the early influence of McGill University's Institute of Islamic Studies and particularly the ideas of W. C. Smith.[59] It is noteworthy that al-Faruqi went to Egypt and lectured on the history of religions, a field of studies which at this time was gaining academic prominence and attention in North America. Each of the lectures demonstrates a clear progression moving from a discussion of why Muslims should and must study other faiths (lecture one) to discerning the nascent elements of Arab religion within the history of religions (lecture six). The last two lectures in this series introduced ideas that are amplified in his book, *On Arabism*, and indicate something of the process of his own thought.

The need for Muslims (and for that matter, al-Faruqi) to study other faiths is not simply a pragmatic requirement for those who live as a minority within a largely non-Muslim country, for obviously Egypt boasts a Muslim majority, but al-Faruqi in his first lecture goes on to list other reasons. For instance, inquiry into and study of non-Muslim faiths is part of the rich historic legacy of Islamic thought, whose influence has extended into modern times. Al-Faruqi cites the medieval thinker Ibn Hazm as one among many who studied other religions and in particular who set out the principles of what is now known as textual criticism.[60] Therefore, the study of others is not something new for Islam. Secondly, the 1960s were witnessing a period of religious revival or awakening and if Muslims wanted to understand this world, then they needed to grasp the religions behind it. Furthermore, to those Muslims who felt threatened that the scientific (read 'Western') study of religion would marginalize Islam, al-Faruqi points out that Islam is a rational faith demanding the use of rational thought, which does not contradict received revelation. It only affirms and supports what Allah has already given. Lastly, al-Faruqi appeals to the place of Egypt as a modern influence on religious thought by pointing out the need to study religion rationally and to understand the power and logic of other religions and cultures. He states: "It behoves us to understand the religions of those worlds in order to understand the forces that move them in order to understand the logic of their culture."[61]

In lecture two, al-Faruqi introduces the methodology of the science of religion. Indeed, if Muslims need to study other religions scientifically, how then is this to be done? After discussing and dismissing the methods of psychology, philosophy and, quite interestingly, phenomenology, he settles on the historical method as the best approach to the study of religion.[62] The fact that phenomenology in this lecture of 1959 is discarded as an inappropriate method requires some attention primarily because later, in 1986, al-Faruqi was to write: "Without a doubt, the phenomenological study of religion is the highest point the academic study of religion has reached in the West."[63]

In fact, within a few years (by at least 1967), with the publication of *Christian Ethics,* al-Faruqi would approach the study of Christian ethics from a phenomenological perspective.[64] However, in 1959 he was still quite critical of this method as something which denied any essence of religion.

The phenomenological method as explained by Rudolf Otto, Gerardus van der Leeuw, Mircea Eliade and W. C. Smith proposed that each religion had its own historic path consistent with each member's personal psychological needs and that this can lead to a level of relativism with religion becoming new every morning. Al-Faruqi's reaction to this was:

> It is up to the science of religion to study it (religions) and figure out its motivations and their manifestations and outcomes. If it does this, it could direct the stream (of religious history) to whatever it wants or at least influence the direction of this path or predict it. The great weakness of this method (phenomenology) is it denies that religion has a substance or an essence, but how can it distinguish these phenomena one from each other to decide which is religious and which is not and then filter these religious phenomena from each other to know which one of them is Buddhist, Hindu, Islamic or Christian? It must then assume what it publicly denies.[65]

In support of the historical method, al-Faruqi cites six reasons, all of them conforming to his view of religion.[66] The main positive feature was that history studied religion in order to determine the logical process of its development within human history including its essence, the testimony of its adherents, the phenomena unique to it and its ready acceptance of data from all the other fields.

The question remains: Why did al-Faruqi make use of phenomenology a few years later? The apparent distance between his position in 1959 and that of 1967 and beyond is not as great as one might assume. Aside from the fact that 1959 marked an early point in his study of *Religionswissenschaft* and that he was still in the process of forming his own ideas, much of his early critique was centred on W. C. Smith's position that religion, particularly Islam, has no essence.[67] It would appear at first glance that al-Faruqi dismissed the entire theory of phenomenology of religion without fully grasping all of its contributions. However, this is not the case. For example, at the end of Lecture Four, he mentions the need to practice *epoché* (suspension of judgment) when approaching the past. This is clearly a feature of the phenomenological method. In due course it will be seen that al-Faruqi adopted and adapted phenomenological concepts into his methodology. In 1959, he made the choice not to mention the philosophical ideas of phenomenology used in his doctoral research in favour of emphasizing history. Years later, however, he would criticise the historical approach as a self-determining process based on evolution.[68]

In Lectures Three to Six, al-Faruqi begins to apply his methodological ideas by laying out an historic schematic of world religions in which each successive religion reveals more of God's message culminating with Islam. In these lectures, one can see the formation of his later theory of Arab consciousness or Arabism. For example, in his third lecture, al-Faruqi divides the world's religions into three broad entities of Eastern/Indian, Western/Greek and Arab/Semitic.[69] He defines and contrasts each through their worldviews specifically in terms of their approach to this present world and that of the supernatural or divine world. The Eastern religions, according to al-Faruqi, sought escape from this world, which is considered to be evil, temporary and illusory, in favour of the eternal and good world. The Western and Greek religious traditions on the other hand viewed these two worlds as intimately connected, with the present world of humanity a poor reflection of the higher world. Hence the gods interacted with this world and came to be represented within the world of people. The Arab and Semitic worldview saw these two realms as completely separate with, however, the superior realm influencing the human world through commands and laws.

He concludes by commenting that Arab religious history is divided into five periods: pre-Abrahamic up to 1800 B.C.; post-Abrahamic until 1280 B.C.; from Moses to Jesus; from Jesus to Muhammad; and finally from Muhammad until the present.[70] The division of the world's religions into groups was not something new for the science of religion, but the divisions within the Arab religious history were inspired more by an Islamic viewpoint.

In the following lectures (Four–Six), the methodological approach to non-Muslim faiths is less a direct study of the other, as it is a by-product of understanding Islam. In other words, al-Faruqi builds his case for the history of the Arab (Islamic) religion and in doing so creates a way to view non-Arab faiths. However, this is slightly more complicated because Judaism and Christianity are not viewed as faiths distinct from Islam, but rather as beliefs whose true essences are pictures of God's message for their time. Full clarity comes with Islam, but this is a perspective available only to those who look at this past through the lens of Islam. Thus, in Lecture Four, al-Faruqi sets out five metaphysical elements[71] and uses these as a means to uncover the gradual unfolding of God's message and law to all humanity in each of his historical divisions of the Arab religion. He concludes that Islam is as old as humanity, but did not always exist as 'Islam'; therefore, Muslims need to search for the religion of God in the pre-*hijrah* periods.[72] To undertake such an investigation requires the use of the phenomenological tool of *epoché* to suspend any preconceptions and ideas a Muslim may possess in order to apprehend history, and to perceive how those in the past understood their religions.[73] Here, as mentioned above, al-Faruqi advocates the use of a tool drawn from phenomenology and applies it to history despite his earlier dismissal of the phenomenological method per se. One might object that the call to practice *epoché* after pre-determining what one will find is not really *epoché* at all, but more of a means to an end.

The last two lectures, very briefly, are at once an application of the five metaphysical principles, in which the peoples of Sumer and Akkadia are highlighted as possessing elements of the Arab religion,[74] and an examination into the migration of people into al-Shām (the region of present day Syria, Lebanon, Palestine, Israel and Jordan), who carried with them these same elements of the Arab religion.[75] Within the fifth lecture al-Faruqi introduces, but does not elaborate in any great detail, his concept of later Jewish racialism that led to the alteration of the Torah rendering God as their own and thereby fostering separateness from other peoples.[76] In contrast, as presented in his final lecture, the Qur'ān preserved the history of the religion of God through the presence of *Ḥanīfiyya* in the pre-*hijrah* period.[77]

One need not assume these six lectures reflect all of his thought, for they may simply be tailored to the audience he addressed. However, since many of these ideas continued to be repeated and refined over the ensuing years, it is not without reason that we can postulate they mirror something of the development of his own thought process.[78] This of course needs some further explanation. In our previous discussion, it was seen that al-Faruqi struggled to find his 'identity' while in the United States after being left stateless in 1948. In the process of self-discovery, he moved toward a rediscovery of his Islamic heritage first by studying Islamic intellectual thought and history at al-Azhar and then by studying the place of Islam in the world of religions at McGill University. During these years, he saw himself as an Arab Palestinian Muslim and kept emphasizing the Arabness of Islam even to the point of developing his theory of Arabism (*'Urūbah*). This was a novel approach, building upon the traditional notion of the progress of religion as espoused by Ibn Hazm in which the single continual message of God's oneness and law was systematically given to all humans. The most prominent of these revelations are found in Judaism, Christianity and Islam. The assertion was that the previous two religions bear some semblance to the original message despite at times conveying gross distortions. In any case, the march to Islam was built upon the need to correct and complete earlier corruptions of the texts given to the Jewish and Christian communities. Al-Faruqi moved from this basic view of religious history and sought to develop a new theory in which the essential spirit or essence of Islam always existed. This was something he called Arabism.

The theory of Arabism published in 1962 reflected some of the struggle undergone by al-Faruqi as he sought to establish himself in a new culture. It combined the philosophical ideas of value, morals and ethics, all of which were the focus of his graduate work in the United States, with his Arab identity situated within the broader context of Islamic thought. He came to study the latter in greater depth at al-Azhar in Egypt and at McGill's Institute of Islamic studies, but as the above summaries of his University of Cairo lectures demonstrated, his basic thoughts regarding Arabism were largely in place by 1959. On one level it helped to answer the question: Who am I? On another level it was a means to remain faithful to his Arab identity and his Muslim faith, all presented within academic discourse cognisant of western developments in philosophy and the study of religion. In this way the theory became an updated attempt at articulating Islam's place as the final expression of Allah to humanity. Its purpose was not to present a theory or method of engagement with non-Muslims. Instead Arabism defined the playing field from which a methodology of dialogue could occur. This idea of definition is quite important because it sets out the premises, ethos, attitude and the perspective that al-Faruqi would develop in the course of his future work on interfaith subjects. So what exactly is this theory of Arabism?

Alternately referred to as Arabism ('Urūbah), Arab consciousness and the Arab stream of being, this theory sought to explain the expression of and obedience to Allah's revealed will and law to humanity throughout history. This was demonstrated particularly in the arena of moral and ethical excellence. It is not identified as Islam, but rather as the underlying essence of a spirit that turns to God's oneness and His ways. In the words of al-Faruqi:

'Urubah is the essence of the person who is an Arab; and this is not only the inhabitant of the Arabian Peninsula, or the political territories of the Fertile Crescent, of Northeast and North Africa, commonly regarded as Arab on account of his Arabic-speaking. In addition to the Arabic-speaking peoples, the Arabs include, unlike any other people on earth, millions of non-Arabic-speaking persons living in territories adjoining the Arabic-speaking lands but stretching as far as Siberia, the Philippines, the Danube, Equatorial and East Africa, who represent comparatively higher or lower degrees of Arabness. But Arabs they all are, since their consciousness – and this is the real and final test of Arabness – is not only determined by the values of 'Urubah, but represents those determinants to itself as elements of, and in terms couched exclusively by, Arab consciousness.[79]

Thus, when al-Faruqi used the word 'Arab,' he did not necessarily limit this term to an historical, geographically defined people. He widened the definition to include anyone who recognises, shares, and adheres "to the values of 'urubah to which they have arrived by their own effort, through literature, masters or friends, and stand ready to assist by means open to them the cause of 'urubah in the world."[80] Further, expropriating the term *ḥunafā'* (plural of *ḥanīf*, literally: 'morally pure'), he expanded this concept beyond its traditional Islamic application to those in the pre-Islamic period who believed in one God and instead defined it as encompassing "the non-Arabic-speaking non-Muslims whose consciousness and lives are determined by its ['*urūbah's*] values without their becoming either Arabic-speaking or Muslim."[81] In other words, any non-Muslims at any point in history who demonstrate any of the values of Arabism are in fact Arabs and *Ḥunafā'*.[82] So, when in the course of the following discussion we see al-Faruqi use the word *Arab*, we must not think of *Arab* as a socio-political or even as an historically ethnic word; instead, we must remain aware of his re-definition of the term to mean someone who exhibits these 'yet to be defined' values of Arabism. Indeed, the purpose of his book was to define, defend and explain what Arabism is.

By embracing an inclusive definition of *Arab* and pushing its origins into the antiquity of history, al-Faruqi was then able to construct a theory in which the presence of Arabness and its unfolding became the very nature of Arabism or the Arab stream of being. Therefore, he was able to write:

> ... Arabism is as old as the Arab stream of being itself since it is the spirit which animates the stream and gives it momentum. 'Urubah is that which agitated the Arabs to seek their liberty and unity in the twentieth century as well as to press northward towards the Fertile Crescent to give its people their language, culture and religion, in four succeeding waves: As Muslims in the seventh century A.D., as Arameans in the fifteenth century B.C., as Amorites in the second and third, and as Akkadians in the fourth and fifth millennia B.C.[83]

This was an expansion of ideas he presented in his Cairo lectures in 1959.[84] Of particular importance is the notion of the longevity and ancientness of Arabism in which "something eternally and unchangeably Arab persisted throughout history and by so doing, this Arab essence gave identity to the Arab stream and continuity to the events that make up its history."[85] It is at this point in the work that al-Faruqi introduces the element of faith and revelation to support his theory. From Sūra Āli 'Imrān (3:110), i.e., "*You are the best people brought forth for mankind. You enjoin what is right and forbid what is wrong and believe in Allah,"* he coins the following syllogism:

> To enjoin the good, forbid evil and believe in God is to be ethically the best;
> The Arabs enjoin the good, forbid evil and believe in God;
> Therefore, the Arabs are ethically the best.[86] [Italics his]

He adds:

> The descriptive statement, 'Ye are the best people brought forth unto mankind,' asserts a historical fact that is eternally true. Like all historical truths this one describes a fact that belongs to history and which no thinking can undo.[87]

Thus, faith meets history, which in turn, supports the theory of Arabism. The goal or purpose of Arabism was to produce an ethically, morally and godly people who believed in and obeyed the one God. This 'essence' existed within human history and found expression in certain periods and among various peoples such as the Akkadians, the Amorites, the Arameans and finally the Muslims. It was both an historic and a religious phenomenon. And it was in the realm of religion that al-Faruqi began to unpack the implications of his theory for inter-religious contact. In fact all of the preceding discussion about Arabism acts as a background for how al-Faruqi viewed, interpreted and approached religions. Having posited the basic idea of Arabism and *Arab*, defined in the broadest manner, he begins to re-read religious history, writing:

> That God is and that He is One was not the conclusion of an 'evolution of the idea of God,' as the historians of religion might say. Nor was it the sudden uncaused proclamation from heaven to Abraham, Adam or Muhammad that theologians usually make it out to be, but the crystallization and goal of a long process of maturing ethical sense.[88]

This does not mean that revelation from God was of no use; rather, that God was slowly, carefully revealing his law and values through history and religion. That it took time for people to understand and remain faithful to this truth of the oneness of God is closer to the point that al-Faruqi wishes to emphasize here.

Within this maturing process as viewed from the perspective of religion, al-Faruqi next introduces the idea that Arab consciousness was divided into three periods or streams known as Judaism, Christianity and Islam. In itself this is not really a new idea. What is different, however, is that he built this theory around the concept of an ancient, almost primordial essence within humanity. This was continually expressed in history and religion, of which Islam is the example of its fullest expression, though not itself equated with Arabism. Again he writes:

> Arab consciousness therefore regards all Judaism, Christianity and Islam as moments of its long and arduous course of growth beginning, in childhood with Adam, and reaching the age of reason in Muhammad, 'the seal of the prophets'.[89]

Thus, Christianity did not build upon Judaism nor did Islam build upon Christianity and Judaism; rather, they were expressions of Arabism each fuller than the former. The reason for this was that humanity, over time grew more susceptible to receiving and realising the fullness of the blessings of God's oneness, His law and the subsequent results of justice and a moral society.

As al-Faruqi amplifies his ideas about Arabism, including its nature, purpose and ethos, one may notice some parallels with the ideas of Ernest Renan (1832-1892). Renan was one of the main nineteenth century architects of the science of philology and its use in the earlier distinction between Indo-European (Aryan) and Semitic languages and races. He argued that the Semites invented religion but little else and that the Aryans invented politics, science, the arts and other branches of knowledge.[90] He spoke of a Semitic spirit expressed in two pure forms – the Hebraic/Mosaic and the Arabic/Islamic.[91] According to Maurice Olender, Renan's theory of language was identical to his theory of religion and thus the Semitic spirit was shaped by language.[92] In his book *Studies in Religious History*, Renan, although recognizing that the term 'Semitic' was an incorrect appellation to represent a group of languages (Hebrew, Phoenician, Syrian, Arabic, and Abyssinian), nevertheless continued to apply the word to race.[93] Thus he wrote about Judaism, Christianity and Islam that: "Now, these three great religious movements are three Semitic facts, three branches of the same trunk, - three translations, unequally beautiful, of the same idea."[94] The Semites used a type of "primitive intuition" to arrive at the notion of a Supreme God and monotheism.[95] Thus the Semitic spirit reflected more than language, or in other words it was defined by religion and race. Renan wrote that Muslim Africa and Asia are regions of the world that are perfectly representative of the 'Semitic spirit' even though their "pure Semite population [race] is insignificant."[96]

Although al-Faruqi only cites Renan once in *On Arabism*, one does notice some parallels with Renan's ideas.[97] For example, while the use of Arab is favoured over Renan's use of Semitic or Semite,[98] al-Faruqi's conception of Arabism as a "spirit which animates the stream [of being] and gives it momentum"[99] brings to mind Renan's idea of Semite (and Aryan) as two twins at the origins of civilization.[100] Moreover, the view that the Arabic language is the source of all Semitic languages and that Arab consciousness preserves "the wisdom of all past generations of Semitic stock"[101] also reflects something of Renan's assertion that all "the original traits of the Semitic genius were preserved by Abraham's descendents."[102] Finally, al-Faruqi agrees with Renan, although Renan preferred to use 'Semitic', that "monotheism is exclusively an Arab thought, a reality of Arab consciousness."[103] For al-Faruqi the Hebrew period, which was championed by Renan, constituted little more than a moment of Arab consciousness.

Since there is very little citation of Renan's ideas by al-Faruqi, we are left to speculate regarding the source of these similarities. Certainly the concept of Semitic was current during al-Faruqi's early academic career and given the influence of Renan's thought in wider academic discourse, it is not surprising that some of these ideas appear in al-Faruqi's work. However, al-Faruqi does not simply re-label Renan's speculations, using Arab in place of Semitic, nor does he merely rework some of Renan's concepts. Instead he develops his own theory, while remaining bound by the general constructs and results of nineteenth-century European preoccupations with philology and the quest for the origins of race and culture through language and religion.

As for the relationship between the concepts of Arab and Semite (Semitic), al-Faruqi proposes that Arab consciousness acted as the 'substrate of all Semitic religions' and constitutes a common ground between religions.[104] In other words, Semitic religions were moments in the consciousness of the Arab stream of being. The implication follows that if Judaism and Christianity were Semitic moments of Arabism, then so too was Islam. However, at this stage al-Faruqi does not identify Islam as a Semitic moment.[105]

In an exchange with Stanley Frost, then Dean of the Faculty of Divinity at McGill University, al-Faruqi was asked to further explain his views on Semite/Semitic and Arab. His lengthy reply is instructive and worth repeating because his explanation reflects nineteenth century European philological theories of Semites and Aryans:

I call this unique transcendence-consciousness Arab, rather than Semitic, because Arab is not the name of an element in the Stream, of "one among many." Judaism, for instance, is Jewish because it is the religion of the Jews who were inhabitants of Judah. But it is also Arab because geographically, ethnically, linguistically and ideologically, the Jews who were inhabitants of Judah were one with the Arabs. The Jews were an element among other elements such as the Phoenicians, the Anaanites, the Ancient Ma'inites, etc. But all these were Arabs. It is true that all Arabs in my sense are Semites, but this all-inclusive sense of "semite" is a relatively modern – I suspect Western – concept. I doubt if any Semitic people has represented to itself its own identity as "semitic." You may ask, but has any of those peoples represented itself as Arab? The answer is yes, the "Arabs" (in the smaller sense of the Peninsula Arabs) have always done so. And since they are the fountainhead of all those other peoples, they may legitimately give their name to the whole. I do not know of any geographic, ethnic, linguistic or ideological evidence which relates the Semitic peoples including the Arabs to Canaan, or to Phoenicia, or to Babylon, or to Judah, so as to furnish as much as a claim that the Arab stream of being is really a Canaani, Phoenician, Babylonian or Jewish stream of being. Only the concept "semite" has laid such a claim, but it has done so on the strength of a modern distension of its denotations by Western scholars. If the Western scholar may, in the 19th century, pick out a concept (viz. "semitic") from the Jewish tradition and give it this all-inclusive sense, why may not I take the concept "Arab" which is far more than a concept and restore to it in the 20th century the all-inclusive denotation which is its due?[106]

Here al-Faruqi is offering 'Arab' as a replacement for 'Semitic,' even though he notes that "all Arabs in my sense are Semites." However, he attempts to draw a distinction between Arab and Semitic/Semite. Arab is viewed as the source of Semite, which he views in the narrower sense as Jewish tradition and in the more all-inclusive sense of the language and peoples of the region (Hebrews, Phoenicians, Babylonians, and Canaanites). However, he does not abandon the term Semitic. For example, he later uses the term Semitic consciousness in place of Arab consciousness.[107] Thus there is some confusion over how his definitions shifted as he used these terms. At times Arab and Semitic are distinct and at other times they are interchangeable. He correctly notes that no one referred to themselves as Semites and recognises that it is a modern western concept. As Gil Anidjar mentions, the Semites, like the Aryans, were "a concrete figment of the western imagination" and have largely been abandoned today as fictitious conceptual terms, reflecting more imagination than fact.[108] However, al-Faruqi, while recognizing the concept Semitic as a western idea, nevertheless continued to work largely within this paradigm. This is, perhaps, reflective of the period in which he penned his theory of Arabism, but it does not account for why he maintained its contours throughout his later academic career.

Once al-Faruqi developed this thesis of Arabism, the remaining task for him was to sift through Judaism and Christianity in search of evidence for this Arab stream of being. Although he uses the term 'essence,' there is no mention of the phenomenological terms eidetic vision (search for essences) or epoché (suspension of personal belief). The study is almost exclusively historical in nature following his earlier support for the method of history.[109] In fact it is the absence of epoché in his approach to Judaism and Christianity that is most notable, given his sometimes quite novel interpretations of the Jewish and Christian scriptures.[110] It would be incorrect, however, to limit al-Faruqi's work on Arabism to his interpretations of Judaism and Christianity, for he also spends some effort on addressing Arab nationalism, the Islamist position and the Arabist synthesis, in which he attempts to show why his theory of Arabism is the most plausible view of religious history. After providing brief summaries of his approach to Judaism, Christianity, and Islamist positions, we will finish with our analysis of Arabism by explaining his ideas about the Arabist synthesis.

Judaism, according to al-Faruqi, was the first moment of Arab consciousness, whose essence is "the recognition and worship of the one God and whose ethic is the universalistic fulfilment of value conceived as His command."[111] However, in the course of history the Hebrews gravitated toward creating an exclusive and separatist view of their unique position under God such that they became the 'chosen ones' and God became their God. Nevertheless, Arab consciousness was striving to include all people under the one God and a remnant of the Hebrew people, identified by al-Faruqi as adherents of 'genuine Judaism', understood and proclaimed this message.[112] Unfortunately the vast majority of Hebrews fought against this message. He writes:

> Having transvalued the teachings of these men, the Hebrews combined the legacy of these God-worshipping hanifs with the separatist, tribalist ravings of their rabbis and this gave us the curious mass of Jew-loving, *goyim*-hating, Lord-of-the-universe, God-of-the-Jews literature which is the Old Testament.[113]

Thus, his vision of Judaism was that of a religion that rejected the essence of Arabism, although there were those such as Abraham, Ishmael, Isaac, Jacob and Moses who remained faithful. This rejection is seen particularly in post-Exilic Judaism when al-Faruqi believed most of the Jewish scriptures were written.

According to al-Faruqi, Christianity was the second moment of Arab consciousness and came as a solution to the "chronic perversion of the Hebrews within the Arab stream of being..."[114] This solution essentially was the message and teaching of Jesus. After arguing that this message can be uncovered by carefully analysing the sayings of Jesus in the Gospels, he goes on to deduce two key components of the latter's teaching.[115] The first is the connection between monotheism and the ethical universalism of human brotherhood. Monotheism was never intended to remain a theoretical belief, but needed to produce a genuine 'value-consciousness.'[116] Thus, he comments:

> That monotheism is nonsense and hypocrisy without ethical universalism, and secondly, that although they may differ in theoretical content, they are identical as elements of value-consciousness – this was the great truth Arab consciousness was

gradually discerning and Jesus Christ came to teach with unprecedented clarity and sincerity.[117]

Using the criteria of ethics, al-Faruqi argues that he could determine the true content of the Gospels through an historical reconstruction of Jesus.[118] This assumed of course that the presentation of Jesus in the Gospels, the Epistles and particularly in Church doctrine and history was somehow deficient, requiring a re-reading of the text based upon the criteria of the ethical sayings and teachings of Jesus. This led al-Faruqi to posit a hierarchy of value as the second key component in the teaching of Jesus. Thus, the higher values ought to have precedence over the lower ones in determining how people live.[119] These higher values were contained within the teaching of Jesus and included such ideas as seeking God's kingdom first.

In contrast to much of traditional Christian teaching, al-Faruqi's Christ came not to redeem humanity, but to provide the means for redeeming oneself through the gradual perfecting of ethical consciousness and practice. Al-Faruqi argues:

He [Jesus] came but to show how man ought to live, how he ought to conduct himself *vis-à-vis* the world and existence. This is the meaning Jesus had of redemption. The sin from which he sought to redeem mankind was man's obsession with an insatiable and distracting pursuit of worldly existence, of lower value. ... Christ's redemption is not a having redeemed but a having provided a method of redemption. It is not the fact of Jesus' passion and crucifixion that constitute redemption, but the moral truth it was his special distinction to bring, with divine grace, to man's consciousness. The historical events of his life, whatever research may reveal them to be, were made necessary by his life's being an exemplification of this moral truth, not a 'price' paid in exchange for the forgiveness of the sins of others. It is offensive to common sense to speak of 'forgiving' a reality or a state of nature, and to moral sense, to contemplate anyone 'paying' for the sins of others.[120]

Therefore the mission of Jesus was to point the way, not be the way. In order to maintain this idea, al-Faruqi needed to demonstrate that Christianity corrupted the message and mission of Jesus.

Simply stated, al-Faruqi tries to identify a cleavage between the true faithful followers and the distorters. Thus, in Christianity, by at least 100 A.D., Arab Christianity, which retained and preserved the truth about Jesus, became separated from Pauline or Western Christianity.[121] Arab Christianity was characterised by pure monotheism, ethical universalism, life-affirmation and rationalism. Western Christianity managed to create the opposite, introducing 'trinitarianism,' mysticism and salvation as a *fait accompli*. Hence, Western Christianity removes any reason for religion because "if universal religion is already achieved, what need is there for religion?"[122]

As was mentioned at the outset of this discussion, al-Faruqi did not set out in *On Arabism* to articulate a methodology of engagement, but rather to prepare the field for subsequent avenues of interfaith discourse. This occurred almost as a by-product of attempting to prove his theory of Arab consciousness. Therefore, he needed to construct Judaism and Christianity in ways suitable to support and substantiate his theory. At the same time he needed to provide an account for why both Judaism and Christianity had so obviously missed the essential core of their faiths. Having demonstrated this to his own satisfaction, he turned to Islam as the third and final moment in the Arab stream of being.

Although Arabism is not identified with Islam, it is nevertheless unthinkable without Islam because the Arab spirit, with its never-ending drive for monotheism, universalism, ethicalism, rationalism and world-affirmation, is realised to its fullest extent within Islam. This identification was the result of Islamist assertions of equating Islam, Arab and nationalism. Al-Faruqi's Arabist synthesis moved beyond these categories to recognise a deeper, underlying spirit. The actual revival or renaissance of this Arab spirit is connected with an axiological systemization of the Qur'ān in which the Qur'ān becomes the highest value, containing a hierarchy of moral values including God's oneness and the actualisation of moral and ethical ideals. Al-Faruqi comments that: "… we may then say that Islam is a body of values constituting an ideal realm, a transcendent supernal plenum of value at the center of which is God."[123] The connection between the Arab spirit and Islam rests on the plane of values, such that:

'Urubah is co-intensive with the values of Islam, just as it has been co-intensive with the values of Jesus, of Moses, Abraham and the other prophets in its earlier stages of development. Nonetheless, 'urubah remains metaphysically different from Judaism, Christianity and Islam. To confuse them with 'urubah is to commit the naturalistic fallacy, to confuse two separate entities belonging to different orders of being.[124]

Indeed, this Arab stream of being is "infinite like time" and it is beyond knowledge to discern its beginning or end because it has always existed, even though humanity's awareness of its presence and reality may have started at a certain time.[125] This is quite a lofty declaration not without theological implications, such as: If Arabism is infinite and eternal, is he not equating this with the existence of God? At the end of On Arabism al-Faruqi addresses the implications of this question and by understanding his explanations, we will grasp the connection between value theory, Arabism and his evaluative method of comparative religious study, the latter of which will be discussed in the following chapter.

The nature of Arabism, the Arab spirit or Arab consciousness is determined by values.[126] We must remember that al-Faruqi is not using Arab in an ethno-linguistic manner, but rather to label people who apprehend and perceive God's values. Arabism or the Arab spirit is the wider collective process of this perception. Thus, God's values determine the spirit and reality of Arabism.[127] According to al-Faruqi, since humanity can only perceive God's values or attributes and not His nature, the realisation of these values in space and time (this world) is the process of Arabism. He writes: "For us humans, therefore, God's will is God in percipi; and since God's will is none other than the ideal realm of values, to know them is to know God in percipi, and to fall under their determination is to obey divine will."[128] Hence, the theory of Arabism is really a theory about values, which are given to us by God and are identified with His attributes. Humanity can perceive these values apart from revelation, such as in philosophy, but God's revelation hastens our acquisition and obedience.[129] By this definition, the above question regarding the equation of Arabism with the existence of God becomes one of equating Arabism not with God's nature but with His attributes. In this sense, al-Faruqi can claim that Arabism is 'infinite like time' and that it pre-exists human awareness.

With this understanding of value and Arabism, we can begin to see how values, expressed by al-Faruqi in Arabism, can be employed as a means to define religion and ultimately evaluate it. His theory provides a means to view each of the three moments of Arab consciousness not in terms of categories of superiority or ethnicity, but rather as levels of the potentiality within each faith to continually strive for the goals set by Arabism (pure monotheism, ethical universalism, rationalism and world-affirmation). In this way, interfaith understanding can begin to develop as each religion attempts to realise common goals. The actual substance of how this can develop is not under scrutiny here; rather, it was the theoretical possibility and potential that Arabism created through which each could engage the other. For example, in the end al-Faruqi partly summarised his view of Christianity in this way:

> Undoubtedly, Christianity was a divine moment, incepted by divine action and aimed at giving man the ideal to live by and the road to follow. It posited and asserted the ideal in its fullness: All men are children of God, the Father who is in heaven. Although its categorical imperative sought the moral perfection of the subject, and assumed the *summum bonum* of ethical striving to be a state of the subject in which he becomes the pure and innocent child united to his Father, it conceived the road to such perfection as one in which the welfare of the neighbour is always the aim of ethical striving. It emphasized the higher moral value, the spiritual and ethical rather than the material and the elemental. It demanded self-mastery and instituted ascetic exercise. All these helped give the Christian ethical ideal an extraordinary moving appeal and power. By it, the Arab spirit made enormous and daring strides forward on the road of ethical fulfilment.[130]

The early part of this developmental stage in al-Faruqi's thought (1948-1962) reflected ideas and approaches generated by his work in philosophy, the study of religion and Arabism. Academically and professionally, he completed his doctorate at Indiana and post-doctoral studies at al-Azhar and McGill. This was a time of personal and academic change reflected in his movement from the philosophy of value to Arabism with its need for comparative history in the study of religion and ultimately beyond into the arena of dialogue. It would seem an entirely natural progression to move academically from Arabism into the study of comparative religion, since it was a necessary requirement for his theory. His interest and work from 1963 to 1968 forms the basis for the later development of his comparative and meta-religious principles, which created the essential foundation for his dialogical applications.

4

COMPARATIVE, META-RELIGIOUS AND DIALOGICAL PRINCIPLES (1963-1968)

This stage is arguably the most important in the thought of al-Faruqi because, once his methodology was developed, he spent the remainder of his career expanding and further applying his ideas. It is important to note that almost all of his articles from this period discuss comparative religion and in some measure dialogical issues except perhaps one, but even here there was some juxtaposition between Islamic and Western perceptions of value.[1] In fact, one notices that even though al-Faruqi is arguably more known for his Islamization of knowledge project, this is a product of his later years and represents only a fraction of his publications.[2] Even in the midst of developing this project, he still maintained a strong commitment to exploring Muslim and non-Muslim interaction and dialogue. Thus, on the basis of his published works, one can claim that Muslim relations with non-Muslims, particularly with Christians and Jews, was his paramount interest within the theme of reviving and preparing the Muslim *ummah* to engage the Western world. However, it must be mentioned that this interest was often within the context of Muslim self-understanding and not an exercise in theoretical ecumenicalism.

This interest is demonstrated in his 1963 article, "On the raison d'être of the Ummah," which at first glance would appear to have little to add to interfaith issues.[3] Upon closer inspection, however, and although much of the article dealt with issues specific to the Muslim *ummah* in relation to *al-ḥayāt al-dunyā* (life in this world) and a refutation of Sufism, he managed to draft comparisons with Christianity and Indian religions and situate his discussion within this wider religious context. There is little, if any, elaboration of methodology, but in the context of humanity's purpose, he does offer some insight into his attitude toward other faiths. He argues that the purpose of humanity is to do good works, which is equivalent to fulfilling God's will as encapsulated in His divine law.[4] The world was created in such a way as to allow people to fulfill their purpose, which is ethical and moral in nature.[5] Without the potential for evil, good would always exist and man's vocation and purpose would cease to be.[6] Without choice, people could not demonstrate or fulfill God's purpose in creation. Simply stated, God created in order to see who is the *better* worker of good deeds. Thus, al-Faruqi viewed Islam as world-oriented, Indian religion as world-escaping and Christianity as world-overcoming.[7] He writes:

> While the redeemed life in Indian religion is not a life in space-time but in *Nirvāna*, life under the grace of Christ is either an *imitatio Christi*, i.e., a seeking of death at the hand of one's enemies; or monotonous proclamation of the news of the *fait accompli* redemption by Christ while awaiting the eschatological end of this-world as if it were a temporary, intermediate interlude, insignificant in itself, but important only on account of that to which it leads. In neither case is the only and final criterion of truthfulness to this-world realized, namely, whether or not man's vocation consists of diverting the causal threads of the cosmos towards a historical space-time reality in which all values are realized.[8]

In contrast, he considered Islam as the only religion that seeks to transform both humanity and the world by striving after good in this world. Therefore, the Christian enterprise is simply incorrect in view of his opening premise that man exists to realise ethical value in this world. Whether or not such an attitude is conducive to dialogue will be seen later.

Remaining with the theme and use of ethics, which by now may be recognised as a constant thread in his general view and approach to other faiths, al-Faruqi contrasts in a short article how Islam and Christianity approach the Hebrew Scriptures.[9] He reveals not only his opinion regarding Christian uses of the Hebrew Scriptures, but also his views on Judaism. These themes, drawn from his theory of Arabism, would be repeated later in his book, *Christian Ethics*. First, he makes a distinction between the Hebrew Scriptures and the Old Testament, with the latter being considered the Christianized version of the former.[10] Second, he states that religion was something characteristic of the Jews, not the Hebrews. In fact, the Hebrew Scriptures merely "present us with a story of the life of the Hebrew."[11] He went on:

> As we understand it today, religion was impossible to the Hebrews. Their 'religion' was their nationalism; and it was this nationalism of the ancestors that became – with its literature, its laws and customs – the religion of later times, of the Exile and post-Exile Jews down to the present day. The Ancient Hebrew worshipped himself; he sang his own praise. His god, Jahweh, was a reflection of his own person, a genuine *deus ex machina* designed to play the role of the other-self in the Hebrews' favourite intellectual game, namely, biographical painting or self-portraiture in words.[12]

Having dispensed with the possibility of the Hebrews practicing religion, let alone being monotheists (he labeled their beliefs as 'monolatry'),[13] he asserts that Christianity views revelation as an event and not as a word or an idea, which has led them to discount the words of God while tending only to His actions. He attempts to support this with the Christian view that since Jesus is the word of God and since he existed within history, divine revelation must be something God does and not something He says.[14] In contrast, Islam views revelation as only ideational,[15] with the focus upon ethicality because God does not reveal Himself, but only His will. God's law can only be revealed in word, not in deed, because moral law is a "conceptually-communicable, ideational schema of a value-content endowed with moving appeal."[16] The Christian approach to the Hebrew Scriptures is viewed as reading its own creed and beliefs into these texts whereas Islam simply views these texts as God's will revealed in ethical concepts and ideas. Examples such as the Christian approach to the covenant, election, the nature of man (in this case Adam and the redeeming act of Jesus) and the nature of God are discussed and dismissed as merely a means to find support and history for Christian dogmatic beliefs. Accordingly:

> Islam may be said to have recaptured the pure Semitic vision, beclouded by the old Hebrew racialism as well as by the new 'Christianism', of a moral order of the universe in which every

human being, regardless of his race or colour, - indeed of his religion in the institutionalized sense – gets exactly what he deserves, only what his works and deeds earn from him on an absolute moral scale of justice.[17]

Thus, Islam validates the Hebrew Scriptures as the word of God by distinguishing the ethically valid from the perverse in Hebrew Scripture.[18]

Using the measure of ethics and morality, al-Faruqi extended his original ideas, first developed in his doctoral work, refined in his theory of Arabism and more concretely articulated in these above two articles, in an attempt to engage and evaluate Judaism and Christianity. Moving away from ethics and morality and in a return to *Religionswissenschaft*, he delivered a lecture in 1964 (subsequently published in 1965) on the twin themes of the nature and significance of the history of religions in Muslim-Christian dialogue.[19] This article became one of his clearest attempts to explain his view of the history of religions and its application to dialogue.

The article sets out to perform a variety of tasks, from explaining al-Faruqi's theory of the history of religions to discussing the place of this field within Christian education and ending with the promise of its significance for Christian-Muslim dialogue. Of these, the latter item is of prime interest for it offers some insight into how he was approaching the concept of dialogue in 1964. However, dialogue does not just happen. It is always dependent upon a method of interpreting the other, whether explicitly articulated or not. Thus, his call for dialogue becomes one application of his theory of the history of religion. Consequently the majority of the article deals with theory.

According to al-Faruqi there are three aspects involved in the history of religion: reportage (the collection of data), construction of meaning-wholes (systematization of the data), and judgment or evaluation of the meaning-wholes.[20] The first appears straightforward, involving a call for a broad, inclusive scope of data discovery including all aspects of human life and religions using every branch of human knowledge.[21] The second requires three steps: organising and classifying this collected data, contextualising it within history and distilling meanings present in the data, which in turn are systematized.[22] These first two tasks require the historian to approach all religions on their own terms and not those of the historian's. In relation to Christianity and his own approach, he comments:

> For me to understand Christianity, for example, according to its own standards, and Christian thought as an autonomous expression of Christian experience is all well and good. But, if I ever omit from this understanding the claim that Christianity is a valid religion for all men, that the Christian faith is not only a true expression of what God may have done for some people but of what He has done or ever will do for the redemption of all men, of man as such, I am certain I would miss the essence and core.[23]

For al-Faruqi, even if one is able to complete the first two aspects in the study of religions, the work of the historian of religions is incomplete. There is still the need to evaluate, and this is the final task.[24] The historian of religion ultimately must assess the systematized meaning-wholes or else risk sliding into a relativistic pluralism and succumbing to a brand of cynicism in which every voice claims competing truths. Thus, the historian of religion must search for truth by evaluating these various claims.

How one sorts through various meaning-wholes led al-Faruqi to advocate a set of meta-religious principles along with the need for an application of *epoché* (suspension of judgment).[25] Although in this article he does not explain a system for meta-religion, he does outline some general thoughts. He remarks that the common genre of meta-religion examines differences as existing on the surface of religions and agreement as existing in the essence of religions.[26] He strongly criticizes this view as little more than confusing essence with representation made possible by a selective use and interpretation of data. In its place he calls for a critical meta-religious theory, which he was to explain in more detail in later publications.[27] Based in part on B. E. Meland's philosophical theory of religion, al-Faruqi suggests that God endowed humanity with the ability to judge and to evaluate divergent meaning-wholes within various religions.[28]

He first applies these principles to Christian education. Essentially, the study of religious history must not have a Christian agenda or become a tool to confirm Christianity. He adds that "Intellectual honesty is here most crucial, and must be satisfied before our loyalty to our religious traditions – indeed even at the cost of this loyalty if such sacrifice is necessary."[29] One would assume this applied to Muslim historians of religions as indeed to all. However, he goes further and challenges his audience with the need to re-assess Christian history by evaluating all the various early traditions and not merely accept what is considered orthodox. One would also assume this challenge would require a re-assessment of all religions.

The second and more interesting application involved dialogue between Christians and Muslims. In this context, dialogue is not about engaging the other in conversation. It is rather about engaging the common heritage of Christianity and Islam found in the Hebrew Scriptures and the formative years of Christianity and Islam.[30] By suspending personal belief (*epoché*), the historian of religion can classify and systematize the Hebrew Scriptural and religious meaning-wholes leading to an identification of Semitic themes, which belong to all three faiths. These Semitic themes can be found in the formative periods of Christianity and Islam because they too share in the Semitic consciousness.[31] This is of course a re-statement of his Arabism theory in which 'Semitic' replaces 'Arab' consciousness probably because it would be more palatable to his Christian audience.[32] In regard to the nature of dialogue between Christians and Muslims, he goes on to make this bold statement:

> The 'Christianity' which Islam *is* [italics mine], therefore, is an alternative to Orthodox Christianity; but it is as much Christianity as Orthodox Christianity is. Neither is Islam's Christianity an alternative posed *in abstracto*, as a discursive contradiction or variation, but *in concreto*, a historical alternative.[33]

Therefore, any dialogue is really in essence a domestic dialogue or a dialogue among family members and not something between opposing religions. By building upon his Arab (Semitic) consciousness theory as a tool for the historian of religions and by introducing the need to classify, systematize and evaluate the relevant religious and historical data, all obtained under *epoché*, al-Faruqi produces a theory of dialogue that, on the face of things, goes beyond categories. He completes this theory by commenting:

> Despite this domestic nature of the contention between Islam and Christianity, neither Christianity nor Islam is really capable of

going over its categories in the examination of the historical facts involved. Only a complete suspension of the categories of both, such as history of religions is capable of, holds any promise. The historical truth involved must be discovered and established. If, when that is done, either Christianity or Islam continues to hold to its old versions and views, it would do so only dogmatically, not critically. And we may hope that under the impact of such re-establishment of the formative history of Semitic consciousness in its Judaic, Christian and Islam moments, the road would be paved for some dogma-free spirits, loyal to that consciousness, to prepare the larger segment of mankind for meeting the challenge of the world-community. So, too, such re-establishment of the history of Semitic consciousness makes possible a new reconstruction of Christian religious thought which does not suffer from dependence upon epistemology.[34]

With the publication in 1967 of *Christian Ethics*, a work that was in process during the early sixties, he offered his most succinct explanation of his theory of comparative religious studies and meta-religion.[35] Before turning to this work, however, a brief summary may prove helpful. Thus far, we have walked with al-Faruqi through his doctoral emphasis upon value theory and ethics, both of which posit God as the definer of value (in its ideal being or essence), with man's role being to actualise this ideal of value. Next we witnessed his early attempts to build a bridge between philosophy and the history of religions using history at first and then adding phenomenology and its offspring *epoché* and eidetic vision. This led him to his Arabism theory of Arab consciousness which he believed ran through eternity, emerging at different points in human history as the religious expressions of Judaism, Christianity and Islam. Armed with the criteria of ethics and morality, he wandered through the *raison d'être* of humanity, the history of religions and finally into dialogical applications. This intellectual movement paralleled the development of his own self-conception moving from a philosopher into an historian of religions and then into a Muslim proponent and practitioner of engagement.

The culmination, thus far, of al-Faruqi's thought on ethics and religion is found in his book, *Christian Ethics*. Here for the first time he weaves together a number of ideas and constructs two basic theories forming the heart of his methodology. These are found in the first part of his book, the introduction, while the rest of the book acts as a rough application examining Judaism and Christianity. The reader, especially after working through his earlier publications, will find a number of repetitions and recurrent themes emerging in this book. After describing some of his presuppositions and the use of *epoché*, we will turn to his principles of comparative religious studies and his theory of meta-religion.

Introduced earlier in this study, the phenomenological tool of *epoché* was a primary component in al-Faruqi's approach to other religions. He made at least two assumptions at the outset. One, the study of religion is not a study of 'scientific facts' because the core of religion is a 'life-fact' and therefore religion cannot be studied as a series of objective cold facts.[36] Two, it is assumed that the non-adherent can understand these 'life-facts' and their meanings. If not, then there would be no possibility of any comparative religion or dialogue.[37] Proceeding from these two presuppositions, he offers his own definition of *epoché*:

> ... to get out of oneself and, putting oneself as it were entirely in parenthesis, to exercise by means of the imagination a leap into the religious factum in question. Then – and there we go beyond the technical sense of *epoché* – standing freely and within the life-fact, one has to 'live' it, i.e., to enable himself, and actually to suffer himself, to be determined by the content beheld alone. Only then can he be said to have apprehended the meaning presented, to have not only surveyed that content as it were for the outside but to have 'been' it.[38]

For al-Faruqi the application of *epoché* must not be a permanent state; rather, it is only a first step toward understanding. He argues for the need to go beyond *epoché* because the alternative is a sort of relativism in which each religion's truth claims are merely apprehended, with no evaluative method in which to judge or compare these claims. Thus after the use of *epoché*, the scholar must discard this initial approach in favour of another in order to evaluate: "What is needed is the establishment and elaboration of the higher principles which are to serve as basis for the comparison of various systems of meanings, of cultural patterns, of moralities, and of religions; the principles by reference to which the meanings of such systems and patterns may be understood, conceptualized, and systematized."[39]

With this we can begin to see how al-Faruqi moved from the pure academic ideals of the historiography of religions toward a means to compare religions. For him the purpose of the comparativist does not end with understanding, but with the evaluation and judgment of the meaning-wholes discovered in various religions. Truth then becomes the paramount concern in the study of religion for, by definition, truth must be universal. He states:

> Religion that is valid only for its adherents is no religion at all. Even at best, such a religion is but a tribalist ethic; just as a truth which is truth only for those who accept it and has no claim to the acceptance of all men, is not truth at all, but a mere prejudice.[40] ... There is no escape, therefore, in the comparative study of religion, for some evaluation of the content examined; and it is the principles of such evaluation that are here in question.[41]

After defining and amplifying *epoché*, al-Faruqi spends the better part of his introduction outlining his methodology. As we will see, there are actually two complementary methodologies proposed.

In the study of religion there are two kinds of principles; theoretical, which governs understanding, and evaluative, which governs judgment.[42] These theoretical principles became al-Faruqi's methodology of comparative religious understanding, while the principles of evaluation became known as his methodology of meta-religion. These two notions had in fact been introduced earlier in his 1965 article "History of Religions," but in *Christian Ethics* they are more fully developed.

Theoretical principles determine how to understand 'life-fact' meanings as presented in a religion, including religio-cultural phenomena, and their conceptualisation and systematization by historians of religion.[43] However, 'to compare' really means 'to evaluate,' that is, to possess some kind of criteria by which to juxtapose different religions. On the surface, it is somewhat difficult to ascertain what al-Faruqi meant when he separated principles of understanding from principles of evaluation. The solution to this confusion rests in what happens after reaching comparative understanding. It is granted that to compare religions requires some evaluative criteria, but this is to be used simply to understand the differences and not to determine where the truth resides.[44] With this caveat in mind, we can outline his five principles of comparative religion.

Principles of comparative religious studies

The first principle is that of internal coherence.[45] Within a religious system there cannot be any self-contradiction between the various elements that constitute that system. He writes: "Internal coherence is therefore a law governing the validity of revelation. This is not to assert a law for, and hence a limitation upon God, but man."[46] Thus, he could not abide by any paradox as a final principle because it posits self-contradiction. He assumed that God can use paradox, if He willed, but He would always provide humanity with clear and rationally apprehensible revelation that would 'fit' under an overarching unity of internal coherence.

Secondly, external coherence between the religious system and wider cumulative human knowledge is requisite. Any advancement in human knowledge affects all other areas of knowledge. Thus he writes that: "Coherence with the larger body of human knowledge is a must for all disciplines, for all genuine discoveries of truth. In the case of religion, no revelation can be an absolute law unto itself but must cohere with human knowledge as a whole, above all with the history of that revelation, the established factor of the accompanying human situation."[47] Thus, all revealed truth is always relational to the human situation. This is vitally important. Al-Faruqi believed that God communicates to man through revelation in a fully comprehensible manner. The alternative is quite possible, but then how would people be able to follow and obey without understanding what God commanded?[48]

Following closely is the third principle that all revealed truths must cohere with the religious experience of humanity. If God is indeed the source of revelation, then His commands will not contradict each other. Therefore, in the fourth principle a religious system's truths must correspond with reality. On this he says: "Contradiction of reality is *ipso facto* invalidation of the system. No theory or view can afford to oppose reality without separating itself, sooner or later, from the life or thought of man. To ignore reality is to be ignored by reality. The data of religious revelation must find corroboration in reality."[49]Al-Faruqi does not elaborate further on what he meant by reality or who determines what reality is, but leaves the impression that there is one agreed upon 'reality' against which humanity can measure truth.

The fifth and last principle is that a religious system ought to serve man's movement towards ethicality and higher value. This latter principle is reminiscent of the theory of Arabism where ethics and morality are the measure of the ever-present Arab spirit and in which man is destined to actualise its ideal. Humanity must have the opportunity to realise its destiny and this is expressed in religion, for it is God who defines the Ideal and reveals how humans are to achieve this end, which is obedience to God's commands. He notes that: "A system which deems this destiny of man already realized, impossible of realization or unworthy of human striving and endeavour, in fact denies the *raison d'être* of morality and religion."[50]

As both an application of the above principles and a precursor to the evaluative principles of meta-religion, he next elaborates on the function and nature of *Religionswissenschaft*. This brief digression was intended by him to help build the case for the need for evaluative principles and it is mentioned here for two reasons. First, it further enlightens us as to his view of the study of religion and second, it offers a small insight into his contextually driven need to move from academic study to evaluation. According to al-Faruqi, an historian of religion should fulfill three criteria: without personal prejudice, understand and communicate religious understanding; openly declare and 'hold in check' any presuppositions or personal involvement in the study; and, create a set of critical and universal principles as a presupposition for study.[51]

It follows then that the nature of *Religionswissenschaft* also comprises three disciplines.[52] First, using empirical means, it seeks to determine how a religious group feels, believes, thinks, knows and judges. This is accomplished via *epoché* where one's understanding of a religion is contrasted with that of its adherents', but not necessarily limited by it. Second, comparison is made between the different religious groups as to how they feel, believe, think, know and judge. This is simply juxtaposition, avoiding the tendency to ignore or limit differences. Finally, comparison is made in the same manner not between groups, but between a group and the "common findings of the religious experience of mankind."[53] Common findings are by nature normative and, when used in comparison, lead to evaluations regarding the place of religion and its doctrines and beliefs within the 'valuational hierarchy'.[54] This call for evaluation and judgment as eloquently voiced by al-Faruqi was really a call for an activist role in the history of religions. That he himself was an activist has been earlier attested and reflects something of his vocation.[55] His approach to the study of religion was not only an academic exercise, but led to evaluations of truth and value. He calls, in his *Christian Ethics*, to other historians of religion to join him:

> The comparativist does not dabble with materials which are dead and removed from contemporary interest, but with religious, ethical, and aesthetic valuations which are alive and always seething with energizing power and moving appeal, not because their adherents are alive – these may have perished with their civilizations without the theoretical chance of a return, millennia ago – but because the religious, ethical, aesthetic values present in their valuations, are always real and alive.[56]

In other words, values never die. The demand for evaluation without falling into relativism requires some external method from which to compare various religious truth claims. This in turn requires a set of external criteria not derived from religion, but suitable to evaluate all religions. It was out of this that al-Faruqi's theory of meta-religion emerged.

Principles of meta-religion

The principles of meta-religion are couched in philosophical language, perhaps reflecting his philosophical training. For ease of introduction these six principles are:[57]

1. Being is of two realms, that is, the ideal and the actual realm of existence.
2. Ideal being is relevant to actual being.
3. Relevance of the ideal being to the actual being is a command.
4. Actual being is as such, good.
5. Actual being is malleable.
6. Perfection of the cosmos is the burden of humans alone.

This may not be what one expected. It seems hardly 'religious'. It is in fact an extension of his doctoral work mixed with his theory of Arabism, but there are constant elements in the form of value and ethics. However, before explaining this theory in more detail, it is important to understand what he was trying to accomplish. He sought to create a theology-free system where rational thought applied to ethics and value would allow comparative religion to move beyond the old categories of theoretical truth and instead come to rest upon humanity's duty and responsibility to realise value in God's will.[58] Meta-religious principles are intended as a means to rationally evaluate these values in various religions. Therefore, before embarking on his explanation of his principles, he assumes for the sake of argument that God does not exist and then derives his ideas from his earlier research into values.[59]

In attempting to understand his six principles of meta-religion as explained in his book *Christian Ethics*, one finds that al-Faruqi does not always offer a detailed and clear explanation. At the outset, he writes: "A full elaboration of them [six principles] belongs elsewhere. For the moment, and in order to proceed to Christian ethics which is our subject, we must content ourselves with the shortest enunciation of these principles."[60] Despite the summary nature of some of his explanations in *Christian Ethics*, some clarification can be found in the last chapter of his earlier book *On Arabism*. This is particularly helpful in understanding his first principle.

Al-Faruqi's meta-religious theory begins with postulating what he considered to be a self-evident truth, that is, that being exists in two realms. He equates the actual realm with the categories of 'is' and 'fact' and the ideal realm with 'ought' and 'value.' In *On Arabism*, if his use of these two concepts is consistent with his later use of them in *Christian Ethics*, the actual realm is defined as the realm of space and matter including humanity, sensory perception and acts of consciousness.[61] This realm is the place of facts, by which I think al-Faruqi meant objects - whether existing as concrete realities such as physical objects or as conceptual ideas that can be perceived and realized in this world, such as love and goodness. Unfortunately in *Christian Ethics*, al-Faruqi does not clearly define what he meant by 'facts.'

The ideal realm is more difficult to understand. By way of explanation al-Faruqi offers: "The ideal is that through which the actual *is* what it *is*." [Italics mine][62] What he means here is not entirely clear. In his previous book *On Arabism*, he defined the ideal realm as transcendent being expressed on two levels.[63] On one level there exists the realm of essence and ideal entities,[64] while on the second there exists the realm of value which constitutes God *in percipi* and from which the actual *ought* follows.[65] Humanity can perceive (*in percipi*) or recognise God's values, but cannot know God in his essence – *in esse*. The realm of value provides the actual realm with its axiological significance or valuableness.[66] Even though al-Faruqi viewed being as existing in two broad realms, he further amplified it as occupying different levels within each of the two realms. He writes:

> Being confronts us on a number of levels. There is first the manifold of sense, the realm of objects in the real world of which our consciousness takes possession through the media of sense and out of which it constructs the body of knowledge known as the empirical sciences. There is, secondly, mental being, the realm of concepts and thought, the acts of consciousness itself, their contents and the relations and dependencies of those contents. There is, thirdly, the ideal being, the realm of essence, of the ideal entities through which the objects of the real world and their relationships are what they are, and out of which our consciousness constructs the a priori sciences. There is, fourthly, the realm of value which, like the third realm, is ideal but which gives real being in which it is instantiated, not its theoretical structure, but its axiological significance.[67]

Al-Faruqi still maintains that there are two basic realms of existence, but that in each realm there are two levels. In *Christian Ethics*, his main concern was not to fully explain each realm of being, but rather to state the claim that being exists in these two distinct realms:

> All that is being asserted is that there are two realms, not one; and we call the argument therefore self-evident because its denial involves one either in thorough scepticism, or in self-contradiction the moment he 'cognizes' or 'evaluates'.[68]

He attempts to illustrate his ideas by appealing to ethics and values. If I understand al-Faruqi correctly, the object (the actual realm or fact) does not belong to the same order of being as the ideal or value realm.

The value of an object or concept is not the same thing as the object itself. To assert this would be to commit the naturalistic fallacy (the identification of value with its object). Therefore, objects or facts in the actual realm can be evaluated and distinguished only by value as it exists in the ideal realm. If values were bound with or defined by objects, then there would be no means to distinguish between the values of different objects. For example, how would we distinguish between the value of someone's love for a pet and someone's love for a child? Can we make this distinction and if so, based on what? The person who loves a pet may well claim that it is like a child to him/her. Without an independent category of 'love,' which exists in the ideal realm separate from the object of that love, in this case a pet or a child, any value distinctions would be the relative opinions of people. However, though people reside in the actual realm, they intuitively appeal to the value of love, as it exists in the ideal realm, and in doing so make a distinction between love for a pet and a child. Therefore in a burning house, the child is saved first and then the pet because the value of human life is considered greater than that of a pet. In this way, al-Faruqi is positing the existence of two realms of ideal and actual of which ideal value resides in the ideal realm and provides the means to measure the valuableness of objects in the actual realm.

Given the existence of two realms, al-Faruqi's second principle maintains that ideal being is relevant to actual being. This relevance is one of dependence. Al-Faruqi writes: "Since the ideal realm acts as principle of classification of the order and structure of actual being, it follows that it [ideal realm] provides the pattern by which the actual is or is not what it is, the standard by which the actual is or is not valuable."[69] Objects in the actual realm, such as trees, are what they are based upon the essence of a tree in the ideal realm. Again al-Faruqi comments that: "Between essences [in the ideal realm] and real existents [in the actual realm], there is an ontological relationship. The structure of the former reappears in the latter."[70] The ideal pattern of a tree is realised in the world of space and time. In addition, value is relevant to its object, that is, an object receives its value or dis-value from the ideal, but the object does not define its own value. The ideal realm also provides the standard by which the actual is judged and valued precisely because value is not in the same category as the object itself. Again al-Faruqi writes: "It [ideal value] is the standard of valuableness, of goodness in its most general sense, which facts [objects], whether by nature or through man's agency, are supposed to realize or embody if they are to be valuable at all."[71]An example may prove helpful. A principle of ideal value is required to differentiate between the different values of objects. If one is building a cabinet, this implies a theoretical model of a type of a cabinet. This assumes there is an external means to distinguish between one cabinet and another. For example a beautifully built cabinet is valued differently than a broken dilapidated cabinet.[72] If one is cutting the wood to make a cabinet, one needs to measure and cut according to a plan. If there were no external criteria determining where to cut a piece of wood, then it would not matter where the cut is made. However, in this case, properly cutting the wood is essential in order to build the cabinet according to the plan. In this example, the plan is the ideal realm and the finished cabinet is the actual realm. The value remains in this ideal realm and we intuitively appeal to this ideal value when evaluating our finished cabinet. Despite the imperfection of this example (in our case the ideal cabinet is a mental construct that we create and not some ideal self-existent cabinet), it does help to illustrate the relationship and relevance of the ideal to the actual realm.

However, al-Faruqi goes even further and posits that the relevance of the ideal to the actual is a command.[73] His use of the word 'command' implies personality, but what he intended was more in line with necessitates. The ideal exists and is either realised or not realised in the actual realm. Whether or not the ideal is realised in this world does not affect the ideal. Going back to our previous example of cutting wood, if there is a line showing where to cut, then that is the ideal. Whether or not I cut on the line does not affect the ideal itself, it only tells me whether or not I am cutting correctly. I will realise this when the cut piece does not fit in the cabinet I am building, necessitating the need to cut it again to that same ideal (line). In order to build properly, the ideal (that line) commands or necessitates that it be followed. Whether or not the builder chooses to follow the ideal in no way changes or influences this ideal line. It is here that al-Faruqi introduces the role of people in actualizing the ideal:

Regardless of whether or not man obeys the command, the ideal realm persists in commanding. It judges the actual situation as praiseworthy or condemnable; whoever enters the situation stands under its command to realise the value in question; and hence, under its judgment as to whether he is, or is not, as he ought to be; whether he has, or has not, fulfilled what he ought to do.[74]

He then goes on to define the ideal as eternal and immutable.[75] The ideal exists, unchanging; however, humanity's ability to understand and realise the ideal changes over time.

There is another aspect of the ideal realm that necessitates obedience, that is, the physical laws of nature. In the words of al-Faruqi, "the theoretical ideal is itself the law of nature."[76] Humanity must obey these natural laws. However, in the area of values, such as goodness, morality and love, people have a choice whether or not to realize or actualize these values in this world. In other words, the valuational ideal does not constrain humanity to conform to it. If it were so, that is, if the valuational ideal gave itself existence, then value and dis-value would be inevitable and the world would be fatalistic in nature. It is here that al-Faruqi introduced the idea of the command of value as a moving appeal to humanity. Human feelings of moral responsibility, moral guilt and conscience, along with the ethical freedom implicit in the ever-present possibility that man may act otherwise than he does, argues against value providing its own existence. Al-Faruqi concludes: "The realm of ideal being, therefore, is relevant to man, as member of the realm of actual being, in that it issues to the latter a 'command' which he can always miss; in that it furnishes for him the desideratum not necessary determination, of his being, his membership in the actual realm, his cosmic stand."[77]

The fourth principle follows with the statement that actual being is good.[78] Since ideal value can be realised in the actual realm and since existence is foundational for all other values to be realised, then existence is itself good. In al-Faruqi's words: "For if it were not valuable to be real, it would not be valuable for any value to be realized. But a value whose realization is not valuable is a contradiction in terms. The value of real-existence stands therefore as an axiom of axiology and morality."[79] Further, existence is valuable because the ideal realm necessitates the value of existence in the actual realm. On this basis he postulates that since the world and humanity exist they are intrinsically if not potentially good. He tends here to equivocate 'good' with 'value' and 'worth' along with 'not evil' or 'not perverse'. Man's existence, since he exists at all, is to bring the good of the ideal world into the actual world. If this is denied, he contends, the denier ends up "merely to exist in a perfectly deedless, actionless, speechless state."[80] Actual being as such is not evil, though it can contain evil, but any religion that views the world as fundamentally evil, without value or worth, forfeits the right to contend for what is and is not valuable for man.[81] The assertion that the realm of actual being is good does not mean it is perfect or that it cannot become better; it means that actual being can improve.[82]

The fifth principle is that actual being is malleable.[83] While the ideal dictates what should be, the realisation of this in reality is subject to a variety of factors. Essentially, just because the ideal realm necessitates something, this does not mean it will happen in the actual realm, furthermore and indeed if it does happen there, it may happen in degrees of fulfillment in the actual realm. For example, on earth gravity affects every mass drawing it to the centre. This is a natural law. However, planes, birds, and kites can all *fly*. When sufficient speed and lift are applied, these objects can temporarily overcome the effects of gravity. As long as the determining factors for flight are present, flight occurs. When these factors are removed the full effect of gravity is seen. Despite flying, planes and birds remain subject to gravity.[84] Therefore, in this sense the actual is malleable. It can be altered and changed while the ideal yet remains. Put another way, the actual can be progressively changed to increasingly meet the requirements of the ideal realm. Man, for example, can improve. He can grow and realise value. Al-Faruqi states it this way: "Whether in his own person or in nature, man can and in fact does give new direction to the causal, forward push of reality, in order to become something else, something other than he would otherwise be. This he does because he is susceptible, in addition to the blind determination of ontological reality, to a determination of another order, to the moving appeal of values, to determination by the ideal valuational realm of being."[85]

The last principle in the theory of meta-religion is that the cosmos is the burden of humanity alone.[86] Here, he formally introduces people as the only agents in creation with the capacity to actualise the ideal. All creation, except man, is under the dominion of the theoretical ideal being and has little choice but to obey the ideal. He writes: "The elements, organic matter, plants, and animals – all are mercilessly subject to inevitable laws. Only man, although he is not free from these laws which operate in him as much as in any other member of the realm of actual being, is capable of deflecting the courses of the causal threads of destiny to ends other than what they would reach if left alone."[87] One example would be medical intervention to save life. This is the distinctive quality of humans. They can temporarily alter the course of the inevitable. He goes further and sees that humanity alone is the conduit through which value is realised. Without humanity, he wonders whether or not the elements of creation would have value:[88]

> His [humanity's] significance in creation is precisely this, that he is the only creature who holds the key to the entrance of the valuational ideal into the actual. Man is the bridge which values must cross if they are to enter the real. He stands at the cross roads of the two realms of being, participating in both, susceptible to both.[89] .... That is man's cosmic status: to bring about such necessarily 'potent' world into likeness with the realm of ideal being, to perfect the world by deflecting its causal potency to ends which embody values.[90]

At the outset of his discussion about the six meta-religious principles, al-Faruqi begins by assuming the non-existence of God. This is done in order to develop criteria for principles of evaluation that were independent of religious assumptions. In this way he hoped to appeal to rational arguments that would be outside religion. If he could construct these principles, then he would have the means to evaluate religions based upon religiously neutral criteria. At the end of his discussion, he re-introduces God into the paradigm and summarizes his meta-religious principles in terms of God and creation.[91]

The philosophical statement and first principle that being exists in two realms, the ideal and actual, is rephrased to state that God, who is the only transcendent being, exists in the ideal realm, while creation, which belongs to the actual realm, exists as actual beings and objects. The second principle - the ideal is relevant to the actual realm - means that God is concerned for this world, and does not merely co-exist with it. His values or attributes become the pattern for value in this world. Morality, goodness, beauty and even objects such as trees are dependent upon God for their existence and value. That such relevance is a command (principle three) means that God's concern for the world is realised through His commands or will and actualized in the responses of obedience by the world of nature, which has no choice, and by people who have a choice. Al-Faruqi explains it in this way:

> That the realm of ideal being is 'composed' of a theoretical order and a valuational order means that God's acts are necessary and unavoidable in the realm of nature, (they constitute the laws of nature); but that they are, besides this, for man is also nature, only commands where man's destiny is concerned. Commands are, precisely, determinants which may or may not 'act,' according as they are or are not obeyed.[92]

The fourth principle, i.e., that actual being is good but incomplete, means God has created the actual realm for a purpose and this is to be realised by man. This purpose is the realisation of God's will in this world expressed through ethical and moral values. It follows then that the actual realm must be malleable or capable of change and improvement. This becomes al-Faruqi's fifth principle, according to which it is possible for people to obey God's commands because the realm of actual being can be gradually perfected to bring about 'ethical felicity.' Finally, the last principle - that perfection of the cosmos is the burden of humans alone - becomes restated thus: the sole responsibility of humanity is to obey God's commands because only people are capable of choosing to obey.[93]

How these principles actually work is the focus of the rest of *Christian Ethics*. According to al-Faruqi, the comparative study of religions (in the 1960s) was concerned with theoretical truth: a 'true' discernment versus a 'false' discernment. The end result is the view that one religion is true and the others false, or at best possessed of only glimpses of the truth. He states: "All that is possible in these circumstances is 'mission', a sinister category in human relations in which the majority of mankind are declared enemies whom it is the duty of the faithful to 'convert'. Naturally, the other party, which is in every case the majority of men, looks upon mission as subversion worthy of the greatest combat effort."[94]

The alternative is meta-religion, allowing one to move beyond the old theological questions and instead examine and analyse value, which is the will of God and the 'ought' that arises from this ideal realm of being. In this way a confrontation between truth and falsehood is avoided. One merely acquires a greater or lesser grasp of truth as he writes:[95]

> The more and the less perception of value are both 'true'. Both are perceptions of genuine value, of the ideal realm of being; and the discrepancy of the less can be filled only with more value-discernment.[96]

This position permits him to find value in all religions, yet find greater value in a few. He goes on to apply this to Judaism and Christianity and evaluates their ethical teachings and applications against what he considered the ideal. In short he portrays Judaism as a form of radicalism, which Jesus came to break with universal brotherhood:[97]

> We may therefore conclude this analysis by saying that Jesus universalized the community ideal of Israel by interiorizing the law, i.e., by making all piety, all ethics, and all virtue dependent upon an inward, radical transformation of the self, which is within the capacity, and thence the prerogative, not only of a chosen race but of all men. This transformation of which only God can be the judge and after which all contention is left for personal conscience, obviates the need for law, indeed for religion in the institutionalized sense and, in final analysis, for Jesus himself as a religious teacher. For by transforming the inner source of all action, no action can take place that is not done under the perspective of the new transformation, which is its very title to ethical goodness.[98]

As for Christianity, he maintains that the ethic of Jesus was lost in western or Pauline Christianity as Jesus became transfigured politically and his message became steeped in the sinfulness of man and the *fait accompli* idea of redemption.[99] According to al-Faruqi, Jesus never organised a church because his main concern was dealing with the deep problem of ethics requiring the radical transformation of people in accordance with the divine will.[100] In the end, al-Faruqi's main negative evaluation of Christianity rests squarely on the question of ethics or more precisely the Christian distortion of the ethic of Jesus. After surveying various Christian intellectuals, including Paul Tillich and Reinhold Niebuhr, al-Faruqi concludes:

The theme behind them all is identical. Human nature is corrupt in its essence by original sin. Even when it stands under grace, as in the life of a baptized Christian, human nature remains corrupt. The function of grace is not to remedy this corruption now, but later, in heaven, or the after-life.[101] .... The overall meaning, therefore, of Christianity being called the religion of redemption, is that it holds as absolute truth, the following two premises: First, in the Christ-event, God has reconciled and therefore redeemed man and the world to Himself, from whom they were alienated by man's sin; and that all that is necessary for the reconciliation and redemption of man and the world has been completed. Second, now that redemption is a *fait accompli*, the morally (sic) imperative is that man life (sic) as redeemed fellows in continuous communion and fellowship with the Godhead, until God decides to put an end to this temporary interlude of man in the realm of real existence.[102]

Thus, he asks, since humanity is redeemed, what need remains to strive for moral excellence?[103]

From this period onward, the twin principles of comparative religious studies and meta-religion were to dominate and shape al-Faruqi's approach and viewpoint of non-Muslim faiths. Although he mentioned non-monotheistic faiths, his primary interest remained with Judaism, Christianity and Islam. In the remaining articles written before 1969, he added a final capstone approach to his previous two sets of methodologies. This was his system of dialogue.

Principles of dialogue

In 1967, al-Faruqi accepted an invitation to participate in a series of ecumenical discussions. The lecture he presented, entitled "Islam and Christianity: Problems and Perspectives," was published in 1968, but an earlier *précis* was published in 1967 as "Islam and Christianity: Prospects for dialogue".[104] We will look at these lectures together.

The first item of interest is the definition and objectives he sets for dialogue. Previously it was seen that dialogue was not between two disparate faiths (Christianity and Islam), but really a domestic dialogue between two movements of Arab consciousness. Each of these movements has a greater or lesser actualisation of the ideal and thus neither is necessarily false, but at different points along the path of realising the will of God. With this as a background, he defines dialogue in a series of statements. That dialogue is necessary is self-evident simply because both Christianity and Islam exist in the world, interact and make ultimate claims to the truth demanding a critical appraisal best done in a spirit of dialogue. Dialogue then, is a "dimension of human consciousness"; it is a "category of the ethical sense"; "it is education at its widest and noblest"; it is "the removal of all barriers between men for a free intercourse of ideas which demands that the sounder claim to the truth win"; and, it is "the only kind of interhuman relationship worthy of man".[105] The ultimate objective for dialogue is the search for and adherence to truth.[106] To this end, and keeping in mind that he was presenting the paper at a primarily Christian gathering, he writes: "We must say it boldly, that the end of dialogue is conversion; not conversion to my, your, or anyone else's religion, culture or political regime, but to the truth. Conversion, as a conviction of the truth, is not only legitimate, but obligatory – indeed, the only alternative consistent with sanity, seriousness and dignity."[107] Since dialogue is so important to both faiths and vital in a world known more for conflict than mutual respect, there is the need to set guidelines for the practise of dialogue. Six such rules are suggested by al-Faruqi:[108]

1. All dialogue is subject to critique.
2. Any communication must obey the laws of internal coherence.
3. Communication must obey the laws of external coherence.
4. Communication must obey the law of correspondence with reality.
5. Dialogue must be free from "canonical figurizations".
6. Dialogue between Muslims and Christians should be centred upon questions of ethics and not theology.

Some of these rules are more straightforward than others. For example, the acceptance of the first condition that all dialogue is subject to critique seems obvious. In support, he appeals to God's revelation of his will. God allows humanity to ask questions in order to understand, although al-Faruqi does not mean that humanity 'dialogues' with God. Therefore, within dialogue neither side is permitted to make dogmatic statements, which are beyond critique.[109] To do so simply refutes the possibility of any meaningful discourse. Internal and external coherence also appear simple enough. The laws of logic must exist in communication, by which he means that no paradox was allowed as a final position. This and the criteria of external coherence were discussed earlier under the principles of comparative religious studies. Coherence with all the history of man, especially religious history, is necessary so that discourse should not fall into the pit of myth, esoteric stories or fanciful and unsubstantiated tales. The un-stated criterion of rationality pervades everything and it goes without saying that dialogue cannot occur between irrational parties. Therefore, external coherence means in part empirically verifiable and rationally understandable histories.[110] Principle number four then becomes almost a corollary, in that dialogue must correspond with reality either as corroboration or refutation. Yet, again as mentioned above, he does not elaborate on what he means by reality. It would seem that he saw it as obvious.

Now the fifth rule of dialogue requires some additional explanation.[111] Dialogue must be free from the 'canonical figurizations' of each religion. By 'figurizations,' he means perceptions and interpretations and by 'canonical,' dominant or dogmatic. Thus, in religious history revelation was separated into concepts in order for the faith community to understand; it was interpreted and then arranged into structures by rational thought and shaped into legal ideas and provisions to guide the community. Once these concepts, structures and legal notions became normative they are said to have been figurized. However, in the history of faith different figurizations emerged from different thinkers and communities creating a variety of representations. Over the course of time disputation and discussion arose over these various figurizations and some became more accepted than others. Some became known as heretical and others as accepted representations of truth and, therefore, were employed as a means to define truth for that faith. In this way, they became canonized as dogma or orthodoxy. In the realm of dialogue, al-Faruqi does not call for a rejection of, but freedom from figurization. Later this will become clearer as we explore some examples he proposed for dialogue.

In the last principle for dialogue, he calls for discourse on ethical rather than theological or ideological questions.[112] He argues that, due to the great number of doctrinal disparities between Christianity and Islam, little progress can be made in dialogue. Each side is not ready to confront all the facets of their ideologies. In addition, questions of theology become questions of faith and doctrine. The lines are drawn and hard to cross without cries of heresy or betrayal. Questions of ethics, however, are less threatening because they become differences in perceptions as opposed to categories of right/wrong or true/false and are rationally approachable by everyone. He writes: "Difference in ethical perception, on the other hand, can mean that one does not see as much, as far, or as deep as the other. This situation calls for nothing but the involved midwifery of value perception."[113] This is a direct application of both the methodologies of comparative religion and meta-religion. The last principle of dialogue, in particular, reminds us of the ideal concept that people, like religion, are at different levels of realising or bringing ideal being into the actual realm.

Not content with simply enumerating this methodology of dialogue, al-Faruqi went on to provide some examples. In his 1967 publication, he offers two possible themes, which would be expanded to three in his more complete 1968 article.[114] In the first theme, he contends that both Islam and Christianity "regard themselves as standing in a state of innocence."[115] He writes: "Gone are the sordid obsessions with innate depravity, intrinsic futility, necessary fallenness and cynical vacuity of man and of the world. Modern man affirms his life and his world."[116] The second theme is that the act of faith is the beginning, not the completion of piety and virtue. In his own words:

The act of faith neither justifies nor makes just. It is only the entrance ticket into the higher realms of ethical striving and doing. It does no more than let us into the realm of the moral life where to realize the divine imperative in the value-short world, to transform and fill to with value, is man's prerogative as well as duty.[117]

Finally, both religions recognise that the mission of man is to be ethical and moral in this world as he strives to fulfill God's will. All people begin equally with a "carte-blanche on which nothing is written except what each individual earns by his own doing or not doing."[118] The initial impression left by these two suggested themes is that, although they may touch on ethics, for Christians these themes are really issues of doctrine and theology. For example, in Christianity the nature of humanity's innocence is a question of theology. Al-Faruqi's above contention that Islam and Christianity regard themselves as standing in a state of innocence belies how that innocence is achieved. Are people born innocent and do they retain that innocence through personal effort or does God declare people innocent through the redemptive effort of Jesus? This would seem to violate his sixth principle of dialogue in which he advocates that questions should be centred on ethics and not theology. This line of thought will be elaborated later. For al-Faruqi, the first task in his articles was to explain in detail what he meant by these themes. On modern man and innocence, the subject of the first theme,[119] he begins by stating: "The notion of Original Sin, of the fallenness of man, appears from the perspective of contemporary ethical reality to have outlived its meaningfulness."[120] Sin is defined here as a moral and not an ontological category, such that death is not dependent upon morality, that is, it is not the result of sin. Moreover, moral sin is always personal and in no way hereditary. Finally, sin is not something done, but something perceived. Thus, wrong perceptions become defined as sin. According to al-Faruqi, remedies such as retaliation, retribution and forgiveness are all inadequate, leaving education as the key solution to sin:

> Education is the unique process of salvation. No ritual of water, therefore – of ablution or Baptism, of initiation or confirmation; no acknowledgement of symbols of authority – no confession or contrition, can by themselves do this job for man. Every person must do it for himself, though he may be assisted by the more experienced and everybody can do it.[121]

The second theme is preparatory for the third, for it deals with justification in terms of declaring or making something good.[122] Belief in something or the act of faith in someone does not make one good. Ethical misperception is not solved by confession or faith; rather, the solution begins with realizing the content of the divine will or its values. Next, education brings the individual into a more complete ethical understanding. Last and most difficult of all is the translation of understanding into the reality of practice. Hence, the act of faith is merely the beginning, where recognition or perception of God's values is seen to be fulfilled in personal life.

The last theme for dialogue depends on rejecting the view that redemption is a *fait accompli*.[123] He explains that modern Muslims and Christians recognise that redemption is not already completed.

Salvation is an ethical duty on the part of man toward God since it flows out of morality. This leads him to write: "The only morality that can flow out of accomplished salvation necessarily robs man's life of its gravity, its seriousness and its significance."[124]

In such a situation there would be no need for moral and ethical striving. He acknowledges that the already saved person is obligated to live a moral life, but the motivation is based on gratitude, not on striving for salvation, and this is deemed inadequate to govern man's efforts. This is why the already saved still sin:

> Thus, it takes something more than redemption, in the sense of forgiveness and release of ethical energies, to achieve salvation, in the sense of ethical felicity, or realizing value in space-time. It takes a life of danger, of disturbing the flow of space-time, of deflecting its threads toward value-realization, the bringing about of the *matériaux* of value and filling the world therewith.[125]

Progressive ethical salvation, available to all and measured against the ethical ideal as it is actualised in the world, is the alternative he tenders. Both Christianity and Islam, he maintains, can agree on this theme for dialogue.

In 1968, he published an article entitled, "Islam and Christianity: Diatribe or dialogue," which discusses the above dialogical ideas in a more refined manner than found in his previous two articles. The ground-rules for dialogue are the same, but written in a more accessible and slightly less philosophical fashion. Thus, they become:

1. No religious pronouncement is beyond critique.
2. Internal coherence must exist.
3. Proper historical perspective must be maintained.
4. Correspondence with reality must exist.
5. Freedom from absolutized scriptural figurization.
6. Dialogue should be conducted on areas where there is a greater possibility of success, such as ethical values.

Immediately one can see how much clearer these rules have become. There is no need to repeat their meanings. His description of the three themes for dialogue is also presented more elegantly. For example, for the first theme he writes:

Contemporary Muslims and Christians are life-affirming in regard to God's creation and hold that man has a unique task to perfect this world. The theological usefulness of the notion of original sin, hereditary, collective, and vicarious sin are gone. Sin is personal and based on free-will; it is primarily located in misperception and its solution is in education rather than forgiveness. Sin is not necessary nor is it predominant in human affairs. For modern Muslims and Christians the way out of the predicament of sin is in human rather than divine hands. Salvation is achieved by continuous education and each person must educate himself.[126]

Although al-Faruqi does not provide examples of dialogue derived from his themes, one can speculate how his ideas might work in practice. A dialogue based on his first theme, for example, might focus on ways to reduce sin (unethical behaviour) through educational avenues, such as learning about the environment, health and employment. This leads to his explanation of the second theme in which he writes:

An awareness of the imperative of doing the will of God exists. Former notions of justification are insufficient. Justification is a continuous process which does not consist of confession to God, but of recognition of real values and the following of the long, hard road in reaching these values. Knowledge is virtue. Neither great sin nor serious repentance is typical of most people, hence the confession of faith has but mediocre value. Justification is psychic release which may enable a man with determination to reach his goal, but is not a value in itself.

According to al-Faruqi, the challenge to follow God's will on earth and to bring about value is not based upon humanity being redeemed by God, but rather on the gradual and persistent effort to obey God. As with the first theme, there are many avenues that Muslims and Christians could discuss and through joint effort seek to realise God's will in the world, such as, working together to reduce poverty or injustice. Finally, he concludes with his third theme:

Every man has an equal imperative to fulfill his moral mission which is yet unfulfilled on a world-wide basis. Redemption is only being accomplished by man rather than already having taken place. Justification and redemption are but a prelude to the perception and pursuit of value (God's will). This is possible to all people and has to take place all the time.

The responsibility to pursue value, which is described as pursuing God's will, and the search for truth may begin with Christian notions of justification and redemption, but in themselves these notions are only a beginning. Al-Faruqi sees that the purpose of humanity is to seek moral excellence. He offers this as his final theme for dialogue and in application extends the boundaries of Muslim-Christian dialogue to include all of humanity. Hence, Muslim and Christian dialogue and their joint efforts to pursue value in the world would benefit all people. In summary these three themes can be reduced to:

1. Man's nature – not sinful
2. God's will – to be realised
3. Man's mission – moral existence and striving leads to salvation

Conclusion

By 1968, al-Faruqi had established and outlined his methodology for dialogue and engagement with non-Muslims. He spent the remainder of his life applying and refining his ideas even in the midst of launching and guiding the Islamization of knowledge project. He had developed and explained three approaches to engagement with non-Muslims, building each succeeding theory upon the former. He wedded comparative religious studies with philosophy in his search to compare and then evaluate different religions. The drive to evaluate, that is to discover truth, led him to search for what he termed 'meta-religious principles' through which all religion could be evaluated. These principles did not replace the initial requirement to compare, but became the means to the final product of finding truth in religion. Dialogue and its principles became an application and contact point of both comparative and evaluative study. The fullness of his dialogical application will be discussed in the following chapter. For now, in summary form, his three methods were:

The principles of comparative religious understanding
1. Internal Coherence.
2. External Coherence – with cumulative human knowledge.
3. All revealed truths must cohere with the religious experience of mankind.
4. The truth of religion must correspond to reality if it intends to establish its claim to be a system.
5. Religion must serve the upward progress of man towards ethically higher value and the Godhead.

The principles of meta-religion
1. Being is of two realms, that is, the ideal and the actual realm of existence.
2. Ideal being is relevant to actual being.
3. Relevance of the ideal being to the actual being is a command.
4. Actual being is as such, good.
5. Actual being is malleable.
6. Perfection of the cosmos is the burden of humans alone.

The principles of dialogue
1. No religious pronouncement is beyond critique.
2. Internal coherence must exist.
3. Proper historical perspective must be maintained.
4. Correspondence with reality must exist.
5. Freedom from absolutized scriptural figurization.
6. Dialogue should be conducted on areas where there is a greater possibility of success such as ethical values.

Commensurate with these principles were the expectations that interfaith interactions, whether on the level of academic comparison or activist dialogue, required freedom to engage the other, true equality between parties, and, the use of rational thought and ethics as foundational tools for both study and dialogue. These expectations become more pronounced as one analyses his writings from the years 1969-1986.

5

METHODOLOGICAL APPLICATIONS
AND RESPONSES
(1969-1986)

After his years at McGill University studying Judaism and Christianity, followed by his teaching posts through the 1960s until he started at Temple University in 1968, al-Faruqi developed his theories and methodological approaches to non-Muslim faiths. His interest and involvement in interfaith relations, beyond study and methodology, had in fact surfaced quite early in his academic career. For example, he attended the 23rd Assembly of the World Council of Churches and the International Missionary Council in New Delhi in 1961.[1] The record of his participation in seminars, conferences, lectures and presentations in the early 1960s is well attested in his personal papers.[2] Not only was this pursued on his own initiative, but also various institutions such as the Vatican and the World Council of Churches, as well as academic and religious organisations, sought out and benefited from his participation. This dramatically increased beginning in 1965, but aside from two published lectures (1964 and 1967), there is little record of the content of this involvement. It is by 1969 that the published record of his thought becomes available and for this reason the refinement and application of his methodology dates from this later period (1969-1986). We will first examine how he applied his methodologies and second, how some non-Muslim participants received his ideas.

Methodological refinement and application

When one surveys the dialogical career of al-Faruqi, it quickly becomes apparent that this was one of his priorities as a scholar and an activist. This can be seen on two levels. First, he was involved at the organisational level and second, he made presentations in various symposia. Since his organisational or institutional involvement was introduced earlier in Chapter One, only a brief summary by way of reminder is needed before examining how he applied his ideas.

Al-Faruqi first became involved in the American Academy of Religion (AAR) in 1972/73, at a time when there was no Islamic Studies section. The original desire for a focus on Islam came from the chairman of the History of Christianity Section, Dr. Franklin Littell, who invited Dr. al-Faruqi to set up a subsection on Muslim-Christian Encounter. By 1976, the AAR had formally accepted the Islamic Studies group and al-Faruqi remained its chair through to 1982. Over this ten-year period the theme of Muslim-Christian/West interaction was prominent, perhaps reflecting both the times and particularly al-Faruqi's interests.[3] In 1977, he joined the board of the Inter-Religious Peace Colloquium (IRPC) and in 1978 replaced Cyrus Vance as the Colloquium's Vice-President after the latter was appointed Secretary of State for the government of the United States.[4] The organisation, also known as the Muslim-Jewish-Christian Conference (MJCC), eventually dissolved as a result of financial constraints.[5] Al-Faruqi provided some insight into why such organisations were important to him when he wrote:

The MJCC meetings were the first to be held in modern times. They were genuinely ecumenical in that they were attended by people of vision who looked forward to inter-religious understanding and cooperation as the only alternative to the hostility which has dominated relations between the three faith communities. They were convinced that ignorance and misunderstanding, the twin feeders of inter-religious hostility, ought to be cut off [for] a serious return to dialogue.[6]

In the year the MJCC dissolved (1980), he became formally involved with the Global Congress of the World's Religions (GCWR) as a board member, a post he held from 1980 until 1982. Of note was his promotion of GCWR before the International Institute of Islamic Thought (IIIT). In 1982, he convened a meeting in Islamabad under the auspices of IIIT and the Islamic University where thirty Muslim professors from around the Islamic world discussed a wide range of subjects related to the Islamization of knowledge. At the end of the gathering, al-Faruqi presented the GCWR to his colleagues and secured unanimous agreement that the Muslim world should participate in the

GCWR and its sponsored events.[7] Thus, it would not be unwarranted to claim that al-Faruqi was as interested in participating in interfaith dialogue as he was in the establishment of interfaith dialogical institutions and partnerships. Clearly, the activity of engagement was something more to him than personal interest as he believed this was a long-term means to bring various faith communities closer together by fostering mutual understanding and cooperation. Two of these three organisations outlived his involvement – the Islamic Studies group (which later became the Islamic Studies Section of the AAR) and the Global Congress of the World's Religions. Not content to help conduct the orchestra, al-Faruqi also wanted to play in the band. He did this though his publications and public presentations.

Al-Faruqi spent the remaining years of his life actively engaged in writing and amplifying his methodological ideas both as theory and in practical discourse with non-Muslims. Having spent time in the previous chapters unveiling his methodology by systematically working through his writings up until 1968, there is neither the space nor the need to do the same with his numerous works of the following two decades. By my count there are over 30 books and articles published after 1968 that are relevant to this study. Although some are identical and published under different titles, the remaining works coalesce around certain themes and ideas, allowing for a conceptual rather than a work-by-work summation and analysis. Thus, the three aspects of his method, namely, comparative religious studies, meta-religion and dialogue are used as filters through which to examine his remaining works. The objective is to determine how his earlier methodological ideas were refined and applied.

As one reads through his later works, it becomes apparent that al-Faruqi applied his methodology in two general ways, both revolving around dialogue. In fact, the principles of comparative religious understanding and meta-religion become subsumed within dialogue. In the vast majority of his applications, the focus was on dialogical themes rather than a purely academic comparative analysis of other religions. In order to engage in dialogue these two sets of principles (comparative religions and meta-religion) are assumed and not always explicitly stated. For this reason, it was first necessary in the previous chapters to examine these foundational principles because they re-emerge in the application of his method of dialogue.

Al-Faruqi sought to apply his ideas in two, often overlapping, ways: internal and external dialogue. Internal dialogue was aimed primarily at a Muslim audience and could be classified as the practice of *da'wah* for the education of fellow Muslims. He appealed to and applied his various principles of comparative and meta-religious analysis to engage and guide Muslims in their relations with the non-Muslim world. For example, the book *The Islamization of Knowledge* dealt with the urgent call for Muslims to reclaim knowledge in all its forms, to Islamize it and create a uniquely Islamic epistemology. One would not really expect to find much about inter-religious interaction in such a work, but in reality some of what he wrote was juxtaposed against primarily Christianity and Buddhism. In contrast, external dialogue involved actual engagement with non-Muslims, which is itself a form of *da'wah* and it is here that al-Faruqi became more directly engaged.

The refinement of his methodological principles is discussed according to this general division between internal and external dialogue. Examples are drawn chronologically from his publications in order to situate his method within the context of his life. However, some articles contribute both to internal and external dialogue and thus appear more than once.[8] The basic criteria in placing articles in one group or the other depends upon the audience addressed and his objectives.

Internal dialogue

For al-Faruqi, the general contextual background for the presence and use of internal dialogue is that of communities of Muslims who are influenced by Western ideas and models of thinking whether they live as a minority group in the West or as Muslim majorities in countries such as Pakistan, Malaysia and Saudi Arabia. Al-Faruqi exemplified this position as he wrestled with his own identity as a Muslim in the midst of Western thought particularly as he resided in a predominantly non-Muslim land. That he found his identity within Islam and the world Muslim *ummah* was previously discussed in Chapter Two, but in the latter years of his activism he sought to call Muslims back to Islam along the same road he trod – education. All of his articles in the category of internal dialogue follow a similar pattern. Whether discussing metaphysics, culture, human rights or even *Tawḥīd* (God's Oneness), he tended to use Christianity as a point of comparison. He also made comparisons with Buddhism, Judaism and occasionally

Hinduism, but these were not mentioned nearly as often as Christianity.

In article after article, he used themes of comparison such as original sin, salvation, ethics and values, aspects of colonialism (economic, educational and religious attempts to dominate) and the interpretation of selected Old and New Testament passages. He even argued for the proper use of transliterated Arabic, which he labelled as Islamic English, with the requisite use of diacritics as a means to educate both non-Muslims and non-Arabic-speaking Muslims on the proper use and pronunciation of Arabic terms, names and ideas.[9] Without labouring through all the remaining articles that touch upon internal dialogue a few examples will suffice to demonstrate his use of comparative religious and meta-religious methodology.

His methodology of comparative religious studies tended repeatedly to follow the pattern of comparing Christian teaching on a variety of subjects with evaluations made in order to demonstrate its differences with the Islamic position. These comparisons served a utilitarian purpose, driven by an Islamic perspective and need. In other words, he set out to address different Islamic subjects and then sought suitable comparisons with Christianity to underline his point. For example, in the published version of a speech delivered at the 1969 Toronto conference of the MSA, he wrote:

> The purpose of this paper is to examine, in an attempt to resolve, those areas of conflict that seem to exist between the Islamic approach to knowledge (learning and inquiry) and its ethical value with those approaches to knowledge and its value as generally explained in the West.[10]

As he often did, he identified the West as Christian and in this talk compared Islam and Christian views on knowledge and ethics. He argued that Islam is an inclusive religion integrating all aspects of peoples' existence whereas Christianity was not so entirely engaged. The idea of a private and personal faith concentrating on a person's soul was one view of Christianity that he chose to emphasize.[11] He pointed to Jesus who asked his disciples to judge by their own conscience and not to be judged by the law of the land.[12] This led to worship and the giving of alms in secret in the belief that God, who sees all, will reward in secret as well.[13] According to al-Faruqi, this resulted in the separation of Church and state and eventually between reason and faith. It is of this separation that Muslims must be wary and they need to re-integrate faith and reason, knowledge and religion, and, practice and ethics. To live as a Muslim in the West meant learning about the West and in this case Christianity in order to see where it differed from Islam in order for the Muslim to live and practice faith according to Islamic principles and not those of the West.[14]

The theme of Islamic education was continued in a lecture given at the First International Conference of Islamic Education in Mecca (1977) and subsequently published in 1979.[15] Here he distinguishes between the Western development of the social sciences in contrast to church-based doctrines and then compared these to Islam. The social sciences rejected the spiritual in favour of rationalism, science and empiricism,[16] while church-based doctrines continued to separate faith and reason and emphasize the personal aspect of religion.[17] Concerning Islam he writes:

> Islam affirms that God's commandment, or moral imperative, is necessarily societary. It is essentially related to, and prevails only within, the social order of the *Ummah*. This is why Islam entertained no idea of personal morality or piety which it did not define in ummatist terms. Even *salāt*, the utterly personal encounter with and worship of God, Islam declared a means to the altruistic and other-related imperatives of morality. Indeed Islam made its religious value dependent upon them. That is why Islam prohibited monasticism and celibacy; transcribed its religious and ethical ideals into *sharīah*, or public law; and restricted its ethical precepts to public institutions which can thrive only if the state itself is Islam. This is the significance of Islam's transcendence of the limits of Christian morality. Whereas Christianity defined salvation in terms of intention, i.e., the personal moment of consciousness, Islam defined it in terms of the act, i.e. public entry into the realm of space, time and society. In the former case, conscience was the ultimate tribunal on earth; in the latter, it consists of public law, public court, public sanctions, and rewards and punishment by God in history.[18]

One of al-Faruqi's main claims is that Christianity focuses on internal and personal forms of piety whereas Islam stresses that such piety must be expressed within society. Even within personal forms of morality, such as in ṣalāt, the benefits do not remain with the pious individual, but extend outward for the welfare of the community. In this way he speaks of personal worship as a "means to the altruistic and other-related imperatives of morality." Thus piety, morality and ethics are included in and expressed through the vehicle of the sharīʿah, or God's and therefore public law, manifested in public institutions under the care of the state. Al-Faruqi's other main claim revolves around salvation, intentions and acts. He writes that Christianity defines salvation in terms of intention, which he declares to be personal whereas Islam defines salvation in terms of the act, which is expressed publicly. He further attempts to clarify this distinction by the assertion that in Christianity the conscience of the individual is the 'ultimate tribunal on earth,' but that in Islam this tribunal is the law of God codified in public law. The distinction made between the intention and the act is unclear. Al-Faruqi seems to say Islam focuses on the act and Christianity on the intention. However, the well-known niyya (intention) ḥadīth locates the value of the act within the intention.[19] Assuming that al-Faruqi was aware of this ḥadīth, the question can be asked: Why separate here the intention from the act? One may argue, and I think it is justified within the context of the quotation, that he was primarily interested in the contrast between private and public morality. According to al-Faruqi, Christianity's emphasis upon individual piety is expressed religiously in monastic terms and soteriologically in personal salvation where an individual is redeemed on the personal level. By contrast, Islam's emphasis is on the community and hence public morality. This is expressed in public law which is based on God's law while the salvation of the community is expressed through public morality in obedience to God's will. However, the contrast between private and public morality is not necessarily a contrast between intention and act. Therefore, al-Faruqi's choice of words is confusing.

Later, in a departure from his focus on education, he would contribute a paper on Muslims and economics.[20] At first glance it would appear to offer very little in terms of comparisons with Christianity or any other non-Muslim faith; however, it seems that al-Faruqi's thought was constantly shadowed by the West and primarily Christian ideas. In this article, he discusses whether a Muslim is definable in terms of his economic pursuits and ends up drafting a theory of anti-materialism based upon the apparent Christian corruption of the statement by Jesus that "man does not live by bread alone." He writes:

> In the hands of the Christians of history, however, this statement of Jesus became the cornerstone of an anti-materialist ideology. It grew to a total condemnation of matter, of the world, of history. It developed an isolationist ethic of asceticism, or political cynicism, of monkery. It became the war-cry of a new religiosity, which transformed the religion of Jesus into Christianism, the religion of Paul, Athanasius, Tertullian, Augustine, of the imperial Roman Church. ... Jesus was sent to the Jews to put an end to their crass materialism and to liberate them from the extreme legalism to which their rabbis had subjected them. His solution had to be the re-emphasis of the spiritual, the internal, the personal, which was weakened or lost in the literalist conservatism of the rabbis. The call was corrupted by his followers into another extremism based on the degrading of the material, the external and public, the societal, "man does not live by bread alone" became the misplaced, abused motto of this movement.[21]

According to al-Faruqi Islam, with Muhammad, re-balanced this by declaring nature good not evil and the material as something to embrace.[22] Thus, it is good and noble - even ethical - for the Muslim to pursue the material aspect of life as long as it is balanced with the spiritual. He goes therefore from defending Jesus as the one who re-emphasized the spiritual in contrast to those of his followers who corrupted his teaching to belittling the Christian interpretation of the life of Jesus. In a somewhat insensitive comment to Christians, he writes:

> Muhammad could have been another Christianist Jesus concerned only with the spiritual world, and giving himself to his enemies for crucifixion. That is by far the easier course. Instead, our prophet faced reality – political, economic, military reality – and made history.[23]

However, we shall leave criticism for a later chapter. One further note is that al-Faruqi does not pursue here the reasons why the West is considered materialistic; only that Islam balances between the extremes. In any case, the point is that even when speaking about Muslims and economics (and any number of other fields), he chose to shape his thoughts around a comparison with Christianity even though this article was a contribution to a book in honour of the Pakistani intellectual Mawdūdī and not so much directed towards dialogue with the West.

In various articles discussing ethics and Muslims,[24] al-Faruqi drew upon comparisons with Christian concepts such as original sin, salvation and the image of God present in humanity. Based upon the presupposition of inherited innocence and the presence of reason as the image of God borne by people, he argued, as he had done previously, that without the Fall of Man, there is no need for a saviour or for salvation. He writes in one article from 1979:

Islām has no soteriology. "Salvation," in its purview, is an improper religious concept which has no equivalent term in the Islāmic vocabulary. Man stands in no predicament from which he is to be "saved." Adam, the first man, committed a misdeed (eating from the prohibited tree); but he repented and was forgiven. His misdeed was an ordinary human mistake; it was the first error in ethical judgment, the first misconduct, the first crime. But, for all its firstness, it was the deed of one man, and hence his own, personal responsibility. It had no effect on anyone else besides him. Not only was it devoid of cosmic effect, but even of any upon his children. It constituted no "fall," neither for Adam himself, nor for anyone else. It did send Adam from Paradise to earth but it changed nothing in his nature, his capacities, his promise, his vocation or his destiny. Man is not "fallen" and hence there is no need to "save" or ransom him. Rather, man stands under an imperative, an ought-to-do, and his worth is a function of his fulfillment or otherwise imperative. Rather than "fall," Islām asserts innocence; rather than "salvation," felicity. Being an exact function of his own deeds, man's felicity or infelicity is his own work, totally. Such felicity does not depend upon anyone's blessing or agency; it is not the effect of a sacrament, or of an ontic participation in a mystical body such as the Church. Islām is free of both.[25]

People can save themselves by doing good and by leading an ethical, moral life. In fact, saving oneself becomes the motivation for doing good. In contrast, the Christian assertion of salvation as a *fait accompli* potentially destroys morality and religion. According to al-Faruqi's reasoning, if someone is saved, then there remains little reason to pursue ethical and moral behaviour because it makes no difference to one's personal salvation. He writes: "The whole career of man on earth is robbed of its achievement-meaning because the ideal has already been achieved and all that needs to be done has already been done."[26] Further and equally disturbing for al-Faruqi was the possibility of a form of racism to emerge out of the Christian idea of a saved person being ontologically different from other people. In the book *Islam and Culture*, he adds regarding moral value and racism:

> The saved person is alleged to be ontologically different from the non-saved. A lost and found *imago dei* is supposed to distinguish the Christian ontically from the rest of mankind. He is only one step removed from the thesis of racism which assigns value to man on the basis of ontology, of their being what they are, not of their doing what they do.[27]

These comments were made in order to demonstrate Islam's position on values. At first glance the comparison with Christianity seems appropriate only if someone were questioning Islamic values from a Christian perspective. However, al-Faruqi may have felt that his fellow Muslims, even if they did not live in the West, were sufficiently influenced by Christian thought to warrant such comparisons.

Similar comparisons were also made in a lecture he presented at a Symposium in Malaysia to honour the millennium of Ibn Sina (1981). In his paper entitled, "Islam and the theory of nature," al-Faruqi continually used Christianity as a referent to what is wrong in comparison with Islam. The incarnation, mixing the sacred and the profane, and viewing nature as evil, were held up for their contrast with Islam.[28] On occasion he could be harsh and derogatory in his comments, such as:

> The orderliness of nature did not make much impression upon the Jewish mind or the Christian mind, both of which were formed in an atmosphere alien to philosophical thinking and

opposed to reason having any role in the faith except surrender. That is why in both instances, no worthy theory of nature developed before they came in contact with Islam. It was under the impetus of Islam, that the first stirrings of reason took place, that the first attempts to make rational sense out of the faith's dogmatically held truth were entered into by the most daring of Jewish and Christian minds. Christianity was particularly opposed to nature as well as to any theorization of it. It had condemned it as a fallen realm of sin, of alienation from God, a devil's arena where evil is necessarily supreme.[29]

Such statements would not necessarily be conducive for external dialogue, but evidently seemed appropriate for internal dialogue.

The last two examples of comparative religious studies to be mentioned here are taken from his works entitled *The Islamization of Knowledge* and *Tawḥīd*. The general motivation for the study of any religion, including Islam, is discussed in the first of these works, where he writes:

> To know oneself is to know how one is different from others, not in material needs or utilitarian realities, but in moral judgment, in spiritual hope. This is all the domain of Islām, of the culture and civilization which Islām built and sustained through the generations. It is achievable only through the study of Islām and its civilization, and the comparative study of other religions and civilizations.[30]

Out of this need to know oneself, he applies his system of comparative religious study and reiterates a number of his comparative principles under the heading 'first principles of Islāmic Methodology'. He emphasizes the need for internal coherence and conformity with reality, and also the fact that religion must serve the upward progress of man towards attaining higher ethical value, as measurements to distinguish Islam from other faiths.[31] This is all contained in the use of rational thought as exemplified in Islam where:

> At least in Islām, unlike the other religions which are dogmatic through and through, faith is never irrational in its role and contribution. It does not stand above reason, just as reason does

not stand above faith. The perception of reason and faith as diametrical opposites, and of man having to choose between them is not Islāmic. That "the Jews require a sign [miracle] and the Greeks seek after wisdom. But we preach Christ crucified, unto the Jews a stumbling block [*skandalon*] and unto the Greeks foolishness .... The foolishness of God is wiser than men ... Not many wise men ... are called: but God has chosen the foolish things of the world to confound the wise; ... the weak things ... to confound the mighty; and base things of the world, and things which are despised hath God chosen, yea, things which are not to bring to nought things that are" (I Corinthians 1:22-28) may be Jewish or Christian or Hindu, but it is the antithesis of the Islāmic position.[32]

That he felt the need to include religious comparisons in a discussion of Islamizing knowledge should by now not be a surprise. However, sprinkled throughout his articles and books he sometimes makes unexpected statements which seem to reflect something more than mere comparison. For example, he comments in the same work: "It is commonplace for man to desire, to grow and to enjoy, to acquire and possess, to love, to marry and procreate, to seize and exercise power, etc. Islām wishes these activities to continue. It does not, like Christianity or Buddhism, condemn and wish them to stop."[33]

Lastly, in his book *Al-Tawḥīd*, al-Faruqi provides numerous examples of the application of both his meta-religious and comparative religious principles.[34] Since the latter has already been documented, a quick word about meta-religion will conclude this section on internal dialogue. The concept of *Tawḥīd* as the essence and capstone of Islamic religious experience and truth was something deeply important to al-Faruqi.[35] It also presented a prime opportunity to apply his theoretical model of meta-religion in terms of an analysis of a worldview or a claim to world truth. First appearing in 1967 as meta-religious principles, he re-introduced and reinterpreted these in 1982 as five core principles of *Tawḥīd.* These became (1) duality, (2) ideationality, (3) teleology, (4) the capacity of man and the malleability of nature, and, (5) responsibility and judgment.[36]

These five aspects of *Tawḥīd* maintain some correspondence with his previous meta-religious principles. However, in *Al-Tawḥīd* al-Faruqi derives principles from the Qur'ān and not from philosophy as he had previously done when first constructing his meta-religious principles. For example, duality corresponds to the first meta-religious principle where being exists in two realms. The other four principles of *Tawḥīd* tend to include concepts drawn from each of the remaining meta-religious principles, such that there is no simple correspondence. The second *Tawḥīd* principle of ideationality includes the concept of relevance between the two realms of existence (meta-religious principle two) and the idea that this relevance is a command (meta-religious principle three). However, ideationality is communicated with reference to humanity. Al-Faruqi writes: "When that will is expressed in words, directly by God to man, or "the laws of nature," the divine will is deducible through observation of creation."[37] In his previous meta-religious principles, al-Faruqi delayed emphasizing humanity's role until his last two principles. Under *Tawḥīd*, humanity is prominent from the second principle onward.

In the third *Tawḥīd* principle, labeled teleology, creation is discussed in terms of its purpose, its perfection and its realisation as the will of its creator. Again this principle reflects the concepts of meta-religious principles three and four (relevance between realms is a command and creation is good). The last two *Tawḥīd* principles correspond with meta-religious principles five and six, but under *Tawḥīd* the sense of moral obligation, responsibility and judgment is more pronounced than found in his earlier meta-religious principles. The main difference between these two sets of ideas is one of application. Throughout his discussion of the principles of *Tawḥīd*, al-Faruqi applies these to humanity, whereas in his original discussion of meta-religion, the role of humanity was left until the final two principles. While at this point there are no comparisons drawn with other religious worldviews, the exercise proves more than merely theoretical. It lays the foundational and universal principle of *Tawḥīd* which is then examined from various perspectives in the remainder of the book, including religious comparisons.[38] We shall limit ourselves here to one illustration, which demonstrates an application of meta-religion in a comparative manner.

According to al-Faruqi, Judaism and Christianity blur the duality of the ideal and actual realms.[39] Both view God as a godhead, that is, Christians postulate the tri-unity of God while the Jews see themselves as 'sons of God' and thus chosen and above other peoples. The distortion is due to the conflict of immanence and relationship with the transcendence of God. In Islam, the ideal is relevant to, but separate from, the actual and is demonstrated as the divine will (ideal) manifest in the created world (actual), rendering the actual realm intrinsically good. Humanity becomes the conduit for this realisation of value.[40] In comparison he writes: "*Per contra*, Christianity had deprecated the world as "flesh," mankind as *massa peccata* (fallen creature), and space-time as that in which the realization of the absolute is forever impossible."[41] Actual being, that is humanity, can realise the good for which she was created and there is no need for any kind of saviour, unlike Christianity.[42] Finally, since actual being is good and it is the task of all people to realise the good (fulfilling the divine will), then the ought-to-be and the ought-to-do is a requirement for everyone.[43] Thus, there is no discrimination between the ontological 'value' of people. He concludes that this was something recognised and taught by Jesus and his earlier disciples, but not followed by later Christian believers.

By now it should be sufficiently clear that in the realm of internal dialogue, al-Faruqi's use of comparative religious studies along with, in some measure, meta-religious principles, constituted a means to an end. As demonstrated, he continually used Christianity as the main referent in discussing various subjects important to his understanding of Islam. It was almost as if Christianity and other non-Muslim faiths provided the boundaries within which discussions had to take place. Rarely did he ignore the beliefs of others in his presentation and description of Islamic values, ethics and positions on knowledge. Even his most acclaimed works on the Islamization of knowledge and in particular *Tawḥīd* were framed in such a way as to be set in relief to non-Muslim faiths. Clearly dialogical methodology, in this case for internal Muslim-to-Muslim use, was an ever-present component in his thought, and proved to be even more so in external dialogical engagement with non-Muslims.

External dialogue

The task at hand in this final section of our study of al-Faruqi's methodology of engagement is to examine the practical applications of his various principles in actual dialogue with the non-Muslim world. As in the case of the above discussion on internal dialogue, we will not sift through every single article or book chapters, but rather introduce some representative examples.[44] Given the importance of this section, however, discussions will be generally more involved than they were for internal dialogue.

In the practice of external dialogue, al-Faruqi's work falls into three broad categories – world religions textbooks, academic publications and public presentations. Over the course of the time period under investigation (1969-1986), he wrote or contributed to four books on world religions designed as textbooks for students. Interestingly, the first contribution was in 1969 (*The Great Asian Religions*) and the last was finalised for publication just prior to his death in 1986 (*The Cultural Atlas of Islam*).[45] Clearly this aspect of writing appealed to him as an historian of religion and as a teacher.[46] There is little need to discuss this category of dialogue beyond noting a few items. First, he maintained his theory of Arabism and its approach to Judaism, Christianity and Islam as moments of the same consciousness.[47] Second, he consistently appeals to the phenomenological method of *Religionswissenschaft* as the best means of approach, along with the practices of *epoché* and eidetic vision.[48]

Although these textbooks did not offer any detailed or sustained comparative analysis of non-Muslim faiths, al-Faruqi was writing for a primarily non-Muslim audience and was intent on explaining Islam. Thus, he was careful to include what he determined to be the Islamic position regarding both Judaism and Christianity. In this way we can speak of these works as part of a larger attempt at external dialogue or, if one prefers, educational *da'wah*. However, in order to meet the wider objective of explaining Islam, he chose to provide only general outlines and comments rather than any detailed analysis. This was left for academic publications and presentations.

Academic publications

The second category of external dialogue consists of publications that include comparative religious analysis and *da'wah* or dialogue. The main feature of these works is their academic nature as published papers. However, these were not subject to the same level of critique as those falling into the category of public presentations, which were open to questions and debate. For this reason, some of these books and articles form only one half of a dialogue often presented as responses to the published works of others, but with the intent of creating a platform for dialogue within the mind of the reader.

One example is his article rebutting W. C. Smith's contention that the essence of the religion of Islam is a product of modern interpretation and not something inherent in it as an historic religion.[49]

Briefly, W. C. Smith argued in Chapter Four of his book, *The Meaning and End of Religion: A New Approach to the Religious Traditions of Mankind*, that Islam as a system and an essence was a relatively modern development.[50] The impact of the reification (giving concrete form) of Islam historically created what is now seen as its essence. He suggested three areas of impact: 1) the influence of reified Near Eastern religions upon the Qur'ān; 2) the reifying hypostases of Greek thought upon Islamic thought; and 3) modern apologetics. Al-Faruqi disagrees with this analysis in his rebuttal, arguing that Islamic religious experience has a critically knowable essence the establishment of which does not violate any of the constituent elements of that experience.[51] In order to demonstrate that Islam from its inception maintained a recognisable essence, he contrasts it with Judaism and Christianity. This was not a novel approach since W. C. Smith had introduced the idea that the reified Near Eastern religions influenced the Qur'ān and Islam and al-Faruqi simply respondsre in kind. However, he chooses to amplify the use of comparison in an effort to show that Islam's contribution to humanity, soteriology and history was and is unique. It is interesting that he opts to discuss soteriology, since this is more of a Christian than an Islamic concept. He comments that:

Indeed, fulfilment of his vocation is the only condition Islam knows for man's salvation. Either it is his own doing or it is worthless. Nobody can do the job for him, not even God, without rendering him a puppet. This follows from the nature of moral action, namely, it is not itself, that is moral, unless it is freely willed and undertaken to completion by a free agent. Without the initiative and effort of man, all moral worth or value falls to the ground. ... Islamic soteriology therefore is the diametrical opposite of that of Christianity. Indeed, the term 'salvation' has no equivalent in the religious vocabulary of Islam. There is no saviour and there is nothing from which to be saved. Man and the world are either positively good or neutral, but not evil. Man begins his life ethically sane and sound not weighed down by any original sin, however mild or Augustinian.[52]

Aside from the themes of ethics and value theory, the innocence and intrinsic goodness of people and the vocation of humanity to fulfill the divine will, which consists of obedience actualized in the good, he once again chooses to contrast the Islamic position with a Christian background. The audience for this article would not necessarily have been Christian, as one might suspect from his frequent referrals to Christianity, but scholars drawn from a wide background.[53] Therefore, it speaks to his method and his perceptions both of the work of some of his colleagues, such as W. C. Smith, and of Islam, since he could have just as effectively argued his case without these numerous comparisons.[54]

A very different application of his approach to non-Muslims is found in his 1979 work on the rights of non-Muslims under a Muslim government. This was an example of al-Faruqi taking his ideas to their logical end and given that he wrote as a minority Muslim in the U.S., it is noteworthy that he would examine the reverse of his position, that is, of minority non-Muslims in a majority Muslim context. First, he categorizes Christianity and Buddhism as universalist religions that which dispense grace and yet condemn the unbeliever.[55] He then describes Hinduism and Judaism as ethnic religions that condemn the unbeliever on religious and secular grounds and last of all defines Islam as *dīn al-fiṭrah* (natural religion) under which all people are equal and have access to revelation (including the uncorrupted message of Judaism and Christianity).[56] From this platform he then offers a number of rights to non-Muslims. Only one will be highlighted - the right to convince others, that is, the right for the non-Muslim to convince the Muslim of the truth of his faith. Although freedom is a prerequisite for open dialogue, this dialogue must nonetheless adhere to certain guidelines. He maintains that public discourse, while upholding the freedom to convince, is subject to restrictions, if it is judged by the Muslim listener or the Islamic state to exceed the intellectual or spiritual nature of the argument.[57] One would assume this would also apply to Muslim arguments if the non-Muslim determined that these violate the intellectual or spiritual nature of an argument, but in this case who decides? Unfortunately, he does not elaborate further and leaves some important questions unanswered, such as the criteria that the Islamic state (or the individual Muslim) should use to monitor and restrict dialogue. For example, are emotional appeals acceptable or can someone refer to esoteric ideas in order to persuade the other? At least al-Faruqi theoretically allows both camps the opportunity to convince each other.

His painful experience over the loss of his homeland also influenced his perceptions and approach to non-Muslims. In particular, his three works on Islam and Israel or Zionism demonstrate how deeply he was affected by the creation of Israel.[58] Al-Faruqi felt Muslim-Christian dialogue has been damaged by the Christian West's support for Israel. He entertained some radical opinions, such as the need to wage war against Israel if it did not allow her citizens access to the Qur'ānic message. As he saw it: "The injustice perpetrated by Zionism is so complex, so compounded and so grave that there is practically no means of stopping it without violent war in which the Zionist army, state and all its public institutions would have to be destroyed."[59] In contrast to such opinions, he returned to his meta-religious principles as a means from which to build dialogue.

In the year of his death (1986), al-Faruqi published an article on meta-religion essentially summarizing his methodology for the study of religion followed by an application described as an Islamic theory of meta-religion. It provides a potential point of comparison with his earlier works.[60] However, upon closer inspection, substantial sections from previous works are simply repeated with little or no revision. The first example is drawn from his 1965 paper, "The history of religions," and the second is a revision of his 1980 paper, "The role of Islam in global inter-religious dependence."[61] The former paper dealing with methodology was discussed earlier while the latter article, focusing more on application, will be examined below. Given these repetitions of ideas and his statement that he would not elaborate a system of meta-religion, the article loses some of its promise as a means to compare his earlier ideas with later ones.[62] Aside from introducing his perspective on the stages of the study of religion along with a new conclusion, the work adds little in the way of new insights into his methodology. It does, however, indicate that he was generally content with his methodology and saw little need for revision. This adds further weight to the earlier conclusion that his methodology reached its final form early in his career, at least by 1968, and that the application of his ideas occupied his later years.

Since a large portion of this article was previously addressed, there is little need at this point to spend much time on it beyond a brief look at two items. First, the article's introduction outlining his perspective on the stages of the study of religion shows some development from his 1959 Cairo lectures (Muḥāḍarāt fī Ta'rīkh al-Adyān). In particular, he originally dismissed various approaches to the study of religion except the historical method, although he did accept some phenomenological concepts such as *epoché*.[63] In contrast, twenty-seven years later, it is the historical method that is found wanting and replaced by the phenomenological.[64]

He retained moreover his general assessment of the development of the study of religion, positing that in the ancient Near East there was little interest in other religions aside from one's own until the Greeks (sixth-century B.C.).[65] Judaism and Christianity are viewed as interested in, but generally condemnatory of, other religions. After some twenty years of writing, al-Faruqi preserves a harsh view of Judaism, stating:

> The religion of the Hebrew patriarchs, and of their states of Israel and Judah down to the Assyrian invasion which blotted out the former, developed with awareness of other religions. The patriarchs regarded them as legitimate for their adherents. ... At later times, however, when the existence of Judah was threatened, the other religions and their gods were severely condemned and any Hebrew participation in them was prohibited. Since insecurity has been the hallmark of Jewish existence ever since, and because all the materials we have about Judaism date from the post-Exilic period and went through a sieve of Jewish hatred for and fear of all *goyim* (non-Jews), we may characterize the attitude of Judaism toward the other religions as one of hatred, fear, and a false complex of superiority or election.[66]

This assessment is quite reminiscent of his books *On Arabism* and *Christian Ethics*, both written in the 1960s. As for Christianity, it does not fare much better. Christianity first inherited the Jewish attitude toward other religions and looks with favour upon Judaism. However, al-Faruqi claims that it so radically re-interpreted Judaism to fit its own theological needs that what was left was something different than Judaism.[67] As Christianity further developed in the period of the Enlightenment, revelation was replaced by reason, leading to scepticism and romanticism.[68] This in turn led to early attempts at the study of religion leading eventually to the development of the phenomenological method.

The second item of interest from the article "Meta-Religion" is his conclusion. Despite his claim for the article that it reviews the characteristics of meta-religion according to Islam, one is hard pressed to reconcile these with his principles of meta-religion expressed in his *Christian Ethics* (1968). In fact, in his 1986 article, he lists eight meta-religious characteristics as opposed to the six found in *Christian Ethics*. Moreover, his 1986 presentation is much closer to his dialogical principles than they are to his original explanation of the principles of meta-religion. This may be seen by first summarizing the Islamic meta-religious characteristics as presented in 1986:[69]

1. "Islamic meta-religion does not a priori condemn any religion." According to al-Faruqi Islam assumes all religions are God sent until historically proven otherwise.
2. "Islamic meta-religion links the religions of history with the divine source...." This is based on the Islamic assumption that God sent all peoples prophets who brought the same message.
3. "Islamic meta-religion grants ready accreditation to all humans in their religious attempts to formulate and express religious truth." That is, since people are born innocent and with the capacity to know God's will, moral law and distinguish between good and evil, they are capable of understanding religion.
4. All religions are in need of rational, self-critical examination of their religious traditions in order to be purged of human additions, emendations and falsifications.
5. Islamic meta-religion affirms that reason and revelation co-exist with one requiring the other. "That is why in Islamic methodology, no contradiction, or non-correspondence with reality, can be final or ultimate."
6. Islamic meta-religion is humanistic "Islamic *par excellence*..." All people are given everything required to know and obey God's will including intrinsic goodness, reason and discernment between good and evil.
7. Creation is made with purpose and that is to realise value.
8. Islamic meta-religion is not just a theory, but also an institution. According to al-Faruqi, the successful application of meta-religion is seen in history and this has proven the validity of the Islamic system.

By comparing these to his 1967 principles, it becomes obvious they are quite different:

Principles of meta-religion (1967)	Principles of Islamic meta-religion (1986)
1. Being is of two realms, that is, the ideal and the actual realm of existence. 2. Ideal being is relevant to actual being. 3. Relevance of the ideal being to the actual being is a command. 4. Actual being is as such, good. 5. Actual being is malleable. 6. Perfection of the cosmos is the burden of humans alone.	1. No *a priori* condemnation of any religion. 2. Religions of history linked with the divine source. 3. Acknowledges all human religious attempts to formulate and express religious truth. 4. All religions are in need of rational, self-critical examination of their religious traditions in order to be purged of human additions, emendations and falsifications. 5. Reason and revelation co-exist. 6. Humanistic *par excellence*. 7. Creation is made with a purpose and that is to realise value. 8. Not just a theory, but also an institution.

This is an unexpected conclusion for a paper on meta-religion as a critical world theology, since the principles are presented as Islamic meta-religious ideas. The absence of complete and direct correlation with al-Faruqi's 1967 meta-religious principles is also confusing because there are obvious differences between the two lists of principles. Thus, his use of the term "meta-religion" is inconsistent and confusing. When one compares his Islamic meta-religious principles to those of dialogue on the other hand, it becomes clear that his intention may have been to Islamize his dialogical ideas while retaining some of his meta-religious principles.[70] In other words, the principles he itemized in 1986 are a mixture of his earlier ideas. This becomes clearer when dialogue and Islamic meta-religious principles are compared. This may be seen in the following table:

Principles of dialogue (1968)	Principles of Islamic meta-religion (1986)
1. No religious pronouncement is beyond critique.	1. No *a priori* condemnation of any religion.
2. Internal coherence must exist.	2. Religions of history linked with the divine source.
3. Proper historical perspective must be maintained.	3. Acknowledges human religious attempts to formulate and express religious truth.
4. Correspondence with reality must exist.	4. All religions are in need of rational, self-critical examination of their religious traditions in order to be purged of human additions, emendations and falsifications.
5. Freedom from absolutized scriptural figurization.	5. Reason and revelation co-exist.
6. Dialogue should be conducted on areas where there is a greater possibility of success such as ethical values.	6. Humanistic *par excellence.*
	7. Creation is made with a purpose and that is to realise value.
	8. Not just a theory, but also an institution.

A comparison of the above dialogical principles from 1968 and the principles of Islamic meta-religion from 1986 demonstrates some correspondence, but in the latter al-Faruqi introduces new principles not previously developed. For example, of the above eight Islamic meta-religious principles, the second and the eighth bear little resemblance to earlier discussions about meta-religion or dialogue. The divine source of religion (principle 2) and the application of meta-religious principles as an institution (principle 8) appear drawn from Islamic presuppositions. The remaining six principles are open to interpretation in terms of correspondence between his lists of 1967 meta-religious and 1968 dialogical principles. For example, the first and fourth Islamic meta-religious principles of 1986 may correlate with the first dialogical principle of 1968. That there should be no *a priori* condemnation (principle 1, 1986) and that all religions must be critically examined (principle 4, 1986) can be viewed as an amplification of the first dialogical principle (1968), which reads that no religious pronouncement is beyond critique. His third Islamic meta-religious principle, which is that Islam acknowledges all human religious attempts to express religious truth and which is explained by al-Faruqi to mean that no contradiction or non-correspondence with reality can exist, does seem to parallel the fourth dialogical principle that correspondence with reality must exist. Islamic meta-religious principle five, that reason and revelation co-exist, may be said to correspond to dialogical principle five, i.e., that there must be freedom from dogmatic interpretations of scripture. Further, the sixth Islamic meta-religious principle, that people are intrinsically good and can discern between good and evil, may correspond to the fourth meta-religious principle (1967) that actual being is good. Finally, Islamic meta-religious principle seven, that the purpose of creation is to realise value, is similar to the 1967 meta-religious principles two and three, which argue that the connection between the ideal and actual realms is a command. Thus, although correlations between his Islamic meta-religious principles (1986) and the principles of dialogue (1968) and meta-religion (1967) are not direct, that is, there is no one-to-one correlation, the Islamic meta-religious principles do contain the main methodological concepts found in his earlier lists of dialogical and meta-religious principles. So instead of a review and summation of his previous work on meta-religion, his 1986 article is in fact a new application in which he blends together earlier ideas, even though his previous theoretical methodology remains largely intact. The ensuing years saw a variety of applications made to his original principles as he mixed and reinterpreted them for different situations and audiences.

Public presentations

Even though this chapter reviews the years 1969-1986, it would be incorrect to maintain that al-Faruqi began to formally engage non-Muslims only during this period. As was mentioned earlier, he did present a paper in 1964 to the Divinity School at the University of

Chicago and in 1967 was invited to read a paper at Woodstock College. However, the frequency of invitations to speak on behalf of Islam increased dramatically in the late 1960s through to the 1980s. The publications of this period reflect how he applied his methodological ideas in different situations.

In 1976, al-Faruqi presented three major papers, two of which were delivered as contributions at symposia on inter-religious engagement and the third at a general academic congress. His first presentation was given at the "Seminar of the Islamic-Christian Dialogue" (Tripoli, Libya – February 1-5, 1976) in which he spoke about the common bases that exist between Christianity and Islam.[71] Its structure is straightforward, divided into a discussion about and application of the various characteristics that each faith holds in common. When one examines what al-Faruqi considered common aspects between Christianity and Islam, one finds a modified form of his principles of meta-religion first articulated in 1967. Here he streamlines his six principles into four and presents them in the form of religious rather than philosophical ideas. Given that both Christianity and Islam accept God, there was little need to begin with philosophical premises such as the Ideal and the Actual. He could posit God as the Ideal being and creation, including humankind, as the Actual without any substantial preamble. So, after a brief introduction of the acceptance of God as part of the 'core' of both faiths, he very briefly summarizes his Arabism theory, concluding that this provided a set of shared core principles. These core ideas formed the basis for all religious manifestations in the 'Arab Theatre' and thus, formed the components or elements of commonality between Christianity and Islam.

His meta-religious principles, by now quite familiar from our earlier discussion, are restated in this 1976 paper in the following manner:

1. Reality is dual (God and creation).
2. God communicates through revelation.
3. Creation is able to fulfill the Creator's purpose.
4. The ontological and moral responsibility of creation.[72]

There seems little need to explain these core principles beyond offering a few comments. Although al-Faruqi states here that God did communicate through revelation, it was rational thought that discerned and apprehended these revelations:

If the creature was created, it must have been so for a purpose entertained by its creator. This purpose cannot be anything but the fulfilment of His will and this must be built into the creature precisely because it is creature. Discovery of any creature's ought-to-be and ought-to-do can, therefore, take place through reason and analysis of this innate pattern in nature. The other way of discovering the will of God is through direct revelation; that is, the immediate communication of the divine will in words. The will of God, i.e., theoretical and axiological truth, is, therefore, knowable by one means or the other, or both.[73]

If humanity is given a purpose, then it must be obtainable and this means man must be innately good and predisposed to know and obey the will of God. Thus people, bound by God's will and the laws of nature, possess the moral ability to realise their purpose through ethics and moral choices.[74] This assumes that God's will is essentially about providing the means for humans to choose between right and wrong.

From these core commonalities, dialogue could occur through a wide range of subjects. Al-Faruqi identifies three broad areas labelled as the 'cooperative endeavour.'[75] The first two revolve around issues of mutual awareness between Muslims and Christians and the third is a summons to jointly address the needs of humanity. In the first area, Christian awareness, he urges Christians to continue on the path of openness and good will to all Muslims. He praises Vatican II's steps toward openness.[76] However, he condemns the alignment of Christendom with what he refers to as "the Zionist-settler state"[77] and calls for it to end:

Nothing is more offensive to our ears, whether Christian or Muslim, as well as to common sense and our sense of history than the attempt by these voices and agencies, to literalize (and thus en-landize and materialize) the divine covenant ceding real estate to a race, the irrevocability of a covenant lifting a race above mankind, the blasphemous straight-jacketing of God by His own promise and His implied "doggedness" in face of the immoral conduct of His "elected people".[78]

This sentiment hearkens back to his critique of Zionism and Jewish particularism found in his books *Arabism* and *Christian Ethics*.[79] That both Christians and Muslims together should condemn this is confirmed by his attempt to posit a common belief about Jesus versus Jewish claims and those of some elements within Christendom to the contrary:

> Nothing is more inimical to Christianity and Islam than the tampering by these agents with Christian and Muslim understanding that Jesus was indeed the word of God, given to his virgin mother, Mary, to fulfil a divinely ordained mission on earth, namely, to liberate man from the chains of liberalism, legalism, and particularism which Jewish leaders had imposed upon their people, and to open anew the gates of salvation and felicity: that he was indeed the Messiah promised by the earlier prophets.[80]

Despite this common front and call to action against Zionism, al-Faruqi does not dismiss the suffering of the holocaust. He instead calls for this suffering to be redressed in terms of compassion, justice and compensation. However, as Christians and Jews find rapprochement in their relations, he insists it must also include Muslims and their concerns.[81]

The second area of cooperative endeavour is Muslim awareness of Christianity. Unlike the first area, Christian awareness of Muslims, al-Faruqi goes on to provide a more detailed discussion. This is potentially enlightening, since as a Muslim he was in a position to provide insight into how Muslims could grow in their awareness of Christianity, as well as identify areas of common action. However, this becomes more of a Muslim critique of Christianity or more precisely Christendom, rather than a discourse on how Muslims could cooperate with Christians. Simply stated, Christians (Christendom) need to change in order for cooperation and relations to develop and grow.[82]

He begins here as he did in *Arabism* by separating Christianity (which is generally good) from Christendom (which is generally bad).[83] Muslims need to distinguish between these two in order for any dialogue to occur.[84] He defines Christianity as God's religion "which cannot be indicted under any condition."[85] He continues: "Christianity as a religion which God taught Jesus and Jesus conveyed, is always innocent and infallible."[86] Having justified Christianity, he rejected whatever he considered unchristian as something resulting from the

Church or Christendom. It is from this position that he critiques colonialism, the mission of the Church and orientalism as betrayals of true Christian teaching and as points of contention with Muslims. It was Christendom, not Christianity that was responsible for and guilty of colonialism and Church mission.[87] Thus, Christianity and in particular the Pope should denounce colonialism.[88]

Muslims also need to become aware of the mission of Christendom. He defines mission as both an imperative shared by Muslims and Christians and also as a betrayal at the hands of Christendom when it was twinned with colonialism. He writes:

> In itself mission is morally and religiously imperative because it is an effort by man to enable other men to benefit from the supreme wisdom, the religious truth, appropriated by the missionary. ... Christianity and Islam are missionary *par excellence*. To them both equally belongs the nobler mind which seeks to share its spiritual possessions because it knows them to be valid and good. Truth always invited the missionary; it wants to be known.[89]

However, he opines that when the mission of the Church was aligned with colonial interests and objectives it ceased to be about truth and more about possession and domination. Thus, on the one hand mission activity is good, even noble, for both Muslims and Christians, but on the other it can be wrong and harmful.[90] He explains that Christian mission's "continued existence and activity constitute a terrible sore in Christian–Muslim understanding and cooperation" and that "Christian mission should postpone its activities for some other time."[91] Al-Faruqi attempts in this way to dissociate the mission activities of Christianity from those of Christendom. However, he creates added confusion by using 'Christian mission' when referring to both Christendom, whose mission activities are wrong, and Christianity, whose mission activities are noble. He writes: "The inevitable connection with colonialism in the past, the persistent subversive machinations of neo-colonialism at present, the fact that parts of the Muslim world, such as Palestine and the Gulf, are still subject to settler-colonialism, makes Christian mission in our generation utterly suspect, rather repugnant."[92] He advises Christians that they must disconnect Christianity from Christendom. So, while condemning Christendom's missionary activities, he endorsed, but calls for the true mission of Christianity to be postponed. He does not indicate the conditions under which his call for postponement should end, but one can assume it would last at least until Christian mission was separated from the activities of Christendom. Further, he notes that it was the colonial spirit that produced orientalism, but he is careful to declare Christianity innocent of its creation.[93] He again calls for Muslims and Christians to condemn the abuses of scholarship that seek to undermine Islam.

The third and final area for cooperative endeavour consists in a detailed invitation for Christianity and Islam to address the various needs of humanity. These needs range from knowledge and personal ethics to materialism and nihilism.[94] Humanism, secularism and scepticism plague modern humanity to such an extent that utilitarianism, existentialism and empiricism have made advances. The antidote to the plight of the world rests on the joint application of the Muslim and Christian teachings of hope, optimism and morality, integrating the spiritual and the material.[95] Al-Faruqi sought to raise the profile of interfaith dialogue from mutual understanding to action, which would benefit each faith community and the world at large. At minimum, he sought out areas where both Muslims and Christians could agree and ought to cooperate to the furtherance of their respective religious convictions, including the realisation of the good for all.

This paper originally delivered before Muslims and Christians, seeks commonalities between faiths by overlooking or de-emphasizing differences although he does introduce some critique of Christendom/Christianity, albeit insubstantial. Earlier in his career he condemned those who simplified religions in order to find similarities at the expense of unique characteristics.[96] He also focuses here less on the differences between Islam and Christianity, and defines Christianity without reference to Christendom and the mission of Christianity as basically compatible with that of Islam – to seek truth. He avoids mentioning for example that Christian mission as mandated by Jesus was to make disciples of all nations, which is tantamount to making them Christians.[97] Al-Faruqi could certainly have interpreted this as a form of proto-colonialism because he viewed Christendom as largely responsible for introducing the concepts of the fallen nature of humanity and the need to be redeemed by a crucified Messiah. This message was driven home by the West in its search for domination, accomplished in part by making people Christians. In any case, he presents here a conciliatory face to dialogue.

In the same year (1976), within a few months of his Tripoli talk, he read two papers at successive conferences. The first, entitled "On the nature of Islamic da'wah," was delivered at a World Council of Churches consultation held at Chambésy, Switzerland (June 26-30, 1976).[98] The second, "Islam and other faiths,"[99] was presented at the 30th Annual International Congress of Human Sciences in Asia and North Africa (Mexico City, August 3-8, 1976).[100] Each paper emphasized different aspects of engagement, with the latter a more general and theoretical presentation than the former. While both articles offer insight into the basic application of his ideas, the Chambésy paper provides an example of direct engagement with Christians.

In his presentation of Islamic da'wah, al-Faruqi reconstructs his theory of meta-religion in yet another way. The basic elements of his meta-religious principles remain in play, but they are cast within the context of da'wah and Tawḥīd. Interestingly, he begins his presentation by discussing the methodology of da'wah, including its definition and nature, and then moves on to the content of da'wah, which in actuality constitutes an application of his meta-religious principles and is thereby more akin to a methodological approach as defined in this study. In the process, he discusses seven aspects or characteristics of Islamic da'wah, although only a few of these will be highlighted.[101] First, he defines da'wah as a non-coercive device requiring that people be convinced, but never forced to accept Islamic teachings.[102] He writes: "Islam puts its trust in man's rational power to discriminate between the true and the false."[103] People are free to disbelieve, but that is at their own peril. Despite this level of free inquiry those who do reject the Islamic message are not viewed too highly by al-Faruqi as he comments regarding the truth of Islam: "It cannot be met with indifference except by the cynic, nor with rejection except by the fool or the malevolent."[104] Second, he emphasizes that da'wah is addressed to Muslims and non-Muslims and that it is a rational intellection and a necessity.[105]

The last aspect to be mentioned is his assertion that Islamic da'wah is ecumenical *par excellence*. This was based on his concept of dīn al-fiṭrah from which all religions emerged. From this common source all religions can be critically analysed to determine how each agrees with the natural religion.[106] He does not mention in this presentation that he had already concluded that Islam was the true embodiment of *dīn al-fiṭrah* or that he was confident that when religions were measured against this primordial ideal, Islam would be identified as the closest.[107]

Having outlined the nature, process and purpose of Islamic *daʿwah*, he discusses its content in terms of meta-religion now re-cast under the umbrella concept of *Tawḥīd*.[108] For ease of comparison, the principles of 1976 are re-arranged to correspond with those of 1967, as seen in the following table is offered:

Principles of meta-religion (1967)	Principles applied (1976)
1. Ideal and Actual realms. 2. Ideal being is relevant to Actual being. 3. The relevance of the Ideal to the Actual is a command. 4. Actual being is as such good. 5. Actual being is malleable. 6. The perfection of the Cosmos is only a human burden	1. God is One (*Tawḥīd*) – reality is dual. 2. God is related to creation as its God. 3. Man is capable of action. 4. Man alone in creation has free-will. 5. Man must actualize the divine will. 6. *Tawḥīd* gives man dignity.

In the 1976 presentation, the order is different than for the principles of 1967, but the same elements remain.[109] There is little need to repeat his principles of meta-religion or their embodiment under *Tawḥīd*. However, his last two points (1976) are clearly written as comparisons with Christianity. Under humanity's need to actualize God's will (principle 5 above), he writes about *daʿwah*:

It does not justify itself as a call to man to relieve himself from the predicament of existence which it regards as suffering and misery. Its urgency is not an assumed 'need for salvation' or for compassion and deliverance from anything. In this, as in preceding aspects, Islamic *daʿwah* differs from that of Christianity. Assuming all men necessarily to be 'fallen', to stand in the predicament of 'original sin', of 'alienation from God', of self-contradiction, self-centeredness, or of 'falling short of the perfection of God', Christian mission seeks to ransom and save. Islam holds man to be not in need of any salvation. Instead of assuming him to be religiously and ethically fallen, Islamic daʿwah acclaims him as the *khalīfah* of Allah, perfect in form, and endowed with all that is necessary to fulfil the divine will, indeed even loaded with the grace of revelation! 'Salvation' is hence not in the vocabulary of Islam. *Falāh*, or the positive achievement in space and time of the divine will, is the Islamic counterpart of Christian 'deliverance' and 'redemption'.[110]

He ends with this comment about the dignity of man under *Tawḥīd* (principle 6):

Christianity calls man to respond with faith to the salvific act of God and seeks to rehabilitate man by convincing him that it is he for whom God has shed His own blood. Man, it asserts, is certainly great because he is God's partner whom God would not allow to destroy himself. This is indeed greatness, but it is the greatness of a helpless puppet. Islam understands itself as man's assumption of his cosmic role as the one for whose sake creation was created. He is its innocent, perfect and moral master; and every part of it is *his* to have and to enjoy. He is called to obey i.e., to fulfil the will of Allah. But this fulfilment is in and of space and time precisely because Allah is the source of space and time and the moral law. Man, as Islam defines him is not an object of salvation, but its subject.[111]

Fortunately the original publishers of the article included a brief record of the questions posed to al-Faruqi by some of the Christian participants.[112] This will be examined below. Unlike his Tripoli presentation, the Chambésy presentation made no mention of common bases from which Muslim and Christians could cooperate. Both talks did, however, provide modified forms of his meta-religious theory, but these were applied for different purposes. Tripoli employed them to build the case for dialogue, whereas Chambésy used them to distinguish Islam from Christian core beliefs within the context of daʿwah and Christian mission. Why the difference in application? It may well have been as simple as different audiences, leading al-Faruqi to be at one time conciliatory and later provocative.

The last in this trilogy of papers was presented a few days after Chambésy in Mexico City. As was asserted earlier, al-Faruqi could never be accused of being an idle scholar! In a very different forum from the previous two, he spoke before an academic audience unencumbered by the need to be either conciliatory or confrontational. The International Congress of Orientalists had decided in 1973 to include Asia and North Africa as areas of interest for the 1976 congress held in Mexico.[113] Al-Faruqi accepted the invitation to address the congress regarding Islam's contribution to the community of world faiths. The purpose of his paper "Islam and other faiths" was to champion Islamic humanism as the basis for inter-religious cooperation and humane universalism. In it he attempts to accomplish this by first identifying the need for universal relations between peoples and religions, second, by introducing a modified form of his meta-religion theory along with implications and applications to other faiths and last by establishing a comparison between Islam and other faiths in order to demonstrate Islam's superior foundation for inter-religious cooperation. Many of the ideas he presents in this paper are repetitions of concepts and methods discussed elsewhere. For example, he reiterates almost verbatim the first four *Tawḥīd* principles discussed in the previous article "On the nature of Islamic da'wah," and re-introduces his idea that Islam is ecumenical *par excellence.* Of specific interest is the way he positions, explains and applies his methodological principles of meta-religion.

He first positions Islam as the solution to the need of humanity to find and apply a means of inter-human relations.[114] He then goes on to explain the implications of his meta-religious principles for other faiths in relation to God, revelation, man and society.[115] Of these, we will only focus on two examples of the application of his method followed by his summary of the Islamic approach to other faiths. First, under the category of 'man,' whom he saw as born perfect and innocent, he repeats the idea of *dīn al-fiṭrah*, which he also calls *Ur-religion* or *religio naturalis.*[116] Al-Faruqi reasons that since all people possess an innate recognition of God as transcendent and holy distinct from religious traditions, it is therefore possible to critically evaluate religion against this norm. In fact, all religions emerged from this primordial faith of which he identifies Islam as its true inheritor. This idea provides the basis for inter-religious relations and hence our second example, which he labels as innate world ecumenicalism.[117] Since this is a key exposition of the application of his theory of inter-relations, we offer this extensive quote:

Islam's discovery of *dīn al-fiṭrah* and its vision of it as the base of all historical religion is a breakthrough of tremendous importance in inter-religious relations. For the first time it has become possible for an adherent of one religion to tell the adherent of another religion: 'We are both equal members of a universal religious brotherhood. Both of our traditional religions are *de jure*,[118] for they have both issued from and are based upon a common source, the religion of God which He has implanted equally in both of us, upon *dīn al-fiṭrah*. Rather than seek to find out how much your religion agrees with mine, if at all, let us both see how far both our religious traditions agree with *dīn al-fiṭrah*, the original and first religion. Rather than assume that each of our religions is divine as it stands today, let us both, cooperatively wherever possible, try to trace the historical development of our religions and determine precisely how and when and where each has followed and fulfilled or transcended and deviated from, *dīn al-fiṭrah*. Let us look into our holy writ and other religious texts and try and discover what change has befallen them, or been reflected in them, in history.' Islam's breakthrough is thus the first call to scholarship in religion, to critical analysis of religious texts, of the claim of such texts to revelation status. It is the first call to the discipline of 'history of religion' because it was the first to assume that religion had a history, that each religion has undergone a development which constitutes that history.[119]

This idea of *dīn al-fiṭrah* became the cornerstone of his proposed system of inter-religious discourse. At least in this presentation, his methodology depends upon its historic existence and adequate apprehension by all people. This will require some scrutiny in the next chapter. For now, suffice it to say that al-Faruqi summarises his Islamic approach to other faiths with great optimism, stating that it is "the best foundation for a religious world-ecumene" and the best way to unite Judaism, Christianity and Islam based on the Ḥanīfī religion of Abraham (*dīn al-fiṭrah*).[120] In fact, he maintains that: "Islam's *dīn al-fiṭrah* is the only idea capable of pulling Western man out of his predicament and launching him on a dynamic and creative road to self-fulfilment."[121] In the end, he makes three comments summarising the Islamic position toward other faiths:

1. Islam is tolerant and assumes all religions to be holy.
2. Islam, using the construct of *dīn al-fiṭrah* as the "single roof" over all faiths, satisfies the only condition for constructive dialogue and interfaith relations.
3. Islam provides the new humanism in which people are defined as inherently good (not fallen, no original sin) leading away from western scepticism and materialism to optimism and the spiritual actualization of the divine will.[122]

When one looks at the common body of ideas that al-Faruqi produced in these three papers, certain general themes appear indicative of his approach. Although he did not mention *dīn al-fiṭrah* in his Tripoli lecture, it was certainly present in content and was used as a means to describe the common bases between Christianity and Islam. This is seen in his use of meta-religious principles and his theory of Arabism where he assumed the existence of a common historic religious consciousness. In his Chambésy presentation, *dīn al-fiṭrah* became a justification for *daʿwah* in as much as it forms the basis for Arabism, a term he did not use, but a concept he explained.[123] *Dīn al-fiṭrah* also appears in his Mexico paper, but there he undergirded it with a fuller explanation. Finally, all three papers presented Islam as the solution, or as the measure against which other faiths should be evaluated. This was not as directly stated in the first lecture as it was in the latter two, but it was implied by the appeal to the ideas of Arabism. Al-Faruqi constructed a system or approach based upon an Islamic perspective and thus it is no surprise that Islam became the prominent guardian and definer of the basis and means of dialogue. This was to be expected from such a passionate Muslim intellectual, but it does not follow that it was the only means of constructing dialogue or even the best or most widely accepted form. Of this more will be discussed later.

From 1979-1986, he presented five more papers touching upon various applications of his approach. At the 1979 American Academy of Religion conference, the Islamic studies committee organised a dialogue between the Jewish, Christian and Muslim academic communities in which he presented a paper, "The nation state and social order in the perspective of Islām."[124] The purpose of this work was to promote Islam as the best example of how society could be ordered. After discussing the family and the nation/tribe as ordering bodies within a society, he reintroduced his Arabism theory to demonstrate universal brotherhood as the best way to order society. Islam was offered as this "ideal's greatest affirmation; and the Islāmic state, its greatest embodiment."[125] Interestingly for our purposes, this paper, written in 1979, presupposes without alteration ideas he first presented in his 1959 lectures in Cairo (Muḥāḍarāt fī Tarīkh al-Adyān) and later elaborated in On Arabism.[126] For example, al-Faruqi states here that the universal community was first established in history under the Akkadians and the Babylonians. Since then the ideal of a universal community was taught by Jesus as an antidote to Jewish ethnocentrism and was finally perfected by Islam. While the applications changed, the basic premise of an idealized universal community remained the same.

Concurrent with his involvement in AAR, he participated in a new forum for inter-religious engagement, delivering two papers at the Global Congress of the World's Religions (1979 and 1980).[127] The first, "The role of Islam in global inter-religious dependence," examined the ideational and practical relation of Islam to other faiths concluding with several concrete Islamic contributions to global inter-religious inter-dependence.[128] The second, "Divine transcendence and its expression," focused upon a comparison between pre-Islamic and Islamic concepts of transcendence.[129] Although both papers dealt with different topics, they shared the similar pattern of comparison between Islam and the other, but for different purposes.

The themes of Arabism and dīn al-fiṭrah and the methodology of meta-religion reappear in the first paper, but are not explicitly labelled as such. In his discussion of Islam's ideational relation to religions, he makes use of Arabism and the principles of meta-religion to demonstrate the common core with both Judaism and Christianity. He summarises it in this way:

> Islam does not see itself as coming to the religious scene ex nihilo, but as a reaffirmation of the same truth presented by all the preceding prophets of Judaism and Christianity. It regards them all as Muslims, and their revelations as one and the same as its own. Together with Ḥanīfism, the monotheistic and ethical religion of pre-Islamic Arabia, Judaism, Christianity and Islam constitute crystallizations of one and the same religious consciousness whose essence and core is one and the same.[130]

Furthermore, this unity is characterized by a number of principles, which upon examination appear to be a re-statement of his meta-religious ideas. He lists these as the ontic reality of God, man's purpose to serve God, the relevance of God to man which is the revelation of God's will (moral ought), man's capability to obey and fulfill God's will, and man's obedience leading to felicity.[131] Interestingly when he turned to discuss other religions, he did not appeal to meta-religion, but chose to re-iterate his *religio naturalis* or *dīn al-fiṭrah* ideas. He emphasized the Qur'ānic position that all peoples received prophets and the same message.[132] For this reason, by virtue of revelation, Islam honours these religions and, by virtue of the rational nature of humanity, Islam holds them responsible to acknowledge God and obey His will.[133] Any differences between religions are the result of disobedience and not due to different revelations.[134]

The relation of Islam to the wider world of atheism, secularism and, one might add (although he does not), any new religions subsequent to Islam, was based on his meta-religious principles and *Ur-religion* (*dīn al-fiṭrah*), which he calls Islamic humanism.[135] In effect Islamic humanism was an application of his meta-religious principles with the concept of *Ur-religion* introduced as a means to show the innate presence of God in human thought. Humanity has a purpose (to worship and obey God) and has been granted all that is required to realise this purpose. Reason in relation to the nature and inherent goodness of mankind provide the basis for a relation between the non-religious and Islam. In a way, al-Faruqi argues that Islam, if permitted, would guide and lead the world into the felicity of God.

Not content with theory, he briefly discusses the practical aspects of Islam's relation to the world.[136] Simply stated, it is to be the creation of a world *ummah* under Islam in which the religious and non-religious could live. He concludes that Islam's historic experience of inter-religious relations is proof of its sincerity and success.[137]

The second paper "Divine transcendence and its expression" deals with divine transcendence discussed in a comparative fashion. It reads as a general summary of his ideas of *On Arabism* and *Christian Ethics*. He dealt specifically with Judaism and Christianity, dismissing other religions from his discourse as gross distortions and digressions of the elements of *dīn al-fiṭrah*.[138] In his discussion of divine transcendence in Judaism, he divides Judaism into pre- and post-exilic periods (just as he did in *On Arabism*), and states that in the former period the Hebrews did not entertain the idea of a transcendent God.[139] However, in the post-exilic period this began to change and was hastened by the influence of Christianity and later Islam.[140]

In al-Faruqi's account, the presence of transcendence in Christianity began with the teaching of Jesus, specifically with his emphasis on universalism and internalism.[141] Unfortunately, al-Faruqi does not clearly define what he meant by internalism, but it appears to revolve around the idea that Jesus called the Jews back to the Arab (Semitic) monotheism of the *ḥunafā'*.[142] As for the divinity of Jesus, al-Faruqi argues that this was a result of interpretative errors made by the companions of Jesus and early theologians, such as Paul, who invested poetic language with literal meanings. Thus Christianity, by labelling Jesus as divine, sought to bridge the gap between the transcendence and the immanence of God.

Al-Faruqi also points to the influences of Gnostic thought and the mystery religions.[143] From Gnosticism Christian theology received the idea that God is wholly spirit and that creation was the result of a series of emanations, such as the logos (word). According to al-Faruqi: "The opening verses of John's gospel bespeak pure gnosticism: and so do those of the Nicene Creed."[144] Thus Gnosticism was a positive influence for transcendence. However, the Christian majority who could not grasp such abstract doctrines declared Christian Gnosticism heretical and insisted upon a human yet divine Jesus, that is, material logos. Al-Faruqi comments that: "Little did they care that the creaturely human Jesus dealt a death blow to the transcendence of the divine logos."[145] The influence of the mystery religions was no less significant and ultimately detrimental to the concept of transcendence in Christianity. Al-Faruqi argues that Christianity adopted the mystery religions' sacraments of participating in the death and resurrection of a god and interpreted these not as myth but as literal reality.[146] In contrast, the worship of the "God of Semitic religion" was spiritual without recourse to sacraments. Again al-Faruqi argues that the spiritual language of Semitic worship was erroneously read literally and this produced the paradox of God's transcendence yet immanence in Jesus. He concludes that Christianity "raised 'paradox' above self-evident truth and vested it with the status of an epistemological principle. Under such principle, anything can be asserted and discussion becomes idle."[147]

In his explanation of the Islamic position of divine transcendence, he appeals to the human capacity to understand the transcendence of

God based on revelation brought by the prophets and common sense granted by the creator to all humanity.[148] Thus in Islam, transcendence is the "ultimate base of all religion, and all anthropology."[149] However, with the capacity to understand comes the possibility to misunderstand. He launches into an extended discussion of the historic challenges Islam faced with anthropomorphism (tashbīh), and the corrective work of the Muʿtazilah and al-Ashʿarī.[150] The details need not concern us. The point to emphasize here is the comparative nature of this paper and the reiteration of his views on Judaism, Jesus and Christianity. The other interesting item is that al-Faruqi critically examined Islam's battle over transcendence, although he claimed the movement away from transcendence was the result of non-Arabic speaking converts. In any case, normally he did not openly criticize Islam in inter-religious papers. He left such critique to works addressed to fellow Muslims such as his article "The Islamic critique of the status quo of Muslim society."[151]

One final paper with a similar title was presented at an Islamic conference for a Muslim audience. At the International Conference of the Fifteenth-Century Hijrah, held at Kuala Lumpur, Malaysia in 1981, al-Faruqi delivered a paper entitled "Daʿwah in the West: Promise and trial."[152] Aside from making some unflattering comparisons with Christianity, he presents in it a detailed analysis of his views on hijrah (emigration) and the muhājir (émigré) particularly in relation to daʿwah.[153] Some of his analysis has been introduced earlier in this study.[154] The focus here will not be on his vision of the muhājir or hijrah, but on the reasons for their existence and need. He discusses in particular the spiritual bankruptcy of Christianity and the West and notes that the solution rests with Islam. Thus, his application calls for daʿwah, hijrah and the muhājirun. Within this Islamic context, he levels strong criticism against the West and Christianity. There is no reason not to believe this was how he perceived Christianity. For the purpose of dialogue, the following opinions would seem difficult to bridge.

Al-Faruqi points to the spread of Islam in the West (America, the United Kingdom and Western Europe) as a result of two factors – the spiritual bankruptcy of the West and Muslim emigration.[155] Of these two, only the first will occupy our attention. For him, Western spiritual impoverishment was manifested in two realms. The first realm was knowledge of man and nature, which saw Christianity surrender reason to faith.[156] Despite Islam's reconciliation of faith and reason, which according to al-Faruqi eventually caused the Enlightenment and the industrial and scientific revolutions, the West turned to Romanticism with its mistrust of reason.[157] This resulted in relativism, naturalism, nationalism, and nihilism. In the second realm of religion, Christianity, or rather Hellenised Christianity, became impotent, devoid of any real substance and as something increasingly incomprehensible.[158] Al-Faruqi presents Christianity[159] as racist, exploitative and unable or unwilling to address the social problems of the world. In his words:

> True, the modern library is full of books and essays which seek to present Christianity as a religion of social concern. Their logic is not convincing because none has dared to address itself to the world – and life-denial endemic to Christianity, or to the paradoxes at the core of its creed. And hardly any call to real universalism and equality has been heeded, whether in society of the Church itself. The sad result was that these attempts of the theologians hardly ever go beyond the classroom. Outside, in the high-rise office buildings where decisions are made, Christian concern is hardly ever a motive or factor whether in politics, education, government or business.[160]

Having outlined the utter failure of the West, he goes on to discuss the solution offered by Islam.[161] He appeals to Islam's view that man is innocent and fully capable of following God's decrees; that man is responsible for himself in order to prove himself worthy and to actualise God's will; that man must adhere to an ethic of action through the law and society (*ummah*) to bring justice and felicity to all; and finally, that these views are held not as dogma, but as "the necessary conclusions of self-evident axioms and empirical facts."[162] These views are reminiscent of his meta-religious principles leaving aside any discussion of the nature of God, which would be unnecessary before a Muslim audience. Faced with this situation it is the obligation of Muslims to emigrate to the West for the purpose of *da'wah*. This theme occupies the rest of his paper.

Non-Muslim reactions to al-Faruqi's methodologies

While the first objective in this chapter was to complete the introduction to the development of al-Faruqi's methodology by examining how he applied his ideas, the second was to provide some reactions to his public presentations. The purpose is to move beyond his words and allow others to provide some additional perspective on how his thoughts and ideas were received. This will entail a discussion of three conferences in which there is a record of exchange between al-Faruqi and other participants.

The Woodstock conference was held in 1967 at the Jesuit seminary located at Woodstock College in Maryland.[163] It gathered together a collection of Catholic and Protestant participants and one invited Muslim guest, al-Faruqi.[164] Of the noted participants were W. C. Smith, who may well have initiated al-Faruqi's inclusion, and Kenneth Cragg, who later engaged him at the Chambésy conference in 1976. At the conclusion of al-Faruqi's paper, questions and comments from some of the participants were invited and he also participated in a panel discussion.[165] The questions were directly related to his paper topic "Islam and Christianity: Problems and perspectives" in which he outlined his vision and means of dialogue.[166] By way of reminder, in his paper he presented a number of dialogical rules in which the ultimate aim of dialogue was the unveiling and acceptance of truth. To this end, he emphasized the potential of ethics as the best starting point as opposed to theology, which he felt held too many pitfalls.

Before questions were entertained, two responders made comments about his ideas. Joseph A. Devenny, in response to al-Faruqi's criticism that Vatican II was inadequate and did not attempt to discuss issues of Christian-Muslim dialogue, sought to align al-Faruqi's six rules for dialogue with various Vatican II documents. Devenny pointed out that while Vatican II did not explicitly use terms such as internal and external coherence or refer to the law of correspondence with reality, these were nevertheless implicitly present.[167] W. C. Smith as the other responder generally praised both the conference for the invitation and al-Faruqi's acceptance as a step forward in building dialogue. He did, however, critique the use of ethics to the exclusion of theology as impractical. Smith commented: "On the point of discussing ethics rather than theology, this is typically Islamic, I suppose, and I am not quite sure it will work. I think any Christian with whom you discuss ethics will soon shift into the theological level that you probably might as well begin there, and so on. However, this sort of thing is part of that dialogue, which would be exciting."[168]

Only two participants are recorded as asking questions of al-Faruqi and two made unanswered comments. Monsignor El-Hayek asked if figurization was possible without revelation to which al-Faruqi replied that revelation was God's work and figurization man's.[169] Once man began the process of thinking about revelation, he inevitably figurized it in order to comprehend and transmit revelation. Dr. Stowe asked why 'dialogue' should replace 'mission'? Al-Faruqi pointed out that 'mission' now has a negative meaning and implies more proclamation than any critical analysis.[170] He then added another important point, which was picked up later in the panel discussion, to the effect that dialogue should be limited to the elite. His reasoning was as follows:

> Now dialogue, I maintain, shall be the prerogative of the intelligentsia because I'm afraid that if I were to open it to everyone, my fellow Muslims, not being educated yet, poor and diseased and so forth, could be brainwashed by you when you come with your pockets full of rice and gold. ... Therefore I'd say that as long as I cannot meet measure for measure the wheat, the gold, the kilowatts of broadcasting stations and the political influence, I'm going to restrict the granting of visas, as Professor Smith has said, and limit the dialogue to the intelligentsia. But only as long as I am the underdog; only as long as I am the poor. Once I become rich, then you can come with all the gold you want, and then the dialogue must be undertaken by the masses at large.[171]

Of the two comments, only Dr. Cragg's will be examined.[172] He chided al-Faruqi on his elevation of Muslim-Eastern Christian relations as enviable, pointing out that there had been little exchange, but merely co-existence based on non-communication. From his years living in the Middle East as the Anglican Bishop of Jerusalem, Cragg could point to the Christian sense of inferiority and psychological oppression, which were non-conducive to any dialogue.[173] He also challenged al-Faruqi's theological position dividing Christians between those who followed the teachings of Jesus and those who followed the Apostles'. According to Cragg both were loyal to Jesus.[174] Finally, he commented that al-Faruqi tended to be 'excessively rational' and that redemption as *fait accompli* did not mean there was nothing left to do before God.[175] In Cragg's words:

This does leave room for the accomplishments that Dr. Fārūqī argued for, but our capacity to move into that vocation is surely not evaporated or diminished by our belief that the stuff of this vocation has already representatively happened in a victory into which we ourselves can enter.[176]

In the panel discussion, al-Faruqi made two comments. The first was to demand evidence from the other panellists for any doctrinal statements that Christianity had made about Islam that were not derogatory and in any way demonstrated respect.[177] There was no recorded response. The other comment re-iterated his call for dialogue and not mission. He also answered a query about limiting dialogue to the intelligentsia. He commented that it is not a permanent limitation and that the "Christian missionary has so far abused that confidence, and because of this abuse he has rendered the non-Christian suspicious of his intentions and his motives."[178]

Although much of the Woodstock conference focused on Christian interests and concerns, it is enlightening that al-Faruqi as a Muslim was asked not merely to present a lecture, but also to participate in the panel discussion. From the exchanges, one can see that he answered questions directly without much movement away from his position. However, the published record limits us.

At the Chambésy consultation in 1976, the context and exchanges were much more heated and direct. Jointly organised by the Commission on World Mission and Evangelism, the International Review of Mission, the Islamic Foundation (Leicester, UK) and the Centre for the Study of Islam and Christian-Muslim relations (Selly Oak College, Birmingham),[179] the consultation was one in a series under the banner of the World Council of Churches (WCC).[180] The first official WCC Christian-Muslim dialogue occurred in 1969 at Cartigny, Switzerland with recognition that certain concepts were controversial such as the Trinity, the crucifixion and salvation. For example, one Muslim participant, Hasan Askari, a Shīite, did concede his need for a suffering God and not just the Islamic God of justice.[181] However, the 1976 consultation saw strong, potentially intractable, differences emerge despite the stated desire to draft "a common code of conduct for mission and to agree on questions of religious liberty, further studies, dialogue and cooperation."[182] This was not realised due to mutual mistrust, but in the end both sides agreed to a broader draft.[183]

Sperber in her work on the history of the WCC Christian-Muslim consultations writes regarding Chambésy:

> The theme was Christian and Muslim *da'wa*. It became a dialogue in which profound theological differences were expressed that could not be bridged pragmatically. Therefore the aggression and accusations were stronger than in earlier dialogues, particularly from the Muslims against the Christians. A joint final statement was adopted, asking for further conferences of the WCC together with the Vatican and with international Islamic organizations, with the aim of mutual understanding and cooperation and of determining procedures for mission more precisely.[184]

The atmosphere of the consultation began with a strong Muslim reaction to the Karachi Bishop Arne Rudvin's keynote address, which was condemned as a message on Christology rather than mission.[185] There was evidently an intense criticism of Christian mission, resulting in a call for it to be denounced.[186] To provide a sense of the proceedings two small exchanges involving al-Faruqi will be mentioned as recounted by Sperber:

> The Muslims confronted the Christians with mountains of accusations about their behaviour, and when the Christians pointed that, in the Middle East, Muslims had also perpetrated a lot of injustice against Christians, the answer given [by al-Faruqi] was: "Unless there is real Christian repentance I don't think this conference will be of any avail. But apparently we are faced by forces that do not want to admit the moral wrongs and mistakes."[187]

Later, the Christians did apologize for colonialism and neo-colonialism in response to the criticism al-Faruqi levelled when he said:

> I personally do not agree to discuss with anyone who argues that there is not neo-colonialism today in, for example, Indonesia... If you don't see that Christians in places like Tanzania and Indonesia are being used by imperialist forces, then there is no point in continuing our conversation.[188]

The point is that al-Faruqi's presentation was delivered not within a disinterested academic setting, but within the hard realities of differences situated in a great deal of emotion. This was seen in the discussions that followed various papers. Of these, al-Faruqi was involved in five of six discussions[189] and in the development of the statement of the conference, which did indicate the participants' desire to see positive progress.[190]

Turning to specific responses by the Christians to al-Faruqi's presentation ("On the nature of Islamic da'wah"), one notices four main lines of questions.[191] The first, led by Father Michael Fitzgerald, dealt with the concept of Islamic *da'wah* as ecumenical *par excellence* and the belief that all religions are *de jure* (legitimate). Essentially, he asked what did al-Faruqi mean by *all* religions? The response was that Islam accepts all religions as *de jure* and then once critical examination yields their core beliefs, these can be evaluated either as truth, untruth or corrupted (mixture of truth and untruth). The exchange that followed is worth repetition:

Al-Faruqi: However, if I discover that another man's religion had been corrupted and falsified beyond recognition, then I have a duty to tell him about the Qur'ān, God's final revelation, to present it to him as rational truth, and invite his consideration. If he says, "I don't want to listen," then either he is malevolent or a fool.

Kenneth Cragg: What you are saying, then, is that God has sent prophets everywhere, but *ex hypothesi* these prophets must be consistent with Islam.

Al-Faruqi: Yes, Islam as religio naturalis, din al-fitrah.

Cragg: But that which in Buddhism is antithetical to Islam and to rationalism is not simply chaff mixed with wheat, if I may put it that way; it is the very wheat of Buddhism. By your analysis here it must then have been a false prophecy which brought the Buddhist to that belief.

Al-Faruqi: I won't say a false prophecy. I would say that a true revelation through an authentic prophet has been thoroughly falsified.

Fitzgerald: But by what historical criteria is the "true" prophet to be identified? And where is the "true" prophecy of which you speak within Buddhism?

Al-Faruqi: I don't know, but it can be researched; the fact that I assume it to be there at the origin is at least a good step in the direction of ecumenical tolerance.

Khurshid Ahmad: It is very possible that rudiments of the true prophecy are to be found even in some pagan religions.

Cragg: It seems rather an escape hatch of a theory, because if a prophet is really a prophet then his message becomes known, it is *balāgh*, communication; and if has not survived historically it must be mythical.

Al-Faruqi: No. At one time it was known. But then later on it became falsified as the Hebrew message became falsified, and the Christian message was falsified.

Cragg: But from an historical point of view that would be entirely conjectural.[192]

This exchange demonstrated a rare series of critical queries about al-Faruqi's concepts of *dīn al-fiṭrah* (identified with Islam by al-Faruqi) and the theoretical core of religions that are considered true (they must agree with Islam). He remained consistent in his arguments, coming full circle, as it were, back to the idea of corrupted religions (those of the Hebrew and Christian message).

The second question dealt with the point that Islamic *da'wah* is rational intellection. Cragg suggested that al-Faruqi's view of man as either fools or those willing to be persuaded neglected a third alternative, that of perverseness by which he meant those who are obdurate. In response, while acknowledging the universal character and presence of sin, al-Faruqi rejected any idea of the fallenness of man. However, he did not provide any account or reason for the universality of sin, just that the Christian reason was wrong.[193] The following is the full exchange:

> **Cragg:** Going back to your [al-Faruqi's] exegesis of the verse in *Surat al-Ahzāb*, we take the point that there is a kind of natural Islam of nature – that is, *islām* with a small "i," as it were – and there is a volitional Islam, on the part of man. But in the conclusion of that verse, after man has accepted the trust, the Qur'ān says: "Indeed he is a wrong doer and rebellious" – which is what the Psalms describe when they speak of thee "froward," i.e. both ill-advised and obstinate. It is this area that I am so deeply concerned about in your paper because, if I may put it this way, there is a certain naïveté about the principles of reason, and about your alternative of the world being either full of fools or of people who are prepared to be persuaded. Is there not a third possibility that there is a kind of quality of ... perverseness? – for which law, exhortation, argument, do not suffice. Indeed they may provoke the very disobedience they condemn. Could it not be that it is this perversity of man which is implied in that particular verse in the Qur'ān? There seems to be a real emphasis upon man as being in trust and at the same time distorting the trust he was given; the trust, if you like, is simply the context of the distortion. Your paper, in its very real concern which we all share for a right and true humanism, neglects this dimension which, perhaps in some emphases exaggeratedly, nevertheless essentially has been at the core of the Christian tradition about man, and the sense of the divine responsibility which Christians understand in terms of that saving intervention which you say is psychotropic folly ... or whatever.

> **Al-Faruqi:** Since we understand the purport of this verse as being to stress the moral aspect of the will of God, it stands to reason that the violation of it is mentioned in the verse rather than its realization. But the realization is mentioned in many other verses in the Qur'ān. The concern here is not really with man's violation as something necessary, but with man's violation as something real. Nobody can deny that men sin and do evil. They are not angels. In the other verse of the Qur'ān which I quoted, the angels

actually argue with God that men will sin. But God says that He has a motive in creating man which the angels do not know. The difference between Islam and Christianity is still very great here. Islam recognizes the universality of sin, and God deals with it by sending down the Qur'ān. He commands the Muslims to continue to deal with it by da'wah. But the concept of the necessity of sin, the fallenness of man, has nothing to do with Islam. To read in this verse any such meaning would be contrary to the meaning intended and the unanimous wisdom of fourteen centuries of Islamic thought.

Fitzgerald: Does the term "rational intellection" refer only to the da'wah itself or does it include also the response to da'wah? And of what nature is this response? Is it in any way comparable to "conversion"? In certain Christian religious philosophies, for example Thomism or Neo-Thomism, there is something similar to the idea of din al-fitrah. Man is said to be capable of the infinite; he does not have a limited horizon, but is always striving to surpass the horizon. But he is faced by a fundamental choice – he has to choose the good which is outside himself, and this is an option which has to be confirmed throughout the whole of life. If a man stops, and turns in on himself, then he is refusing his own nature. Now this sense of conversion has been described by C. S. Lewis in his autobiography as "joy," which includes an element of ecstasy. It is not therefore entirely rational, but this does not mean to say that it is irrational, rather that it is non-rational.[194]

This discussion between al-Faruqi and Cragg did raise some important conceptual disagreements regarding humanity's capacity and willingness to use reason in relation to God. Essentially, Cragg was trying to persuade al-Faruqi that humanity's unwillingness to obey God was not only bound by ignorance, but also by rebellion. This reality was acknowledged by al-Faruqi, but not as a necessity. In other words humanity has the potential to disobey, which is freedom, but it is not a necessity to violate God's will. The main difference between these discussants was over the source of disobedience. Was it inherent within people to rebel, such that they could not but do otherwise or was it a potentiality, which may or may not be realized?

This led directly into the third question about sin, in which Bishop Arne Rudvin felt al-Faruqi had misunderstood the Christian doctrine of original sin as a necessity. He noted that man was not created originally as a sinner, but chose this path. This was brushed aside by al-Faruqi as something of pre-history. For him the reality remained that Christianity condemned all people:[195]

> **Rudvin:** Comment has recently been made on the dogma of original sin. Now I was brought up in the Christian denomination – Lutheran – which has probably been the most emphatic in its insistence upon the dogma of original sin, and I would say that Dr. al-Faruqi's understanding of it is not really correct. He infers that it's a necessary trait of creation, but this is exactly what it is not. The whole conception of original sin, or the fall, in Christianity is an insistence that man's empirical situation today, which is hopeless and sinful, is not part of creation. The dogma about original sin means that we see man as he is empirically, and we emphatically deny that he was created that way.

> **Al-Faruqi:** But you define the state of innocence as Adam before the fall – well, that is not history, and what troubles me is that Christianity declares all men to be sinful in essence throughout the entire history of creation. The fall in Christian thought means that all men are by nature sinful, not just that all men sin in the same way as we might say that all men have noses! The fall means guilt, crime, and Christianity seems to condemn all men as being necessarily guilty.

> **Rudvin:** But here you are presenting your own conclusions as the substance of Christian doctrine. I would summarize the whole doctrine of original sin like this: we recognize that empirical and practical man is in an awful mess, and all men are in the same mess, and have been throughout history, but we deny – or we insist, we cry out – that this is not what man was created to be. Man is not a sinner of necessity, but by his own will.

> **Lamin Sanneh:** I would like to approach this issue from another direction – from the angle of revelation. The problem of revelation is not just the question of divine initiative – God

willing and wanting to reveal Himself to man in the form of a code of laws – but it is also intertwined with the problem of human volition and how man has resisted, indeed rebelled against, and sometimes persecuted the spokesmen of God, the prophets. Muhammad came as a reminder, certainly, which underscores the idea of Islam as *din al-fitrah*; but he also came as a *warner* – a warner because man is recalcitrant, a disputatious being who will argue with the divine initiative and struggle against it. The Qur'ān itself accepts the problem that to secure man's obedience is itself a highly ambiguous and problematic issue, because the intent to seek man's obedience carries with it the risk of man's refusing to give his obedience.[196]

The discussion then moved from humanity to God's role in His creation. In this fourth lengthy exchange, Cragg argued that there is a connection between God and His creation, such that God is involved, concerned and not indifferent to what happens with it. Cragg labelled this as divine responsibility and that its exercise in creation in a "certain sense compromised" God's omnipotence. At issue was the transcendence of God. Al-Faruqi advocated that God could create without any compromise to Himself. It is possible for God to care and this was demonstrated by providing humanity with freedom and moral responsibility, including divine revelation to follow. However, God is in no way responsible for humanity's choices. In the end it seems Cragg and al-Faruqi talked past each other. While Cragg argued that transcendence did not exclude the influence of creation upon God, but that the act of creation itself affected God, al-Faruqi focused on the aspect of God's responsibility and accountability for what happens within His creation, specifically in regard to God's not being responsible for the misdeeds of humanity. Both agreed that God cares and is not indifferent to creation and humanity, but they disagreed over the nature of His involvement. This question reappeared in a later discussion between al-Faruqi and Cragg.

Al-Faruqi argued that God is purely transcendent without any self-revelation beyond providing humanity with a perception of His attributes and Cragg argued that God can be transcendent yet can still reveal Himself. Cragg appeared to direct the discussion with al-Faruqi making counterpoints. It ended with Cragg's reproving him for setting limits around God and by pointing out that the question really is about the degree of God's involvement with his creation and in particular humanity. Al-Faruqi replied that the question was not the degree but the kind of involvement. He further added that Cragg's position was in effect a reduction of God's transcendence, which Cragg denied. The discussion begins with al-Faruqi's response to Sanneh's comment at the end of discussion three:

> **Al-Faruqi:** You [Sanneh] spoke of God "willing and wanting to reveal Himself to man." God does *not* reveal Himself. He does not reveal Himself to anyone in any way. God reveals only His will. Remember one of the prophets asked God to reveal Himself and God told him, "No, it is not possible for me to reveal Myself to anyone."

> **Cragg:** Do you make this distinction absolute? Is not the will expressive of the nature?

> **Al-Faruqi:** Only the nature *in percipe*. In other words, the will of God is God *in percipe* – the nature of God in so far as I can know anything about Him. This is God's will and that is all we have – and we have it in perfection in the Qur'ān. But Islam does not equate the Qur'ān with the nature or essence of God. It is the Word of God, the Commandment of God, the Will of God. But God does not reveal Himself to anyone. Christians talk about the revelation of God Himself – by God of God – but that is the great difference between Christianity and Islam. God is transcendent, and once you talk about self-revelation you have hierophancy and immanence, and then the transcendence of God is compromised. You may not have complete transcendence and self-revelation at the same time.

> **Cragg:** But no more can you have complete transcendence and creation.

> **Al-Faruqi:** Yes, you can. Because creation is, in the Qur'ān's words, *kun fa yaqun* [yakūn], "be and it is." Creation is a commandment of God (Q. 3:47 *et al.*).

Cragg: Yes, but the creation of man is an involvement of the divine will with the human answer, as Dr. Sanneh has been arguing. And therefore it is possible to say that to some extent the transcendent is now in the custody of man.

Al-Faruqi: But God created creation by His command. I as a creature have no right to inflate myself and the rest of creation to such a degree as to say that without His creation God would flounder.

Cragg: But if I may say so modestly, you proceed into an extravagance. The point we are trying to get is whether in Islam there is a divine responsibility – as I believe there is – and I believe this binds Christians and Muslims very closely together – a divine responsibility relating to this creation and to man in particular. This is, I believe, the proper corollary of a belief in creation, and of a belief in revelation and the succession of the prophets. God cares about being obeyed and seeks obedience through the sequence of prophets. Now we on the Christian side are going to go further and say: Yes, God seeks this obedience in redemptive terms. But I'll leave that aside for the moment. This principle must surely be established that the will of God is involved in the creation, and therefore involved in man the creature, offering him the trust (*amānah*) and giving him the vice gerency (sic) (*khilāfah*). God, so to speak, has gone out on a limb. The omnipotence of God is, we could say, in a certain sense compromised, to the extent that an element of what this omnipotence is seeking is now squarely entrusted to man.

Al-Faruqi: Not really. I as a human being can create a computer or an automaton to do certain things and not to do other things, but the existence of the automaton is certainly no compromise of my own inventive power or my superior mind.

Cragg: But your analogy breaks down. Man is not a computer. As you yourself said in an earlier session, he is a volitional being and what is required of him is a volitional Islam. This cannot be automatic, for it must always turn upon the will of man.

Ahmad: I do not see the logic of saying that because God has created man as a volitional being His Omnipotence and Sovereignty are in any way compromised. God can be caring. God is caring. But that doesn't mean that He abandons part of His Sovereignty or Transcendence. On the one hand, as we find in the Qur'ān, God is caring and loving – *Raḥmān, Raḥim, Wadūd* – and He desires man's obedience and worship; but on the other hand, the Qur'ān also makes it clear that God is in no way dependent or in need of man's worship. If men refuse to worship God and to obey Him, God is not affected. It is not God Who seeks completion in our worship, but rather we who seek completion through worshipping Him.

Cragg: Now we have really come to something which is crucial. In my view if you want an unmitigated transcendence then you have got to go to Buddhism where the absolute is totally dissociated from the immanent and historical. But unmitigated transcendence for me is a contradiction in terms. I have introduced the term "compromise," which is an unfortunate term because it suggests bargaining with truth. But if we are going to use this word, then it would seem to me that an indifferent transcendence would be the compromise. It is not that God cares and comes that compromises him. The abeyance of this would compromise him because it would be a kind of abdication.

If I may say so, it seems to me that what we have to try to do is to think more deeply about what we mean by omnipotence. Omnipotence is not the ability to do all things, but rather the ability to be undefeated. It means that God will subdue all things unto himself. It means a final competence. But having said this, I as a Christian am of the conviction that there are certain things about which we can say: "God ought." I find it a terribly desolating and finally contradictory concept to believe in unobligated deity. That is deism. Theism, to which we here are all committed, must mean divine involvement for this, as I have said, is implicit in creation itself. You cannot create and be as if you hadn't. You cannot have law and be indifferent to what happens to it. You cannot educate and be indifferent to what is happening in education. The whole succession of prophets seems to argue a divine solicitude; *jāhiliyyah* matters. If you have a false god it matters. Now this is not fiction; it is not a play on words. God is involved in the wrong that *jāhiliyyah* does to him. I would say that this is where, if we are open together, Islam has to be open at a deep level to what Christians are saying, just as we Christians want to be open to what you are saying. Can we think of the *Allāhu akbar* as a genuine accountability and responsibility to the human situation? Is not that within the meaning of transcendence?

Al-Faruqi: No. Allah is not responsible for our misdeeds.

Cragg: ... If He isn't, quite simply I would prefer to an atheist. An indifferent or a silent heaven ...

Al-Faruqi: I would deny accountability or responsibility on the part of God for my misdeeds. I do not mean to say that God is indifferent, that God is a cynic. Of course He cares. But God has given me freedom and moral responsibility. He has given me all the equipment needed for knowing His will, and even if I am lethargic of mind He has given me the quick rule of thumb by which to know His will – the *shari'ah*, the law, which I can read easily in books. Now if it is my will, despite all this, to disobey Him, then I am responsible and I have to bear the burden – not God. How can the Judge, how can the Source of the law, how can the King be responsible for the misdeeds of the subject? But of course if His citizenry turn out to be gangsters, He will use His authority as Judge and King. Men do fail in their responsibilities – this is an uncontrovertible, empirical fact – and Islam recognizes it fully. The Qur'ān tells us that God is Merciful, and that it is out of His mercy and grace that He has given us revelation through the prophets in order to correct us.

Cragg: Well, I think we agree that transcendence is not non-involvement. What is at issue is the degree of this involvement ...

Al-Faruqi: The kind of involvement ... not the degree. The nature of involvement.

Cragg: But the Qur'ān says *kataba 'alā nafsihi al-raḥmah* – "He has written the mercy upon his soul" (Q. 6:12). Now that is a verse which takes the will of God into the nature of God. Let's take the metaphor of a shepherd, for example. What is the degree of his responsibility? We think of shepherdhood as requiring the utmost of exposure, search, compassion, concern, and would not think a shepherd responsible if he were to say: "Here I have got a fold, and I will sit in it folding my hands." However, whatever a shepherd does under the constraint of his nature is not limitation: it is fulfillment. It would be the repudiation of this which would constitute limitation.

Here we are talking about the degree of the divine relationship to the human predicament. On the one hand you say there is a divine involvement because God cares about man, but his relationship is didactic, hortatory, educational – revelatory in terms of propositions. But is there the possibility of a relationship more tragic, more compassionate? We are not wanting to say that God is less great but differently greater. Now let God be God. It is possible that you can be found forbidding things to God in the interest of what you think is His dignity, and we ought to beware of this.

Al-Faruqi: I am forbidding man, not forbidding God.

Cragg: But you are forbidding God, implicitly at least, for you say there are things that it is not appropriate for God to do. You are forbidding God the sovereign freedom of manifesting his transcendence in whatever way he chooses – which may be to condescend to man's condition in terms of incarnation. What I am saying is, let God himself be the arbiter of what is appropriate to transcendence. This is all I am pleading for.

Al-Faruqi: What does this mean, "Let God be the arbiter of his transcendence"? After all there is this revealed text in the Qur'ān which says: *laisa kamithlihi shay* – "there is nothing like unto Him" (Q. 42:11). It is we who must beware of what is appropriate when talking about God and about transcendence.

Rudvin: If care means that you are really involved, then, what you care for affects you ... it may even hurt you and cause you to suffer.

Al-Faruqi: In no way can God be hurt. If you want to use the word "hurt" poetically, maybe I will wink my eye and let it go ... with plenty of poetry! But if you start saying that something hurts God, therefore He has to take action, then I say that you are putting a condition upon the divinity of God.

Cragg: But if you say anything about God, if you use any human description of him, then you are by implication making God share in humanness. So you are involved in the paradox if you are to use the divine names at all. This is not at stake between us. Once again, the question is the degree to which one can interpret the status of the divine self-spending, which is the heart of the Christian faith – "Being in the form of God he took upon himself the form of a servant." You mentioned kingship a moment ago. We have a marvellous example of kingship in Shakespeare in *Henry V*, when the king lays the crown aside and shows a simple concern to get alongside the common soldier in a dire situation. Is this less kingly than sitting in the palace on a throne? I think most of us would agree that it is not.

Al-Faruqi: No. It is not less kingly but the how of it needs to be specified. If you are saying that the king next started polishing the soldier's shoes and carrying his ordinance box, then this is not kingly. But remember that a Muslim believes that God is nearer to him than his jugular vein, and that our success is dependent upon him. But to interpret this as a specific reduction of God's transcendence is not permissible.

Cragg: Reduction is not permissible certainly, but this is not reductionist. This is the whole point.[197]

Although the above quotations are lengthy, they constitute a unique record of critical discussions between primarily al-Faruqi and Cragg. These exchanges followed al-Faruqi's presentation on "Islamic *da'wah*" and reflected questions by the Christian side of the dialogue. The questions revolved around al-Faruqi's understanding of *dīn al-fiṭrah*, the influence of sinfulness upon rational thought and God's transcendence. As seen in the Woodstock exchanges, al-Faruqi consistently maintained his position and ideas, such as his interpretation of *dīn al-fiṭrah*, his assumption that rational thought is fully capable of discovering the nature of *dīn al-fiṭrah* and his views on God's transcendence.

The last conference presentation, which included a record of discussion, was read at the Global Congress of the World's Religions in 1979.[198] Previously discussed, "The role of Islam in global inter-religious dependence" examined the theoretical and practical relation of Islam to other faiths concluding with several concrete Islamic contributions to global inter-religious dependence. The discussion that followed was more subdued than the Chambésy consultation, but not without some direct questions.[199] The main difference between the two was that at Chambésy there were two distinct sides of faithful followers, while at GCWR there were people from a variety of religious traditions. Thus, the types of comments were more general and few of them posed ask any critical questions about his paper. Questions ranged from the Iranian revolution, which happened just prior to the congress, to jihād, to questions of authority in Islam and tolerance. There is little need to review these questions or answers. Al-Faruqi was not overly taxed.

The movement from the theoretical methodology of dialogical principles into the practice of dialogue demonstrated al-Faruqi's openness and desire not only to study other faiths, but also to meet them in conversation. It was not always a cordial affair and although he advocated the need for dialogue, he tended to limit it to the educated elite and held that it was certainly not for the masses. Whether or not his methodological approach was repeatable or even valuable has not been the focus of our investigation thus far. The first priority was to allow al-Faruqi to articulate and apply his ideas. In the next chapter we turn to an evaluation of his method.

PART THREE

CRITICAL ANALYSIS AND CONTRIBUTIONS

6

A CRITIQUE AND ANALYSIS

Thus far, al-Faruqi's methodology has been presented without much attention to its efficacy as a model or means for interfaith dialogue. The primary interest in Part Two was to grasp the details of his methodology as it developed over the course of his life. Now in Part Three, we are ready to analyse his contribution to the field of Muslim-Christian interfaith engagement and dialogue. Al-Faruqi clearly stated that the goal of comparative religious studies and of dialogue itself was to seek truth through evaluation. Therefore, it would seem both appropriate and necessary according to the dictates of al-Faruqi to evaluate his ideas.

The general objective of this evaluation is to examine the theoretical and practical viability of his approach. This is discussed on two levels. The first assesses the theoretical feasibility of his ideas in terms of their conceptual elements including internal coherence, his presuppositions and the overall cogency of his method. The second level examines the practical aspects of the application of his ideas as presented in his writings and in his various interfaith discussions. Here attention is focused upon the application of his method and its observed usefulness in promoting and sustaining dialogue.

Theoretical feasibility

The process of assessment begins with some of the theoretical presuppositions al-Faruqi brought to his study of religion. This will be followed in turn by assessments of his methodology in comparative religious studies, a critique of the theory of Arabism along with his views on Judaism and Christianity, and an analysis of his principles of meta-religion and dialogue.

Theoretical presuppositions

Everyone brings certain presuppositions to everything studied. The issue is not necessarily the existence of our presuppositions, but what we do with them or rather how they influence our perceptions of others. Al-Faruqi came to the study of other religions through the field of philosophy and as such carried certain ideas that influenced his assessments of religion, particularly Christianity and Judaism. The most pronounced of these was his advocacy and reliance upon rationalism or reason.

The over reliance on rationalism both to understand and evaluate religions is the most cited critique of al-Faruqi's overall methodology.[1] Within this presupposition there are at least two epistemological aspects that need to be considered. The first is how we know and the second is how we can discern truth. In al-Faruqi's philosophical work on ethics and value, he adopted the Kantian view that ideals exist *a priori*, as does truth.[2] These concepts or ideals have application only when there is experience. Thus, reason can only exist in conjunction with experience. Values then in their ideal being are independent of humanity, but they enter the actual realm through people.[3] Without the mind and thought there is no knowledge. The mind contributes forms of sensibility necessary for understanding experience, all of which occurs in space and time.[4] As al-Faruqi moved into the study of religion he continued to apply ethics and value in their *a priori* state, apprehended through reason, as a means to compare and evaluate various religious traditions and teachings. He presumed that truth exists apart from people but that it is correctly comprehensible through reason. Kant himself categorically ruled out any knowledge of God because God is beyond space and time and thus beyond our experience.[5] Therefore, God is not an object of possible experience and hence is closed to our knowledge. This would not have posed a problem for al-Faruqi since, if God wishes to be known through His attributes, that is, *in percipi*, He can enter our space and time through revelation. There is, however, no way to undeniably prove that truth exists *a priori*, but it was an assumption al-Faruqi was willing to concede. Apart from the concern that experience, which is subjective, serves as the means through which truth or value is observed, the application of reason can serve to restore a balance by bringing a measure of objectivity to our understanding of what is true.

Rationalism was the primary method used by al-Faruqi in the study of religion.[6] He dismissed mysticism as subjective and therefore not a critical means of knowledge. However, is rationalism the only means of acquiring knowledge? Rationalism is characterized by its stress upon the innate or *a priori* ability of humans to use reason in order to know something.[7] Thus, what is knowable or demonstrable by human reason is true. This is in contrast to empiricism where the stress is on the senses to provide a means to know something. There are, however, certain limitations with rationalism. First, reason or logic alone is only a negative test for truth. It can be used to eliminate the false, but in and of itself cannot establish what must be true. It can only demonstrate what is possibly real and not what is actually real.[8] Second, there is no rationally inescapable way to establish the first principles of reasoning. They are intuitive but non-demonstrated givens.[9] In other words, reason cannot be used to prove reason because it has no way to prove the laws of thought upon which reason is based. If attempted, this becomes circular reasoning. In like manner, the law of non-contradiction is only a test for falsity and not for truth. Demonstrating that a view is not contradictory to itself does not necessarily show that it is true.[10] The point is that logic and reason cannot be used to prove one view is true. It can only show which ones are false.[11] One may argue in reply that revelational rationalists, among whom al-Faruqi may be numbered, have access to knowledge of the truth and therefore are able to discern which view is true. The problem with this argument is that one would need to be omniscient in order to definitely and finally apply the consistency test for truth. Since this is not possible, the situation for the use of reason to determine truth remains the same. For example, either there is a car in the parking lot or there is not. One statement is true and the other is false, but which is true? Reason alone cannot provide the answer or give guidance to determine which is true. One needs to actually go and see (experience) or rely on the trusted testimony of another (trusting another's experience). The fact is that al-Faruqi did not rely exclusively on rationalism because as a Muslim he trusted in the testimony of the prophets, just as a Christian or a Jewish person trusts in the prophets.

The purpose of the above discussion is to demonstrate that al-Faruqi attempted to use reason to show that Judaism and Christianity historically, ethically and as scriptures became distorted and untrue. However, he assumed Islam was true and did not apply his method of analysis to his own faith nor did he really discuss the tension or relationship between reason and faith. This should not surprise us, since Christians and Jews also assume their faiths are true and then work to evaluate others from this starting point. However al-Faruqi went further by stating, though not demonstrating, that Islam was rationality *par excellence*, thus making Islam the measure of all faiths. This is simply not possible by applying reason alone. Douglas Jay, in his review of *Christian Ethics*, recognises that al-Faruqi offered rational principles as a means to judge all religions objectively, but Islam was cited as the embodiment of rationality, thus rendering Islam the normative standard by which all others are judged.[12] This became a form of circular reasoning, especially as reason does not provide normative standards in religion in the same way that it does in science.[13] Peter Ford in his critique noted that al-Faruqi did not address the issue of authority from which judgments are to be made.[14] Who exactly decides which is true and what are the principles that underlie these judgments? At the end of the day, as noted by Esposito, the criteria of 'what makes sense' was used to determine what would be accepted and what would be dismissed.[15] If something did not make sense to al-Faruqi, such as the divinity of Christ, it was rejected. The rejection was not presented as one man's opinion, but as something against reason and therefore universally rejected by anyone who used reason. Indeed, in *Christian Ethics*, he argued that his critique was not Islamic, but human, an *absolute* critique.[16]

A corollary presupposition to the use of reason was paradox. Reason could not permit paradox and al-Faruqi was particularly dismissive of any hint of such a conclusion, especially if it was posited as a final position. Cragg mentioned: "For al-Faruqi, paradox was evasion, the sign of an untidy mind or a perverse will."[17] However, the problem with such a position, aside from the fact that Christians with whom he wished to engage do not generally hold to his complete dismissal of paradox, is that it is not really held by Muslims either. For example, the ninth-century controversy over whether or not the Qur'ān was created was a result in part of Mu'tazilite rational reasoning that if the Qur'ān is uncreated, then it is eternal. Since only Allah is eternal, there is an obvious problem. So they reasoned the Qur'ān must have been created at some point. However, Islamic history demonstrates that Sunni consensus reached the conclusion that the Qur'ān was not created. An eternal God and His eternal word are in some measure a paradox. How can both be eternal and yet God be one (*Tawhīd*)? This in particular is important because Christianity dealt with the issue of the Word of God, Christ and the nature of God centuries earlier.

Al-Faruqi did not address this nor did he acknowledge any paradoxes within Islamic thought. For example, he promoted Abraham as a contact point in trialogue between the three Monotheistic faiths, but he did not mention the paradox shared by all three concerning the story of the sacrifice of Abraham's son.[18] God asked Abraham to leave the rational, ethical and universal realm of "Thou shall not kill" and move into the realm of belief and trust. In essence, God asked Abraham to violate the God-given command not to kill in order to obey God's command to sacrifice a human life. If Abraham practiced pure reason as al-Faruqi advocated, then Abraham may well have reasoned that since God would not contradict His command not to kill, given that God's will must be consistent, then this must not be a command from God. Such a response would have led to disobedience, yet Abraham transcended the realm of pure reason and entered subjective faith. This illustration suggests other critiques for al-Faruqi's methodology, which will be brought up later.[19] For now the point is taken that paradox exists. One may not like it, but it is just as present in Islam as it is in Christianity and Judaism. Although, al-Faruqi appears not to have addressed the presence of paradox in Islam,[20] he did offer two comments. First, paradox should not be the *final* position because he believed that God communicates to us in understandable ways and for al-Faruqi reason was the primary, if not the only, means we have to discern truth. For example, paradox may appear to exist, but with further revelation and advances in our understanding such paradox may turn out to be explainable. In Christianity the nature of Christ as both God and man is a paradox situated at the core of Christian faith. Al-Faruqi found it difficult to rationally accept this paradox as the final position and instead viewed it as a distortion. Second, al-Faruqi recognised that there are aspects of God's expression of Himself *in percipi* that escapes our limited ability to understand. Therefore, we must accept certain aspects of God's revelation in terms of faith and trust. This is true for the majority of religious believers. Certain doctrines and teachings are accepted based upon trust in the prophets who were given such teachings by God, such as the above example of the Divinity of Christ.

There is one final presupposition to mention before moving on to an analysis of his principles of comparative religious studies, meta-religion and dialogue. This was his appeal to *dīn al-fiṭrah*, which he identified as being embodied in Islam.[21] He presupposed that since humanity is good and innocent and possesses an innate recognition of God as transcendent and holy, apart from religious traditions, this could be used as a reference from which to critically evaluate all religions.[22] He postulated that the natural religion of humanity was recognised by Islam as the basis for all religion. If one could isolate and articulate the essence and characteristics of this *dīn al-fiṭrah*, then it could be used by anyone to see how every religion measured up in comparison. The assumption is that *dīn al-fiṭrah* is the truth and the ideal. However, the idea of *dīn al-fiṭrah* raises certain questions. Is the natural religion of humanity a reduction of the world's religions to their common denominators? Is it an identifiable body of characteristics and beliefs that are independent of the world's religions? Or does it contain aspects that can be reconciled with Islam? Al-Faruqi viewed *dīn al-fiṭrah* as something innate in humanity and expressed in various religions, but over time these expressions became corrupted. This implies that Islam potentially suffers from the same possibility of accretions and distortions that can be corrected by comparing Islam to *dīn al-fiṭrah*. The difficulty is to demonstrate the characteristics of *dīn al-fiṭrah*. It is not sufficient to work from existing faiths to derive this natural religion. If we could discover *dīn al-fiṭrah*, it would revolutionize comparative religion by acting as a meta-religious means to evaluate all religions.

Aside from the problem of identifying this natural religion both as a concept and as an historic entity, al-Faruqi maintained that Islam best represented *dīn al-fiṭrah*. Now it follows logically that if the original Ḥanīfī religion of Abraham (*dīn al-fiṭrah*) is the measure of all religion and that if Islam is identified as the closest to it, then Islam becomes the best measure of all religion.[23] The problem is that the criteria he used to build his notion of natural religion were based upon Islamic ideas, thus becoming another example of circular reasoning.[24] If, as will be seen, this interpretation of *dīn al-fiṭrah* is used as a basis for comparative religious studies or for dialogue, it undermines the process. If the idea of *dīn al-fiṭrah*, as al-Faruqi proposed, is valid, then the presupposition of *taḥrīf* (distortion of the Christian and Jewish Scriptures) is a logical possibility, but if *dīn al-fiṭrah* was not identical to

Islam, then this could also imply that *taḥrīf* potentially exists in Islamic Scripture. This is not of course al-Faruqi's position. In fact the term *naskh* (abrogation or withdrawing one verse for another) and not *taḥrīf* is used to indicate places within the Qur'ān where there are differences between verses.[25] One assumption in *taḥrīf* is that every prophet brought the same message, but this tends to ignore each individual prophet's historical context. This leaves it up to the reader to determine these commonalities while ignoring the differences and contexts.[26] It also presupposes that the Islamic reading of the prophets is normative. Once again this is an Islamic starting point and is mentioned not to delve into the topic too deeply, but rather to point out that al-Faruqi assumed this position as a basic presupposition.[27]

These three theoretical presuppositions (reason/rationalism, no paradox, *dīn al-fiṭrah*) undergird al-Faruqi's methodologies of religious comparison and dialogue. Although he is adamant about the prime place of reason, in reality he was not as extreme in its use to the exclusion of everything else. For example, he appealed to experiential and evidential arguments in support of the truth of Islam.[28] Larry Poston commented: "The example of his own [a Muslim's] life, his commitment to the values he professes, his engagement, constitute his final argument."[29] However, the same could be said of a Christian or Jewish believer as they appeal to their lives as evidence for the validity of their faiths. Furthermore, he did not fully explain how faith and reason are related.[30] He made mention of this primarily in the context of a critique of Christianity which he felt placed faith above reason. Given these presuppositions, we can now turn to an analysis of his various methodologies.

Phenomenological methodology in comparative religious studies

In this section, the phenomenological principles of *epoché* and eidetic vision, along with a critique of Arabism and al-Faruqi's interpretations of Judaism and Christianity, will be our focus. His movement from philosophy to religious studies was marked by his continued use of reason and also some concepts from the phenomenology of Edmund Husserl. In particular, this included the notion of *epoché* or bracketing in which the scholar suspends personal belief and judgment in order to apprehend the beliefs and views of the subject under study. By nature, *epoché* is a subjective element because it depends upon the skill and ability of the user to enter into the other's world without imposing their critical judgments. The relative success of its practice is in part measured, but not limited by, those who are being studied. On the other hand eidetic vision is the practice of identifying the essence or 'whatness' of various phenomena. As with *epoché*, the practitioner cannot superimpose any preconceived structure without the risk of misapprehending the very phenomena he seeks to grasp. Therefore, *epoché* and eidetic vision become the art of suspension of personal evaluative criteria both as presuppositions and structure. There are potential problems with these two practices if they are used simultaneously. *Epoché*, which suspends criticism, and eidetic vision, which suspends objectivity, leaves the findings of the phenomenologist personal and unverifiable. Al-Faruqi advocated the initial use of *epoché*, but concluded that at some point critical thought must be applied to evaluate what the use of *epoché* discovered. However, he did not really discuss when exactly one can know that one has adequately appreciated and understood the religious beliefs, ideas and practices of others and therefore suspend the use of *epoché* and turn to critical judgment. As a theoretical idea, *epoché* is attractive and intuitively employed by most people who practice empathy and a desire to understand. However, as an academic tool it needs to be used carefully and al-Faruqi was quite correct to discuss its temporary nature and the need to evaluate. It would seem suspension and evaluation are interdependent with one informing the other. Whether or not al-Faruqi successfully used *epoché* in practice will be examined later under the section on practical applications. For now, *epoché* as he presented it in *Christian Ethics* appears to have been reasonably applied.

Eidetic vision was not generally mentioned by al-Faruqi, although it is sufficiently close to *epoché* that in some measure it was implicitly present in his thought.[31] For example, he proposed that a careful and unbiased reading of the Christian Scriptures would allow the ethic of Jesus to emerge and be systematised as meaning-wholes. This in turn would permit him to evaluate, not only how far Christendom had moved away from that ethic, but also how the ethics of Jesus may be compared with other religions, such as Judaism and Islam. This can be claimed as a practice of eidetic vision because an unbiased observation accepting phenomena at face value on its own terms and in its own context would allow the ethical teachings and practice of Jesus and of his followers to emerge and be organised into categories. It however, assumes that the Christian Scriptures, in particular the Gospels, are accurate and uncorrupted.[32] Since he believed both the Jewish and Christian Scriptures were altered, he would need to decide which remained true and from this authenticated collection draft his ethic of Jesus. Thus, he would need to prove or give some kind of evidence for which parts of Scripture he accepted. This would render him both judge and jury, deciding in advance, on which data he would practice *epoché*.

A critique of Arabism

The theory of Arabism with its view that there is an Arab consciousness or spirit that runs through the history of humanity manifesting itself spiritually in different moments (Judaism, Christianity, Islam) was something continually present in al-Faruqi's evaluation of religions. Its centrality as a theory in his writings requires at least some comment.

The theory of Arabism was premised upon a number of presuppositions all of which al-Faruqi assumed rather than attempted to justify. He presumed the eternal message of God was His oneness or *Tawḥīd* and that Judaism, Christianity and Islam were centred in this same message. This message was given to all people but expressed most notably in the three monotheistic faiths, while the concept of *taḥrīf* (corruption of scripture) accounted for the emergence of different moments of Arab consciousness. If the theory of Arabism were presented as an Islamic interpretation of the history of religions, little would be left to say since his presuppositions are basically Islamic and monotheistic. However, since al-Faruqi claimed much more than this by positing this theory as universal and applicable to all religions, it is open to a more serious critique.[33] Aside from the nature of the above presuppositions, one needs to examine his definition of 'Arab' and his subsequent use of Sura 3:110.

As one may recall, he defined 'Arab' not as an ethnic concept to describe a people, but as a category including anyone who recognises and shares or adheres to the values of Arabism throughout the course of history. Presumably before the term 'Arab' was ever coined within history, the concept existed. The values of Arabism are a belief in and obedience to *tawḥīd*, and the practice of justice, ethicality and universal brotherhood. He bases this interpretation upon Sura 3:110 ("You are the best of all peoples, evolved for mankind. Enjoining what is right, forbidding what is wrong, and believing in Allah") from which he creates a syllogism:

1. To enjoin the good, forbid the evil and believe in God is to be ethically the best
2. The Arabs enjoin the good, forbid evil and believe in God
3. Therefore, the Arabs are ethically the best

Aside from sounding racial and nationalistic (as Ford noted), the syllogism itself contains problems.[34] Premise two excludes everyone except Arabs and al-Faruqi provides no conclusive support for why it should be accepted as true.[35] Could there not be non-Arabs who enjoin the good, forbid evil and believe in God? Yes, of course, but al-Faruqi simply redefined 'Arab' to include such non-Arabs. This begs the question somewhat and does not demonstrate the truth of the second premise, as one reviewer of the book pointed out.[36] When this verse was revealed, was it understood to refer to the Arabs of Muhammad's time or did it also refer to the more inclusive definition al-Faruqi advocated? He did not discuss this in any way. On one level it appears that while attempting to be faithful to his own religious beliefs, he attempted to make an exclusive verse inclusive. Further, as Ford mentioned, the assertion that only the Arab people have kept Arab consciousness pure while others (Jews and Christians) have altered the divine message is difficult to sustain historically.[37]

The other main critique of his theory was his selective view of Judaism and Christianity. Judaism was seen to have fallen into racialism and exclusivism, which ontologically favoured one people as chosen by God over all the rest. Jesus came to break this distortion with the universal message of interiorised ethics. However, is this all that Judaism and Christianity taught and teach? It may fit well into his theory, but it leaves out much that both the Jewish and the Christian believer would see as essential. As Cragg noted "there were times when his assessments of Judaism and Christianity left the reader wondering whether he had ever really taken their point."[38] Of course such an assessment can also be made of a Christian who represents Islam in ways a Muslim would not.

Understanding and interpreting Judaism and Christianity
Al-Faruqi's interpretation and views of Judaism and Christianity are at times puzzling and at other times ostensibly unfounded. A few examples will help to demonstrate that he viewed Judaism and Christianity in ways that supported his Arabism theory.

Regarding Judaism, al-Faruqi's view was sometimes unabashedly critical. He believed that the Hebrews, after the exile and in the post-exilic period, created an exclusive and separatist system with themselves at the centre as the chosen people of God. The seed of this exclusivism was present earlier, but only manifested itself later as a distortion of the universal nature of the Arab spirit. However, he went further and viewed the Jewish Scriptures as "Jew-loving, *goyim*-hating, Lord-of-the-universe, God-of-the-Jews literature."[39] Religion, he wrote, was impossible to the Hebrews who created a nationalistic faith with God belonging only to them.[40] This position was not unique to al-Faruqi, as may be seen from a perusal of the writings of authors such as Renan.[41] There were Hebrews, however, who are portrayed by al-Faruqi as faithful to the true religion such as Abraham, Ishmael, Isaac, Jacob and Moses. One curious omission from his analysis of Judaism is the tradition in the Hebrew Scriptures of God bestowing his blessing upon non-Jews along with indications of God's future blessings on various Gentile nations.[42] One might question why, if the Jewish Scriptures were written to promote Hebrew racialism, are there such positive references to Gentiles? If the Hebrews after the exile constructed an exclusivist religion, why did they not expunge such contradictory texts that showed God's favour extended to non-Hebrews?[43] Further, he ignored any references to God calling the children of Abraham, Isaac and Jacob, 'His people' and ignored God's commands that they remain separate from the nations around them.[44] In an ironic twist Duran Khalid notes that Muslim self-understanding is as a 'chosen community,' a term not usually employed by Muslims who see it as a Jewish reference to exclusivism. He writes: "And yet, in the final analysis, the concept of choseness is fairly much the same in both religions."[45]

One other important critique of al-Faruqi in his use of both Jewish and Christian Scripture was his tendency to practice eisegesis rather than exegesis. That is, he tended to read into the text meaning that was not there in order to support his thesis. For the sake of brevity only one example will be discussed regarding Judaism.

In *On Arabism*, al-Faruqi set out to discuss the foundations of Jewish separatism by examining Genesis 34 and the story of Jacob and the Shechemites. In what follows, he interpreted the events in a manner that lent support to his thesis of Jewish separatism and as a rejection of an opportunity to practice universalism. Briefly, the story follows

Jacob, his twelve sons and his daughter Dinah as they migrated to the land of the Shechemites from whom Jacob bought a piece of land. Dinah went to visit the daughters of the land, was seen by Shechem the prince who then, in al-Faruqi's words, 'ravished the maid'. Al-Faruqi in his account wrote that Dinah and the Prince fell in love and what took place was not rape. In fact, after the event, the Prince sought to console Dinah with his desire to wed her and offered an alliance between his people and Jacob and his sons. However, the Hebrews wanted to remain exclusivist and devised a clever plan to consent to the marriage on the condition that the men of Shechem become circumcised, which they did. Taking advantage of the pain that ensued, the sons of Jacob went and killed all the men and stole their possessions including the women and the children. Thus began Hebrew separateness. Unfortunately, this reading ignores a number of elements in the text.

There are a series of misgivings about his interpretation of this story. First, he interpreted Genesis 34:2, which reads "and when Shechem the son of Hamor the Hivite, prince of the country, saw her, he took her, and lay with her, and defiled her," not as an act of rape, but consensual intercourse.[46] However, the Hebrew word (לקח – *laqach*) translated as 'took' implies 'to seize,' 'to use,' 'to capture' which is better interpreted to mean non-consensual contact.[47] This is supported by the comment that Shechem defiled or humiliated Dinah.[48] Further, and more importantly, he portrayed the Shechemites as honourable and noble in their desire to join the Hebrews, despite Jacob's relative poverty. Al-Faruqi writes regarding the Shechemites and their king:

His [the Shechemites] was an established, prosperous, happy little kingdom. Jacob's lot, on the other hand, was that of an uprooted nomad with little or no retinue, a few heads of cattle and a few pieces of silver to pay for his occupancy of a little land outside the gates of the city. But the king was so open-hearted and had such faith in the brotherhood of all men that he not only agreed to the son's betrothal to the foreign, rootless girl but went all the way to Jacob to deliver what is and remains a classic in the literature of human brotherhood. Such an attitude would be taken by all mankind as challenging and disarming at the same time. How many could rise up as high as the Shechemites in the matter of brotherly love and cooperation? The Shechemites offer of fraternization was something nobody could have rejected – except the Hebrews![49]

Yet again a full reading of the text indicates that Jacob was not necessarily a poor, wandering nomad with meagre possessions, but someone with such wealth that Hamor the King and his son Shechem could reason before their people that by consenting to circumcision they would eventually possess all of Jacob's wealth through inter-marriage.[50] Furthermore, it was not the case, as al-Faruqi read it, that all the sons of Jacob attacked and killed the men of Shechem; rather, it was only Dinah's brothers, Simeon and Levi, who took revenge for their sister, who had during all this time remained in the house of Shechem.[51] After the deed was done, all the sons of Jacob rose up and took possession of the property of the Shechemites. The purpose of this story was not to demonstrate Hebrew exclusivism per se, but it was a story of revenge perpetrated by two of Jacob's sons for the honour of their sister. Even Jacob disapproved of the extent of the revenge fearing retaliation by other inhabitants of the land who would hear of this event.[52] The response of his sons is telling: "Should he treat our sister as a harlot?"

The point of this rather extended discussion is that al-Faruqi chose this passage as the foundation for his argument on Jewish racial exclusivism. Clearly, he read the text to suit his purpose, but his interpretation cannot be fully supported. Even if one were to grant that Dinah was indeed not raped, the reason for the revenge was not necessarily to keep the Hebrew clan 'pure' and exclusive, but because Dinah was defiled. Were the actions of Jacob's two sons reprehensible? Yes. Was it for the sole purpose of racial purity? No. It was to avenge family honour and their sister.[53]

The intention here is simply to demonstrate that al-Faruqi was overzealous in pursuit of evidence supporting his Arabism theory. Some of his views on Judaism were hardly conducive to dialogue and understanding and were at times inaccurate. It must be remembered that he suffered greatly with the creation of Israel in 1948, losing his homeland, and it would be natural for him to retain a negative view of what he later termed Zionists. It does seem that there are occasions when his academic scholarship is clouded by this anger, thus rendering him less effective as a proponent of the study of religion and a participant in dialogue. However, in other writings he does work to distinguish Zionists from other Jewish people whom he sees as relatively benign, but again this is overshadowed when he calls for the dismantlement of Israel.[54] One is left with the picture of a man struggling to reconcile different positions – academic, personal, and religious.

Al-Faruqi's interpretation of Christianity displays some of the same problems as with Judaism. Here his criticism is based more on his appeal to rationalism. As above, it is beyond the scope of this analysis to itemize and discuss all his views about Christianity and thus only a few representative examples will be presented here. At the outset it can be said that al-Faruqi, depending upon which source is quoted, displays both negative, dismissive opinions and positive, conciliatory attitudes. By surveying his writings for his views on Christianity, one can see a wide range of opinions.

First, he theorized that the mission of Jesus was in large part a corrective measure to right a fallen Judaism, which had become mired in exclusive racialism.[55] The message of Jesus was pure monotheism combined with ethical universalism where the law was interiorised, leading to a 'radical transformation of the self'.[56] However, he created a problem when he went on to say: "This transformation of which only God can be the judge and after which all contention is left for personal conscience, obviates the need for law, indeed for religion in the institutionalized form and, in final analysis, for Jesus himself as a religious teacher."[57] One can ask: If the law is no longer required because ethics is a matter of inner transformation, then what need is there for *Sharī'ah*? Zebiri points out that he sought to reintroduce the need for *Sharī'ah* in an interesting way.[58] He argued that: "From the standpoint of the purely moral worth or unworth of man, Islamic law is not concerned with effects or with bringing their being into real existence."[59] Instead, Islamic law was "solely concerned with man's actual and effective transcendence of himself to the reality of space-time, with his disturbance of the ontological poise of the cosmos, his efficacious diversion of the flow of events – regardless of any and all effects."[60] By this al-Faruqi meant humanity should influence all creation by seeking to apply the inner ethic that Jesus taught in order to transform society and all of creation. In other words, the ethic of Jesus was concerned with the inner man where morality rested upon the determination of the self by the will of God, and *Sharī'ah* externalised this inner ethic into society. Al-Faruqi believed that Jesus did not extend the inner transformation of the individual to include the world of 'space-time.'[61] His message was governed by the conscience, but left no measure for the external application of the inner ethic. Islam completed the message of Jesus with a re-introduction of law that "man should live dangerously, should break forth into space-time, disturb it, and transfigure the universe into the divine pattern which is the Will of God."[62] One may ask: What was al-Faruqi's interpretation of the command of Jesus to 'love your neighbour as yourself'? Assuming a correct understanding of al-Faruqi, he viewed this command as reflecting a personal ethic and not as something that would take the inner ethic and introduce it into the space-time of community and thus further the realisation of God's will. Is it really possible to claim an inner morality and ethic without any external evidence in support? For example, according to Jesus, the proof that someone followed him and his teaching was based upon the presence and demonstration of love for one another, which is an external demonstration of an inner ethic.[63]

Second, aside from rejecting such Christian doctrines as God in Christ,[64] redemption (called by al-Faruqi *saviourism*) and the sinfulness of all people (pejoratively labelled as *peccatism*),[65] he divided Christianity into the real Arab Christianity, which preserved the ethic of Jesus, from Christendom or Western Christianity created by Paul and Augustine.[66] He viewed groups such as the Ebionites, Gnostics, Marcionites, Manichæans, Arians, and Nestorians as preserving the Arab spirit within Christianity.[67] On the other hand, Church history demonstrates that each of these groups was viewed as heretical. Further, he went on to claim that because Semitic Christianity eventually became Islam, Muslims could therefore be called true 'Christians'.[68] As Esposito noted, al-Faruqi claimed the right to reconstruct Christianity showing Christians where they went wrong.[69] However, he went on to say that he "doubted that most Muslims, including Isma'il al-Faruqi, would be willing to accept a Christian's reconstruction of Islamic tradition."[70] In fact, some might argue that this was happening under the guise of orientalism, and that in a way al-Faruqi was merely turning the tables.[71]

Third, al-Faruqi continued his creative approach to interpreting Christian texts, just as he had done with certain Hebrew Scriptures. He built a theory of secularism and anti-materialism around a study of Matthew 6:1-18 and Matthew 4:4, respectively. In the first passage,

Jesus taught that deeds of righteousness must be motivated for God's and not the public's sake. Thus, acts of piety, be these fasting, prayer or almsgiving, should be performed in such a way as to not draw attention to oneself. Further, Jesus called for complete dependence upon God for all material needs so that the focus of life was not wealth, but God. Al-Faruqi interpreted this passage as creating a separation of the church from the state and of faith from reason.[72] It is, however, an unexpected reading for at least two reasons. First, while righteous acts are motivated for God, they are done for the benefit of others, such as giving alms to the poor and forgiving people who harm you. This would tend to support the argument that, while righteous behaviour is primarily undertaken for the sake of God, it is exercised for the sake of others and thus there is integration between Christians and society. It is unclear exactly how al-Faruqi arrived at the conclusion of the separation of church and state from this passage because Jesus addressed not the church, but individuals. He may have interpreted Matthew 6:1-18 in such a way as to mean that since practicing righteousness is focused on God, this somehow renders the church and state separate. If he had appealed to the words of Jesus in Mark 13:17, when he said, "Render to Caesar the things that are Caesar's, and to God the things that are God's", his assertion would have been stronger. Second, al-Faruqi's interpretation would seem to oppose his view of the internal ethic of Jesus. Here Jesus is teaching that correct behaviour should *not* be done to impress other people (internal ethic), but should benefit others (externalized ethic). Thus, the way to measure true internal ethical motives is to behave in an ethical manner for God's sake by helping people anonymously. Thus, the credit for the actions belongs to God. This does not seem to preclude the church and state from working together.

The other example, from Matthew 4:4, is drawn from the temptation of Jesus where he rebuked Satan with the familiar words, "man does not live on bread alone but by the word of God." As for this verse, al-Faruqi claimed that it, "became the cornerstone of an anti-materialist ideology," and "was corrupted by his [Jesus'] followers into another extremism based on the degrading of the material, the external and public, the societal, 'man does not live by bread alone' became the misplaced, abused motto of this movement."[73] Unfortunately, he did not provide further justification for this claim, which marks quite a step from the text to the explanation.[74] In one final example, al-Faruqi dismissed as a paradox Christian attempts to develop a Christian-led social concern because the kingdom of Jesus is not of this world.[75] Thus, Christians who sought to develop social concern would be denying the teaching of Jesus about his kingdom. For this reason, al-Faruqi would deny Christian ethics a place in society or any world influence.[76] Indeed Christians could only ethically exist on the level of personal internalized ethic. However, the teaching of Jesus about the kingdom does not lend itself so easily to al-Faruqi's conclusion. Jesus taught his followers to collectively express social concern as indeed he and the early church demonstrated.[77] Furthermore, if al-Faruqi sincerely believed this about Christians, how could he have hoped for Muslims and Christians to connect through ethics and morality?

There is perhaps no need to continue outlining his views and critique of Christianity because my concern is with his methodological approach to non-Muslims. Certainly his views on Judaism and Christianity play an important role, but there are other aspects of his ideas that we need to consider.[78] Regarding Christianity, the last word can be left to Esposito, who studied under al-Faruqi, and commented: "Faruqi's judgment that Jesus' revolution was betrayed by Christianity, and thus his distinction between Christianism and true Christianity, struck many Christians as resulting from an analysis that used reason to arrive at Muslim conclusions rooted in Islamic revelation and belief."[79] The point of these critiques is to show that not only did his interpretations radically depart from those of Jews and Christians, but that it was from this position that he entered dialogue. The remainder of the theoretical section of this analysis will focus exclusively on his methodology.

A critique of the principles of comparative religious studies

It was noted in Chapter Four that the principles of comparative religious studies, which were basically outlined in al-Faruqi's book *Christian Ethics*, became subsumed within his later methodology of dialogue. At this point in our analysis, we will limit our interest only to his five principles of comparative religious study. The five principles were:

1. Internal coherence.
2. External coherence with cumulative human knowledge.

3. All revealed truths must cohere with the religious experience of mankind.
4. The truth of religion must correspond to reality if it intends to establish its claim as a system.
5. Religion must serve the upward progress of man towards ethically higher value and Godhead.

The first principle of internal coherence demands there can be no internal contradiction. For al-Faruqi this meant that if paradox exists in a religious system, then the system violates the principle. As shown earlier, the issue of paradox is present also in Islam, though not to the same degree as it is in Christianity. However, al-Faruqi never dealt with the issue beyond his critique of religions other than Islam such as the Christian doctrine of the Trinity. He did not address the issue of the eternality of the uncreated Qur'ān nor did he examine the issues of predestination and freewill. This is not to argue against the principle itself, for internal coherence is valid and a necessary condition of truth, but it is not an adequate theory for truth.[80]

External coherence with the wider, cumulative extent of human knowledge meant that religious truth must remain consistent with any advancement in human understanding. This seems a relatively necessary condition because religious truth must be truth across history and human culture. However, there are some potential problems. Al-Faruqi was unclear whether or not human understanding, imperfect as it is, becomes the measure of religious truth or whether this truth measures human understanding. People may advance knowledge to a point where a certain religiously held truth becomes suspect, but next year they may discover new knowledge allowing a religious truth to be reinstated. It may have been better to speak of empirical adequacy rather than external coherence for the former recognises that people are involved in observing and interpreting both religious truth and other types of knowledge. This principle is quite close in nature to his third principle, i.e., that religious truth must cohere with the religious experience of mankind. This means that God would never contradict his commands. Again, this was addressed above in the context of God's alleged contradictory command to Abraham to sacrifice his son and yet not kill his fellow man.

The fourth and fifth principles are also not without questions. Al-Faruqi spoke of the need for religious truth to correspond with reality, yet he left the concept 'reality' undefined. To whose reality did he refer and who decides? This is merely pointed out because at times he would assume certain things such as 'reality' as self-evident. Some elaboration on his part would have helped, but one could posit that 'reality' referred to the normal perceptions of life encountered by people across cultures and time. However, what is 'normal'?

The last principle, that religion *must* serve the upward progress of man towards ethicality and higher value, seems particularly *Faruqian*. It assumes that the purpose of religion is ethics and that humanity's purpose in turn is to achieve ethical perfection, which it seems, is to equate it with complete obedience to the will or law of God. This final principle, perhaps unlike the others, tends to promote a presupposition as a principle. Esposito commented that al-Faruqi did not deal with the charge that one person's principles are another's presuppositions.[81] Thus, a Christian might wish to re-write this last principle based upon her presuppositions and her reading of Scripture to emphasize a restoration of humanity's relationship with God, which would include ethics and value, but not be limited by it. As an aside, one may ask: Who decides what is the measure of higher ethicality and does not this change with the history of humanity? Some of these points will be re-visited later in our analysis of dialogue, but for now we turn to an assessment of his principles of meta-religion.

A critique of the principles of meta-religion

When the principles of comparative religion and meta-religion were coined, al-Faruqi drafted them as a means to answer two questions that he faced in the study of religion. The first, comparative religion, was intended to deal with the question of understanding, while the second, meta-religion, focused on questions of evaluation. By way of reminder, the meta-religious principles were:

1. Being is of two realms, that is, the ideal and the actual realm of existence.
2. Ideal being is relevant to actual being.
3. Relevance of the ideal being to the actual being is a command.
4. Actual being is as such, good.
5. Actual being is malleable.
6. Perfection of the cosmos is the burden of humans alone.

In *Christian Ethics*, he framed it in this way:

> The principles which we are seeking fall into two kinds: Those which govern understanding, or the theoretical principles, and those which govern judgement, or the principles of evaluation. The former regulate our grasping of meanings presented, the religio-cultural phenomena, and our conceptualization and systemization of them. They are the same principles which govern our understanding of all other phenomena, and constitute the foundation of human knowledge in general. The latter are specialized and though they are as axiomatic as the theoretical principles, they constitute the foundation of all religio-culture. They are alternative to the principles of understanding but taking them for granted, they look beyond them to the religio-cultures to which they bring, when applied, a new order of meaning.[82]

It appears al-Faruqi sought to derive a set of philosophical principles based on reason that could be utilised to evaluate or measure religions not against each other, but against some universal standard. If this is a correct understanding of his purpose, then it appears to have been an ambitious undertaking and one not without problems. There is no intention in the present critique to work systematically through each of his principles because part of the problem is that his meta-religious principles were originally drafted in philosophical language and he never really fully articulated his theory.[83] He did, however, write that these principles are self-evident.[84]

In his 1965 article, "History of religions: Its nature and significance for Christian education and the Muslim-Christian dialogue," the ideas of B. E. Meland are introduced as creating a framework for meta-religion.[85] In his response, Meland provides us with some interesting critiques regarding al-Faruqi's view of history and the universality of religious norms, which in turn becomes a critique of meta-religion.

Since meta-religion assumes principles of historical understanding, Meland first discusses al-Faruqi's view of history.[86] Historical facts, as assumed by al-Faruqi, existed and could be discerned, studied, systematized and evaluated. However, despite the desire to create an overarching platform from which to measure and evaluate historical material, Meland points out that it is more complicated than presumed by al-Faruqi. The apprehension of undisputed historical facts, which can be used to serve as a guide or norm for judging the accuracy of all claims of faith, is open to serious question. The relationship between faith and history is not separate, but interdependent. Thus, there is some question as to whether or not anyone can isolate these 'facts.' Meland notes that "History, so it seems, strangely and ironically, rests back upon documents which turn out to be reports of faith."[87] This does not make history fictitious; rather, it demonstrates that events and reports are inseparable. Al-Faruqi proposed that such 'facts' could be isolated and then used as an evaluative tool regarding faith. However, these historical 'facts' are 'facts' of faith and faith mediates history. Since they rest with faith, how can they be used to measure faith? In essence the critique questions the possibility of finding a meta-religion simply because faith and history is too complex to find an umbrella system of universal measurement.

The second question raised by Meland revolves around the possibility of universal religious norms.[88] Meta-religion depends upon finding and applying universal norms from which the particular can be evaluated. If one could discover such universals, then the particulars of each religion could be measured against these norms just as al-Faruqi surmised. So the question becomes: How can these universal norms be found? The main problem is that the particulars or aspects of faith imply universals, but such universals are not available independently from the particular and therefore cannot be used to measure these particulars. For example, knowledge about universals exists within lived experience and becomes a form of ontological vision of man's existence as it pertains to God's creative act. In other words, existence can be attributed to a creative act of God. Thus, one can propose as universal that all people, regardless of faith and culture, exist as part of God's creation. However, al-Faruqi meant more than this and sought to establish on the basis of universal religious norms a means to distill each religion's universal components and thus possess criteria to compare and evaluate. Meland opines that this is a relapse into the Enlightenment habit of seeking universal judgments in rational abstraction where concrete historical realities are incidental.[89] He writes: "... the point I am making is that the generalizations drawn from specific occurrences within a cultural history are not *prima facie* universal judgments that can be recognized as such outside the cultural imagery. When they are projected within any religious faith, they bear the imprint of cultural history."[90]

One other general comment regards the principles themselves. One assumes that meta-religious principles are applicable to all religions. However, one wonders if the two realms of the ideal and actual would be accepted as a starting point by all religions, such as Buddhism or even Hinduism, where the actual is really illusory. His theory tends to be more suited to monotheistic faiths.

The last observation revolves around the consistency of the theory of meta-religion. By this is meant that al-Faruqi started out seeking to establish a series of evaluative principles that were not derived from any religion and therefore could stand above as a means to measure all religions. However, by 1986, in his publication of "Meta-Religion: Towards a critical world theology," meta-religion becomes wholly identified with Islam. Although much of the article was a combination of material drawn from previous works,[91] his conclusions were new.[92] It would seem odd to speak of meta-religion according to Islam because the point of meta-religion was to be supra-religious. As mentioned earlier in Chapter Four, there is some confusion over his use of meta-religion. Originally these were six principles and, as articulated in the 1986 article, they became eight Islamic meta-religious characteristics. These resemble his dialogical principles more than those of meta-religion.[93] This issue of inconsistency, which is seen elsewhere,[94] appears to be due to his attempts to move from his theoretical ideas to their practical application. It appears that he tweaked the various disparate forms of his 'meta-religious' principles for application as dialogical principles.

A critique of the principles of dialogue

The principles of dialogue were stated theoretically, but it is in their application that we see al-Faruqi refine and amplify its meaning. The principles of dialogue were:

1. No religious pronouncement is beyond criticism.
2. Internal coherence must exist.
3. Proper historical perspective must be maintained.
4. Correspondence with reality must exist.
5. Freedom from absolutized scriptural figurization.
6. Dialogue should be conducted in areas where there is a greater possibility of success such as ethical values.

However, for the moment our analysis will be restricted to theoretical aspects. Since these principles were based upon the principles of comparative religious study and meta-religion, much of the critique has already been discussed. Thus, only two of the six dialogical principles will be mentioned along with his proposed dialogical themes and conditions.

Freedom from absolutized scriptural figurizations (principle 5) was a topic first introduced in his 1967 presentation on dialogue at the Woodstock conference, although it existed in embryonic form throughout *Christian Ethics*.[95] It was later elaborated in more detail in "Islam and Christianity: Diatribe or dialogue."[96] The premise as explained seems quite reasonable as it recognises and accepts that perceptions of faith and doctrine are a product of time and space and these on occasion need to be re-examined and understood for new contexts.[97] Such figurizations occur in Islam and Christianity and his call is for those involved in dialogue to be open to re-examining these historical ways of interpreting belief. However, it is in the details that some problems arise and it is these details that are quite important because he posits this as a principle for dialogue. For example, are there any non-negotiable figurizations that would traverse time and space? If so, what are these for Islam and Christianity and who decides if these should or should not be re-examined?[98] The general examples he provided arise out of the Protestant Reformation and Ibn Taymiyya's and Ibn 'Abd al-Wahhab's attempts at reform. These are fine examples, but they were largely internal intra-faith discussions and not something amenable to dialogue between faiths. When al-Faruqi does provide more concrete examples he focused only on re-figurizing the Christian ideas of sin and redemption, a theme, which repeatedly occupied his attention since *Christian Ethics*.[99] His approach was basically an Islamic reading of these two central tenets of Christianity, according to which he redefined sin as misperception to be overcome by education and ethical behaviour and redemption as something people do and achieve largely on their own. His definition of figurization moved from a rethinking of concepts in religious belief, where the faith community re-works its collective understanding for a new day, to a wholesale rejection of past understanding for something radically different. It is one thing to ask Christians or Muslims in dialogue how their historic understandings of sin or redemption can be understood and applied today and quite another to ask them to reject such understandings for something quite different. This is a bit contrary to what he later wrote about figurization.[100] It seems his theory and his practice differed.

The sixth principle, that dialogue should be conducted in areas where there is a greater possibility of success, such as ethical values, is generally a good idea. When two disparate parties sit down to talk, it is wise to choose less controversial topics for discussion. His reason for the choice of ethics is interesting. He felt that questions of theology quickly become questions of faith and doctrine. The lines become drawn and are hard to cross without cries of heresy or betrayal. Questions of ethics, however, are less threatening because they are differences in perceptions as opposed to categories of true and false.[101] Theoretically this looks like a promising suggestion, but he did not discuss the presuppositions inherent in the use of ethics. Would everyone agree on all the facets of ethics such as marriage, polygamy, divorce, alcohol consumption, birth control or abortion?[102] He also tended to gloss over the differences in ethics between Judaism, Christianity and Islam and he avoided any discussion of the relationship between faith and ethics.[103] The call for ethics also neglected the reality that for Christians, ethics are based on theology. If one starts out with ethical topics, theology is not far behind because ethics are based upon the nature of God. Interestingly, later when al-Faruqi introduced themes for dialogue, he chose sin, justification and redemption![104] These certainly contain questions of ethics, but they are also theologically charged.

The final critique is not based on the principles of dialogue, but upon one of their prerequisites, freedom and equality. Al-Faruqi often noted that equality between interlocutors is a requirement for true dialogue. He was correct of course as he was when he cited the need for freedom to voice one's opinions. The problem arises in his article "Rights of non-Muslims under Islam: Social and cultural aspects."[105] He posits that within Islamic lands, if the listener (Muslim) or the Islamic state judges that discourse exceeds the intellectual or spiritual nature of the argument, it is subject to restriction.[106] One would assume this would apply to the non-Muslim listener as well, especially if presented with arguments they deem to violate the intellectual or spiritual nature of an argument. But then who decides? Under such conditions, could dialogue really flourish?

Assessment of theoretical feasibility

After examining various facets of al-Faruqi's theoretical ideas, one is left with the need to offer some general overall assessment. In answer to the question of whether his work is theoretically feasible, one is left with some doubts. His adamant commitment to reason as the central and virtually only criteria from which to derive methodology and evaluation of religion is problematic as was his refusal to entertain any paradox even when speaking about God who is beyond human reason. Despite his best intentions to derive principles that were free from theology, he ended up re-introducing Islam as *dīn al-fiṭrāh* and as reason *par excellence*, thus making Islam the rational measure of other faiths.

In his theory of Arabism, his definition of 'Arab' suffered from some of the same problems as nineteenth-century definitions of Semitic and Aryan. The existence of a primordial essence within humanity, which emerges as moments of monotheistic consciousness and ethical behaviour, labelled by al-Faruqi as 'Arab,' is difficult to historically verify. As yet no other scholar has picked up the baton to further this line of thought. His interpretations of Judaism and Christianity are at times unrecognisable to the adherents of either and his ambition to create a forum for dialogue became mired in his re-figurization of both faiths. There seems little question that he understood what Christians and Jews believed. The breadth of his scholarship remains intact, but he chose to bridge the gaps between the faiths by reinterpreting instead of meeting the other. This was not unique to al-Faruqi, but represents a tendency by many participants in interfaith dialogue. One cannot question his intentions or desire for dialogue, but the path he chose, at least on a theoretical level, creates sometimes more problems for dialogue then it solves.

The ambition to discover and articulate a meta-system from which to compare and evaluate all religions remains largely unfilled. This was not because of any substantive inadequacies on his part, but rather the nature of the project appears unachievable. His persistent desire to use ethics as the measure and the content of dialogue was perhaps more reflective of Muslim concerns than of those he wished to engage.

In the end, despite some theoretical misgivings, al-Faruqi did attempt something different in dialogue. He sought to overcome the imbalance of power and dominance of the Christian West in relation to Muslims by creating a rational platform from which participants could engage in dialogue. Such a platform could theoretically help to remove the relative political and economic weakness of Muslims in the emerging post-colonial period and offer a more equitable means on which to build dialogue based on rational thought. On this theoretical level he offered something in dialogue that was unique among Muslims and Christians and despite some flaws his attempt is worth serious consideration. Indeed, his methodological principles are repeated as rules for interfaith dialogue including theological dialogue in the recent book *Interfaith Dialogue: A Guide for Muslims*.[107]

Passion for engagement and the personalities behind such a desire can do much to overcome theoretical shortcomings. Thus, it is with the practical applications of his ideas that we conclude this analysis. It must be remembered that al-Faruqi sought to apply his ideas and not merely leave them on the design table. Indeed, we have the distinct advantage to witness and analyse his use of his own ideas as a practitioner and not merely as a theoretician.

Practical applications

To offer an analysis of how al-Faruqi applied his ideas in debate and dialogue one must rely on the limited record of published interactions and the reactions of those who engaged him in dialogue. One can also observe to what extent he was able to meet his own expectations in the use of theoretical tools, such as *epoché* and whether he was able to fulfil the criteria he demanded of historians of religion.

Practical assumptions

We shall begin by mentioning some of the assumptions he made upon entering dialogue with Christians. Aside from the aforementioned theoretical presuppositions such as rationalism, he also brought along the assumption that Christian mission and *diakonia* were wrong and even harmful because he viewed their objective as being to possess and dominate the other.[108] This is a general statement that needs some explanation. While he endorsed and praised mission as a moral imperative shared by Muslims and Christians, he sought to separate Christianity from Christendom.[109] The latter, united with colonialism, used mission as a means to extend imperialism. This type of mission was correctly condemned. However, there remains ambiguity over what constitutes good and bad Christian mission. Without due distinction, he states that the continued existence of Christian mission was a "terrible sore in Christian-Muslim understanding and cooperation" and that it should be postponed for some other time.[110] It seems that the mission of Christendom should be immediately stopped and true Christian mission should be delayed. However, if true mission is a moral and religious imperative, why then did he call for the Christian side to postpone their activities? The short answer was that the Muslim peoples were not yet ready to engage Christian missions because of inequalities of education, economics and political power.[111] As a practitioner of dialogue, al-Faruqi needed to believe that engagement could occur. However, this interaction in effect was to be limited and theoretically directed by Muslims, such that Christian activities would be restricted. On one level this attitude is understandable because Christians in the 1960s initiated much of the dialogue and sought to maintain the status quo by inviting select Muslims to respond even as the Christian West held the reigns of political and economic power. On another level al-Faruqi viewed Christian mission as a means to serve the purpose of Western domination and power. This view was too simplistic and assumes Christian mission was a monolithic movement, when in fact it is more complex and diverse.[112]

A second assumption he made was that education is the answer to improving and fostering dialogue. This applies within the Muslim community and between religious faiths. He argues that careful rational thought would ultimately uncover the truth in all religions, and such an exercise would allow each participant to apply such truth. As a Muslim participant, al-Faruqi held a third set of assumptions about Judaism and Christianity. As was seen earlier, he disagreed with a number of Jewish and Christian doctrines, such as the need for salvation not being based upon any inherent role of sin. This position might be expected of a Muslim interlocutor, but he went further and characterized the attitude of Judaism toward other religions as "one of hatred, fear, and a false complex of superiority or election."[113] This continued with Christianity, which he asserted possessed an "attitude of hatred and condemnation of the other religions."[114] One can ask: Is there not a third alternative? Are there no Christians and Jews who are genuinely interested in interfaith study and dialogue who do not suffer from a complete sense of superiority or a spirit of condemnation, but who still believe their view is correct? Al-Faruqi would agree that such do exist, but in his writings this was seldom made explicit.[115] Instead, he tended to speak about Judaism and Christianity as if they were single-minded institutions without nuance and variety. Despite a mixture of attitudes and beliefs on all sides, dialogue can and does occur because one does not really categorize dialogue as between the religions of Christianity and Islam, but between individual Muslims and Christians or between groups and communities of Muslims and Christians. Although one can view Roman Catholicism as more monolithic with its one earthly head, the Pope, this is not as prominent with other branches of Christianity and certainly not in Islam. Thus, it seems a little disingenuous for someone to characterize Judaism, Christianity or Islam with such categorical, sweeping statements.[116] The final practical assumption was his advocacy of ethics as the best theme for dialogue rather than theology. This will be mentioned below when we discuss his practice of dialogue.

Use of comparative religious studies and meta-religion

It is clear that al-Faruqi favoured the phenomenological approach to the study of religions. Furthermore, he strongly advocated the use of *epoché* and to a lesser extent eidetic vision. The question arises: How successful was he in the use of these two phenomenological tools? In *Christian Ethics*, he spent a great deal of time explaining, defending and amplifying *epoché*, but as one examines the book and his many articles, it becomes apparent that the ideal was not easily realised. This has been recognised by others when reading al-Faruqi. Zebiri comments that it was difficult for al-Faruqi and some other Muslim thinkers to practice *epoché* and describe Christian beliefs in a detached way and so instead they felt the need to refute them.[117] A related question arises out of the three criteria he listed that an historian of religion needs to fulfil. These were: to understand and communicate religious understanding without personal prejudice; to openly declare and 'hold in check' any presuppositions or personal involvement in study; and, to create a set of critical and universal principles as a presupposition for study.[118] Once again as with *epoché*, al-Faruqi struggled to personally realise these criteria.[119] Of course, this can equally be said of some Christian scholars. As mentioned above, there seems little question that he knew the doctrines of Christianity and Judaism, but he chose at times to communicate this knowledge in a pejorative manner. Perhaps it points to something al-Faruqi could not abide, such as the notion of paradox, according to which the historian of religion must hold in tension personal belief and the beliefs of those under study, especially when personal belief directly opposes the beliefs of others.

Turning to meta-religion, al-Faruqi originally proposed a set of six principles by which religions could be evaluated on a neutral or theology-free basis. Throughout the preceding chapters much has been said about this theory, but the question remains, does it actually work? Is it a useful methodology for comparing and analyzing religions? One must remember that al-Faruqi, above all, sought 'truth.' Christian, Jewish, Muslim and other religious claims to truth can be tendered, but truth by its very definition is exclusive. Thus, he sought some way to determine and distinguish the signature of truth from among its many claimants. Given this intention, it is normal to question the practical feasibility and usefulness of his theory. At the outset, in his very first principle (Ideal and Actual realms), he posited that reality has a dual nature and only a dual nature. Is this an acceptable criterion, for example, in Buddhism or Hinduism? It certainly is how a monotheist interprets reality, but is that necessarily the same for non-monotheists? What about reincarnation, karma or the need to free oneself from all desire in order to move beyond the realm of illusion? Is the realm of illusion the actual realm? It would seem that meta-religion is really better designed to measure and compare monotheistic faiths. This is fine, but the theory should be amended to that of meta-monotheistic religious principles. That would seem to be a more accurate label. If one limits the principles to the monotheistic faiths alone, does it work?

The answer to the question of applicability rests upon which version of meta-religious principles is consulted. Originally, these principles were presented in philosophical language and then developed as time progressed into various versions. It can become a little confusing because al-Faruqi seemed to modify, emphasize and re-label the principles for different occasions. The number of principles at times ranged from four to eight, as with his last published discussion of meta-principles cast as a critical world theology, which ended up purely Islamic in character.[120] Therefore, it is difficult to know what one is applying. Moreover, since his evaluative principles were based on measuring ethics and values in a rational way, one may even question whether this is the best way to engage other monotheistic faiths. Hendrik Kraemer, in his introduction to *Christian Ethics*, writes:

However, I sincerely doubt that his philosophical metareligious principles are the right way to arrive at communication and dialogue. I would urgently invite him to reconsider his theory. The crucial question, it seems to me, is whether, by judging religion on the basis of rationality, he is doing justice to the spirit of either Christianity or Islam. Both are based on a Revelation of God, different as their understanding of Revelation may be. As such they establish their own norm, which is God's inscrutable, gracious will. Their self-understanding derives from the content and meaning of this act of God. The response to God's act is faith, surrender, obedience. Rationality as *normative* standard belongs to science and techniques, not to religion, for the truth and value of no religion can be demonstrated by rational reasoning. My personal opinion is that dialogue and communication do not need a preconstructed philosophical common standard of judgement, but only sincere desire on the part of men of faith to meet each other, to understand each other as they understand themselves, to enter each other's spiritual reality, to give account of their own faith and be witness there of, to be open to criticism and willing to exercise self-criticism. These are severe demands which require patience and self restraint as well as forthrightness, humility, forbearance and mutual respect.[121]

Al-Faruqi may well have responded that, without rationality, how can one evaluate different faiths when the objective is to discover truth? Kraemer's argument is that judgment is not the primary objective in dialogue; rather, its purpose is to understand another's faith as well as one's own through openness to criticism and self-critique. The question is not necessarily who is right and who is wrong, but what is the best way to live together. This is fine if all the interlocutors share a level of equality without any large disparities between societies. Issues of justice, poverty and perceptions of being dominated by another faith also influence dialogue. While al-Faruqi's meta-religious principles were an attempt to find a more neutral way to assess religions and deal with issues, such as morality, ethical behaviour and justice, the project may be unachievable because rationality is limited. However, this is not to argue that rationality should be abandoned. Instead the expectations of reason need to be tempered by the realisation that it is one part of the larger project of discerning truth. This leads us into the discussion of dialogical engagement, which ultimately was where al-Faruqi focused most of his applications.

Analysis of dialogical engagement

The place to begin our examination is with his concept of dialogue. The object and purpose of dialogue for al-Faruqi was the desire to discover the truth and the primary avenue taken was through a rational application of a comparative analysis of ethics and value based upon meta-religious principles.[122] To this end he drafted a number of dialogical principles to guide and oversee this effort. These principles of dialogue were:

1. No religious pronouncement is beyond critique.
2. Internal coherence must exist.
3. Proper historical perspective must be maintained.
4. Correspondence with reality must exist.
5. Freedom from absolutized scriptural figurization.
6. Dialogue should be conducted on areas where there is a greater possibility of success, such as ethical values.

Although he rejected paradox as rationally sloppy and ultimately unacceptable, dialogue itself contains a certain level of paradox. This is particularly acute in interfaith dialogue. Such a venture requires the participants to somehow maintain faith and allegiance to their own beliefs and at the same time assent to the legitimacy of others who are attempting to do the same.[123] Thus, it requires juggling at least two different – often opposing - sets of beliefs. This is to be accomplished amidst unresolved and even contradictory issues between faiths and the interpretations of dialogue participants. There is no real 'independence' from the other participant; indeed, it is more like a dance, albeit to different tunes and steps. Dialogue is often based on personally predetermined criteria and, in the end, upon the person as they are. Cragg writes that dialogue is "an actual pluralism of mind and soul" which seems "not only daunting, but spiritually impossible."[124] This is further complicated within the paradox of the divine will engaging humanity. Using al-Faruqi's terms, the divine has allowed His law to be realised in the actual realm among imperfect yet innocent humanity who are expected to recognise, obey and maintain this law.[125] Since God's law communicated through revelation in the prophets is a perfect law, how then could imperfect man hope to keep it perfectly? Al-Faruqi did not address any aspect of the potential for paradox in dialogue. Nevertheless, he believed dialogue was not only necessary, but also imperative.

In his quest to apply the sixth principle of dialogue, i.e., that it should be conducted in areas where there is a greater possibility of success, he saw ethical values as the best way to engage the other. Aside from the doubt expressed by W. C. Smith as to whether discussing ethics rather than theology will work in practice, one is hard pressed to see any substantial application of ethics in al-Faruqi's presentations before Christians.[126] It seems he spent most of his time explaining why ethics is the best course to follow rather than demonstrating it in practice. When one surveys all his published presentations, only two papers discuss ethics in application. The first, published in 1968, lists three areas of discussion on "the contemporary ethical reality of Muslims and Christians."[127] These are man's innocence, the importance of the act of faith, and the yet to be fulfilled moral vocation of man.[128] Sin is interpreted as ethical misinterpretation, which is a possibility, but the Christian participant would not accept it as a definition and any subsequent dialogue would see the introduction of theology. For Christians, whether or not man is 'innocent' is at its core an issue of theology. Al-Faruqi viewed the act of faith as a question of justification in which faith neither justifies nor makes just. It is only the entrance-way into moral and ethical behaviour. Finally, the moral vocation of man is interpreted by al-Faruqi as nullified by the Christian notion of redemption as a *fait accompli*.[129] It is unclear how these ethical ideas would offer a greater possibility of success for dialogue between Muslims and Christians. Indeed, it was after al-Faruqi's presentation that W. C. Smith questioned the viability of ethics as a focus for dialogue. There could be other more mutually beneficial aspects of ethics to guide dialogue, such as questions of justice or poverty, but al-Faruqi did not mention these possibilities.

The other example of practical application is seen in his presentation at the Tripoli symposium. Here he simply introduced a wide range of topics, not all of which were ethical in nature. These revolved around Christian and Muslim mutual awareness and the enigmatic label 'public human affairs', under which he listed knowledge, personal ethics, family, race, materialism, colonialism and nihilism.[130] His treatment of each reads, on the one hand, as a critique and, on the other, as a call for Muslims and Christians to unite to solve any problems.[131] In the end, it appears that his call for ethics as the basis for discussion remained mostly theoretical.

Given that he was a frequent participant in dialogue, it is fair to ask about his attitudes and style of engagement. These are subjective categories based on the views of those who met and debated al-Faruqi and thus they share a certain level of bias. He is reported as possessing a reputation for being provocative, tenacious, stubborn and at times belligerent, but he was also viewed as a stimulating colleague and a warm-hearted friend.[132] It depended upon the context. For example, Cragg, who engaged al-Faruqi on more than one occasion, noted his frustration during the Chambésy consultation in 1976. Cragg recounted a discussion regarding a distinction between the fact of incarnation, its possibility and the implications of restricting what the divine can do. In the midst of the debate, al-Faruqi retorted that by this argument, God might become a brick. Cragg felt that al-Faruqi's hasty ridicule foreclosed mutual reflection and deeper discussion and Cragg cited this as a warning against the damage of dismissiveness.[133] In relation to al-Faruqi's dismissal of Christian doctrine, Cragg writes, "The charges are many and categorical and often formulated in terms that provoke despair about genuine encounter rather than inform a will to it."[134] To somewhat balance these recollections, Cragg also wrote in the same article that: "These paragraphs do not pretend to suffice in tribute, criticism, and exposition concerning the work of a formidable, lively, resourceful, belligerent, and tenacious practitioner of dialogue; we mourn his passing and esteem his legacy."[135] Clearly, there was mutual respect between the two.

One additional aspect of al-Faruqi's approach to dialogue was that it should be restricted to the elite. At a 1967 presentation, he stated that dialogue should rest with the intelligentsia, because the Muslim masses are ill equipped to engage Western Christians.[136] Here the sense is of protecting Muslims until they are educated and prepared to interact on the level of formal dialogue. This is understandable, given the context of the post-colonial period. However, al-Faruqi did not mention the dominating influence of the West through media, education and technology that was already shaping and informing Muslim viewpoints. Thus, a form of dialogue was already in process, but it was on the level of general influence and not formal dialogue. At the 1976

Tripoli address, he seemed to retract his notion of restricting dialogue to the elite by calling for a wide and public dissemination of shared purpose and cooperation if there is to be any lasting fruit.[137] Interestingly, Yushau Sodiq also cited the complaint of elitism in his analysis of teaching Islam in American universities, but in a different way. He mentioned that the advanced level of al-Faruqi's English precluded the use of his texts for freshman courses in universities![138]

Lastly, in this discussion of the application of his dialogical ideas, we encounter the requirements he set out for participants in dialogue. He called Christians and Jews to give up much of their history, theology and scripture in order to enter dialogue.[139] For example, asking Christians to accept Muhammad as a prophet would be the same as asking Muslims to accept Jesus as the Son of God. Doing so would amount to 'confessional suicide.'[140] For many, this is too great a price to pay for dialogue. In principle, he argued for balance in dialogue, but in practice he asked the other to make sacrifices he would not ask of himself. On the other hand, Cragg noted that, for Muslim participants, al-Faruqi maintained an interesting position. If in the course of dialogue a Muslim was rationally convinced of the Christian message, then theoretically such a person could embrace the faith of Christianity. However, al-Faruqi's position on conversion from Islam was traditional: it constituted treason to the Islamic state punishable by banishment, life imprisonment and even capital punishment.[141] Such a point of view created an uncertain climate for dialogue and seemed out of step with al-Faruqi's expressed openness to rational thought, truth and the right to convince the other.

Assessment on practical application

Al-Faruqi spent a great deal of time and effort developing and applying his theories of dialogue. To the question of whether his methodologies were viable in practice, one can reply in the affirmative. His methods worked quite well, but perhaps only for him. From his perspective, his principles of dialogue were rational and useful in creating the structure and opportunity for interfaith communication. However, for others his methods were less workable. One cannot speak of a *Faruqian* way of dialogue, yet since dialogue is a personal activity motivated by a variety of reasons, this is not an unexpected conclusion. Al-Faruqi sought engagement as a result of who he was as a Muslim and the role he accepted in living out his faith. However, his principles and ideas were presented as completed methodologies. By 1968, his theoretical methods had been set and although in the ensuing years his application required some adjustment, he avoided the opportunity to build upon the critiques of the non-Muslims he had engaged by revising his methodology and not just his applications. Although he approached the field proposing his ideas as a means of dialogue for everyone, this was overly optimistic. Even with his meta-religious principles, he adjusted and refined these to fit various contexts of application, but the basic theoretical premises remained the same. He seemed to move back and forth from defending Islam to challenging Christianity and Judaism rather than finding common ground on which to build.[142] However, it must be remembered that he was and remains the pioneer among modern Muslims who learned about and sought to engage the other.

7

AL-FARUQI'S CONTRIBUTIONS
TO DIALOGUE

The continued challenge for Muslims and Christians to achieve a level of mutual understanding and to find ways to live together is not something that is easily faced nor can it simply be ignored. The issues of Muslim-Christian dialogue began in centuries past and are still an important characteristic of twenty-first-century domestic and international relations. The days of polemic are not over, but there is a recognition that polemic is unhelpful if the goal is to talk with or understand each other. How this is to be done and with whom is a repeated question. In this brief chapter, we will start with al-Faruqi, recapping his ethos, legacy and influence, and then move on to examine ways in which to build upon his contributions to interfaith dialogue.

Al-Faruqi and Muslim interlocutors

Within the history of Muslim thought on non-Muslim faiths and among his peers, where can we place al-Faruqi? Historically, he built upon the traditional position of Qur'ānic religious *ummahs* and the Qur'ān's authority to judge all other religions. He accepted the concept of *Ur-religion* (*dīn al-fiṭrah*) in which any dialogue was actually within one religious tradition even if these traditions were divergent and considered distorted versions of Islam. He maintained the medieval concern to define and defend Islam while strengthening the *ummah*. This concern has remained a feature of Muslim modernist thought. Reference to individual thinkers, such as Ibn Hazm, and the use of biblical criticism are features of his work. He drew upon the objectivity displayed by the Qur'ān commentator, al-Shahrastani (1086–1153), and the use of *taḥrīf* developed by Ibn Hazm and Ibn Taymiyya. One could even label him as a neo-Muʿtazilite for his emphasis on reason and ethics, but he also employed philosophy, history and scripture, as did his predecessors.[1] Lastly, he advocated the use of phenomenology in the study of religions in much the same manner as al-Biruni (973-1048).

Contemporary influences are more difficult to itemize. However, he did share the modernist position with such influential intellectuals as Muhammad 'Abduh, particularly in regards to re-building the Muslim community in the midst of a world influenced by western hegemony and thought. Dialogically, he was perhaps more influenced by non-Muslim thinkers such as W. C. Smith. He shared an interest in and saw the need for dialogue despite his less than sometimes irenic stance. Among his peers, he was more apt to use rational philosophy combined with historical and literary criticism within his overall approach to dialogue.

Legacy of al-Faruqi

Al-Faruqi's legacy and influence represented a new beginning in the history of contemporary Muslim-Christian and Muslim-Jewish dialogue. He did not merely possess good intentions or a desire for improved interfaith understanding. He made a conscious choice to pursue the academic study of Judaism and Christianity within a predominantly Judeo-Christian environment and to actively practice dialogue with non-Muslims by developing a set of methodologies that he hoped would foster interfaith relations and at the same time strengthen the Islamic *ummah*. He became a pioneer in contemporary Muslim thought and approach towards non-Muslims.

His ideas in practice displayed both strengths and weaknesses. That he restricted the acquisition of knowledge to the rational excluded a number of valid and useful avenues of engagement. For him, stories, myths, poetry, imagination, intuition and love are absent as means of explaining the difficult if not the inexplicable.[2] For example, sometimes love and imagination defies internal coherence, but they can offer ways of understanding that is unavailable to rationalism. How does one rationally explain love? Love can be the driving force behind dialogue and indeed community, just as Jesus taught his followers to "love your neighbour as yourself."[3]

Despite criticisms of and weakness in both his theoretical methodology and his practical applications, one can identify a number of positive contributions. He clearly demonstrated a desire and commitment to study and engage those of other faiths. He recognised the need to move beyond the confines of polemic, including the tendency to distort the beliefs of others. Whether or not he was successful is a question asked of all dialogical participants and in his case his ambition never realised its fulfillment, although the same can potentially be said of everyone. The combination of theoretical and academic work formed the basis for his practical involvement. This is particularly important to remember because he avoided the role of an armchair critic and chose to expose his own faith to the challenges of interfaith dialogue. Going further, he encouraged fellow Muslims to be open to dialogue.[4] This is evidenced by his requiring the Muslim students he taught to take courses in other religions in order to prepare them for the task of living with and engaging other faiths. With the goal of searching for 'truth' in an atmosphere of freedom and equity, he developed his principles of dialogue, which, even if one disagrees with them, indicate the serious and thoughtful way he sought to place interfaith conversation on a new, mutually evaluative plane. Finally, in the midst of the Church-driven desire for engagement he became a pioneer among Muslims not only in the sense of accepting the challenge, but also in seeking ways to improve the level of discourse. One of these was his adamant emphasis upon ethics as the starting point for dialogue. This theme of ethics will be revisited below.

Some contributions from contemporary Muslim scholars

The voices of his contemporaries in some measure echo al-Faruqi's ideas. Among the handful of Western-based Muslim scholars, all have offered their own perspectives and methodologies, although up to this point none has surpassed al-Faruqi's systematic attempts at creating methodologies for dialogue. One of the most widely known and appreciated dialogical voices is that of Mahmoud Ayoub, who taught at Temple University in the position al-Faruqi once occupied.[5] For Ayoub, dialogue is more than conversation and implies working together for better mutual understanding while maintaining the distinctive characteristics of each religion.[6] He appeals to the example of the delegation of Christians from Najrān who sought either to convince Muhammad to become a Christian or to reach a peace covenant allowing them freedom and social independence.[7] Despite irreconcilable theological differences, both communities exercised mutual tolerance and accepted the existence of the other. Like al-Faruqi, Ayoub stresses ethics over theology as a theme for dialogue.[8]

Al-Faruqi saw education as the prime means for preparing Muslims to engage non-Muslims and in a similar way Ayoub sees the classroom in colleges and universities as an important avenue for encounter as students learn and interact with other faiths.[9] However, Muhammad Arkoun (1928-2010) cautioned that academic courses on religion are often taught in isolation from other religions, leaving little opportunity for a critique of other faiths.[10] This can be remedied in part by offering comparative courses on religion. The contributions and work on interfaith dialogue by Ayoub is more irenic than al-Faruqi's, but they each have a similar desire to engage primarily Christians.[11]

Other prominent contemporary Muslim scholars involved in dialogue, such as Seyyed Hossein Nasr, Hasan Askari, Abdulaziz Sachedina, Khurshid Ahmad, Shabbir Akhtar and Mohammed Talbi offer complementary ideas to those of al-Faruqi.[12] Nasr, who was a colleague of al-Faruqi at Temple University, is interested in philosophical and theological issues, advocating an epistemology of a single reality (oneness of God) as a means to guide Muslim-Christian dialogue.[13] Whereas al-Faruqi shunned theology as a generally unproductive area for interaction - instead favouring ethics - Nasr recognises the central place of theology in Christian thought and the need to include it within dialogue. However, after outlining a number of obstacles to dialogue, Nasr does recognise the difficulties that theology presents, writing: "It is perhaps better therefore, to accept on the formal level certain differences as being precisely irreducible on that level and then go on to cultivate mutual respect even if one is not able to gaze at the principal Unity in which all formal differences are resolved."[14] Thus, in some measure he agrees with al-Faruqi about the potential intransigence of theology as the basis of dialogue, but insists that it cannot be ignored in the way al-Faruqi advocated.

Hasan Askari, like W. C. Smith, notes that plurality not only exists within the community of diverse world religions, but also that plurality is actively present within each religion.[15] This is something not made explicit by al-Faruqi who centred his thought upon Sunni Islam. Yet even within Sunnism, he tended to present a more monolithic face to Islam while recognising some plurality within Christianity and Christendom. Askari, like al-Faruqi, focuses on Jesus, but for different reasons. Al-Faruqi examined the ethic of Jesus in his book *Christian Ethics* as the binding commonality between the monotheistic faiths. Askari also views Jesus as the 'common sign' and the foundation of mutual friendship between Muslim and Christian;[16] however, he goes on to present the Qur'ānic Jesus as the only correct and proper interpretation, thus reducing his effectiveness in dialogue.[17]

Another contemporary voice in dialogue is that of Abdulaziz Sachedina. Like al-Faruqi, Sachedina advocates the central role of ethics as the major theme for interfaith relations and accepts that the Qur'ān contains a theology that "regards religious pluralism as a divinely ordained system of human co-existence."[18] Sachedina believes that before Islam engages other faiths it must first conduct a dialogue with its normative tradition in order to discover a relevant theology for the twenty-first century.[19] He believes that Muslim and Christian dialogue must occur cognisant of the wider context of secularism along with the political, social and economic challenges that each body of believers mutually encounter. Unlike al-Faruqi, Sachedina calls for a more inclusivist position regarding the traditions of other faiths. He writes that: "No Christian or Muslim can sit in dialogue when in the depth of their hearts, because of a prejudicial attitude, they fail to accept the salvific efficacy of the other's religious tradition."[20] This is not an easy position to maintain. It is easier to recognise or respect such salvific efficacy rather than accept it. Al-Faruqi, by practicing *epoché* (suspension of judgment), appreciated and understood another faith's religious traditions, but in the search for truth he could not hold to Sachedina's call to accept the salvific efficacy of other faiths. Therefore, al-Faruqi would limit Sachedina's expectation to the early stages of dialogue and study, but this would have to give way when each faith is evaluated in the manner al-Faruqi proposed.

One of the organisers of the 1976 Chambésy dialogue, in which al-Faruqi demonstrated his acumen for debate within dialogue, was Khurshid Ahmad. Born in Delhi, Ahmad grew up among Muslims, Hindus, Christians and Sikhs and this encouraged his later study of comparative religions.[21] He later moved to England where he helped to establish the Leicester Islamic Foundation in 1968 (it became active in 1973). There are many similarities between Ahmad and al-Faruqi in their respective approaches to dialogue. Both have a holistic vision of Islam as a world community.[22] Both believe every religion has an element of the divine message which encourages meaningful dialogue, although Ahmad does not mention the concept of *dīn al-fiṭrāh*.[23] Al-Faruqi and Ahmad also agree that freedom and equality are essential if dialogue is to become fruitful. Finally, dialogue as an inherent component in Islam includes the characteristic of *da'wah* in which each discussant is permitted to persuade the other of the truthfulness of their beliefs.[24] This does not necessarily mean conversion or mission. It is rather seen as a normal aspect of conversation between two passionate parties.

Shabbir Akhtar, a British Muslim who taught in Malaysia and who now teaches in the United States, has written three books, one of which, *A Faith for all Seasons*, offers some insights similar to those of al-Faruqi and other contemporary Muslim participants in dialogue.[25] On one level he echoes al-Faruqi's emphasis on the need to study another faith before entering into dialogue. Akhtar writes that: "... a Muslim cannot reasonably claim to be seriously engaged in dialogue with Christians unless he can possess a thorough knowledge of the Christian faith, and, if at all possible, exercise imaginative sympathy with the ideals of that faith."[26] On another level, while Akhtar sees the importance of reason, he does recognise that all faculties should be "recruited in the service of faith."[27] On the issue of faith and reason, something which al-Faruqi did not discuss in detail, Akhtar offers a position with which al-Faruqi would likely have agreed when he writes that: "The devout hope is that they [faith and reason] will not conflict; faith may well be mightier *than* reason but it is surely mightiest *with* reason. But where they clash, the philosopher, no less than the believer, cannot hesitate about which loyalty comes first."[28] The main difference between Akhtar and al-Faruqi is that Akhtar more readily acknowledges that the challenges offered by the modern world, such as secularism, not only affect Islam and Christianity, but that each faith should work together to counter the negative influences of modernity upon faith. He goes further, calling for Muslims to learn from Christian experiences in dealing with these challenges of modernity and openly admires the spirit of self-criticism present in liberal Protestant theology.[29]

One final Muslim contributor to dialogue, who like al-Faruqi became an active participant in interfaith work in the 1960s, is the Tunisian scholar Mohammed Talbi.[30] Although little of his academic career was based in the West, he considers himself a western educated scholar and writes in French. Many of Talbi's dialogical ideas are similar to those of al-Faruqi. For example, Talbi calls for the practice of *ijtihād* (independent reasoning) in order to reassess Islamic thought and faith just as al-Faruqi sought to Islamize knowledge.[31] Both scholars agree that Muslims need to break out of their isolation and re-engage the world, albeit on Muslim terms and not those of the West. Dialogue is thus a means of intellectual self-examination. Talbi writes: "Now the precise purpose of dialogue, whatever the circumstances, is to reanimate constantly our faith, to save it from tepidity, and to maintain us in a permanent state of *ijtihād*, that is a state of reflection and research."[32] In dialogue, Talbi has called for equality, freedom, respect and that interlocutors must neither hide their convictions nor compromise them.[33] Furthermore, he insists dialogue must be free from efforts to convert each other. In a similar vein to al-Faruqi, Talbi's call for dialogue takes on a serious tone when he writes: "So then if present-day Islam does not succeed, through dialogue with all systems of thought without exception or exclusion, in renewing the spirituality of its followers and in assimilating, as in the past, all values which are not opposed to its Witness, it will certainly be on its way to failing its mission on earth."[34] Finally, like Sachedina, Talbi accepts the salvific efficacy of other faiths and criticizes any dialogue in which one or more sides presupposes the others are condemned solely based on different convictions.[35] As we noted in the above discussion concerning Sachedina, al-Faruqi could have accepted this as a starting point, but only in terms of understanding and not evaluating the other.

General presuppositions in dialogue

The above contemporary Muslim scholars continue to write and engage non-Muslims and quite naturally have moved the boundaries of dialogue forward since al-Faruqi's death. In a synthesis of their contributions one can begin to outline some general presuppositions and positions in dialogue. Each may differ in application, but there are similarities in the underlying expectations and requirements for dialogue.

Among the presuppositions behind dialogue, at least for the individual participant as demonstrated by al-Faruqi, is the possession of a strong personal faith.[36] That is, they are convinced of the truth they have discovered in their faith and thus are secure enough to venture into dialogue. Discourse may emerge out of a personal or common need and for a variety of other reasons, but those engaged need a clear sense of where they are and what they believe before moving into interfaith dialogue. There must also be self-confidence in their relationship to their own faith that permits criticism. Leonard Swidler adds:

> Persons entering into interreligious, interdialogical dialogues must be at least minimally self-critical of both themselves and their own religious and ideological traditions ... such an integrity and conviction must include, not exclude, healthy self-criticism. Without it there can be no dialogue – and, indeed, no integrity.[37]

This applies to all participants (Christian and Muslim) and leads to the second prerequisite – respect. Al-Faruqi called for an equality between Muslims and Christians, but how is 'equality' to be defined or measured? Since this is a complicated term to define and apply, it is suggested that mutual respect would be a better objective.[38] This allows participants to be who they are without the requirement or pressure to modify their beliefs for the sake of dialogue.

The third presupposition is that of the freedom to believe and to engage the other without fear. For example, in the course of dialogue if one party becomes convinced of the other's position, there should be freedom to embrace it without fear of the reaction of others. This is perhaps an overly ambitious idea, but one worth striving towards despite the obstacles. Al-Faruqi contributed to this in two opposing ways. He accepted the need for freedom for discourse in as much as he emphasized its objective was to uncover the truth. Both sides are to be free to persuade and convince the other, but at the same time he also viewed Muslims who reject Islam as traitors to their faith, *ummah* and state.[39] These two positions are almost mutually exclusive and can only restrict Muslim efforts at dialogue.

The tools of dialogue require intelligent and informed discourse along with a generous and open attitude toward the other. The fourth presupposition is that the acquisition of knowledge is open to various ways of knowing, not just rationalism. As seen, al-Faruqi advocated rational thought and dismissed mysticism, but not all share this opinion. Sachedina argues that unless Muslim thinkers are willing to go beyond the episteme in the classical sources, Islam will continue to remain unresponsive to the pluralism of today's global community.[40] The way we approach our own traditions is as important as the tools we use to acquire knowledge of the self and others. Askari provides a slightly different perspective, writing: "It is sometimes easier to reflect with the aid of poetic metaphors, particularly when one has to tread the difficult space between two massive traditions. Where the conceptual finds the door solidly barred against all entry, the symbolic carves its way in."[41] Openness to experiencing the other's rituals and ethos of faith can greatly enhance dialogue as each strives to exceed intellectual understanding even to the point of grasping the emotive elements of the heart. Christianity and Islam cannot be reduced to dogma and doctrine without missing the richness of a living faith. To restrict dialogue to intellectual matters risks defining religion in ways the adherents would not.

One final presupposition to engagement is the goal or goals of dialogue. Mission and da'wah can create a level of suspicion on each side. For example, questions of ulterior motives, such as the goal of conversion that can drive the other's interest in dialogue, may limit each party's willingness to engage the other. Al-Faruqi viewed various forms of Christian mission as damaging to engagement and either called for it to cease or be postponed, but he permitted Islamic da'wah. However, honest witness of one's beliefs within an atmosphere of respect and mutual understanding is potentially far less divisive. The goals of dialogue do vary, but at a minimum mutual understanding, respect and building trust and friendship should have a prominent place, even when parties agree to disagree. This may appear somewhat näive, but the alternatives border on the cynical. Despite finding points of disagreement and at times facing frustration over al-Faruqi's approach and attitude, those Christians who knew and engaged him write of their fondness and respect for him.[42] This at least indicates the presence of mutual respect, friendship and trust as outcomes of dialogue and interaction.

The above presuppositions or prerequisites are not exhaustive, but they do reflect some of the emphases of al-Faruqi in his theoretical and practical work on dialogue. As with other participants in dialogue, his ideals were not fully realised, but his attempt and consistent willingness to dialogue demonstrated both his commitment and the value he placed on discourse with Christians.

Ethics as a theme for dialogue

Al-Faruqi's main thematic focus upon ethics and moral behaviour to the exclusion of theology as the prime means for dialogue was previously criticized, but the idea and importance of ethics has reappeared in both religious and secular circles. His work on ethics is one of his main contributions to dialogue and something from which to build.

Al-Faruqi was not the first to emphasize ethics, as Izutsu points out in his work *Ethico-Religious Concepts in the Qur'ān*. Izutsu notes that: "Islamic thought at its Qur'ānic stage, makes no real distinction between the religious and the ethical."[43] Moral behaviour is based on divine commands and prohibitions producing social ethics, which are exercised between people in community. Relations between humanity and God are governed by ethico-religious concepts from which social ethics are derived. Since this is foundational to Islamic thought it is to be expected that Muslim scholars would offer ethics as a means for dialogue with Christians. However, al-Faruqi's contribution was to search for the ethical in Judaism and Christianity and not just in the Qur'ān. Combined with his principles of dialogue, his analysis and synthesis of ethics formed the basis for application in dialogue. Contemporary Muslim scholars involved in dialogue in some measure continue to stress this thematic avenue for conversation.

Abdulaziz Sachedina views ethical discourse as the main component in interfaith relations in which religious communities recognise the need to express the human spirit or spirituality and the accompanying ethical values in order to build and structure society.[44] As mentioned earlier, Ayoub also advocates the use of ethics as a more viable means for engagement than theology. Ziauudin Sardar, who writes on contemporary Islam among other topics, proposes a joint ethical programme to address social, political and intellectual issues in a post-modern world. Each faith in order to survive in a secular world beyond personal belief will need to develop a joint ethical front with other religions. In fact, he calls Muslims and Christians to "move beyond 'dialogue' to find a common ground for genuine discussion and continuous pragmatic action."[45] One example of this was the 1994 UN Cairo Conference on Population and Development. Led by the Vatican, various Muslim voices were added to critique family planning proposals that minimised reproductive freedom in an effort to balance population and resources.[46] Taji-Farouki, who teaches as the University of Exeter, offers other examples of joint action ranging from UN calls for a common core of humanistic values to Prince Hassan of Jordan's desire for a universal ethic from which to build a new international humanitarian order.[47] There are numerous other Muslims who could be added to this list who advocate ethics as a common meeting place for discourse and action.[48] However, the idea of 'ethics' has moved beyond a theme for Muslim and Christian discourse emerging in non-religious discussions and thought.[49] This is interesting and important for it moves the potential for dialogue beyond Christian and Muslim interaction to include all people regardless of religious or non-religious persuasion.

Margaret Somerville is an ethicist who advocates a shared ethic between peoples, cultures and disciplines not on the basis of religion, but on common humanity and the universal responsibilities that bind people together.[50] A search for a shared ethics will help to emphasize what we have in common and that we belong to the same moral community. She proposes two foundational principles, which are a deep respect for life and also for the human spirit.[51] Spirituality is regarded as an inherent characteristic common to all people, but expressed in different ways. Somerville labels this spirituality as the 'human spirit,' which is the drive to find meaning in life.[52]

In her book, *The Ethical Imagination: Journeys of the Human Spirit*, she seeks to identify the values that are held in common by humanity, and then imagines different ways in which we can discover these shared values. Thus, she appeals to the importance of stories, myths, poetry, imagination, examined emotions (understanding what and why we feel the way we do), intuition (especially moral intuition), and the human spirit as means to grasp human ethics. Somerville writes: "It's not that reason, common sense, objective facts, and science are unimportant to ethics – on the contrary. Rather, the problem is that they are often assumed to be the *only* matters important to ethics."[53] She goes on to suggest there are multiple and diverse ways of knowing, which encompass the mind, body, heart and spirit.[54] Myths and stories can capture and express realities that cannot be put directly into words or shared any other way. For example, awe and wonder are indescribable, but stories can help to communicate such experiences. The key is to hold all ways of knowing in a dynamic balance.

Al-Faruqi's emphasis on ethics and ethicality as the primary means of thematic contact between Muslims and Christians is based on the belief that the message of revelation is the same for all three monotheistic faiths. His search for ethics in Judaism and Christianity although based *a priori* on Islamic ethics was in fact a search for a shared ethics. Once found and articulated he believed this shared ethics would be a means not just for dialogue, but also for cooperative efforts between religions to realise the goals of bettering human societies. Somerville for her part seems to be seeking the same thing, but from a different direction. She begins not with revelation and religion, but with the commonality of human values across cultures and time looking empirically for what we value and hold as ethical ideals. She does not dismiss religious contributions, but does note that even atheists hold ethical values and expectations. In order to grasp and understand ethics and value she advocates the use of a variety ways of knowing. Al-Faruqi tended to focus only on reason and revelation. However, as Somerville notes, reason can be a concept of uncertain meaning leading to disagreement in relation to ethics.[55] For example, she explains that for lawyers 'reason' has a narrower definition than it does for philosophers and theologians.

By way of application, Muslim and Christian cooperative efforts can be focused on justice, addressing the concerns of poverty, ecological issues and economics. In the wider community of humanity, beyond religion, different groups and ideologies can find areas of common ground. Somerville suggests the example of feminist concerns finding common cause with religious beliefs. Some feminists regard surrogate motherhood as degrading to women while some religious people regard it as denigrating human procreation and harming the rights of children.[56] This would be an example of shared ethics finding consensus in application.

Al-Faruqi's contributions to dialogue can be extended beyond Muslim-Christian-Jewish discourse, if the use of ethics as a common platform for interaction is applied beyond the sphere of religion, as Somerville suggests. This is one way to build upon his ideas including broadening the ways of knowing beyond the prominence of reason. One can only speculate how he would have reacted to the work of ethicists such as Somerville, but the cooperative efforts between Christians and Muslims on the ethical and moral plane surely would have been heartily approved.

Although Muslim approaches to non-Muslims have progressed beyond al-Faruqi's ideas, his presence is still felt. However, his theoretical methodology of approaching other faiths remained his own. No other Muslim scholar thus far has sought to build upon the idea of meta-religious principles or the theory of Arabism. On the other hand, al-Faruqi's principles of dialogue in practice are generally assumed. For example, the presupposition that no religion is beyond critique is widely accepted, as is internal coherence, historical perspective, correspondence to reality, and the need to focus on areas of dialogue where there is the possibility of greater success, such as ethics.[57] These may seem obvious principles, but al-Faruqi developed and articulated these in relation to dialogue and its application, the latter being far more difficult. In this way, he laid the practical methodological groundwork on which others can build. Thus, overall his contribution to dialogue is rich. He provided theoretical tools of methodology; actively applied these in discourse and the example of his passion, commitment and person became an example for other Muslim dialogical participants.

CONCLUSION

In this study of the development of Isma'il al-Faruqi's methodological approach to dialogue with non-Muslims, a number of questions formed the boundaries of our inquiry. In particular these revolved around four different interconnecting aspects, including the reasons behind his lifelong interest in interfaith dialogue, the methodologies he developed, their application and a critical assessment of his work.

Part One sought to discover the reasons why al-Faruqi focused a large part of his academic career on Muslim-Christian dialogue. After introducing the life of al-Faruqi, attention turned to an application of Marya Schechtman's identity theory and her four features of self-narrative (survival, moral responsibility, self-interested concern and compensation). This led to a number of conclusions. Al-Faruqi's self-conception was that of a Muslim émigré who suffered the scars of forced exile from Palestine and who in the process of re-discovering his identity as a Muslim in the West found his place as a leader, an activist and an educator. He defined himself as a Muslim Arab Palestinian who belonged to a world Islamic *ummah*. His passion was to change the way Muslims thought and approached their world using the modernist Muslim reformer approach of education, blending Islamic traditional sciences with modern Western concepts. He saw himself as an activist engaging his faith in study and dialogue with the world beyond Islam.

The development of his methodology paralleled the development of his self-conception as a Muslim. It was not that his 'Muslimness' or his belief in Islam and identity as a person depended upon his emigration and life in the West, for he was a Muslim before leaving Palestine; rather, it was the context of the West that shaped and refined his self-understanding as a Muslim. This is not something unique. Many immigrants re-evaluate and re-identify themselves in their new context adapting, adopting and rejecting elements of their new host culture and that of their home culture. That al-Faruqi broadened his understanding of Islam from an ethnic cultural identity (an Arab Palestinian Muslim) to that of a Muslim who lived as part of a world *ummah* occurred in the context of establishing his new life in the West. The means or mode of this development was in wedding education with his struggle as a minority status Muslim. As he resolved these identity issues, he met the academic dynamic of religious and philosophical studies through which new questions were asked of his faith. As he re-adapted his faith in this new environment, he chose to define it in comparison to other faiths. So pervasive is the presence of these types of comparisons that one is led to conclude that al-Faruqi found it difficult in his writings to express his Islamic ideas without reference to other faiths. This is merely an observation, but it does return us to the construction and shaping of his self-conception and identity as discussed in Chapters One and Two. One can simply ask: Why did he feel the need to consistently compare Islam to such faiths as Christianity? Was it because he lived and addressed Muslims in the West or was it something deeper? For example, lectures presented in Pakistan, Saudi Arabia and Malaysia continued to use non-Muslim faiths as tools for comparison. If addressing a purely Muslim audience, why the need? Part of the answer lay in his self-conception. In essence, his identity as a Muslim matured through the course of philosophical and religious studies. Thus, he expressed his identity as much in terms of what he did not believe as in what he did believe. This is not as necessary in a Muslim majority environment, but becomes more essential in a Muslim minority environment.

Al-Faruqi's loss of his homeland to Western (Christian, Jewish and secular) interests through the creation of Israel and the global impact of colonialism, combined with his perception of the weakness of Muslim states, led him to re-identity himself within the context of non-Muslims. For this reason alone, it would not be unexpected to see his constant use of non-Muslims as a referent when discussing Islamic topics. What is less expected was his life-long interest and commitment to interfaith study and dialogue. In Chapter Two it was suggested that this was bound up within the development of his Muslim identity in the West and expressed through the Islamic concept of *da'wah*. *Da'wah* as practised with Muslims and non-Muslims dealt with a range of related topics, such as the Islamization of knowledge and interfaith dialogue. All was done in order to strengthen Muslims who lived in a world full of non-Muslims. Thus, his methodology was bound to his self-identity and grew in proportion to the needs of the Muslims he encountered living in the West. Philosophical and religious studies provided the tools for engagement, but the interest and commitment came from him as a person. It was not merely a means to an end nor was it reduced to fulfilling an obligation to practice *da'wah*.

My contention is that his interest in dialogue and the study of other faiths was part of who he was and that this was inseparable from his own self-conception. His renewed discovery of his 'Muslimness' grew commensurate with his academic knowledge and was shaped by his interaction with other Muslims. His twin passions for scholarship and for his fellow Muslims found expression in the application of intellectual thought and was realised through activism. By the time he entered McGill University in 1958, this activism was recognised by his colleagues and his studies became driven by the greater need to define and situate Islam within the wider world. Thus, interfaith dialogue - whether for internal Muslim consumption or for external non-Muslim interaction - served the same purpose, which was to strengthen Muslims and the *ummah* to live, thrive and in the end extend the teachings of Islam to non-Muslims. This applied equally to the individual and the community. For al-Faruqi, education and knowledge was the vehicle through which to achieve these goals, whether in reforming Muslim universities, mentoring and training the Muslim students he recruited or in engaging non-Muslims and thus educating them about Islam whilst challenging their own faiths.

During his methodological formative years (1948-1968), the Christian church became increasingly open to dialogue with non-Christians. This dialogical ecumenical spirit coincided with al-Faruqi's career, providing him with opportunities to apply his ideas in active dialogue. At the same time, academic growth in the study of religion began to move into interfaith dialogue, epitomized by W. C. Smith, with whom al-Faruqi studied. *Religionswissenschaft* provided al-Faruqi with methodological tools, which he merged with his philosophical training, ultimately producing his meta-religious and dialogical principles.

In Part Two we witnessed that his methodology of engagement emerged as a set of three approaches. His early attempt at comparative religious studies resulted in his theory of Arabism. From there he went on to develop two methodologies for the study of religion. The first guided acquisition of knowledge about a religion (principles of comparative religion) and the second was designed to evaluate each religion against a universal standard, which he labelled as meta-religious principles. This is seen most clearly in his book *Christian Ethics*. His principles of dialogue were based upon these two earlier methodologies for the study of religion. Theoretically, once proper understanding of a religion is achieved, one can then evaluate this religion in relation not to other religions but to a fixed universal standard, which he called *dīn al-fiṭrah* or *religio naturalis*. From this platform, dialogue between faiths in relation to the *dīn al-fiṭrah* can emerge as a search for truth. His application of dialogue became an extension of himself in the form of *daʿwah* practiced inwardly among his fellow Muslims and outwardly engaging non-Muslims.

In Part Three, two questions were asked of his methodologies. In terms of theoretical feasibility, his Arabism theory is interesting and quite novel, but is also open to serious criticism and as mentioned no scholar has since promoted it. As for the meta-religious principles, it was found that the project to find a universal means to evaluate all religions based on *dīn al-fiṭrah*, was again quite problematic, if not overly Islamic in spirit. His theoretical principles of dialogue are understandable and useful. However, his strong emphasis and dependence on rationalism to the exclusion of other forms of knowledge acquisition and his dismissal of paradox ignored both Christian and Muslim attempts to explain the unexplainable. On the application side of his work, his practice of dialogue was adequate for his use, but not necessarily for others. His insistence upon re-interpreting Judaism and Christianity hindered the depth of his engagement. For example, his attempt to redefine Christianity based upon Islamic ideals is not really dialogue. His desire, commitment and emphasis on dialogue are unquestionable, but the application of his ideas never overcame his Islamic presuppositions. He simply asked too much of Jews and Christians as partners in dialogue. Neither religion could reject, as he asked, their core beliefs for the sake of dialogue without the effort becoming futile.

His contribution in the field of dialogue and the Muslim study of religions was that of a pioneer whose sincerity and ambition is to be applauded. Despite theoretical and practical weaknesses of his thought, he moved Muslim-Christian interaction forward as he developed his methodologies. Here for the first time a Western-trained Muslim scholar studied Judaism and Christianity and produced methodologies which resulted in the potential for deeper levels of engagement. Not only was he committed to interfaith dialogue, but he also encouraged Muslims to study and engage others for the mutual benefit of all communities. His dialogical theme of ethics, although originally expressed in opposition to the theme of theology, interestingly has become more prominent since his death. Ethicists such as Margaret Somerville see a shared ethics as a means to bring all people together in common cause whether religious or non-religious. In this sense, al-Faruqi anticipated the future even as Muslim and Christian communities find tentative ways to cooperate in an increasingly secular and post-modern world. Dialogue has certainly moved past al-Faruqi, but his contribution, passion and role in its development cannot be ignored.

APPENDIX

INTERFAITH MEETINGS, CONFERENCES AND ORGANISATIONS[1]

1959

May   Muḥāḍarāt fī Ta'rīkh al-Adyān (Lectures on the History of Religions) delivered at the Faculty of Arts at Cairo University.[2]

1961

November–
December   Attended the 23rd Assembly of the World Council of Churches and the International Missionary Council in New Delhi.[3]

1962

March-April   Ten-lecture series on the relation of Islam to nationalism at the Institute of Higher Arabic Studies in Cairo.[4]

June-July   Twenty-lecture series on the history of religions given at al-Azhar University in Cairo.[5]

1963

Winter   Ten lectures given on comparative religion at the University of Cairo.[6]

Autumn   Public lecture on comparative religion at Syracuse University.[7]

May 16	Seminar: *Culture of Two Worlds,* Islamabad, Pakistan. Presentation: "Religion in the life of the people in the East and West."[8]
Spring	Presented a series of lectures at the Institute of Higher Arabic Studies in Cairo on "Particularism and universalism in the Old Testament."[9]

1964

January 26	Spoke to the Baptist graduate students at the Baptist University of Chicago at their Sunday seminar. The seminar topic was *Christianity and non-Christian Religious Perspectives and Questions* and al-Faruqi's talk was entitled, "The problem of Christian-Islamic rapprochement."[10]
April 30	Lecture entitled, "History of religions: Its nature and significance for Christian education and the Muslim-Christian dialogue," given to the faculty at the University of Chicago Divinity School.[11]

1965

March 4, 17	Invited by Grace Gospel Church in Syracuse, New York to address the church on "Islam, Scripture and samples of prayer" including answering questions on life in a mosque and Muslim views of God. He was invited to return March 17 to respond to a rector's summary of al-Faruqi's earlier presentation to the church.[12]
April 22-24	Invited by P. T. Raju to present a paper at a conference on "Comparative philosophy and culture" held at the College of Wooster, Wooster, Ohio.[13]
October 10	Spoke at the First Universalist – Unitarian Church at Auburn, New York on the subject of "Islam as a religion for modern man."[14]

1966

May 2-7   Delivered a lecture entitled, "Science and traditional values in Islamic society," at a symposium on *Science in South Asia* held at the Rockefeller University in New York.[15]

May 4-11   Participated as a discussant in the Gallahue Conference at Princeton on the topic, "Religious pluralism and world community."[16]

October 29   Keynote speaker at the International Relations Committee Eastern Zone for teachers K-12. The focus was on Islam.[17]

November 28   Presented a lecture entitled, "A Muslim view of man," in the lecture series "Religious Confrontation" hosted by Macalester College.[18]

1967

Late 1966/early 1967   Gave first lecture in the series for the inter-college seminar on Islamic civilization at the Department of History at SUNY, Albany.[19]

April 21-22   Read a paper, "An Islamic view of the West: Anathema, blessing or challenge," at Stanford University's Islamic Society conference on Islam and the West.[20]

Spring   Helped organise the conference, "Asia: The knowledge gap," at Maxwell Graduate School and the South Asia Programme of Syracuse University. He chaired the session, Islam and Communism in Asia.[21]

Summer   Panelist and presented a lecture, "Islam and Christianity: Prospects for dialogue," given at an ecumenical conference at the Jesuit seminary located at Woodstock College.[22]

September 14   Lecture given on the Middle East at the Western College for Women, Oxford, Ohio.[23]

October 13-14	Presented a lecture on "The general history of Muslim peoples" hosted by the New York State Department of Education and presented to various groups from colleges of New York state.[24]
October 19	Panellist at the 3rd annual Pre-teach-in-week on religion and international affairs held at the University of Toronto. The panel examined religious factors in the Arab-Israeli war.[25]
November 16-18	Organised symposium on Pakistan on the modernization of an Islamic state at Syracuse University.[26]

1972

| January 18 | Gave a lecture entitled, "Islam and Christianity," delivered at the University of Durban, South Africa.[27] |

1973

| April 12 | Participated in the Religion and Science Colloquium (location is not mentioned).[28] |

1975

August 7	Lecture on Islam given at the Chautauqua Symposium on World Religions.[29]
October 24-26	Presented a paper to the Society for the Scientific Study of Religion entitled, "Islam, the state and political power."[30]
November 20	Participated in a panel discussion at the MSA chapter at the University of Windsor on the topic, "The concept of God in Islam and Christianity."[31]

1976

| February 1-5 | Lecture, "Common bases between the two religions in regard of convictions and points of agreement in the spheres of life," at the "Seminar of Islamic-Christian Dialogue" held in Tripoli, Libya.[32] |

April 12	Spoke on "Islam and other faiths" at the International Islamic Conference, London. The Conference focus was "Islam and the future of Humanity."[33]
June 26-30	Presentation entitled, "On the nature of Islamic daʿwah," was delivered at a World Council of Churches consultation held at Chambésy, Switzerland.[34]
August 3-8	"Islam and other faiths," presented at the 30th Annual International Congress of Human Sciences in Asia and North Africa, Mexico City.[35]
1976-1982	Chair of the Islamic Studies Group of the AAR until 1982.[36]

1977

April 15	Invited by Joseph Gremillion to become a member of the Board of Directors of the IRPC. Accepted and listed on the Board Aug 4, 1977 until 1979.[37]
June 6-10	Delegate to the "Conference on Religious Workers for Lasting Peace, Disarmament and Just Relations among nations" held in Moscow.[38]
November 12	Invitation to speak on "Jerusalem in Islamic perspectives" at Duke University's Interfaith Colloquy on Jerusalem in the "Perspectives of the Three Great Monotheisms" jointly sponsored by the Arab-American Student Association and the Triangle Friends of the Middle East.[39]

1978

February 20	Lecture on "Jerusalem in Judaism, Christianity and Islam," Harvard Islamic Society.[40]
February 27	Letter of thanks received for a lecture on Islam at Cornell University from Cornell United Religious Work.[41]

March/April	Delivered a series of 10 lectures on Islamic civilization at Cairo University. The last lecture was on Islam and the other religions.[42]
April 17	Lecture on "Jerusalem in Judaism, Christianity and Islam," Indiana University.[43]
July 24-28	Read paper, "Rights of the non-Muslims in Islam and the Islamic concept of human rights," at the Muslim Minorities Seminar in London.[44]
September 9	Spoke at the Standing Conference on Interfaith Dialogue in Education. No location or topic mentioned.[45]
September 8-10	Spoke on "Islam and the language of transcendence," at the World Congress of Faiths at York, UK.[46]
September 13	Spoke on "Da'wah and jihad in Islam," at the British Association for the History of Religions at Oxford.[47]

1979

August 20-22	Invitation to speak at the Islamic Cultural Studies Conference organised by North Brisbane College of Advanced Education in conjunction with Queensland University.[48]
August 31	Invitation to speak at the Islam and Christianity Conference at Mannix College (Layton, Victoria, Australia) and organised by the World Assembly of Muslim Youth (YAMY).[49]
September	Spoke on "The historical development of the new era," at the MIT Islamic Society.[50]
September 18	Letter of invitation to speak on the impact of religion and the world political scene sponsored by the Stanford Forum for World Affairs, Stanford Connecticut.[51]
October 10	High School address at Westtown School in Westtown, Pennsylvania.[52]

October 22	Addressed the Catholic Women's Club in Philadelphia.[53]
November 17-20	AAR paper, "The nation state and social order in the perspective of Islām."[54]
November 26	"The role of Islam in global inter-religious dependence" at the Global Congress of the World's Religions.[55]
December 3-5	Presentation on "The Islamic faith and the problem of Israel and Jerusalem" at the International Seminar on Jerusalem, London.[56]

1980

September 30	Spoke on "Islam: Religion and way of life," at Duke University's Institute for Learning in Retirement Programme.[57]
1980-1982	Board member of the Global Congress of the World's Religions (GCWR) 1980-1982.[58]

1981

February 1	Accepted invitation to join the Board of Advisors for the Islamic Foundation in Leicester, UK.[59]
May	Three lectures entitled "Islam and Judaism," "Islam and Christianity," and "Islam and Secularism," given at the Department of Religious Studies at the University of Oregon.[60]
September 22	Responder to a panel discussion on Islam from Christian, Jewish and Hindu perspectives at the World Conference on Religion and Peace.[61]
November 17-19	Paper on "Revelation and authority," at the International Progress Organisation Symposium on the Concept of Monotheism in Islam and Christianity, Rome.[62]
November 24	Lecture, "Daʿwah in the West," at the Hijra International conference in Kula Lumpur, Malaysia.[63]

1982

February 21, 22	Guest speaker at Indiana University Lilly Seminar on "Jerusalem: Symbol of interfaith understanding."[64]
March 21, 22	Three lectures given at Colgate University, Hamilton, New York.[65]
April 6, 7	Spoke at Macalester College, Saint Paul, Minnesota at the invitation of the Muslim students.[66]
May 20	Presented lecture, "The place of social sciences in an Islamic curriculum," for the series "Muslim education in the modern world," held at the University of London's Department of Comparative Education.[67]
October 29	Interfaith Conference of Metropolitan Washington presentation on the theological and historical perspectives of Islam on the Holy land in order to facilitate understanding of the current Middle East situation.[68]
Autumn	"Divine transcendence and its expression," at the Global Congress of the World's Religions.[69]

1983

January 28-29	Talk on the "Moslem religion" at the Congregation Beth Yeshurun in Houston, Texas. The conference was on "Religious resurgence in comparative perspective: Selected cases from Christianity, Islam and Judaism."[70]
March	Spoke at the University of Lagos Campus in Nigeria.[71]
June 12	Spoke on "The Islamic critique of the social status quo of Muslims" at Georgetown University Symposium on *New Perspectives on Religion and Politics in the Middle East.*[72]
November 10	Declined an invitation to the London Interfaith Festival (September 11-17) due to a conflict with his teaching commitments at Temple University.[73]

1984

February 2   Participated in the conference, "Introduction to the world of Islam," at Greenburgh. Sponsored by the National Conference of Christians and Jews, INC.[74]

February 24   Spoke at the Presbyterian and United Church of Christ in Philadelphia.[75]

June 12   Spoke on "The issue of global economic disparities from the perspective of Islam" at the 5th General assembly of the World Future Society held at the University of Baltimore in Maryland.[76]

1985

Date unknown MSA lecture "Nature of man in Islam and other religions." Letter was undated, but found in PPBox 1985.[77]

September 22 Spoke at the Islamic-Christian Dialogue Group of Milwaukee.[78]

October 25-27 Lectured on Western methodology and Islamic thought in Washington D.C.[79]

November 4, 11, 18, 25 Four lectures given on the theme the religion and culture of Muslims at First Methodist Church of Philadelphia. Letter provided no year, but in PPBox 1985.[80]

Annual Conference of UKIM "The path of da'wah in the West," delivered at the United Kingdom Islam Mission conference (UKIM).[81]

1986

April   Rice University "Christian-Muslim workshop" presentation.[82]

May 6   Spoke at the First Unitarian Society of Plainfield's Forum on Islam. His lecture was the Islamic Religion.[83] This was likely his last presentation before his death.

NOTES

Introduction

1   For example, see Kate Zebiri, *Muslims and Christians Face to Face* (Oxford: Oneworld, 1997); Jacques Waardenburg, (ed.) *Muslim Perceptions of Other Religions: A Historical Survey* (New York: Oxford University Press, 1999); idem, (ed.) *Islam and Christianity: Mutual Perceptions since the mid-20th Century* (Leuven: Peeters, 1998); Leonard Swidler, (ed.) *Muslims in Dialogue: The Evolution of a Dialogue* (Lewiston, New York: The Edwin Mellen Press, 1992); Ataullah Siddiqui, *Christian-Muslim Dialogue in the Twentieth Century* (New York: Palgrave Macmillan, 1997); Douglas Pratt, *The Challenge of Islam: Encounter in Interfaith Dialogue* (Burlington, VT: Ashgate, 2005); Yvonne Yazbeck Haddad and Wadi Z. Haddad, (eds.) *Christian-Muslim Encounters* (Florida: University Press of Florida, 1995); Jean-Marie Gaudeul, *Encounters and Clashes: Islam and Christianity in History*, 2 vols., (Rome: Pontifical Institute for Arabic and Islamic Studies, 1984); Hugh Goddard, *A History of Christian-Muslim Relations* (Edinburgh: Edinburgh University Press, 2000); idem, *Muslim Perceptions of Christianity* (London: Grey Seal, 1996).

2   Seyyed Hossein Nasr, 'Islamic-Christian dialogue: Problems and obstacles to be pondered and overcome', *ICMR*, vol. 11, no. 2, (2000), pp.213-227; Tariq Ramadan, *Western Muslims and the future of Islam* (Oxford; New York: Oxford University Press, 2004); Mahmoud Ayoub, 'Islam and Christianity between tolerance and acceptance', *ICMR*, vol. 2, no. 2, (1991), pp.171-182; Hasan Askari, 'The dialogical relationship between Christianity and Islam', *JES*, vol. 9, no. 3, (1972), pp.477-487; Khurshid Ahmad, 'A Muslim response', in Joseph Gremillion and William Ryan, (eds.) *World Faiths and the New World Order: A Muslim-Jewish-Christian Search Begins* (Lisbon: The Interreligious Peace Colloquium, 1978), pp.171-193; Mohammed Talbi, 'Islam-Christian encounter today: Some principles', *MECC Perspectives*, no. 4-5, (July/August, 1985), pp.7-11; Hasan Hanafi, *Religious Dialogue and Revolution: Essays on Judaism, Christianity and Islam* (Cairo: Anglo Egyptian Bookshop, 1977); Akbar S. Ahmed, *Journey into America: The Challenge of Islam* (Washington, DC: Brookings Institution Press, 2010). Al-Faruqi has written over 30 books and articles dealing with this topic including *Christian Ethics: A Historical and Systematic Analysis of Its Dominant Ideas* (Montreal: McGill University Press, 1968). This list is not exhaustive and others could be

added, but the above authors have become more prominent through their publications, influence and presence in dialogue and the study of other faiths.

3   Jane I. Smith, *Muslims, Christians and the Challenge of Interfaith Dialogue* (New York: Oxford University Press, 2007), p.125.

4   Although Isma'il al-Faruqi did not use a hyphen when he wrote his surname as al Faruqi, the current convention is to write his name with a hyphen as in al-Faruqi. For the sake of consistency this convention is retained throughout the book.

5   Jane I. Smith recalls that al-Faruqi tolerated little disagreement with his ideas and his sharp intellectual ability made it difficult to survive long in debate with him. Smith, *Challenge of Interfaith Dialogue*, p.125.

6   Zebiri, *Muslims and Christians Face to Face*, p.139. Regarding al-Faruqi's contribution to contemporary Muslim studies of Christianity, Zebiri writes: "There seems little point in quoting others on matters with which al-Faruqi deals more thoroughly and more competently." Zebiri, p.139. This sentiment is repeated by Nawwab who writes: "Al-Fārūqī – who had the strongest academic background of any Muslim in comparative religion in modern times – was the foremost activist of the Muslim community in interfaith dialogue till his death in 1986." Isma'il Ibrahim Nawwab, 'Muslims and the West in history', in Zafar Ishaq Ansari and John Esposito, (eds.) *Muslims and the West: Encounter and Dialogue* (Washington, DC: Georgetown University, Center for Muslim-Christian Relations, 2001), pp.42f.

7   Jane I. Smith, 'Muslims as partners in interfaith encounter', in Zahid H. Bukhari, Sulayman S. Nyang, Mumtaz Ahmad and John L. Esposito, (eds.) *Muslims' Place in the American Public Square* (Walnut Creek, CA: AltaMira Press, 2004), p.188.

8   Kenneth Cragg, 'Ismā'īl al-Faruqi', in *Troubled by Truth: Life-Studies in Inter-Faith Concern* (Edinburgh: The Pentland Press Ltd., 1992), p.127.

9   Zafar Ishaq Ansari, Foreword to Ghulam Haider Aasi's book, *Muslim Understanding of other Religions: An Analytical Study of Ibn Ḥazm's Kitāb al-Faṣl fī al-Milal wa al-Aḥwā' wa al-Niḥal* (Pakistan: IIIT, 1999), p.vii.

10   John L. Esposito, 'Ismail al-Faruqi: Pioneer in Muslim-Christian relations', in *Makers of Contemporary Islam,* John L. Esposito and John O. Voll (eds.) (New York: Oxford, 2001), p.33.

11   Jacques Waardenburg, *Muslim and Others: Relations and Context* (Berlin and New York: Walter de Gruyter, 2003), p.227, footnote 38.

12   Kenneth Cragg, 'Ismā'īl al-Fārūqī in the field of dialogue', in Yvonne Yazbeck Haddad and Wadi Z. Haddad, (eds.) *Christian-Muslim Encounters* (Florida: University Press of Florida, 1995), p.400.

13   Marya Schechtman, *The Constitution of Selves* (Ithaca, NY: Cornell University Press, 1996).

Chapter One

1   From his CV letter of March 1, 1963, PPBox 1963. Repeated by Muhammad
    Shafiq, *Growth of Islamic Thought in North America: Focus on Isma'il R. al Faruqi*
    (Brentwood, MD: Amana Publications, 1994), p.5. The only source which
    questions this date of birth is Ilyas Ba-Yunus who lists the date as 1922, 'Al-
    Faruqi and beyond: Future directions in Islamization of knowledge', *AJISS*,
    vol. 5, no.1, (1988), p.13. Every other source consulted including al-Faruqi's
    own CV consistently cites 1921. For example, M. Tariq Quraishi, 'The legacy
    of Isma'il al-Faruqi', *Islamic Horizons*, vol. 15 (Special issue August–
    September, 1986), p.32; Islamic Horizons, 'A Glance at the life of Isma'il R.
    al-Faruqi (1921-1986)', *Islamic Horizons*, vol. 15, (special issue August-
    September, 1986), p.21; Ralph Braibanti, 'A memorial tribute', *Islamic
    Horizons*, vol. 15, (special issue August-September, 1986), p.78; Impact
    International, 'Prof. and Mrs. Ismail Faruqi–first degree premeditated
    murder', *Impact International*, vol. 16, no. 11 (13-26 June, 1986), p.5; and John
    L. Esposito, 'Ismail R. al-Faruqi: Muslim scholar-activist', in Yvonne
    Yazbeck Haddad, (ed.) *The Muslims of America* (New York: Oxford University
    Press, 1991), p.65. Al-Faruqi mentions his father's occupation (PPBox 1963)
    and Shafiq (p.7) adds Isma'il's father's name. Stanley Brice Frost in his
    foreword to al-Faruqi's *Christian Ethics*, on page v, writes: "His family had
    for generations wrested a way of life out of the ungenerous Palestinian
    soil", which implies a family history of land cultivation. This does not
    preclude his father being a *qāḍī*.
2   Cragg, 'Ismā'īl al-Fārūqī in the field of dialogue', p. 406. Ilyas Ba-Yunus, 'Al-
    Faruqi and beyond', p.13. There is also a report that al-Faruqi was related
    on his father's side to the prominent al-Husseini family of Jerusalem. ADC
    Special Report, *The al-Faruqi Murders* (Washington: ADC Research Institute,
    1986), p.4. Chedli Klibi, the Secretary General of the League of Arab States,
    in his message at the al-Faruqis' memorial convocation mentioned Isma'il
    was a "member of a most distinguished Palestinian family," but he did not
    name the family. ISNA, 'Memorial convocation: Isma'il Raji al Faruqi, Lois
    Lamya' al Faruqi', (Washington: ISNA, September 26, 1986).
3   Quraishi, 'The legacy of Isma'il al-Faruqi', p.32.
4   Shafiq, *Growth of Islamic Thought in North America*, p.7.
5   Frost, 'foreword', p.v.; M. Tariq Quraishi, *Ismail al-Faruqi: An Enduring Legacy*
    (Plainfield, IN: The Muslim Students Association, 1987), p.5.
6   Frost, 'foreword', p.v.; Shafiq, *Growth of Islamic Thought in North America*, p.7.
7   Frost, 'foreword', p.v.; Al-Faruqi in his Fulbright-Hays application letter (12
    August 1973) noted that he was fluent in Arabic, French and English, the
    last learned at AUB. He also read Urdu, Persian and German. PPBox #1 1967.
8   PPBox, 1963. Shafiq, *Growth of Islamic Thought in North America*, p. 7.
9   Ibid. It is unclear what the term *ḥākim* meant under the British mandate in
    Palestine. Al-Faruqi used the words 'district governor' in an English letter
    (PPBox, 1963) and *ḥākim* in an Arabic letter (Isma'il al-Faruqi, 'Self-

portrait', *Impact International,* vol. 16, no. 11, (13-26 June, 1986), p.6). More specifically, we do not know what duties al-Faruqi performed in this capacity.

10   Braibanti, 'A memorial tribute', p.77. With the end of the British mandate, the position al-Faruqi occupied ceased to exist. It is in this sense that Baribanti speaks of al-Faruqi as being the last governor (*ḥākim*) in the Galilee district. Braibanti chose to translate *ḥākim* as governor, but this may be misleading as senior posts were often held by the British. Therefore, I have chosen to translate *ḥākim* as 'magistrate'.

11   Ba-Yunus, 'Al-Faruqi and beyond', p.13.

12   Al-Faruqi, 'Self-portrait', p.6.

13   Shafiq, *Growth of Islamic Thought in North America,* p.7.

14   Altalib noted al-Faruqi told him of his involvement in the armed struggle as a teenager. However, the details remain unclear. Altalib did not mention, as Shafiq did, that al-Faruqi's motivation was for revenge. Altalib interview (IIIT Herndon, VA, October 29, 2007).

15   Shafiq, *Growth of Islamic Thought in North America,* p.8.

16   Lois Ibsen was born on July 25, 1926 in Montana. In 1950, when she was 25 years old, she married Isma'il. At some point she converted to Islam and adopted the name Lamyā' (لمياء). According to Hasan Hanafi, Lois became a Muslim after marrying Isma'il. Hasan Hanafi interview (University of North Carolina, Chapel Hill, 7 April 2007). She completed a B.A. in Music at the University of Montana and an M.A. in Music at the University of Indiana. In 1960, she studied Islam at the Institute of Islamic Studies, McGill University and then at the Universities of Pennsylvania, Syracuse and Temple. She completed her Ph.D. in 1974 at Syracuse in Music, Art and Religion. She taught at Temple, Butler and Indiana Universities along with universities in Pakistan and the Philippines. Together with Isma'il she raised five children (2 boys and 3 girls). Islamic Horizons, 'Dr. Lamya' al-Faruqi: The woman behind the man (1926-1986)', *Islamic Horizons,* vol. 15, (special issue August-September, 1986), p.19.

17   Shafiq, *Growth of Islamic Thought in North America,* p.8.

18   Quraishi, 'The legacy of Isma'il al-Fārūqī', p.32. These books were Khalid Muhammad Khalid's *From Here We Start,* translated by Isma'il al-Faruqi, (Washington, DC: American Council of Learned Societies, 1953); Mirrit Butrus Ghali's *The Policy of Tomorrow,* translated by Isma'il al-Faruqi, (Washington, DC: American Council of Learned Societies, 1953) and Muhammad al-Ghazali's, *Our Beginning in Wisdom,* translated by Isma'il al-Faruqi, (Washington, DC: American Council of Learned Societies, 1953).

19   Frost writes: "He [al-Faruqi] sold them [homes] as a finished achievement, a poem (with his tongue only half in his cheek) of gracious living." al-Faruqi, *Christian Ethics,* p.v. Esposito notes that the Faruqis' home in Wyncote was beautifully decorated and built indicating Isma'il's continued

interest in this trade beyond his years working in this field. Esposito interview (Georgetown University, 30 October 2007).

20 Al-Faruqi, *Christian Ethics*, p.v.; Quraishi, 'The legacy of Isma'il al-Fārūqī', p.32.

21 Esposito, 'Ismail R. al-Faruqi: Muslim scholar-activist', p.66.

22 Steve Johnson, 'On justifying the good, a glimpse at Isma'il al-Faruqi's doctoral dissertation', *Islamic Horizons*, vol. 15, (special issue August-September, 1986), p.69.

23 Esposito, 'Ismail R. al-Faruqi: Muslim scholar-activist', p.66.

24 In his CV letter of March 1, 1963, al-Faruqi indicates he travelled in 1952 throughout the Muslim world studying under the leading men of learning and religion. The longest period was spent at al-Azhar. PPBox 1963. Shafiq specifically mentions that the al-Faruqis went to Syria. Shafiq, *Growth of Islamic Thought in North America*, p.8. Braibanti further mentions al-Faruqi received a Rockefeller Fellowship for this time period. Braibanti, 'A memorial tribute', p.78. While, the website listing the Rockefeller archives does not list a fellowship for the dates 1954-1958, it does confirm fellowships granted to Isma'il for 1958-1961 and 1963. (28 June 2013) <http://dimes.rockarch.org/xtf/view?docId=ead/FA387/FA387.xml;query=al-faruqi;brand=default;chunk.id=ref29700;doc.view=contents#ref29715>. Al-Faruqi himself mentions fellowships for Cairo, but provides neither the date nor the fellowship granter. PPBox 1967.

25 Shafiq, *Growth of Islamic Thought in North America*, p.8.

26 Fazlur Rahman, 'Palestine and my experiences with the young Fārūqī, 1958-1963', *Islamic Horizons* vol. 15 (Special issue August-September, 1986), p.39.

27 Ibid.

28 In his CV letter of 1963, al-Faruqi mentions he was invited to McGill in 1958 where he spent the year conducting seminars and research in the history of Islamic thought, taught Arabic and supervised student research in Islamic philosophy. PPBox 1963.

29 Quraishi, *Ismail al-Faruqi: An Enduring Legacy*, p.18.

30 As an example, one can point to the guidance W. C. Smith provided his Ph.D. student Mahmoud Ayoub. According to an interview with Ataullah Siddiqui in London, April 20, 1991, Ayoub spoke of how W. C. Smith encouraged him to re-examine his own Islamic roots which in due course he did and he finally returned to them. This is of course anecdotal, but it does show Smith did not try to dissuade Ayoub from his Islamic faith and heritage. Siddiqui, *Christian-Muslim Dialogue in the Twentieth Century*, p.98.

31 Rahman, 'Palestine and my experiences with the young Fārūqī', p.39.

32 There is some discrepancy over the duration of al-Faruqi's two appointments. Fazlur Rahman wrote that the fellowship at the Institute was for two years and for one year at the Divinity school. Rahman, 'Palestine and my experiences with the young Fārūqī', p.40. Frost, at the

time Dean of the Faculty of Divinity, wrote the opposite. *Christian Ethics*, p.v.

33   Al-Faruqi, *Christian Ethics*, p.vi.

34   A letter written by al-Faruqi states in 1960 he was appointed as a visiting Professor at the Faculty of Divinity where he studied Christianity from an Islamic point of view. The appointment lasted for two years. PPBox 1963.

35   Rahman, 'Palestine and my experiences with the young Fārūqī', p.39.

36   Ibid. Interestingly, when the Faruqi family was making arrangements to go to Pakistan they included their Ford Country Squire Station wagon among the items to be shipped from Montreal (letter of 12August 1961). PPBox 1964.

37   Rahman, 'Palestine and my experiences with the young Fārūqī', p.42. A letter in PPBox 1964 indicates al-Faruqi accepted the offer to work at CIIR on 17 March 1961 and official joined the CIIR on 2 October 1961.

38   Rahman, 'Palestine and my experiences with the young Fārūqī', p.42.

39   Ibid. His theory of Arabism is discussed in chapter three. During lectures in Cairo, several students protested about his Arabism theory by asking: "What fables (*asatir*) are you telling us?" In a letter dated 11 November 1963, al-Faruqi responded to a letter critiquing his Arabism theory written by Cuyler Young. In his defence, Isma'il noted that the intellectuals of Cairo (al-Azhar and Cairo Universities) along with those of CIIR and Karachi University at first reacted against Arabism, but as they learned more they "acclaimed it enthusiastically." PPBox 1963.

40   PPBox 1964.

41   In a document listing his academic activities he provides the dates for these lectures. IHAS, (March-April 1962), al-Azhar, (June-July, 1962) (PPBox 1964) and more vaguely the winter of 1963 for the University of Cairo lectures. He also returned in the spring of 1963 to lecture again at IHAS. PPBox 1963.

42   See PPBox 1963 and also PPBox 1964.

43   PPBox 1964. Shafiq, *Growth of Islamic Thought in North America*, p.13.

44   One of the reasons al-Faruqi left Montreal for Pakistan was the opportunity to create a curriculum, which would prepare Muslims both in the traditional Islamic sciences, but also in western methodologies in order for Muslims to address their own concerns in the world. He drafted a detailed curriculum which included a section on comparative religion for graduate students. PPBox 1961-1962. See also Shafiq, *Growth of Islamic Thought in North America*, pp.18f. However, aside from other reasons, he became dissatisfied over the pace of implementing the Islamic studies programme that he envisioned and so he decided to leave. His letter of resignation penned 5 August 1963 was received by Rahman and made effective for 15 September 1963. PPBox 1963. See also Shafiq, *Growth of Islamic Thought in North America*, p.20. In a personal letter to friends dated 12 December 1963, al-Faruqi mentions a 'falling out' with Fazlur Rahman. PPBox 1963. As to

his general feelings, he wrote earlier in 22 March that, "Unfortunately, Islamic Studies here [CIIR] are not serious at all; and the Institute has neither the will nor the desire to put its work on any kind of academic footing." PPBox 1963.

45 Shafiq, *Growth of Islamic Thought in North America*, p.20. See also PPBox 1963, which contains a number of letters of inquiry into Post Doctoral Fellowships and teaching positions as he contemplated leaving CIIR. Among these were letters to Yale, the Universities of Texas, Michigan, Washington (Seattle), Pennsylvania, Toronto, Harvard, Portland State College, Columbia, Syracuse, Utah and the Catholic University of America. PPBox 1963.

46 In contrast to the difficulty in securing employment after his resignation from the CIIR in 1963, he was greeted with numerous offers the following year from Duke, UCLA, Princeton, Portland, McGill and Chicago. He chose Syracuse due to its excellent development possibilities and his desire to live in a cold place after the desert of Karachi. He quipped, "Chicago is all white with snow, and the temperature is zero this morning. So many of our friends here bear grim faces because of this. Not the Faruqi's. They smile, kick the snow on the street as they walk, and pray Allah for more." Letter of 12 December 1963. PPBox 1963.

47 Esposito, 'Ismail R. al-Faruqi: Muslim scholar-activist', p.66.

48 Esposito, 'Teaching Islam the old fashioned way-living it!', *Islamic Horizons*, vol. 15 (Special issue August-September, 1986), p.49.

49 Braibanti commented the Faruqis served as "a shepherds to the Muslim flock in and around Philadelphia." Braibanti, 'A memorial tribute', p.79. See also Shafiq, *Growth of Islamic Thought in North America*, p.37. Dr. Wright, quoted by Qurashi: "He [al-Faruqi], along with his wife, would greet them [students] at the airport on their first arrival to the U.S., find shelter for them, and feed them physically as well as mentally." Quraishi, 'The legacy of Isma'il al-Fārūqī', p.33.

50 Quraishi, 'The legacy of Isma'il al-Fārūqī', p.34.

51 Esposito, 'Teaching Islam the old fashioned way', p.49.

52 MSA was founded in 1963 on the campus of the University of Illinois at Urbana-Champaign by a conference of Muslim students from around the U.S. and Canada. (28 June 2013) <http://msanational.org/about-us/>. According to Ghamari-Tabrizi, the MSA has been the most successful Muslim immigrant association in the USA. The MSA grew rapidly in the mid-1970s and by 1983, 310 MSA student chapters existed with more than 45,000 members. Behrooz Ghamari-Tabrizi, 'Loving America and longing for home: Ismail al-Faruqi and the emergence of the Muslim diaspora in North America', *International Migration*, vol. 42, no. 2 (2004), p.70.

53 Quraishi, *An Enduring Legacy*, p.8, comments that al-Faruqi's first contact with MSA was in 1962 at someone named 'Umar's house in Philadelphia. However, this is a year before MSA was founded and al-Faruqi was in

Pakistan (1961-1963). In a previous article (Quraishi, 'The legacy of Isma'il al-Fārūqī', p.32), he says the first contact was in 1963 in Philadelphia. This would seem more plausible given that by 1963 al-Faruqi was present in the U.S. and that this was the year the MSA was founded. Quraishi in both his works is inconsistent with his dates of first contact. However, Shafiq states first contact was made 21 January 1965 while at Syracuse when al-Faruqi contacted Ahmad Sakr then MSA secretary general for some *'Id* cards. Sakr sent the cards and invited al-Faruqi to become involved even writing to other members of the MSA (Ahmad Totonji, then chairman of the Public and Information Sector, and Munthir Aldruby, then member of the Religious Relation Committee) urging them to contact al-Faruqi. Shafiq, *Growth of Islamic Thought in North America*, p.21. Hisham Altalib recalled first contact was probably in 1963 or 1964 in Philadelphia in connection with AbuSulayman, who was a Saudi political science graduate student with whom al-Faruqi would later establish the International Institute of Islamic Thought (IIIT). Dr. Altalib also would invite Dr. al-Faruqi to speak to MSA groups at various campuses in the USA. Altalib interview (IIIT Herndon, VA, October 29, 2007).

54   Al-Faruqi's influential presence among the students involved in the MSA provided leadership and inspired various students. Shafiq, *Growth of Islamic Thought in North America*, p. xvii. According to Ba-Yunus, al-Faruqi was able to articulate and explain the principles of Islam in Western concepts demonstrating the applicability of Islam. Ba-Yunus goes on to write: "There is little doubt that he became instrumental in changing the image of the MSA from that of being rigidly conservative to an organization with very knowledgeable and rational practitioners and advocates of Islam." Ba-Yunus, 'Al-Faruqi and beyond', p.14.

55   'AbdulHamid AbuSulayman, *The Islamic Theory of International Relations: New Directions for Islamic Methodology and Thought* (Herndon, VA: IIIT, 1987). This was originally a Ph.D. thesis written in 1973 at the University of Pennsylvania. Al-Faruqi met AbuSulayman through the MSA. Ghamari-Tabrizi writes: "His [al-Faruqi's] connection with AbuSulayman was a turning point in his career; it transformed his individual search for Muslimhood into an institutional effort which resulted first in the formation of the Association of Muslims Social Scientists (AMSS), established 1971, and later to the establishment of the IIIT in 1981." Ghamari-Tabrizi, 'Muslim diaspora in North America', p.70. AbuSulayman was able to raise funds from patrons in Saudi Arabia, Pakistan and Malaysia in order to realize the establishment of these institutional organizations.

56   Ba-Yunus, 'Al-Faruqi and beyond', pp.15f.

57   The AMSS is an academic forum bringing together Muslim and non-Muslim scholars to debate social issues from an Islamic perspective. Al-Faruqi's strong connections with the MSA, his intellectual ability and reputation and his organizational ability were key components in the establishment of

the AMSS. AMSS of North America pamphlet from the AMSS 36th Annual Conference held at the University of Maryland, 26-29 October 2007.

58   Ba-Yunus, 'Al-Faruqi and beyond', p.15. See also the AMSS pamphlet "Building knowledge, research and praxis," 2007 produced by Laila Sein at IIIT.

59   Ba-Yunus, 'Al-Faruqi and beyond', p.16.

60   The founding document of IIIT (8 October 1980) lists the President as 'AbdulHamid AbuSulayman and the Secretary-treasurer as al-Faruqi. The initial registration address for IIIT was listed as 323 Bent Road, Wyncote, Pennsylvania, the home of the Faruqis. PPBox #2 1980.

61   Braibanti, 'A memorial tribute', p.76.

62   Ibid., p.78.

63   Ibid. See also PPBox #1 1985 where on February 1, 1985 he joined the Leicester Islamic Foundation.

64   Islamic Horizons, 'A Glance at the life of Isma'il R. al-Faruqi (1921-1986)', Islamic Horizons, vol. 15, (special issue August-September, 1986), p.21.

65   Shafiq lists a number of universities he assisted with Islamic studies programmes and mentions his involved in the founding of the International Islamic Universities of Islamabad, Pakistan and Kuala Lumpur, Malaysia. Shafiq, Growth of Islamic Thought in North America, p.31.

66   Islamic Horizons, 'A Glance at the life of Isma'il R. al-Faruqi (1921-1986)', p.21. Braibanti, 'A memorial tribute', p.76. To this list one can add Egypt, Nigeria and South Africa (PPBox #1 1967), London (PPBox #2 1985), Australia (PPBox 1986).

67   Esposito, 'Teaching Islam the old fashioned way', p.51.

68   There are at least five main articles detailing aspects of Christian-Muslim interaction and influence between 1963-1968. (1963) 'A comparison of the Islamic and Christian approaches to Hebrew scripture', Journal of the Bible and Religion, 31, (1963), pp.283-293. Reprinted in Ataullah Siddiqui, (ed.) Ismail Raji al-Faruqi: Islam and Other Faiths (Leicester: IIIT, 1998), pp.109-126; (1965) 'History of Religions: Its nature and significance for Christian education and the Muslim-Christian dialogue', Numen, no. 12 (1965), pp.35-65, 81-86. Reprinted in Siddiqui, (ed.) Ismail Raji al-Faruqi, pp.161-194; (1967) 'Islam and Christianity: Prospects for dialogue', Sacred Heart Messenger, (September 1967), pp.29-33; (1968) 'Islam and Christianity: Diatribe or dialogue', JES, vol. 5, no. 1, (1968), pp.45-77. Reprinted in Siddiqui, (ed.) Ismail Raji al-Faruqi, pp.241-280; (1968) 'Islam and Christianity: Problems and perspectives', in James P. Cotter, (ed.) The Word in the Third World (Washington: Corpus Books, 1968), pp.159-181 and discussion pp.181-220.

69   For his own account of the creation of the Islamic Studies Group of the AAR, see Isma'il al-Faruqi, 'Introduction: The Islāmic Studies Group, American Academy of Religion', in Isma'il al-Faruqi, (ed.) Islamic Thought and Culture (Herndon, VA: IIIT, 1982), pp.1-3. See also PPBox #1 1979 for his papers on various aspects of the AAR.

70 Esposito, 'Teaching Islam the old fashioned way', p.49.

71 For details see al-Faruqi, 'Introduction: The Islāmic Studies Group', pp.1-3.

72 Isma'il al-Faruqi, 'Abstract of programs for nine years', in Isma'il al-Faruqi, (ed.) *Islamic Thought and Culture* (Herndon, Va.: IIIT, 1982), pp.4-8.

73 See Chapter Five.

74 Joseph Gremillion, (ed.) *Food/Energy and the Major Faiths* (Maryknoll, NY: Orbis Books, 1978).

75 Gremillion, *Food/Energy and the Major Faiths*, p.282. See Gremillion's invitation letter to al-Faruqi to join the board of IRPC dated April 15, 1977. The first board meeting occurred 20 September 1977 in New York. PPBox 1977.

76 Gremillion and Ryan, (eds.) *World Faiths and the New World Order*, p.237. Al-Faruqi co-wrote the foreword with the President, Matthew Rosenhaus, p.viii.

77 Isma'il al-Faruqi, (ed.) *Trialogue of the Abrahamic Faiths* (Herndon, VA: IIIT, 1982), p.ix.

78 Isma'il al-Faruqi, 'The role of Islam in global inter-religious dependence', in Warren Lewis, (ed.) *Towards a Global Congress of the World's Religions: Conference Proceedings at Los Angeles* (Barrytown, NY: Unification Theological Seminary, 1980), pp.19-53.

79 Lewis, *Towards a Global Congress of the World's Religions*, p.11.

80 Among the boards on which he served were the journal *Islamic Studies* published by the Institute of Islamic Research in Pakistan and *The Journal of South Asian and Middle Eastern Studies*. Braibanti, 'A memorial tribute', pp.78.

81 Shafiq lists a number of merit awards such as salary increases as well as numerous grants from Temple University and a few grants from Saudi Arabia's World Assembly (1976, 1977, 1981). Shafiq, *Growth of Islamic Thought in North America*, p.27.

82 Gordon Barthos, 'Scholars' slayings shock U.S. Arab community', *The Toronto Star* 17 August 1986, Sun, B8. *Factiva* (25 May 2010) <http://global.factiva.com/aa/?ref=TOR 0000020080607di8h00ysq>.

83 Lee Linder, 'Arab Professor, Wife Killed; Daughter Stabbed', *The Associated Press* 27 May 1986, *Factiva* (25 May 2010) <http://global.factiva.com/aa/?ref=asp0000020011119 di5r00h9t>.

84 Impact International, 'Prof. and Mrs. Ismail Faruqi–first degree premeditated murders', p.5.

85 Lee Linder, 'Police press hunt for killer of Arab Professor and wife', *The Associated Press* 28 May 1986, *Factiva* (25 May 2010) <http://global.factiva.com/aa/?ref=asp000002001 1119 di5s00hn1>.

86 Lee Linder, 'Coroner says assassin killed Anti-Zionist scholar, wife', *The Associated Press* 29 May 1986, *Factiva* (25 May 2010) <http://global.factiva.com/aa/?ref=asp000002001 1119 di5t00hvd>.

87 Impact International, 'Prof. and Mrs. Ismail', p. 6.

88 'Arab scholar, wife Killed', *The Washington Post* 28 May 1986, A18, *Factiva* (25 May 2010) <http://global.factiva.com/aa/?ref=wp00000020020504di5s00io 6>.

89 Linder, 'Police press hunt'.

90 Impact International, 'Prof. and Mrs Ismail Faruqi', p.6.

91 Linder, 'Coroner says assassin'.

92 Impact International, 'Prof. and Mrs. Ismail Faruqi', p.6.

93 Linder. 'Coroner says assassin'.

94 Ibid.

95 Shafiq, *Growth of Islamic Thought in North America*, p.4.

96 Linder, 'Police press hunt'.

97 Barthos, 'Scholars' slayings shock U.S. Arab community'.

98 Impact International, 'Prof. and Mrs Ismail Faruqi', p.6. He did receive irate letters and threats in 1984 over the publicity of his views on the need to dismantle Israel, which he had expressed in his book, *Islam and the Problem of Israel*, pp.112-114.

99 Impact International, 'Prof. and Mrs Ismail Faruqi', p.6.

100 Sun-Times Wires, 'Islamic scholar, wife slain at home near Philadelphia', *Chicago Sun-Times* 28 May 1986, Five Star Sports Final, 26. (25 May 2010) <http://global.factiva.com/ aa/?ref=chi0000020011119di5s00jul>.

101 Linder, 'Police press hunt'.

102 Quraishi, 'The legacy of Isma'il al-Faruqi', p.34.

103 Isma'il al-Faruqi, 'Islamic faith and the problem of Israel and Jerusalem', in Salem Azzam, (ed.) *Jerusalem: The Key to World Peace* (London: Islamic Council of Europe, 1980), p.80.

104 Islamic Horizons, 'Faruqi killings spark response', *Islamic Horizons*, vol. 15, (special issue August-September, 1986), p.22.

105 Shafiq, *Growth of Islamic Thought in North America*, p.1.

106 G. N. Kashif, 'Al-Faruqi's memorial: A tribute', *Islamic Horizons*, vol. 16, (November 1986), p. 5. There was a Diplomatic Advisory Board, comprised of over 70 diplomats from over 50 countries and an Advisory Committee, comprised of over 200 members including members of Congress, the Senate, academics, and entertainers. The Advisory Committee was chaired by three Christians (Dr. Arie Brouwer, General Secretary of National Council of Churches of Christ in the USA, the Reverend Jesse Jackson, Director of the Rainbow Coalition, Bishop James W. Mallone, President, National Conference of Catholic Bishops) and a Muslim, Dr. Abdullah Omar Nasseef, Secretary General, Muslim World League. ISNA, 'Memorial convocation'.

107 Shafiq, *Growth of Islamic Thought in North America*, p.3.

108 Ibid.

109 ISNA, Memorial convocation. Islamic Horizons, Faruqi killings spark response', p.23.

110 AP, 'Black Muslim charged in slaying of Islamic Scholar and his wife', *The New York Times Abstracts* Late City Final Edition, 18 January 1987, *Factiva* (25 May 2010) <http://global.factiva.com/aa/?ref=nyta000020011118dj1i003lm>. See also 'Alleged Black Muslim charged in murders', *Houston Chronicle* 18 January 1987, *Factiva* (25 May 2010) <http://global.factiva.com/aa/?ref= hou0000020011118dj1i002zy>.

111 Islamic Horizons, 'Letters to the Editor', *Islamic Horizons*, vol. 15, (special issue August-September, 1986), pp.4-10.

112 Ibid., p.4.

113 Ibid., p.5. It appears moreover that the former organisation began thereafter to allow a Muslim observer to be appointed to the NCCC as part of the Memorial Committee's efforts in coordination with ISNA.

114 Ibid.

115 Ibid., p.7.

116 Kashif, 'Al-Faruqi's memorial', p. 5; Shafiq, *Growth of Islamic Thought in North America*, p.3. For the memorial programme, see ISNA, 'Memorial convocation'.

117 Jailani Harun, 'Anwar hits out at self-proclaimed Islamic champions', *Business Times* 2, 1 March 1995, January 1987, *Factiva* (25 May 2010) <http://global.factiva.com/aa/?ref= btmal00020011102dr3100b02>.

118 Islamic Horizons, 'Faruqi killings spark response', p.23.

119 Shafiq, *Growth of Islamic Thought in North America*, pp.4f.

120 Associated Press, 'Alleged Black Muslim charged in murders'.

121 Ibid.

122 Ibid. Shafiq, *Growth of Islamic Thought in North America*, p.5.

123 Associated Press, 'Black Muslim charged in slaying of Islamic Scholar and his wife'.

124 Associated Press, 'Young guilty, sentenced to death in Faruqi killings'. *The Associate Press* 11 July 1987, *Factiva* (25 May 2010) <http://global.factiva.com /aa/?ref=asp0000020 011118dj7b00rrh>.

125 Associated Press, 'Young guilty, sentenced to death in Faruqi killings'.

126 Ibid.

127 Ibid.

128 Ibid.

129 Richard Carelli, 'Court agrees to clarify death penalty appeals'. *Patriot News*, Final, A3, 29 March 1994, *Factiva* (25 May 2010) <http://global.factiva.com /aa/?ref=pathar 0020011029dq3t009u7>.

130 Adam Bell, 'Inside the Capitol'. *Patriot News*, Final A3, 11 March 1996, *Factiva* (25 May 2010) <http://global.factiva.com/aa/?ref=pathar0020011014ds3b 005a1>.

131 Associated Press, 'Authorities say 1986 murder may yield clues about terror groups'. *Associated Press Newswires* 23 September 2001, 12:39, *Factiva* (25 May 2010) <http://global.factiva.com/aa/?ref=aprs000020010923dx9n00q8o>.

Chapter Two

1 Yvonne Yazbeck Haddad, 'The dynamics of identity in North America', in John L. Esposito and Yvonne Yazbeck Haddad, (eds.) *Muslims on the Americanization Path?* (New York: Oxford University Press, 2000), pp.19-46; Yvonne Yazbeck Haddad and A. Lummis, *Islamic values in the US* (New York: Oxford, 1987). Haddad in her article ('The dynamics of identity', pp.29f) discusses the impact of Fazlur Rahman, Seyyed Hossein Nasr and al-Faruqi upon Muslims in North America. Mohommed A. Muqtedar Khan, 'Constructing the American Muslim community', in Yvonne Yazbeck Haddad, Jane I. Smith, and John L. Esposito, (eds.) *Religion and Immigration: Christian, Jewish, and Muslim Experience* (New York: Altamida Press, 2003), pp.175-198; idem, 'Muslim and identity politics in America', in *Muslims on the Americanization Path?*, pp.87-101. Khan in the latter article lists five sources of meaning (subjective, intersubjective, ideal, structural and historical) that influence the process of identity formation in North American Muslim society. He writes: "Subjective sources are essentially dependent on the self-narrative of the individual and contingent primarily on how a person interprets past experiences. This subjective identity emerges through an autobiographical discourse that is politically self-conscious. Isma'il al-Faruqi and Seyyed Hossein Nasr are good examples of individuals who have sought to define themselves through self-narrative." p.88. Although he does not explain why he considers these two as good examples, he does cite Marya Schechtman's work on self-narrative.

2 Ghamari-Tabrizi, 'Loving America and longing for home', pp.61-86.

3 Ibid., p.65.

4 Ghamari-Tabrizi argues that al-Faruqi's "experience of displacement and his "Islamization" project neither represented an "intentional hybridity", nor led to the emergence of an "organic hybridity."" Ghamari-Tabrizi, 'Loving America and longing for home', p.62. As Stanley Brice Frost comments about al-Faruqi: "He became a man of two worlds, intelligently at ease in both and at peace in neither." *Christian Ethics*, p.v.

5 Interestingly, even al-Faruqi was drawn into a brief study of this topic. In 1965, at a conference addressing 'The Problem of the Self', he presented a paper entitled 'The self in Mu'tazilah thought', *International Philosophical Quarterly*, vol. CI, no. 3, (September 1966), pp. 366-88; reprinted in Poolla Tirupati Raju and Albury Castell, (eds.) *East-West Studies on the Problem of the Self* (The Hague: M. Nijhoff, 1968), pp.87-107.

6 John Perry, 'The problem of personal identity', in John Perry, (ed.) *Personal Identity* (Berkley and Los Angeles: University of California Press, 1975), pp.3-12.

7 Schechtman, *Constitution*, p.7.

8 John Locke, *An Essay Concerning Human Understanding*, edited by Peter H. Nidditch (Oxford: Clarendon Press, 1979, first published in 1690). It should be noted the nature of self was studied by others such as Aristotle, Plato,

Leucippus, Democritus, Epicurus and Muslim authors. For example see Plato, *The Dialogues*; Aristotle, *De Anima* Book II, Ch. 1,2; al-Ash'ari, *Maqālāt al-Islāmiyyin wa Ikhtilāf al-Musallīn* vol. 2, edited by Muhammad M. D. 'Abd al Hamid (Cairo: Maktabat al Nahḍah al Miṣriyyah, n.d.), pp.24-25.

9   There are many prominent theorists. Here only a few are mentioned. For additional reading see: Derek Parfit, *Reasons and Persons* (Oxford: Clarendon Press, 1984); Harry Frankfurt, 'Identification and externality', in Amélie Rorty, (ed.) *The Identities of Persons* (Berkley and Los Angeles: University of California Press, 1976), pp.239-252; Alasdair MacIntyre, 'The virtues, the unity of a human life, and the concept of a tradition', in Stanley Hauerwas and Gregory L. Jones, (eds.) *Why Narrative* (Grand Rapids, MI.: Eerdmans, 1989), pp.89-111; John Perry, 'Can the self divide?', in *The Journal of Philosophy*, 69 no. 16, (September 7, 1972), pp.463-488; idem, 'The Importance of being identical', in Amélie Rorty, (ed.) *The Identities of Persons* (Berkley and Los Angeles: University of California Press, 1976), pp.67-90; Harold Noonan, *Personal Identity* (London: Routledge, 1991); John-Paul Sartre, *Being and Nothingness* (New York: Washington Square Press, 1956); Charles Taylor, 'Responsibility for the self', in Amélie Rorty, (ed.) *The Identities of Persons*, pp.281-324.

10   See Marya Schechtman, 'Personal identity and the past', *Philosophy, Psychiatry and Psychology*, vol. 12, no.1, (2005), pp.9-22. For responses, see Grant Gillet, 'Schechtman's narrative account of identity', *Philosophy, Psychiatry and Psychology*, vol. 12, no.1, (2005), pp.23-24 and Markus L. A. Heinimaa, 'Past personal identity', *Philosophy, Psychiatry and Psychology*, vol. 12, no.1, (2005), pp.25-26.

11   Schechtman in the preface to her book expresses her disappointment with analytical philosophy's inability to apply "rigorous standards of argument and investigation to basic problems of human existence." The work of theorists addresses concerns that "seem far removed from the compelling identity issues familiar to us from lived experience, psychology, and literature." Finally, she writes: "Here I focus on our experience of life as lived history, investigating how personal identity is linked to the capacity to construct coherent autobiographical narratives and to enter into the activities and social interactions that define the lives of persons." *Constitution*, p.ix.

12   Ibid., pp.1f.

13   Ibid., p.2.

14   Ibid., pp.67f.

15   Ibid., p.68.

16   Ibid., pp.34, 36.

17   "Indeed, the Lockean puzzle cases indicate that much of the importance we attach to biological survival is parasitic on the more fundamental importance of psychological survival." Ibid., p.87.

18   Noonan, *Personal Identity*, p.9.

19 For example, Schechtman writes: "A bartender may be interested in determining whether the body before him is really the same one born twenty-one years ago because he is worried about legalities. But the law that requires a person to be twenty-one years old in order to drink is based on the idea that under normal conditions there is a rough connection between age of a body and the maturity of the subject associated with it." Schechtman, *Constitution*, p.69.

20 However, it is true that certain physical attributes can provide information about one's character and beliefs. The reidentification question tells us how to identify al-Faruqi in either/or terms. Either this person is al-Faruqi or it is not. For example, either a photograph is a picture of him or it is not. We can see his eye colour, the shape of his face, his stature, recognise his voice and even recognise pictures of him when he was a young man. What the reidentification question cannot answer are the questions about who he was as a person, scholar, mentor, and so on. These involve elements of value, belief, desire and are not either/or questions, but questions of degrees. More will be discussed regarding this further along in the study.

21 Schechtman, *Constitution*, p.25. Absent from this list are the more esoteric features such as spirit or soul, which remain under the purview of metaphysics and theology.

22 Ibid.

23 Ibid., p.73.

24 Ibid., p.74.

25 Ibid., pp.76f.

26 Ibid., p.87.

27 Ibid., pp.80f.

28 Ibid., pp.82-85.

29 Ibid., p.86.

30 Ibid., p.93. Among those who argue that persons are self-creating are: John-Paul Sartre, *Being and Nothingness*; Harry Frankfurt, 'Identification and externality'; Daniel Dennett, *Elbow Room: Varieties of Free Will Worth Wanting* (Cambridge: MIT Press, 1990), pp.74-100. Theorists who favour the idea that the lives of people are narrative in form are: Alasdair MacIntyre, "The virtues, the unity of a human life, and the concept of a tradition"; Jerome Bruner, *Acts of Meaning* (Cambridge: Cambridge University Press, 1990); Mark Freeman, *Rewriting the Self: History, Memory, Narrative* (London: Routledge, 1993).

31 Schechtman, *Constitution*, p.93.

32 Ibid., p.95.

33 Ibid.

34 Ibid., p.98. One may object that this assumes every culture and language constructs identity in the same ways. Schechtman's theory is sufficiently broad to account for personal identity within different cultures and it is not necessarily symptomatic of an individualistic society such as the

United States. Despite this assertion, her work was not framed to account for identity in different cultures. For the purposes of this study, al-Faruqi came to live in the U.S. and his identity was shaped by this host society. In this way Schechtman's work is applicable.

35   Bruner, *Acts of Meaning*, pp.43f.
36   Schechtman, *Constitution*, p.112.
37   Ibid., p.142.
38   Ibid., pp.114-130.
39   This applies equally to those writing autobiographies. Each of us has blind spots in which we are unable to see ourselves objectively. We may have forgotten parts of our history or desired to forget painful periods or even remember events incorrectly because they suit the self-image or self-conception we hold. It can be quite a revelation to discover you are not the person that you think you are.
40   Esposito, 'Teaching Islam the old fashioned way', p.49.
41   Al-Faruqi, 'Self-portrait', p.6.
42   "So al-Faruqi seemed to experience stages or steps of self identity and not a process of hybridization. It appears almost as complete discrete movements." Ghamari-Tabrizi, 'Muslim diaspora in North America', p.69.
43   Altalib interview (IIIT Herndon, VA, 29 October 2007). Also al-Faruqi while at CIIR wrote a letter (1 December 1961) in which he explained the need to increase the work hours for the faculty, library and students. PPBox 1964.
44   There is no indication how he learned English. This likely happened at the American University of Beirut.
45   Rahman, 'Palestine and my experiences with the young Fārūqī', p.40. Cragg, 'Ismāʿīl al-Fārūqī in the field of dialogue', p.400.
46   Quraishi, 'The legacy of Ismaʿil al-Fārūqī', p.32.
47   Maysam al-Faruqi, 'Tawhid: the measure of a life', *Islamic Horizons*, vol. 15, (special issue August-September, 1986), p.47.
48   Ibid.
49   Personal interview with Hasan Hanafi (University of North Carolina, Chapel Hill, 7 April 2007). Hanafi first met Ismaʿil in 1968 when al-Faruqi delivered a number of lectures at Cairo University and thereafter began a lifelong friendship. One result was Hanafi becoming a Visiting Professor at Temple from 1971-1975.
50   Al-Faruqi, 'Self-portrait', p.6.
51   Ghamari-Tabrizi, 'Muslim diaspora in North America', p.67.
52   Esposito, 'Ismail R. al-Faruqi: Muslim scholar-activist', p.72.
53   Ibid., p.67.
54   Ibid., p.66.
55   See Chapter Six for a critique of the theory of *'Urūbah*. Al-Faruqi in response to a critique of his Arabism theory pointed out that various scholars in Pakistan and Egypt eventually accepted his theory. PPBox 1963. However, it remains unclear who actually accepted his theory.

56 Rahman, 'Palestine and my experiences with the young Fārūqī', p.39.
57 Ibid., p.42.
58 Ibid., p.41.
59 Isma'il al-Faruqi, 'Muḥāḍarāt fī Ta'rīkh al-Adyān' (Lectures on the History of Religions), pp.65-74. Fazlur Rahman also comments that while he delivered lectures on Islam, al-Faruqi did the same on Arabism. Rahman, 'Palestine and my experiences with the young Fārūqī', p.41.
60 Al-Faruqi, *Christian Ethics*, p.vi.
61 Rahman, 'Palestine and my experiences with the young Fārūqī', p.39.
62 Ibid., pp.39f.
63 Ibid., p.40.
64 Esposito interview (Georgetown University, 30 October 2007).
65 Rahman, 'Palestine and my experiences with the young Fārūqī', p.40.
66 Ibid.
67 Ghamari-Tabrizi, 'Muslim diaspora in North America', p.67.
68 Rahman, 'Palestine and my experiences with the young Fārūqī', p.42.
69 Esposito, 'Ismail R. al-Faruqi: Muslim scholar-activist', p.72.
70 Isma'il al-Faruqi, *Al-Tawḥīd: Its Implications for Thought and Life* (Kuala Lumpur: IIIT, 1982; 2nd edition Herndon: IIIT, 1992), p.20.
71 See al-Faruqi's answers to questions about his Arabism put to him by Stanley Frost. Ataullah Siddiqui, 'Ismail R. al-Faruqi: From 'Urubah to Ummatic concerns', *AJISS*, vol. 16, no. 3 (1999), pp.4-6.
72 Shafiq, *Growth of Islamic Thought in North America*, p.20.
73 Ghamari-Tabrizi, 'Muslim diaspora in North America', p.70.
74 Quraishi, 'The legacy of Isma'il al-Fārūqī', p.32.
75 Ba-Yunus, 'Al-Faruqi and beyond', p.14.
76 Quraishi, *Ismail al-Faruqi: An Enduring Legacy*, p.9.
77 Ibid., p.i.
78 Ghamari-Tabrizi, 'Muslim diaspora in North America', p.70.
79 However, as Ghamari-Tabrizi notes, al-Faruqi's project of a homogenous *ummah* ultimately failed because it did not correspond to the real-life experiences of Muslims of the West. He neglected the international diversity of Muslims and this is reflected in the *ummahs* they chose to create and live within despite the common faith elements shared by all Muslims. Ghamari-Tabrizi, 'Muslim diaspora in North America', p.61.
80 Ba-Yunus, 'Al-Faruqi and beyond', p.14.
81 Esposito, 'Ismail R. al-Faruqi: Muslim scholar-activist', p.72.
82 Esposito, 'Teaching Islam the old fashioned way', p.51.
83 Esposito interview (Georgetown University, October 30, 2007).
84 Shafiq, *Growth of Islamic Thought in North America*, pp.37f; Esposito, 'Teaching Islam', p.49; Quraishi, 'The legacy of Isma'il al-Fārūqī', p.33.
85 Ghamari-Tabrizi, 'Loving America and longing for home', p.66.
86 Quraishi, *Ismail al-Faruqi: An Enduring Legacy*, p.12. Shafiq also comments: "Al Faruqi paid special attention to Muslim students. He advised them on

what courses to take, kept himself informed of their progress, and sometimes even checked their assignments and read their papers, all the while showing them how their work could be improved. He was not content with average performance – if a student received a "C," he would say that he or she "had brought shame to all of us"- and continually encouraged them to work harder in courses taught by non-Muslim professors. ... If a Muslim student was not doing his utmost to acquire an education, or if he was neglecting his practice of Islam, al Faruqi would not encourage him to remain at Temple." Shafiq, *Growth of Islamic Thought in North America,* p.37.

87   One example of the level of his interest is reflected in a series of subscription requests in 1962 for the *Journal of Theological Studies*, the *Canadian Theological Journal*, *Interpretation*, and the *Harvard Theological Review*. PPBox 1964.

88   Schechtman, *Constitution*, p.87.

89   Maysam al-Faruqi, 'Tawhid', p.47.

90   Ghamari-Tabrizi, 'Muslim diaspora in North America', p.76.

91   Isma'il al-Faruqi, 'Da'wah in the West: Promise and trial', Paper presented at the International Conference of the 15th Century *Hijrah*, held at Kuala Lumpur, Malaysia, 24 November – 4 December 1981. Reprinted in Siddiqui, (ed.) *Ismail Raji al-Faruqi*, pp.319-351.

92   About un-Islamic émigrés, he writes: "In most cases, they are beggars at the western altar of knowledge; or receivers at those of western affluence and economic development. This is not a foreigner's judgement; but the way Muslim immigrants see themselves. To see themselves in this light is typical of the mentality of immigrants." al-Faruqi, "Da'wah in the West," 331. He also quite pointedly includes the following: "That is also why the immigrant is necessarily a parasite to the country that adopts him, regardless of his productiveness. Whether such production is physical or professional, the immigrant's labour is an arithmetical addition to the country's production. His contribution merely increases what is already there, even if it consists of pure research in a laboratory or library. That he has fitted himself into it is the assumption of his employment, and the guarantee of his success. The immigrant's adjustment to his adoptive country and culture signifies this recognition of and acquiescence to the latter's superiority. The immigrant may be able to invent a new tool or machine, discover new facts, or originate a new way of doing things or solving problems. But as to ability to turn the country and its culture to a radically new orientation, and hence to the exploration of horizons genuinely new, the immigrant has none. *Ex hypothesis* he is devoid of other horizons, incapable of rising above the country and its culture to a vantage point from which to see other horizons. For, as an immigrant, he is *of* the old country though presently not *from* the new country, though not quite *of* it. The adoptive country accepts him with its hopes pinned on his

children; or better, grandchildren. In himself, he is a liability; at best, mere material or instrument for its own predetermined march." al-Faruqi, 'Da'wah in the West', p.332.

93 The untrained immigrant is seen by al-Faruqi as being exploited by the Western host as cheap labour. He even sees duplicity in the Church's reaction. He scornfully writes:
"In these circumstances, the advocates of the Christian Church, rejected by their own Western élites, approach the Muslim *déraciné* with their missionary bait. Not that they are truly concerned about his miserable plight and seek to change it, but that they offer it to dampen and silence his rebelling conscience, to cause him to resign to his sad fate as that of a humanity waiting to be ransomed by a crucified god." Ibid., p.335.

94 Ibid., p.345.

95 On this subject he complains: "How many Muslim babies have to be born, how many have to be nursed and sustained, how many have to be fed and protected while going to elementary and secondary school and college – and how many of these succeed through all these stages sufficiently to enter the professions? How many parents, guardians, governments and institutions have to spend in energy and care, and how much has the ummah to spend of its material resources to send one doctor or engineer to professional school or higher educational institution? In short, how many Muslims have to die – yes, do die! – that one Ph.D., M.D. or engineer may be produced? Such a final product of inestimable value is the Muslim immigrant whom the Muslim world presents to America or Europe on a silver platter – free, absolutely free of charge! The West itself would have had to spend the same amounts of everything, if not ten times more, to produce such a creature out of its own population. Now it is getting that person as a free gift. The whole Muslim world is pouring its 'human butter' into the jars of America and Europe, and it is doing so in the constant flow that is known as the 'brain drain'." Ibid., p.333.

96 Ibid., p.334.

97 Ibid., p.343.

98 Ibid., pp.338f.

99 Ibid., p.339.

100 Six elements are identified by al-Faruqi as achievements of the 'Vision of Islam'. These are 1) Islamic vision can remove possible feelings of guilt which were created by leaving one's homeland; 2) Islamic vision can remove the sense of guilt due to success in one's new life in which the *muhājir* may be overwhelmed by feelings of gratitude to his new country forgetting that success is from God not his host country; 3) Islamic vision provides a new challenge and promise to exercise *da'wah*; 4) Islamic vision provides criteria with which to understand, judge and seek to transform North America and the West; 5) Islamic vision provides love and desire to

see North America and the West transformed by God; and, 6) Islamic vision provides a sense of mission. Ibid., pp.340-342.

101 Al-Faruqi advocates a succinct view of students studying in the West. In essence, they are not serving themselves but the *ummah*. Therefore they should view themselves as the 'last of their species' meaning they are sent to acquire all the available knowledge so that they can return, teach it to the *ummah* in such a way that there no longer remains the need to send another student to the West. Ibid., p.343.

102 Jane I. Smith, *Muslims, Christians and the Challenge of Interfaith Dialogue*, p.125.

103 Al-Faruqi, 'Islam and Christianity: Diatribe or dialogue', p.248.

104 Louis Moore, 'Christian and Moslem workshop at Rice/Visionaries look to future of understanding', *Houston Chronicle* 1 Star, 12 April 1986 *Factiva* (25 May 2010) <http://global.factiva.com/aa/?ref=hou0000020011119di4c00 fx1>.

105 Shafiq, p.xvii.

106 Ghamari-Tabrizi, 'Muslim diaspora in North America', p.66, 70. See also Ba-Yunus, 'Al-Faruqi and beyond', p.25.

107 Schechtman, *Constitution*, pp.82-85.

108 Al-Faruqi, *Christian Ethics*, p.v.

109 Aside from interfaith issues, al-Faruqi displayed interest in addressing the many problems in the Islamic world especially in education and among young Muslim students in America and elsewhere. Basically this can generally be placed under the Islamization of knowledge project.

110 Nasr, 'The essence of Dr. Faruqi's life work', *Islamic Horizons*, vol. 15 (Special issue August–September, 1986)', p.26.

111 Esposito, 'Ismail R. al-Faruqi: Muslim scholar-activist', p.76.

112 Al-Faruqi, *Trialogue*, p.xi.

113 Dr. Esposito confirmed this observation. He notes how al-Faruqi enjoyed being a world Muslim leader and how, along with Fazlur Rahman and Seyyed Hossein Nasr, he was one of the "big three in the West for Islam." Esposito interview (Georgetown University, 30 October 2007).

114 Halide Salam, 'Lamya': A tribute to a friend', *Islamic Horizons* 15, (special issue August-September, 1986), p.45.

115 PPBox 1978.

116 Ghamari-Tabrizi, 'Muslim diaspora in North America', p.62.

117 PPBox #1 1979.

118 Quraishi notes: "What made al-Faruqi so important to the community in Philadelphia was his cementing role, his ability to maintain personal contact with everyone." Quraishi, *Ismail al-Faruqi: An Enduring Legacy*, p.10.

119 Esposito, 'Ismail R. al-Faruqi: Muslim scholar-activist', p.64.

120 Nasr, 'The essence of Dr. Faruqi's life work', p.26.

121 Ghamari-Tabrizi, 'Muslim diaspora in North America', p.66.

122 Maysam al-Faruqi, 'Tawhid', p.47.

123 The interpretations of Dr. al-Faruqi's identity by others need not be seen as alternative or in competition to that of his own self-conception. As Schechtman has explained, one's self-narrative is bounded by the restraints of fact and interpretation confirmed by the perspectives of others who know the person. Therefore, the few perspectives offered help to fine tune and confirm his presentation of himself.

124 Ghamari-Tabrizi, 'Muslim diaspora in North America', p.72.

Chapter Three

1 Cragg writes: "The trauma of those events needs to be understood in any reckoning with his religious thought." Cragg, 'Isma'il Al-Faruqi', p.128.

2 For a comprehensive survey of the history of the study of religion, see Jacques Waardenburg, ed., *Classical Approaches to the Study of Religion* 2 vols. (The Hague: Mouton, 1973).

3 Al-Faruqi, *On Justifying the Good*, p.iv.

4 Ibid., pp.vi, ix-x.

5 Al-Faruqi, 'History of Religions', pp.168-170.

6 Ibid., pp.176-183.

7 Al-Faruqi, *Christian Ethics*, pp.1-49.

8 Al-Faruqi, 'Muḥāḍarāt', p.65. See also R. Arnaldez, 'Ibn Ḥazm, Abū Muḥammad ʿAlī b. Aḥmad b. Saʿīd', *Encyclopaedia of Islam* 2nd edition. Edited by: P. Bearman, Th. Bianquis , C.E. Bosworth , E. van Donzel and W.P. Heinrichs. Brill, 2007. Brill Online. McGill University. (28 June 2013) <http://referenceworks.brillonline.com/entries/encyclopaedia-of-islam-2/ibn-hazm-COM_0325>.

9 Al-Faruqi, *Christian Ethics*, p.viii.

10 Ibid., pp.3-11.

11 Ibid., pp.21-32.

12 Ibid., p.10.

13 Ibid., pp.4, 8.

14 Al-Faruqi, 'Meta-Religion: Towards a critical world theology', p.20. This article was originally read as a paper at the Third International Conference on Islamic Thought held in January 1982 in Islamabad, Pakistan, but published in 1986.

15 Al-Faruqi and Lois Lamyaʾ al-Faruqi, *The Cultural Atlas of Islam*, p.xii.

16 For more detailed information on the rise of the ecumenical movement, see John Azuma, 'The integrity of interfaith dialogue', *ICMR*, vol. 13, no. 3, (2002), pp.269-280; Jacques Waardenburg, 'Muslims and Christians: Changing identities', *ICMR*, vol. 11, no. 2, (2000), pp.149-162; N. Goodall, *The Ecumenical Movement* (Oxford: Oxford University Press, 1966); Pierce R. Beaver, *Ecumenical Beginnings in Protestant World Mission* (New York: Nelson, 1962).

17 Zebiri, *Muslims and Christians Face to Face*, p.7.

18   Max Scheler, *On the Eternal Man* translated by Bernard Noble (London: SCM Press, 1960); idem, *Man's Place in Nature* translated and introduction by Hans Meyerhoff (Boston: Beacon Press, 1961); idem, *Formalism in Ethics and Non-Formal Ethics of Value: A New Attempt Toward the Foundation of an Ethical Personalism* 5th revised edition, translated by Manfred S. Frings and Roger L. Funk (Evanston: Northwestern University Press, 1973); Nicolai Hartmann, *Ethics* 3 vol., translated by Stanton Loit (London: Allen, 1932); idem, *New Ways of Ontology* translated by Reinhard C. Kuhn (Chicago: Henry Regency, 1952).

19   The basic question of his dissertation was: How can the good be known? He spent some effort to address what he considered to be obstacles to the understanding of 'the good' of which he labelled as fallacies.

20   Isma'il al-Faruqi, *On Justifying the Good: Metaphysics and Epistemology of Value* (Unpublished Ph.D. Dissertation, IN: University of Indiana, 1952), p.v.

21   G. E. Moore, *Principia Ethica,* rev. ed., edited and with an introduction by Thomas Baldwin. (Cambridge: Cambridge University Press, 1993). Moore discusses the naturalistic fallacy in the first four chapters of his book. However, in his preface to the second edition, Moore discusses the lack of clarity in his use of 'good' and the consequent problems this created for his theory of naturalistic fallacy. He mentioned that the term 'good' is ambiguous and his assertion that 'good' is indefinable is only one of its many possible predicates. He notes that there is no simple answer to the question: "What is the naturalistic fallacy?" He outlined three possibilities: 1) Identifying goodness with some predicate other than goodness; 2) Identifying goodness with some analyzable predicate; 3) Identifying goodness with some natural or meta-physical predicate. Moore retained the idea that goodness is a fundamental ethical concept, but expressed some uncertainty whether it is 'unanalyzable.' (Moore, 'Preface to second edition', pp.3-27). Oliver Curry also points out that there is more than one naturalistic fallacy. He lists eight versions including Moore's (identifying good with its object) and Hume's (moving from *is* to *ought*). Oliver Curry, 'Who's afraid of the naturalistic fallacy?', *Evolutionary Psychology*, vol. 4 (2006), pp.234-247; See also William K. Frankena, 'The naturalistic fallacy', *Mind*, New Series, vol. 48, no. 192 (October, 1939), pp.464-477.

22   Moore, *Principia Ethica*, p.61 (Section 10, paragraph 1).

23   Ibid., p.64 (Section 12).

24   Ibid., pp.59f (Section 7).

25   Ibid., pp.3-16.

26   Moore wrote: "... and what is the naturalistic fallacy? These are questions as to which I am very confused in the book; and, though I cannot undertake to expose all the confusions of which I am guilty with regard to them, I think it will be useful to try to make some points clear." Moore, *Principia Ethica*, p.16.

27 1) Identifying goodness with some predicate other than goodness (that is goodness is a fundamental ethical concept); 2) Identifying goodness with some analyzable predicate; 3) Identifying goodness with some natural or metaphysical predicate. Ibid., pp.16-27.

28 Writing several years later, al-Faruqi expressed some critique over Moore's example of colour in his explanation of value as a simple, irreducible quality. He felt that such a description failed to 'explain why such a quality as goodness should be so unlike all other attributes.' In other words, it fails to explain why goodness as a value is unique. According to al-Faruqi, value and colour are not in the same class or category. He offered no further elaboration on this viewpoint. However, he did continue to appeal to the naturalist fallacy. Al-Faruqi, *On Arabism*, p.254.

29 Hume writes: "In every system of morality, which I have hitherto met with, I have always remark'd, that the author proceeds for some time in the ordinary way of reasoning, and establishes the being of a God, or makes observations concerning human affairs; when of a sudden I am surpriz'd to find, that instead of the usual copulations of propositions, *is*, and *is not*, I meet with no proposition that is not connected with an *ought*, or an *ought not*. This change is imperceptible; but is, however, of the last consequence. For as this *ought*, or *ought not*, expresses some new relation or affirmation, 'tis necessary that it shou'd be observ'd and explain'd; and at the same time that a reason should be given, for what seems altogether inconceivable, how this new relation can be a deduction from others, which are entirely different from it." David Hume, *A Treatise of Human Nature*, Edited with an introduction by Ernest C. Mossner (New York: Penguin Books, 1985, c1969), [Book III, Part I, section I], p.521.

30 Aside from his Ph.D. thesis on value, he reiterated his understanding of value in his first book, *On Arabism*, where he discusses the existence, knowability and realization of value in this world. *On Arabism*, pp.253-270.

31 Al-Faruqi, *On Justifying the Good*, p.5. See also A. P. Brogan, 'Objective pluralism in the theory of value', *International Journal of Ethics*, vol. 41, no. 3, (April 1931), pp.287-295.

32 The debate over monistic axiology continues. Brand-Ballard goes on to analyse Brad Hooker's defence of monism in his book *Ideal Code, Real World* (Oxford: Oxford University Press, 2000). See Jeffery Brand-Ballard, 'Why one basic principle?', *Utilitas*, vol. 19, no. 2, (June 2007), pp.220-242.

33 Brand-Ballard, 'Why one basic principle?', p.220.

34 Al-Faruqi, *On Justifying the Good*, p.v.

35 Ibid., pp.1f.

36 Citing Kant's contribution of describing 'moral law' as a 'fact of reason,' al-Faruqi agreed with Hartmann that value is a genuine 'Prime Mover' in the Aristotelian sense and that "this 'fact of reason' is really only the fact of the a priori emotional intuition of value." Al-Faruqi, *On Arabism*, pp.257, 262.

For the former and latter ideas of Hartmann, al-Faruqi cited Hartmann, *Ethics*, vol.1, pp.239-241 and pp.176-179 respectively.

37 Al-Faruqi, *On Justifying the Good*, p.vi. Al-Faruqi's use of the expression 'order out in a system' is unclear. He may have meant arranging value in terms of a hierarchy, that is some values are placed above others, and hence the following statement of 'reveal the relations' would apply to determining the relative position of the valuableness between different values.

38 Hartmann, *Ethics*, vol.1, pp.183-244.

39 Al-Faruqi, *On Justifying the Good*, pp.vi-vii. See also Hartmann, *Ethics*, vol.1, pp.239-241.

40 Al-Faruqi, *On Justifying the Good*, p.xi. See also Hartmann, *Ethics*, vol.1, pp.223-224 and pp.99ff.

41 Al-Faruqi. *On Justifying the Good*, p.xiv.

42 Ibid.

43 Ibid., p.280.

44 Ibid., p.302.

45 Plato and Aristophanes. *Four texts on Socrates: Plato's Euthyphro, Apology, and Crito, and Aristophanes' Clouds* translated with notes by Thomas G. West and Grace Starry West; introduction by Thomas G. West. (Ithaca, NY: Cornell University Press, 1998), pp.41-61.

46 See Daniel Gimaret, 'Mu'tazila', *Encyclopaedia of Islam*. 2nd edition. Brill Online. McGill University. (28 June 2013) <http://referenceworks. brillonline.com/entries/encyclopaedia-of-islam-2/mutazila-COM_0822>. For a comprehensive analysis of Mu'tazilites in history and its subsequent reappearance in the twentieth century see Rudi Caspar, 'Un aspect de la pensée Musulmane moderne: Le renouveau du Mo'tazilisme', *Mélanges Institut Dominicain d'études Orientales du Caire*, vol. 4 (1957), pp.141-202. See also Detlev Khalid, 'Some aspects of neo-Mu'tazilism', *Islamic Studies*, vol. 8, no. 4 (December, 1969), pp.319-348.

47 Richard C. Martin, Mark R. Woodward and Dwi S. Atmaja, *Defenders of Reason in Islam* (Oxford: Oneworld, 1997), p.16.

48 Ibid., 16.

49 Cook discusses in considerable detail Mu'tazilite and Hanbalite positions on the question of commanding the good and forbidding the wrong. Michael Cook, *Commanding Right and Forbidding Wrong in Islamic Thought* (Cambridge: Cambridge University Press, 2000), pp.87-192 (Hanbalites); pp.195-226 (Mu'tazilites).

50 The idea that God defines ultimate value is a Hanbalite position, since God determines value. However, al-Faruqi took elements from both the Hanbalite and Mu'tazilite positions.

51 Al-Faruqi, *On Arabism*, p.213. In order to explain some of his thought, we are appealing to his book which was published after his dissertation work.

52 Ibid., p.219. According to al-Faruqi, values cannot tell us about the nature
    or essence (*in esse*) of God because He is beyond human understanding and
    knowledge. However, His values can tell us about his will and attributes,
    which we can perceive (*in percipi*).
53 "God's attributes are precisely values." Ibid., p.220.
54 See Ahmad Amin, *Ḍuḥā al-Islām* (al-Qāhirah: Matbaʿat Lajnat al-Taʾlīf wa-al-
    Tarjamah wa-al-Nashr, 1952), pp.47-49.
55 Muhammad ʿAbduh, *The Theology of Unity*, translated by Isḥāq Musaʿad and
    Kenneth Cragg (London: George Allen & Unwin, 1966).
56 Al-Faruqi, *On Arabism*, pp.162, 251.
57 Maysam al-Faruqi, 'Tawḥīd', p.47.
58 Al-Faruqi, 'Muḥāḍarāt', pp.65-74.
59 In the second lecture ('Muḥāḍarāt', pp.67f), al-Faruqi mentioned Smith by
    name and openly opposed his views on the relationship of essence and
    religion. Further, it seems unlikely, but not impossible that al-Faruqi
    studied the history of religions at al-Azhar. For example he may have
    studied Ibn Ḥazm's *Kitāb al-Faṣl fī al-Milal wa-al-Aḥwāʾ wa al-Niḥal*. It seems
    more likely that he was exposed to the western tradition of the history of
    religions at McGill. This probability increases when one considers W. C.
    Smith's prominence and influence as a theorist of comparative religion.
60 Lecture One in 'Muḥāḍarāt', p.65.
61 Ibid., p.66. "Yajduru binā an natafahhama adyāna hadhihi al-ʿawālim li-
    natafahhama al-quwā al-muḥarrika fīhā li-natafahhama manṭiqa
    thaqāfatihā."
62 Lecture Two in 'Muḥāḍarāt', pp.67f.
63 Al-Faruqi, 'Meta-Religion: Towards a critical world theology', p.20.
64 Al-Faruqi. *Christian Ethics*, p.viii.
65 Lecture Two in 'Muḥāḍarāt', p.68. "Liʿilmi al-adyāni an yadrusahu wa
    yatabayyanu al-quwā al-muḥarrikati fīhī wa zawāhiruhā wa natāʾijuha. Wa
    in faʿala dhalika fa-inahu yastaṭīʿu tawjīha al-majrā ilā ḥaythu yurīdu aw
    ʿalā al-aqalli an yuʾaththiru fī ittijāhi al-majrā aw yatanibbʾa bihi. Wa al-
    ḍaʿfu al-akbaru fī hadhā al-madhhabu anahu yunkiru ana lil-dīni jawhar aw
    dhāt. Wa lakin, kayfa lahu faṣlu al-zawāhiri ʿan baʿḍahā al-baʿḍ wa farzu mā
    huwa dīnī minhā thumma farzu al-zawāhiri al-dīnīya ʿan baʿḍihā al-baʿḍ li-
    maʿrifati mā huwa būdhī wa hindūkī wa islamī wa masīḥī minhā? Lā budda
    lahu idān min an yaftariḍa khilsatan mā yunkiruhu ʿalaniyyan."
66 Ibid. The reasons for accepting the historical method are: 1) It accepts the
    data provided by all the other descriptive methods; 2) It accepts logic and
    reason as tools to reach truth; 3) It preserves the essence and divine nature
    of religion as something which is not the product of humanity; 4) It
    assumes religions have history and they develop; 5) It accepts the
    testimony religious people have about their own religion; 6) It accepts that
    each religion has unique phenomena.

67 Later in 1973, al-Faruqi formally critiqued Smith's position that Islam lacked an essence. See Isma'il al-Faruqi, 'Essence of Religious Experience in Islam', *Numen*, vol. 20, no. 3, (1973), pp.186-201. Reprinted in Siddiqui, (ed.) *Ismail Raji al-Faruqi*, pp.3-20.

68 Al-Faruqi, 'Meta-Religion: Towards a critical world theology', p.19.

69 Lecture Three in 'Muḥāḍarāt', p.68.

70 Ibid., p.70.

71 Lecture Four in 'Muḥāḍarāt', p.70. The five metaphysical elements are: 1) The otherness of God; 2) The connection between the other world and the created world; 3) The necessary is obligatory; 4) Whatever happens is the best; 5) The potential of improvement.

72 Ibid., p.71. He goes on to note that Muslims have left the pre-*hijrah* study to westerners who cannot be expected to treat it honestly. Later in 1962, al-Faruqi addressed this question in his article 'Towards a historiography of pre-Hijrah Islam', *Islamic Studies*, vol. 1, no. 2, (1962), pp.65-87.

73 Lecture Four in 'Muḥāḍarāt', p.71.

74 Lecture Five in 'Muḥāḍarāt', p.72.

75 Ibid., p.73.

76 Ibid.

77 Ibid.

78 Ideas such as the essence of religion, the five periods of Arab religious history, the use of *epoché* and the stream of Arab religiosity identifiable within history are all themes that continue in his later works.

79 Al-Faruqi, *On Arabism*, p.ix.

80 Ibid.

81 Ibid.

82 This interpretation and use of Ḥunafāʾ differs from that of Husayn Muroeh (1910-1986). Writing in Lebanon in the late 1960's, Muroeh investigated Islamic history in his book *Al-Nazaʿāt al-Māddiyya fī al-Falsafa al-ʿArabiyya al-Islāmiyya* (Material Tendencies in Arab-Islamic Philosophy) 2 vols. (Beirut: Dār al-Fārābī, 1988). He limited the Ḥunafāʾ to the pre-Islamic period and, according to Rula Abisaab, defined this collection of people as a "religious-speculative trend rising in the milieu of an agricultural area like al-Yamama which drew to it proselytes from among the stable communities of the Peninsula, particularly Mecca." This was a period of transition from pagan to monotheism situated within a social history and political economy reflecting a series of adaptations of Jewish and Christian belief. The Ḥunafāʾ eventually gave way to the emergence of Islam. Unlike al-Faruqi, Muroeh did not make ḥunafāʾ applicable to anyone, but only to those who lived in a specific area in the pre-Islamic period. Thank you to Dr. Rula Abisaab for drawing my attention to her work on Ḥusayn Muroeh who was a contemporary of al-Faruqi. The above quotation is from her unpublished essay 'Beyond the modular and the authentic: Early Islamic

history according to Ḥusayn Muroeh', Institute of Islamic Studies, McGill University, 2008.

83 Al-Faruqi, *On Arabism*, pp.2f.

84 See Lecture Five in 'Muḥāḍarāt', p.73.

85 Al-Faruqi, *On Arabism*, p.3.

86 Ibid., p.5. It appears that the use of 'Arab' in this verse does not refer to the way al-Faruqi earlier defined Arab yet he does not make this entirely clear. At times he tends to use 'Arab' to refer to an ethnic people who in this case received the Qur'ān, but elsewhere he attempted to say the word 'Arab' meant much more. For a full discussion about how this verse was interpreted and applied, see Michael Cook's *Commanding Right and Forbidding Wrong in Islamic Thought*.

87 Ibid., p.6.

88 Ibid., p.12.

89 Ibid., p.11.

90 For a concise investigation into the forces and scholarship underlying the development of the terms Aryan and Semitic up to 1892 (death of Renan), see Maurice Olender, *The Languages of Paradise: Race, Religion and Philology in the Nineteenth Century*, translated by Arthur Goldhammer (Cambridge, Massachusetts: Harvard University Press, 1992). Originally published as *Les langues du Paradis: Aryens et Sémites, un couple providential* (Paris: Gallimard le Seuil, 1989).

91 Ernest Renan, *Histoire générale et system comparé des langages sémtiques* (Paris: Calmann-Lévy, 1877), p.14.

92 Olender, *The Languages of Paradise*, p.55.

93 Ernest Renan, *Studies in Religious History* (London: Mathieson & Co., 1895), p.61.

94 Ibid., p.62.

95 Ibid.

96 Ernest Renan, 'Nouvelles considérations sur le caractère general des peoples sémitiques, et en particulier sur leur tendance au monothéisme', *Journal Asiatique* (1859), pp.214-282 and pp.417-450.

97 Renan's *The History of the Origins of Christianity* (London: Mathieson & Co., n.d.) is cited by al-Faruqi, *On Arabism*, p.72.

98 Al-Faruqi did not abandon the use of Semitic and sometimes used Semitic and Arab interchangeably.

99 Al-Faruqi, *On Arabism*, pp.2f.

100 Ernest Renan, *Oeuvres complètes*, ed. H. Psichari, (Paris: Calmann-Lévy, 1947-1961), vol. 8, p.578.

101 Al-Faruqi, *On Arabism*, p.8.

102 Renan, *Studies in Religious History*, p.67.

103 Al-Faruqi, *On Arabism*, p.12 compare to Olender, *The Languages of Paradise*, p.14.

104 Al-Faruqi, *On Arabism*, p.11.

105 In a later article in 1964, al-Faruqi clearly states that: "Islam is a Semitic religion whose formative years were spent in Arabia, the cradle of all things Semitic." Al-Faruqi, 'History of religions', p.190.

106 Al-Faruqi's reply (9 December 1961) was to a letter from Stanley Frost, (12 September 1961). See Siddiqui, "Urubah to Ummatic concerns', pp.5f.

107 Al-Faruqi, 'History of religions', p.192 and *Al-Tawḥīd*, p.20.

108 Gil Anidjar, *Semites: Race, Religion, Literature* (Stanford, CA: Stanford University Press, 2008), p.6.

109 See lecture Two in 'Muḥāḍarāt', p.68.

110 One example is his interpretation of Genesis 34: 1-34. Al-Faruqi, *On Arabism*, pp.31-37.

111 Al-Faruqi, *On Arabism*, p.16.

112 Ibid., pp.16f.

113 Ibid., 17.

114 Ibid., p.58.

115 In order to discover the essence of Christianity, al-Faruqi proposed two tests. The first was to examine in a patient, scholarly and unbiased way all the utterances of Jesus in the Gospels in order to group these into categories that are internally coherent according to moral and common sense. The second test was to determine if these categories of sayings are coherent with the history of revelation. He added two caveats. One must, historically speaking, consider the results of scholarly research in Biblical history and archaeology and one must, religiously speaking, accept that the prophets sent by God bore the same essential message. Ibid., p.62.

116 Ibid., p.63.

117 Ibid., p.64.

118 Cragg writes: "Thus he [al-Faruqi] brought an intriguing Muslim element to the long nineteenth and twentieth century 'quest for the historical Jesus', an element to which many looked eagerly during his career at McGill." Cragg, 'Isma'il Al-Faruqi', p.140.

119 Al-Faruqi, *On Arabism*, p.65.

120 Ibid., p.67.

121 The idea that Western Christianity distorted the message of Jesus was first voiced in al-Faruqi's article, 'On the significance of Reinhold Niebuhr', *Canadian Journal of Theology*, vol. 7, no. 2, (1961), pp.99-107. Reprinted in *Muslim Life*, vol. XI, no. 3 (Summer 1964), pp.5-14. He critiqued the ethics of Reinhold Niebuhr whom he saw as perpetuating Western Christianity's split personality desiring on the one hand to uphold the spirituality of Jesus while on the other upholding the materialism of the world. The essence of his critique is a rejection of Christian doctrine of sin and its effect upon human nature including the resulting societies that were created. This is treated more fully in his book *Christian Ethics*.

122 Al-Faruqi, *On Arabism*, p.94.

123 Ibid., p.200.

124 Ibid., p.207.
125 Ibid., p.198.
126 Ibid., p.220.
127 Ibid., pp.211f.
128 Ibid., p.244.
129 Ibid., p.262.
130 Ibid., p.221.

Chapter Four

1 Al-Faruqi, 'The problem of the metaphysical status of values in the western and Islamic tradition', *Studia Islamica*, vol. 28, (1968), pp.38-63.

2 The Islamization project was a means to prepare and strengthen Islam to take charge of its own destiny rather than succumb to western dictated models and assumptions of knowledge. This included the influence and impact of non-Muslim religions upon Islam as well as Islamizing education. See Cragg, 'Isma'il al-Faruqi', p.129.

3 Al-Faruqi, 'On the Raison d'être of the Ummah', *Islamic Studies*, vol. 2, no. 2, (1963), pp.159-203.

4 Ibid., pp.159f.

5 Ibid., p.162.

6 This implies that God allows evil to exist to fulfill a greater purpose in humanity.

7 Al-Faruqi, 'raison d'être', p.163.

8 Ibid., p.164.

9 Al-Faruqi, 'A comparison of the Islamic and Christian approaches to Hebrew scripture'. Reprinted in Siddiqui, (ed.) *Ismail Raji al-Faruqi*, pp.109-126. This was one of three research papers al-Faruqi wrote during his years in the Faculty of Divinity at McGill University. PPBox 1963.

10 Al-Faruqi, 'A comparison of the Islamic and Christian approaches to Hebrew scripture', p.111.

11 Ibid., p.110.

12 Ibid.

13 Ibid., p.111.

14 Ibid., p.112f.

15 By 'ideational' al-Faruqi means that Islam views revelation as ideas or concepts expressed in words and not in events. He writes: "'Thus saith the Lord' is the only form revelation can take." Ibid., p.114.

16 Ibid.

17 Ibid., p.119.

18 Ibid., p.122. It is interesting that while he criticizes Christian interpretations of the Hebrew Scriptures as dogmatic and deterministic, he views Islamic interpretations as free from dogma. He goes on to state that the Qur'ānic principle or viewpoint is that only part of the Old Testament is God's word. Thus, using an ethical approach, which is 'governed by

absolute and immutable ethical laws,' Islam can separate the ethically valid from the perverse in Hebrew Scripture. This would seem to be an Islamic reading of the Hebrew Scriptures based upon Islamic predetermined assumptions that one could argue are every bit as deterministic as his critique of Christian approaches. For some reason, he did not notice that his assertions where in fact an 'Islamized' use of the Old Testament finding support for what Islam already accepted and ignored anything else as accretions and distortions. This is evident in that he ignored Jewish interpretations of their Scripture. It is more methodologically sound to first attempt to explain Jewish interpretations of Hebrew Scriptures and then make comparisons with Christian and Muslim views.

19 The lecture, presented by al-Faruqi, was entitled 'History of religions', pp.35-65, 81-86. It was delivered to the faculty of the Divinity School at University of Chicago on 30 April 1964. During this year al-Faruqi was visiting lecturer of the History of Religion at the Divinity School.

20 Al-Faruqi, 'History of religions', p.161. Al-Faruqi does not provide a clear definition of 'meaning-wholes.' If I understand him correctly, 'meaning-wholes' refer to the process of classifying and systematizing religious data such as beliefs, rituals, terms and concepts and distilling their religious meanings which are then systematized enabling future comparison and evaluation with the 'meaning-wholes' of other religions. For his explanations, Ibid., pp.168-171.

21 Ibid., pp.161-167.

22 Ibid., pp.168-172. He writes: "It is particularly here that history of religions shows its purely scientific character. Within the one religion, the task of organizing the data into a systematic whole, of relating doctrinal, cultic, institutional, moral and artistic facts into the history of civilization concerned as a whole, is a purely scientific affair, despite the fact that the materials with which the historian of religions works are unlike those of the natural or social scientist. The scientific character of enquiry is not a function of the materials, but of what is done with them." Ibid., p.171. This last statement was criticized by a Professor Lang who commented that it is the method that gives us our data and determines the phenomenon. Thus method is a complex relationship between objectivity and the 'relatedness of the data to the interpreter'. Ibid., pp.206f, footnote, 13.

23 Ibid., p.173.

24 Ibid., pp.172-183.

25 Ibid., pp.172, 175. "There is hence no escape for history of religions from developing a system of principles of meta-religion under which the judgement and evaluation of meaning-wholes can take place." Ibid., p.176.

26 Ibid., p.177.

27 In particular his book *Christian Ethics* and his 1986 article 'Meta-Religion: Towards a critical world theology', pp.13-57.

28 Al-Faruqi, 'History of religions', pp.178-183. Meland provided a response which accompanied al-Faruqi's article in the reprinted version by Siddiqui. Meland, 'Response', pp.87-95. Reprinted in Siddiqui, (ed.) *Ismail Raji al-Faruqi*, pp.194-203.

29 Al-Faruqi, 'History of religions', p.185.

30 Ibid., pp.189-191.

31 Ibid., p.190.

32 On al-Faruqi's use of Arab and Semitic/Semite, see the discussion in Chapter Five.

33 Al-Faruqi, 'History of religions', p.191.

34 Ibid., p.192.

35 In a letter dated 17 March 1961, al-Faruqi writes that his Rockefeller grant for his project of a Muslim study of Christian ethics would end 31 December 1961. Thus, he was working hard to complete the manuscript and hand it in to the Faculty of Divinity (McGill University). PPBox 1964.

36 Al-Faruqi, *Christian Ethics*, p.3.

37 Ibid., p.8.

38 Ibid., p.4.

39 Ibid., pp.9f.

40 Ibid., p.10.

41 Ibid.

42 Ibid., pp.11-14.

43 Ibid., p.11.

44 Ibid., p.15.

45 Ibid., p.12.

46 Ibid., p.11.

47 Ibid., p.13. This idea is a foundational component of later thinkers such as Abdolkarim Soroush. Charles Fletcher, *The Methodology of Abdolkarim Soroush: A preliminary study* (Islamic Research Institute, Islamabad. Occasional Papers, no. 70), 2006. Originally published in *Islamic Studies*, vol. 44, no. 4, (2005), pp.527-552.

48 One might add that while God's commands could be understandable, it in no way follows that people can understand it perfectly or that people will, out of ignorance or desire, corrupt the meaning of God's commands.

49 Al-Faruqi, *Christian Ethics*, p.14.

50 Ibid., p.15.

51 Ibid., pp.15f.

52 Ibid., pp.16-19.

53 He is careful to discredit the idea that common findings mean common denominators that are isolated from context and then superimposed upon a religion. He writes: "Common findings of the religious experience of mankind are those religious truths which natural comprehension had found to be true, desirable, and imperative and which the religious experience of mankind has corroborated." Ibid., p.19.

54   Ibid.
55   See Chapters One and Two.
56   Al-Faruqi, *Christian Ethics*, p.19.
57   Ibid., pp.22-32.
58   Ibid., p.33. One may argue that al-Faruqi's system is not really theology-
     free for he assumes ethics, values and laws are given by God and reflect His
     will for humanity.
59   Ibid., p.22.
60   Ibid. Al-Faruqi mentioned that he would provide a full elaboration of these
     meta-religious principles in a book entitled, *A Perspective of the History of
     Religions in the Near East*, which was never published.
61   Al-Faruqi, *On Arabism*, p.253.
62   Al-Faruqi, *Christian Ethics*, p.22.
63   Al-Faruqi, *On Arabism*, p.250.
64   Ibid., p.253.
65   Ibid., p.266.
66   Ibid., p.253.
67   Ibid., p.253.
68   Al-Faruqi, *Christian Ethics*, p.23.
69   Ibid.
70   Al-Faruqi, *On Arabism*, p.258.
71   Al-Faruqi, *Christian Ethics*, p.24.
72   The broken cabinet may be valued as an antique or may retain sentimental
     value and thus for one person it may be valued higher than a beautifully
     build cabinet. Based only on functionality or appearance the beautifully
     built cabinet could be valued higher than the broken one.
73   Al-Faruqi, *Christian Ethics*, pp.24-26.
74   Ibid., p.25.
75   Ibid., p.26.
76   Ibid., p.25.
77   Ibid., p.26.
78   Ibid., pp.27f.
79   Ibid., p.27.
80   Ibid.
81   Ibid., p.28.
82   Ibid.
83   Ibid., pp.28-30.
84   Of course even in the act of flight, the object is subject to gravity, unless
     the object leaves the earth's gravitational field.
85   Al-Faruqi, *Christian Ethics*, p.30.
86   Ibid., pp.30-32.
87   Ibid., p.30.
88   One may reply that it is God who determines value. In the book of Genesis
     God made the world and 'declared it good.' Therefore, the value of the

world in its actual form and not just in the ideal is independent of humanity. It is not known how this fits with al-Faruqi's assertion that humanity is given the task to realize the value that God has set in the ideal realm allowing man to bring it about as it were in the actual realm of reality. Can something be good and beautiful in the actual realm without the presence of people? For example, the discovery of the beauty and wonder of life in the ocean depths only recently available to people does not mean that such beauty did not already exist. It only means that we can now appreciate and label it as such. For God who created, was not this always valuable?

89 Al-Faruqi, *Christian Ethics*, p.30.
90 Ibid., p.31.
91 Ibid.
92 Ibid.
93 Al-Faruqi writes that the last principle is "... to obey God's command, to perfect His creation is to be moral and thus to fulfill the requisites of the human viceregency of God on earth." Ibid.
94 Ibid., p.34.
95 Ibid., p.31.
96 Ibid.
97 Ibid., p.52. In his opinion, the Hebrews sought to value population and politics, which is the racial and ethnic purity as God's chosen people. "For them, human life was valueless unless it carried their own political idea." According to al-Faruqi, in contrast, the Hebrews valued community higher than individuals and emphasized the Torah law more than moral law. Ibid., p.77.
98 Ibid., pp.88f. Note also the ethic of Jesus was viewed by al-Faruqi as the ethic of intent, that is, intention is more important than the act itself. Ibid., p.78.
99 Al-Faruqi built his case against western Christianity or Christendom (Semitic Christianity seemed to be acceptable) first by seeing that Christianity reinterpreted Hebrew scripture as salvation history (*Heilsgeschichte*) thus providing justification for the Hebrew racialism because it was leading to the incarnation and redemption of humanity. Ibid., p.55. Then he viewed Paul and later Augustine as degrading humanity with original sin. Ibid., pp.158-163. After the Nicene Creed until today, according to al-Faruqi, Christianity has redefined the image of God in humanity as something present only in Christ and through him present in a Christian. Ibid., p.180. This he believed brought us back to a form of racialism. Al-Faruqi believed that the concept of the universal nature of sin in humanity, for which he coined the word 'peccatism,' was introduced by Paul not Jesus. Ibid., pp.194-203. Later, in a summary of western Christianity, he writes: "Peccatism, saviourism, millennialism, and paradox held complete sway." Ibid., p.294.

100 Ibid.

101 Ibid., p.223.

102 Ibid., p.229.

103 Interestingly this possible conclusion was addressed by Paul and others in the New Testament, but al-Faruqi did not mention their explanations. For example, in the book of Romans Paul writes: "What shall we say, then? Shall we go on sinning so that grace may increase? By no means! ... count yourselves dead to sin but alive to God in Christ Jesus. Therefore do not let sin reign in your mortal body so that you obey its evil desires. Do not offer the parts of your body to sin, as instruments of wickedness, but rather offer yourselves to God, as those who have been brought from death to life; and offer the parts of your body to him as instruments of righteousness. For sin shall not be your master, because you are not under the law but under grace." Romans 6: 1-2, 11-14. (*NIV*)

104 Al-Faruqi, 'Prospects for dialogue', pp.29-33; idem, 'Problems and perspectives', pp.159-181 and discussion 181-220. The latter article includes a number of responses to al-Faruqi's statements, which will be examined in Chapter Six.

105 Al-Faruqi, 'Prospects for dialogue', p.30; idem, 'Problems and perspectives', pp.167f.

106 Al-Faruqi, 'Prospects for dialogue', p.30.

107 Al-Faruqi, 'Prospects for dialogue', p.30; idem, 'Problems and perspectives', p.168.

108 Al-Faruqi, 'Prospects for dialogue', pp.31-32; idem, 'Problems and perspectives', pp.169-172.

109 Al-Faruqi, 'Prospects for dialogue', p.31.

110 Ibid.

111 Al-Faruqi, 'Prospects for dialogue', p.31; idem, 'Problems and perspectives', p.170.

112 Al-Faruqi, 'Prospects for dialogue', p.31; idem, 'Problems and perspectives', p.171.

113 Al-Faruqi, 'Prospects for dialogue', p.32.

114 In 'Prospects for dialogue' the first two themes actually correspond to the first and third themes in the article 'Problems and perspectives'. The second theme in the latter article was omitted by al-Faruqi in his earlier and shorter article.

115 Al-Faruqi, 'Prospects for dialogue', p.32; idem, 'Problems and perspectives', p.172.

116 Al-Faruqi, 'Prospects for dialogue', p.32.

117 Al-Faruqi, 'Problems and perspectives', p.172.

118 Al-Faruqi, 'Prospects for dialogue', p.32.

119 Al-Faruqi, 'Prospects for dialogue', p.32; idem, 'Problems and perspectives', pp.173-175.

120 Al-Faruqi, 'Prospects for dialogue', p.32.

121 Ibid., pp.32f.

122 Al-Faruqi, 'Problems and perspectives', pp.175f.

123 Al-Faruqi, 'Prospects for dialogue', p.33; idem, 'Problems and perspectives', pp.176-178.

124 Al-Faruqi, 'Prospects for dialogue', p.33.

125 Al-Faruqi, 'Problems and perspectives', pp.177f.

126 All three quotations are from al-Faruqi, 'Islam and Christianity: Diatribe or dialogue', Reprinted in Siddiqui, (ed.) *Ismail Raji al-Faruqi*, p.242.

Chapter Five

1 PPBox 1964.

2 The appendix chronologically lists al-Faruqi's involvement in various aspects of interfaith discourse. Of particular note is the number of invitations he accepted to speak at churches, synagogues and to other religious groups.

3 In letter dated 19 April 1979, al-Faruqi invited the President of the Vatican Commissions for Non-Christians, his Eminence Cardinal Sergio Pignedoli, to lecture on "Relations of the Catholic Church with Muslims and Jews" for the 1979 AAR convention. PPBox #1 1979.

4 Gremillion, (ed.) *Food/Energy and the Major Faiths*, pp.viii, 6, 237.

5 Funding came from the Ford, Rockefeller, DeRance and Rosenhaus foundations along with a five individual gifts from friends. Matthew Rosenhaus (president) and al-Faruqi wrote in 1978 "... we see that the IRPC's future will depend upon relatively small contributions such as they are offered, motivated by faith and conviction and by love." Gremillion and Ryan (eds.) *World Faiths and the New World Order*, p.viii. Further, in 1979 al-Faruqi could write that the IRPC is the sole American ecumenical institution representing Abrahamic-faith communities nationally and on the scholarly level, worldwide. PPBox #1 1979.

6 Al-Faruqi, ed., *Trialogue*, p.x.

7 Al-Faruqi, 'Islamabad regional meeting', in Henry O. Thompson, (ed.) *The Global Congress of the World's Religions, Proceedings of 1980-1982 Conference* (Washington, DC: The Global Congress of the World's Religions, Inc., 1982), pp.141-43. Among the action points listed, GCWR was seen as a vehicle to present Islam and its solutions to the world's problems, such as justice and peace along with a promotion of mutual understanding and cooperation.

8 For example, one section of al-Faruqi's 'Essence of religious experience in Islam', pp.192-199 and reprinted in Siddiqui, (ed.) *Ismail Raji al-Faruqi*, pp.9-17 was included in al-Faruqi's book *Al-Tawḥīd*, pp.1-9.

9 One may correctly question the inclusion of a monograph on Islamic English. However, al-Faruqi would likely have argued that, for the purposes of dialogue, one needs to avoid mistranslation and misinterpretation of fundamental terms such as *īmān* (conviction not faith) *jihād* (self exertion in the cause of Allāh including peaceful and violent means as needed) and

ṣalāh (act of worship not prayer which is duʿā). *Toward Islamic English* (Herndon, VA: IIIT, 1986), pp.23, 27f, 36. He also writes: "The immutability and permanence of Arabic has saved al Qurʾān al-Karīm from the hermeneutical problems besetting the Old and New Testaments, as well as the Hindu and Buddhist scriptures..." Ibid., p.13.

10   Al-Faruqi, 'The challenge of Western ideas for Islam', *Islamic Literature* vol. 15, no. 9, (September, 1969), p.39.

11   Ibid., p.39.

12   Ibid. He did not provide a reference for the paraphrase of the teaching of Jesus, but since he drew upon the Sermon on the Mount from Matthew 5-7, he may have referenced Matthew 7: 1-2 where it says: "Do not judge lest you be judged. For in the way you judge, you will be judged; and by your standard of measure, it will be measured to you."

13   Matthew 6: 1-18.

14   Al-Faruqi, 'The challenge of Western ideas for Islam', p.42.

15   Ismaʿil al-Faruqi, 'Islamizing the social sciences', *Studies in Islam*, vol. 16, no. 2, (April 1979), pp.108-121. Reprinted in Ismaʿil R. al-Faruqi and Abdullah Omar Naseef, (eds.) *Social and Natural Sciences: The Islamic Perspective* (Sevenoaks, UK: Hodder and Stoughton, 1981), pp.8-20.

16   Ibid., p.11.

17   Ibid., p.14.

18   Ibid.

19   The ḥadīth reads: "Narrated by ʿUmar bin Al-Khaṭṭāb: Allah's Apostle said, "The reward of deeds depends upon the intention and every person will get the reward according to what he has intended. So whoever emigrated for Allah and His Apostle, then his emigration was for Allah and His Apostle. And whoever emigrated for worldly benefits or for a woman to marry, his emigration was for what he emigrated for."" *Ṣaḥīḥ al-Bukhārī*, translated by Muḥammad Muḥsin Khān, (Istanbul: Hilāl Yayınları, 1979) vol. 1, book 1, number 1. (Also repeated in vol. 1, book 2, number 51; vol. 3, book 46, number 706; vol. 5, book 58, number 238; vol. 7, book 62, number 8; vol. 8, book 78, number 680; vol. 9, book 86, number 85)

20   Ismaʿil al-Faruqi, 'Is the Muslim definable in terms of his economic pursuits?', in Khurshid Ahmad and Zafar Ishaq Ansari, (eds.) *Islamic Perspectives: Studies in Honour of Mawlānā Sayyid Abul Aʿlā Mawdūdī* (Leicester: Islamic Foundation, 1979), pp.183-193.

21   Al-Faruqi, 'Is the Muslim definable in terms of his economic pursuits?', p.184.

22   Ibid., p.185.

23   Ibid., p.187.

24   Articles such as al-Faruqi's, 'Islam and human rights', *Islamic Quarterly*, no. 27, (1983), pp.12-30, discusses ethics, morality and human rights. He contrasts the Islamic doctrine of innocence at birth (contra Christianity) and equality between all peoples (contra Hinduism). 13f. See also his 'Islam

and the theory of nature', *Islamic Quarterly*, no. 26 (1982), pp.16-26, where he discusses how nature is to be used in ethical and moral terms contrasting Islam and the Christian West. pp.25f.

25 Isma'il al-Faruqi, 'On the metaphysics of ethics in Islam', *Listening*, no. 14, (1979), p.22.

26 Isma'il al-Faruqi, *Islam and Culture* (Kuala Lumpur: Angkatan Belia Islam Malaysia, 1980), p.34.

27 Ibid., p.22.

28 Al-Faruqi, 'Islam and the theory of nature', p.18.

29 Ibid., p.20.

30 Isma'il al-Faruqi, *The Islamization of Knowledge: The Problem, Principles and the Workplan* (Islamabad, Pakistan: National Hijra Centenary Committee of Pakistan, 1982), p.15.

31 Ibid., pp.35-40.

32 Ibid., pp.34f.

33 Ibid., p.39.

34 Al-Faruqi, *Al-Tawḥīd*. The book covers an array of topics from metaphysics to aesthetics in which al-Faruqi chooses to compare Islam to Christianity and Judaism.

35 Isma'il al-Faruqi, 'Tawhid: The quintessence of Islam', *Journal of South Asian and Middle Eastern Studies*, vol. 8, no. 4, (1985), p.9. "Tawhid is that which gives Islamic civilization its identity by binding all its constituent parts together and thus making them an integral, organic body which we call civilization." Al-Faruqi also translated works on *Tawḥīd*, such as Al-Wahhab, *Sources of Islamic Thought: Three Epistles on Tawḥīd by Muhammad ibn 'Abd al Wahhāb*. Unfortunately, al-Faruqi does not mention the original sources for these "three little-known epistles," but he does provide the names of each: Epistle 1, *The First Principles and their Proofs*, Epistle 2, *Four Basic Rules*, Epistle 3, *Clarification of Misunderstandings*. The other work al-Faruqi translated on *Tawḥīd* was Muhammad ibn 'Abd Al-Wahhab, *Kitab al-Tawḥīd: Essay on the Unicity of Allah, or, What is Due to Allah from His Creatures*, translated by Isma'il R. al-Faruqi (London: IIFSO, 1980). This work consists of 67 short chapters mainly drawn from the Qur'ān and the Hadīth and written for didactic purposes.

36 Al-Faruqi, *Al-Tawḥīd*, pp.9-15.

37 Ibid., p.11.

38 He examined knowledge, metaphysics, ethics, the social order, the *ummah*, the family, political and economic order, the world order and finally aesthetics using *Tawḥīd*. The list of comparisons is too extensive to itemize.

39 Al-Faruqi, *Al-Tawḥīd*, pp.29f.

40 Ibid., p.30.

41 Ibid., pp.30f.

42 Ibid., p.31.

43 Ibid., pp.31f.

44 There are roughly twenty articles and books that represent different attempts at external dialogue.
45 Al-Faruqi, Chan, Raju and Kitagawa, *The Great Asian Religions* (1969). Al-Faruqi, *Historical Atlas* (1974). Al-Faruqi, *Islam* (Niles, IL: Argus Communications, 1979). Al-Faruqi and Lois Lamya' al-Faruqi, *The Cultural Atlas of Islam* (1986).
46 One notices that approximately every five years from 1969 onward, he participated in the publication of world-religions texts: *The Great Asian Religions* (1969); *Historical Atlas of the Religions of the World* (1974); *Islam* (1979); *The Cultural Atlas of Islam* (1986).
47 "It [Qur'ān] presents them [Judaism and Christianity] as moments in a continuing divine revelation whose essence is one and the same, namely, that God is, that He is one, and that man is to serve and obey Him by fulfilling the divine command, which is the summun bonum (16:36)." Al-Faruqi, *Great Asian Religions*, p.323. See also *Historical Atlas*, p.246; *Islam*, xii and *Cultural Atlas*, pp.43-69. He maintained this theme throughout his career.
48 He wrote of phenomenology that it: "... requires that the observer let the phenomena speak for themselves rather than force them into any predetermined ideational framework; and, let the eidetic vision of essence order the data for the understanding and be corroborated by them." Al-Faruqi, *Cultural Atlas*, p.xii.
49 Al-Faruqi, 'Essence', pp.186-201. Reprinted in Siddiqui, (ed.) *Ismail Raji al-Faruqi*, pp.3-20.
50 W. C. Smith, *The Meaning and End of Religion: A New Approach to the Religious Traditions of Mankind* (New York: Macmillan Company, 1963), pp.80-118.
51 Al-Faruqi, 'Essence', pp.186-201.
52 Ibid., p.15.
53 The article originally published in *Numen*, is the official journal of the History of Religions Association and given the nature of this field in the 1960s and 1970s, the focus was upon religions other than Judaism, Christianity or Islam.
54 Indeed, as he began to outline the essence of Islamic religious experience, which was reprinted in his book *Al-Tawḥīd*, he included comparisons with Christianity. Al-Faruqi, *al-Tawḥīd*, pp.12-16.
55 Isma'il al-Faruqi, 'Rights of non-Muslims under Islam: social and cultural aspects', *Journal of Muslim Minority Affairs*, no. 1, (1979), p.91. Reprinted in Siddiqui, (ed.) *Ismail Raji al-Faruqi*, p.282.
56 Al-Faruqi, 'Rights of non-Muslims', pp.284-287.
57 "In case the non-believer recourses to immoral practices such as bribery or any means of coercion and attraction extraneous to the intellectual or spiritual nature of the argument, the Muslim auditor ought first to reject the presentation and denounce its author. Moreover the Islamic state then has the right – nay, the duty – to interfere and stop the public discourse.

The state is obliged to protect its citizens against such means. But the honest-to-God presentation, from which ever side it comes, must be allowed to proceed without let or hindrance from any source." Al-Faruqi, 'Rights of non-Muslims', p.294.

58 Al-Faruqi, *Islam and the Problem of Israel.* idem, 'Islamic faith and the problem of Israel and Jerusalem', pp.77-105. idem, 'Islam and Zionism', in J. L. Esposito, (ed.) *Voices of Resurgent Islam* (New York: Oxford University Press, 1983), pp.261-267.

59 Al-Faruqi, 'Islamic faith and the problem of Israel and Jerusalem', p.80. He further wrote: "Islam demands of its adherents and institutions to make the word of God known to all mankind. It recognizes no state authority which shuts off a people from hearing the word of God. True, Islam can only present the word of God and cannot force its acceptance. But when the presentation of the word of God is itself prohibited or proscribed, the Islamic state is obliged to confront the prohibiting authority and break it up. It is not therefore beyond the jurisdiction of the Islamic State to transcend its own frontiers and to wage *jihad* or holy war against such Zionist State wherever it may set up its house to imprison its adherents therein. If, contrary to its nature, the Zionist State were to open its frontiers and permit its citizens to be exposed to the word of God, then the Islamic State can take no further action against it." Ibid., pp.84.f

60 Al-Faruqi, 'Meta-Religion: Towards a critical world theology', pp.13-57. Reprinted as 'Towards a Critical World Theology', in *Toward Islamization of Disciplines*, pp.409-453.

61 The section in the article 'History of Religions' dealing with the methodology of the study of religion (pp.161-164; 168-184) is included in 'Meta-Religion: Towards a critical world theology'" (pp.20-35). idem, 'The role of Islam in global inter-religious dependence', pp.19-38. Almost the entire article of 'Role of Islam' (pp.21-37) is included in 'Meta-Religion: Towards a critical world theology' (pp.40-56).

62 Al-Faruqi writes: "It is not within the purview of this essay to elaborate on a system of meta-religion." Al-Faruqi, 'Meta-Religion: Towards a critical world theology', p.29. This comment is rather strange since the title of the article is about meta-religion as a component in world theology and yet he avoids any detailed discussion of his system of meta-religion. It may be that he felt he already covered this topic in *Christian Ethics*, but he does not make this reference for his readers.

63 Al-Faruqi, Lecture Four in 'Muḥāḍarāt', p.71.

64 Al-Faruqi, 'Meta-Religion: Towards a critical world theology', p.19f.

65 Ibid., pp.14f.

66 Ibid., p.15.

67 Regarding Christianity, he writes: "Consequently, the on-going, living Judaism that did not dissolve into Christianity and all other religions were evil, demonic, to be utterly rejected and vanquished. This attitude of

hatred and condemnation of the other religions on the part of both Judaism and Christianity, including their relation to each other has persisted for millennia." Ibid., p.16.

68 Ibid., p.17.

69 Ibid., pp.56f.

70 Principles of dialogue as outlined in his 1968 article "Islam and Christianity: Diatribe or dialogue," Reprinted in Siddiqui, (ed.) *Ismail Raji al-Faruqi*, pp.250-255.

71 Isma'il al-Faruqi, 'The Muslim-Christian dialogue, a constructionist view', *Islam and the Modern Age*, vol. 8, no. 1, (1977), pp.5-36. Also as 'Common bases between the two religions in regard of convictions and points of agreement in the spheres of life', in *Documents and Researches of Seminary [Seminar] of the Islamic-Christian Dialogue* (Tripoli, Libya: Popular Office of Foreign Relations, Socialist Peoples Libyan Arab Jamahiriya, 1981), pp.229-264. Reprinted in Siddiqui, (ed.) *Ismail Raji al-Faruqi*, pp.211-240. The 'Seminar of the Islamic-Christian Dialogue' was jointly sponsored by Muammar Qadhafi and the Vatican.

72 Al-Faruqi, 'The Muslim-Christian dialogue, a constructionist view', pp.8-10.

73 Ibid., p.8.

74 Ibid., p.9.

75 Ibid., pp.11-30.

76 Ibid., p.12. On March 28, 1967, al-Faruqi responds to Rev. Basetti-Sani's manuscript regarding spiritual pilgrimage and Vatican II that the latter "is only a warm up with more to go". PPBox #1 1967.

77 Al-Faruqi, 'The Muslim-Christian dialogue, a constructionist view', p.12.

78 Ibid.

79 See al-Faruqi, *On Arabism*, pp.16-48; See al-Faruqi, *Christian Ethics*, pp.50-66.

80 Al-Faruqi, 'The Muslim-Christian dialogue, a constructionist view', p.12.

81 Ibid., p.13.

82 Ibid., p.14.

83 Al-Faruqi, *On Arabism*, pp.100-110.

84 He writes: "It is a great intellectual achievement to do so, and it is a spiritual necessity if Christian-Muslim dialogue is to continue and succeed." Al-Faruqi, 'The Muslim-Christian dialogue, a constructionist view', p.14.

85 Ibid.

86 Ibid.

87 "Through colonialism, Christendom, and not Christianity, robbed the Muslim of his liberty to express his thought, to assemble which his peers, to act in any field, including the education of himself and his children." Ibid., p.15.

88 Ibid., p.16.

89 Ibid.

90 It is interesting that in al-Faruqi's distinction between Christianity and Christendom, he did not make a similar distinction between Islam as a religion, which like Christianity is good and "Islamdom" as a power structure, which like Christendom is bad. See Patricia Crone, 'Post-Colonialism in Tenth-Century Islam', *Der Islam*, vol. 83, no. 1 (2006), pp.2-38.

91 Al-Faruqi, 'The Muslim-Christian dialogue, a constructionist view', p.17.

92 Ibid.

93 Ibid.

94 The topics he addressed were knowledge, personal ethics, family, race, materialism, colonialism and national competition, and nihilism.

95 Al-Faruqi, 'The Muslim-Christian dialogue, a constructionist view', p.30.

96 Al-Faruqi, 'History of religions', p.177. As an example, he cites Friedrich Heiler, 'The history of religions as a preparation for the co-operation of religions', in Mircea Eliade and Joseph Kitagawa, (eds.) *History of Religions: Essays in Methodology* (Chicago: University of Chicago Press, 1959), pp.132-160. See also Raimundo Panikkar, *The Unknown Christ of Hinduism* (London: Darton, Longman & Todd, 1964).

97 Matthew 28: 18-20.

98 Al-Faruqi, 'On the nature of Islamic da'wah'. See also al-Faruqi, *Islamic Da'wah: Its Nature and Demands* (Indianapolis, IN: American Trust Publications, 1986). Reprinted in Siddiqui, (ed.) *Ismail Raji al-Faruqi*, pp.305-318.

99 Al-Faruqi, 'Islam and other faiths', in *Middle East 1*. ed. Graciela de la Lama (30th International Congress of Human Sciences in Asia & North Africa, 1976), (Mexico: Colegio de México, 1982): 153-179. Reprinted as "Islam and other faiths," in Altaf Gauhar, (ed.) *The Challenge of Islam* (London: Islamic Council of Europe, 1978), pp.82-111; Reprinted in Siddiqui, (ed.) *Ismail Raji al-Faruqi*, pp.129-160.

100 The congress first started in 1873 as the International Congress of Orientalists and convened regularly until 1973. In 1976 the name was changed to the International Congress of Human Sciences in Asia and North Africa to reflect Islamic subjects. Two sessions later, in 1984 the name was permanently changed to the International Congress for Asian and North African Studies (ICANAS). See (29 June 2013) <http://www.umass.edu/wsp/sinology/conferences/icanas.html>.

101 These characteristics are that *da'wah* is: 1) Not coercive; 2) Not a psychotropic induction, that is *da'wah* must not be the result of magic, illusion, or any other form of deception. Conversion must be a conscious rational decision for the sake of Allah alone made in good conscience. This eliminates converting children or those with intellectual disabilities; 3) Directed to Muslims and non-Muslims; 4) Rational intellection; 5) Rationally necessary; 6) Anamnesis, by which al-Faruqi means that the message of Islam is not new, but a rediscovery of the primeval religion or monotheism found in every person. This innate knowledge is implanted at

birth by God; 7) Ecumenical par excellence. Al-Faruqi, 'On the nature of Islamic da'wah', pp.305-314. Quotations are drawn from the reprint in Siddiqui ed. *Ismail Raji al-Faruqi*, pp.305-318.

102 Al-Faruqi, 'On the nature of Islamic da'wah', pp.305f.

103 Ibid., p.306.

104 Ibid.

105 "The directing of da'wah to Muslims as much as to non-Muslims is indicative of the fact that, unlike Christianity, Islamicity is never a *fait accompli*. Islamicity is a process. It grows, and it is sometimes reduced. There is no time at which the Muslim may carry his title to paradise, as it were, in his pocket. Instead of 'salvation', the Muslim is to achieve felicity through unceasing effort." Ibid., p.308. "As rational intellection, da'wah shows that in Islam, faith has to do with knowledge and conviction, whereas in Christianity it is, as Blaise Pascal (1623-62) found out, a blind wager." Ibid., p.310.

106 "The task of dialogue, or mission, is thus transformed into one of sifting the history of the religion in question. Da'wah thus becomes an ecumenical cooperative critique of the other religion rather than its invasion by a new truth." Ibid., p.314.

107 See 'Islam and other faiths', p.139 where al-Faruqi equates Islam with *dīn al-fiṭrah*.

108 Al-Faruqi, 'On the nature of Islamic da'wah', pp.314-18.

109 The correlation of his 1976 presentation with his 1967 principles is rearranged as: 1) God is One (Tawḥīd) – reality is dual; 2) God is related to creation as God; 3) Man alone in creation has free-will; 4) Tawḥīd gives man dignity; 5) Man is capable of action; 6) Man must actualize the divine will.

110 Al-Faruqi, 'On the nature of Islamic da'wah', pp.316f.

111 Ibid., pp.317f.

112 This portion was not included by Siddiqui in his reprint, but it is found in al-Faruqi, *Islamic Da'wah: Its Nature and Demands*, pp.11-19.

113 See the above note 102.

114 "Our need for a sure and promising foundation on which to build a world-order of human relations, at once humane and universalist, imposes upon us to listen, to consider, and to learn from Islam." Al-Faruqi, 'Islam and other faiths', p.130.

115 Ibid., pp.133-150.

116 Ibid., p.139.

117 Ibid., p.140.

118 'de jure' is defined as a legitimate religion despite its divergence from *religio naturalis*.

119 Al-Faruqi, 'Islam and other faiths', p.140.

120 Ibid., p.152.

121 Ibid., p.154.

122 Ibid., pp.153-155.
123 Al-Faruqi, 'On the nature of Islamic da'wah', pp.311f.
124 Al-Faruqi, 'The nation state and social order in the perspective of Islām', in al-Faruqi, *Trialogue*, pp.49-61.
125 Ibid., p.60.
126 See Lecture Five of 'Muḥāḍarāt', p.72; See also *On Arabism*, pp.1-13.
127 Al-Faruqi's involvement will be discussed later in this chapter.
128 'The role of Islam in global inter-religious dependence', pp.19-53.
129 Isma'il al-Faruqi, 'Divine transcendence and its expression', in Henry O. Thompson, (ed.) *The Global Congress of the World's Religions, Proceedings of 1980-1982 Conference* (Washington, DC.: The Global Congress of the World's Religions, Inc., 1982), pp.267-316. Reprinted in Siddiqui, (ed.) *Ismail Raji al-Faruqi*, pp.21-70.
130 Al-Faruqi, 'The role of Islam in global inter-religious dependence', p.75.
131 Ibid.
132 Ibid., p.77.
133 Ibid., p.78.
134 Ibid., pp.79f.
135 Ibid., pp.82, 84.
136 Ibid., pp.85-91.
137 Ibid., pp.91f.
138 Al-Faruqi, 'Divine transcendence', pp.21-26.
139 Ibid., pp.26f.
140 Ibid., pp.27f.
141 Ibid., p.30.
142 Ibid., p.31.
143 Ibid., pp.35-44.
144 Ibid., p.35.
145 Ibid., p.37.
146 Ibid., p.39.
147 Ibid., p.44.
148 Ibid., p.45.
149 Ibid.
150 Ibid., pp.48-52.
151 Isma'il al-Faruqi, 'The Islamic critique of the status quo of Muslim society', in Barbara Freyer Stowasser, (ed.) *The Islamic Impulse* (London: Croom Helm, 1987), pp.226-243. Uncharacteristically this article makes no mention of or comparisons with other religions.
152 Al-Faruqi, 'Da'wah in the West: Promise and trial', pp.319-351.
153 Ibid., pp.329-350.
154 See Chapter Two.
155 Al-Faruqi, 'Da'wah in the West: Promise and trial', p.320.
156 Ibid., pp.320-322.
157 Ibid., pp.322f.

158 "The incarnation of God, the trinity, salvation as *fait accompli*, the Kingdom of God as here and not-here, God's death and resurrection, vicarious guilt, suffering and merit, original sin and fallenness, the Church as the body of God – all these have remained utterly opaque and incomprehensible. Subscription to these views hardly ever went beyond lip-service." Ibid., p.323.

159 The context here is 'Hellenised' or 'Western' Christianity and not necessarily Christianity itself. Unfortunately al-Faruqi does not always make his distinctions explicit and this creates confusion.

160 Al-Faruqi, 'Da'wah in the West: Promise and trial', p.325.

161 Ibid., pp.325-328.

162 Ibid., p.327.

163 Established in 1869, the College was located in Maryland until 1969 at which time it moved to New York City, but was dissolved in 1974.

164 Joseph A Devenny, 'Comment by Joseph A. Devenny', in James P. Cotter, (ed.) *The Word in the Third World* (Washington, DC: Corpus Books, 1968), p.181.

165 'Discussion', in Cotter, (ed.) *The Word in the Third World*, 193-197. 'Panel discussion', in Cotter, ed., *The Word in the Third World*, pp.198-219.

166 For a detailed discussion of this presentation please see Chapter Four.

167 Joseph A. Devenny, 'Comment by Joseph A. Devenny', in Cotter, ed., *The Word in the Third World*, pp.182-188.

168 W. C. Smith, 'Comment by Wilfred Cantwell Smith', in Cotter, (ed.) *The Word in the Third World*, p.192. This was demonstrated in the discussion following al-Faruqi's presentation on Islamic *da'wah*. This exchange is presented later in this chapter.

169 'Discussion', in Cotter, (ed.) *The Word in the Third World*, p.193.

170 Ibid.

171 Ibid., p.194.

172 W. C. Smith's comment was general in nature about the shift in Protestant mission, its method and ethos. Ibid., pp.194f.

173 Ibid., p.195.

174 Ibid., p.196.

175 Ibid.

176 Ibid., p.197.

177 'Panel discussion', in Cotter, (ed.) *The Word in the Third World*, pp.202f.

178 Ibid.

179 The five-day consultation was jointly arranged by David Kerr (Director of the Centre for the Study of Islam and Christian-Muslim relations at Sally Oak Colleges, Birmingham) and by Khurshid Ahmad (director general of the Islamic Foundation, Leicester). World Council of Churches, *Christians Meeting Muslims: WCC Papers on 10 Years of Christian-Muslim Dialogue*, p.129.

180 For extensive discussions of the various WCC sponsored meetings, see Jutta Sperber, *Christians and Muslims: The Dialogue Activities of World Council of*

Churches and their Theological Foundation, pp.7-50; Dick Mulder, 'Developments in dialogue with Muslims: World Council of Churches', in G. Speelman, J. van Lin and D. Mulder, (eds.) *Muslims and Christians in Europe: Breaking New Ground* (Kampen: Uitgeverij Kok, 1993), pp.153-161; Stuart E. Brown, (ed.) *Meeting in Faith: Twenty Years of Christian-Muslim Conversations Sponsored by the World Council of Churches* (Geneva: WCC Publications, 1989).

181 Sperber, *Dialogue Activities*, p.94.

182 Ibid., p.101.

183 Mulder summarizes the results of the Chambésy consultation in this way: "Muslims are still reluctant to take a new step in their relations with Christians because their suspicion of Christian intention continues. The reason is the undeniable fact that many of the Christian missionary services today continue to be undertaken for ulterior motives. Taking advantage of Muslim ignorance, of Muslim need for education, health, cultural and social services, of Muslim political stresses and crises, of their economic dependence, political division and general weakness and vulnerability, these missionary services have served purposes other than holy – proselytism, that is, adding members to the Christian community for reasons other than spiritual. For sure, there is also a small passage in the final document telling the conference was grieved to hear that some Christians in some Muslim countries have felt themselves limited in the exercise of their religious freedom and have been denied their right to church buildings, but the criticism from the Muslim side was much more elaborated and the conference strongly urged the Christian Churches and religious organizations to suspend their misused diakonia activities in the world of Islam. It did not urge the governments of certain Muslim countries to grant full religious freedom to their Christian citizens." Mulder, 'Developments in dialogue', p.156.

184 Sperber, *Dialogue Activities*, p.32.

185 Sperber writes: "Bishop Arne Rudvin from Karachi had given a keynote speech on Christian mission in which he claimed that individually mission was a matter of saving human beings and globally of the lordship of the crucified and risen Christ as the Son of God which should be recognized by all people. Mission was the transmission of a message, the gospel, the content of which could not be the subject for a discussion or dialogue. His address was subject to vigorous criticism from the Muslim side, which presented Christianity as blind belief in irrational arguments." Ibid., p.157. See also Ibid., pp.94, 98, 164f.

186 Ibid., p.79.

187 Ibid., p.101. Sperber quotes from a discussion at the end of the consultation. See 'Towards a modus vivendi', *International Review of Missions*, vol. 65, no. 260, (October 1976), p.455.

188 Sperber, *Dialogue Activities*, p.150. This is a quote from the discussion that followed two papers on Indonesia and East Africa. See 'Christian mission in

the Muslim world', *International Review of Missions*, vol. 65, no. 260, (October 1976), p.446.

189 Al-Faruqi's presence is seen in the five following discussions: Arne Rudvin, 'The concept and practice of Christian mission', *International Review of Missions*, vol. 65, no. 260, (October 1976), pp.374-390 (discussion portion from pp.385-390); his own paper 'On the nature of Islamic da'wah' (discussion pp.400-409); Muhammad Rasjidi and Ali Muhsin Barwani 'Christian mission in the Muslim world', *International Review of Missions*, vol. 65, no. 260, (October 1976), pp.427-447; 'Discussion on religious freedom', *International Review of Missions*, vol. 65; no. 260, (October 1976), pp.447-452; 'Towards a modus vivendi', *International Review of Missions*, vol. 65, no. 260, (October 1976), pp.452-457.

190 'Statement of the conference', *International Review of Missions*, vol. 65, no. 260, (October 1976), pp.457-460.

191 The record of the exchanges after al-Faruqi's presentation is drawn from its first publication in the *International Review of Missions* vol. 65, no. 260, (October 1976), pp.402-409. However, al-Faruqi's presentation at the 1976 Chambésy consultation was reprinted in 1986 as *Islamic Da'wah: Its Nature and Demands* and the publishers included an apparently edited version of the exchanges, which differ from that published in 1976. For example, while exchanges one and three remain the same between the 1976 and 1986 versions, the publishers of the 1986 reprint lengthened exchange two by inserting material drawn from the 1976 record of exchange four. Aside from context, I am assuming that the first published record (1976) by one of the hosts of the consultation to be the most accurate.

192 Al-Faruqi, 'On the nature of Islamic da'wah', pp.402f.

193 Ibid., p.404.

194 Ibid., pp.403f.

195 Ibid., p.405.

196 Ibid., pp.404f.

197 Ibid., pp. 405-409.

198 Al-Faruqi, 'The role of Islam in global inter-religious dependence', pp.19-53 (discussion pp.38-50).

199 For example Osborn Scott asks about the term infidel and whether or not it was a derogatory term, to which al-Faruqi replies, "It is indeed a derogatory term and why shouldn't it be? It only applied to those who did not recognize God." Ibid., p.38.

Chapter Six

1 See Cragg, 'Ismā'īl al-Fārūqī in the field of dialogue', p.400. Esposito, 'Ismail al-Faruqi: Pioneer in Muslim-Christian relations', pp.35. Jay, 'Review of *Christian Ethics*', pp.288f. Ford, 'Isma'il al-Faruqi on Muslim-Christian dialogue', pp.273, 278. Kraemer in al-Faruqi, *Christian Ethics*, p.ix.

2 Al-Faruqi, *On Justifying the Good*, p.280.

3   Ibid., 302. This is not to say that God does not or cannot extend his goodness and values into creation, just that he chose to create humans in order for this to occur. He did not *need* to do this, but chose to do so in creation.

4   Norman L. Geisler and Paul D. Feinberg, *Introduction to Philosophy* (Grand Rapids, MI: Baker, 1980), p.88.

5   Ibid.

6   Al-Faruqi, *Christian Ethics*, p.32.

7   Norman L. Geisler, *Christian Apologetics* (Grand Rapids, MI: Baker, 1976), p.29.

8   Ibid., p.45.

9   Ibid., p.46.

10 Ibid., p.137.

11 Geisler writes: "There is no way by logic alone to prove that all views except one are contradictory, thus forcing one to adopt as true the only remaining one." Ibid., p.137.

12 Jay, 'Review of *Christian Ethics*', p.288

13 Ibid., p.289.

14 Ford, 'Isma'il al-Faruqi on Muslim-Christian dialogue', p.278.

15 Esposito, 'Ismail al-Faruqi: Pioneer in Muslim-Christian relations', p.33.

16 Al-Faruqi, *Christian Ethics*, p.32 and *Historical Atlas*, p.33.

17 Cragg, 'Ismā'īl al-Fārūqī in the field of dialogue', p.400.

18 This is the well-known argument of 'teleological suspension of the ethical' developed by Søren Kiekegaard's *Fear and Trembling*, translated by Walter Lowrie (Princeton: Princeton University Press, 1968).

19 See the later section on practical applications and the paradox that potentially exists in interfaith dialogue.

20 Cragg, 'Isma'il Al-Faruqi', p.290.

21 Al-Faruqi, 'Islam and other faiths', p.139.

22 Ibid., p.140.

23 Ford, 'Isma'il al-Faruqi on Muslim-Christian dialogue', p.275.

24 Al-Faruqi, 'Islam and other faiths', p.138. For a similar critique of circular reasoning see Zebiri, *Muslims and Christians Face to Face*, p.142.

25 Hava Lazarus-Yafeh, 'Taḥrīf', *Encyclopaedia of Islam*. 2nd edition. P. Bearman, Th. Bianquis, C. E. Bosworth, E. van Donzel and W. P. Heinrichs, (eds.), (Brill, 2008). Brill Online. McGill University. (29 June 2013) <http://referenceworks.brillonline.com/entries/encyclopaedia-of-islam-2/tahrif-SIM_7317>; John Burton, 'Abrogation', *Encyclopaedia of the Qur'ān*. General Editor: Jane Dammen McAuliffe, Georgetown University, Washington DC. Brill, 2008. Brill Online. McGill University. (29 June 2013) <http://referenceworks.brillonline.com/entries/encyclopaedia-of-the-Quran/abrogation-COM_00002>.

26 Cragg, 'Ismā'īl al-Fārūqī in the field of dialogue', p.402.

27 Zebiri, *Muslims and Christians Face to Face*, p.142.

28   Al-Faruqi, 'On the nature of Islamic da'wah', p.33.
29   Larry Poston, *Islamic Da'wah in the West* (New York: Oxford University Press, 1992), p.4.
30   Al-Faruqi, *Islamization of Knowledge*, p.34f.
31   He did specifically mention eidetic vision in his book *Cultural Atlas*, but in practice its presence in his approach was more implicit. Al-Faruqi, *Cultural Atlas*, p.xii.
32   Al-Faruqi, 'On the nature of Islamic da'wah', pp.400-409.
33   Al-Faruqi, *On Arabism*, p.ix-x. In his preface, al-Faruqi claims his theory is for everyone and not just those whom he considers and defines as possessing the Arab spirit.
34   Ford, 'Isma'il al-Faruqi on Muslim-Christian dialogue', p.273.
35   The appeal to revelation would not necessarily be accepted by a non-Muslim. So to maintain a belief in the verse's truthfulness, al-Faruqi redefines Arab. However, one wonders how many Muslims would read the verse in this way.
36   Malik, 'Review of *On Arabism*', p.337.
37   Ford, 'Isma'il al-Faruqi on Muslim-Christian dialogue', p.276.
38   Cragg, 'Ismā'īl al-Fārūqī in the field of dialogue', p.399.
39   Al-Faruqi, *On Arabism*, p.17.
40   Al-Faruqi, 'A comparison of the Islamic and Christian approaches to Hebrew scripture', p.110.
41   Renan, *Studies in Religious History.*
42   For example, Isaiah 19: 19-25 reads: "In that day there will be an altar to the LORD in the heart of Egypt, and a monument to the LORD at its border. It will be a sign and witness to the LORD Almighty in the land of Egypt. When they cry out to the LORD because of their oppressors, he will send them a saviour and defender, and he will rescue them. So the LORD will make himself known to the Egyptians, and in that day they will acknowledge the LORD. They will worship with sacrifices and grain offerings; they will make vows to the LORD and keep them. The LORD will strike Egypt with a plague; he will strike them and heal them. They will turn to the LORD, and he will respond to their pleas and heal them. In that day there will be a highway from Egypt to Assyria. The Assyrians will go to Egypt and the Egyptians to Assyria. The Egyptians and Assyrians will worship together. In that day Israel will be the third, along with Egypt and Assyria, a blessing on the earth. The LORD Almighty will bless them, saying, "Blessed be Egypt my people, Assyria my handiwork, and Israel my inheritance."'" (*NIV*)
43   It is not sufficient to cite *taḥrīf* as a reason because it does not provide any account for why the text was not removed.
44   For example Exodus 19: 3-6; Leviticus 20: 22-26; Deuteronomy 7: 1-11. However, al-Faruqi could argue that these references were added in order to support Jewish exclusivism, but without an *a priori* presupposition

against this notion, there is no reason to question the integrity of these texts.

45 Khalid Duran, 'Muslims and non-Muslims', in Leonard Swidler, (ed.) *Muslims in Dialogue: The Evolution of a Dialogue* (Lewiston, NY: The Edwin Mellen Press, 1992), p.87.

46 Al-Faruqi, *On Arabism*, p.31.

47 In the Septuagint, the word לקח– *laqach* is translated into the Greek as λαβων (from λαμβανω), which means 'take with the hand, lay hold of any person or thing in order to use it'. The verb in isolation could mean consensual or non-consensual contact.

48 The Hebrew and Greek (from the Septuagint) are respectively – עכה – *'anah* meaning 'to afflict, oppress, humble, be afflicted, be bowed down'; εταπεινωσεν (from ταπεινοω) meaning 'to make low or bring low, abase or humble'. This adds weight to the above proposed translation of non-consensual contact.

49 Al-Faruqi, *On Arabism*, p.32.

50 Genesis 30: 43 demonstrates the wealth that Jacob accumulated and this is re-iterated in Genesis 34: 21-23. "We can marry their daughters and they can marry ours. But the men will consent to live with us as one people only on the condition that our males be circumcised, as they themselves are. Won't their livestock, their property and all their other animals become ours? So let us give our consent to them, and they will settle among us. All the men who went out of the city gate agreed with Hamor and his son Shechem, and every male in the city was circumcised." (*NIV*)

51 The characters are significant in this story because Simeon, Levi and Dinah shared the same mother, Leah. Dinah was the youngest of Leah's children by Abraham. The other brothers were born of different mothers. Thus it is important to see who exacted revenge. It was two of Dinah's blood brothers who defended her honour. (Genesis 35: 23-26) The story of Dinah's birth is found in Genesis 30: 20f.

52 Jacob's response to Simeon and Levi was: "You have brought trouble on me, by making me odious among the inhabitants of the land, among the Canaanites and the Perizzites; and my men being few in number, they will gather together against me and attack me and I shall be destroyed, I and my household." (Genesis 34: 30) (*NIV*) See also Genesis 49, which records Jacob's last words. Of note are his thoughts on Simeon and Levi (verses 5-7) which reads: "Simeon and Levi are brothers; their swords are implements of violence. Let my soul not enter into their council; let not my glory be united with their assembly; because in their anger they slew men, and in their self-will they lamed oxen. Cursed be their anger, for it is fierce; and their wrath, for it is cruel. I will disperse them in Jacob, and scatter them in Israel." (*NIV*) It is clear years after this event that Jacob still harboured distaste for his son's actions. Of his remaining sons, only Reuben, his first born, was to receive such a negative report.

53 For further comment, see John L. Sailhamer, *Genesis*, in Frank E. Gaebelein, (general editor), *The Expositor's Bible Commentary*, vol. 2, (Grand Rapids, MI: Zondervan, 1990), pp.212-216.

54 His call for the state of Israel's dismantlement drew strong reaction, particularly as this portion from his book, *Islam and the Problem of Israel*, was reprinted in Esposito's *Voices of Resurgent Islam* and then quoted in several Jewish newsletters. Esposito wrote to al-Faruqi warning him of the presence of his comments appearing under banners of 'Perish Judea!' in the Near East Report (27 January 1984). As for responses, Jay Meyers, a member of the Executive Committee of the Temple University Law Alumni wrote a direct letter demanding a personal meeting and clarification. Al-Faruqi responded with a letter dated 27 February 1984 saying that his work was being taken out of context and that he was open to a meeting. He also received a number of irate letters with the common theme of 'you and me, anywhere, anytime.' Perhaps this should not have surprised al-Faruqi, for his manuscript was rejected by several publishers, such as Open Court, Houghton Mufflin, Dover, Harper & Row and McGraw-Hill before it was accepted for publication with reservations by the Islamic Foundation in the UK. When questioned about his opinion by the eventual publisher, he responded that he was explaining why Israel should be dismantled, but was not calling for it actually to be done. He wrote in 9 April 1979, "It is intended to instruct Muslims why it should be dismantled and what should be put in its place." Further, he wrote, "The book is not intended to convince Muslims or non-Muslims that Israel must be dismantled. It is not a plea!" Finally, he offered that the book's audience would primarily be Muslims and would be read almost exclusively by Muslims. However, the book found a wider audience. PPBox #1 1984.

55 Al-Faruqi, *On Arabism*, pp.58, 64.

56 Al-Faruqi, *Christian Ethics*, p.88.

57 Ibid.

58 Zebiri, *Muslims and Christians Face to Face*, p.145.

59 Al-Faruqi, *Christian Ethics*, p.253.

60 Ibid., p.253.

61 Ibid.

62 Ibid.

63 "By this all men will know that you are my disciples, if you have love for one another." John 13: 35. (*NIV*)

64 Cragg, 'Ismā'īl al-Fārūqī in the field of dialogue', pp.403f. Cragg points out that al-Faruqi did not seriously study Christology but seemed to dismiss *a priori* the incarnation and redemption.

65 Al-Faruqi viewed saviourism and salvation as a *fait accompli* which, he believed, creates complacency because already attaining salvation removes any further reason for ethical behaviour or human responsibility. Zebiri, *Muslims and Christians Face to Face*, p.151. A Christian could argue that before

you can do the will of God, the will of God must first be done in you and this is the result of redemption. Regarding his idea of *peccatism*, a word al-Faruqi coined to refer to 'original sin,' he reinterpreted the Genesis account of the Tree of the Knowledge of Good and Evil as a fabrication. He claimed what transpired was actually not disobedience, but the innate drive in humanity for knowledge; thus Adam and Eve were not condemned nor punished by God. He created them to seek knowledge and truth, which is what they did. Thus, al-Faruqi believed that in order to enhance and protect the exclusivist claims that the Jews were alone the children of God, the Jews emphasized the sacrificial system to obtain forgiveness. This system was not available to the rest of humanity because God chose Israel. Christianity carried on this Jewish teaching, but universalized it making hereditary the concept of sin for all people. Ibid., p.150.

66 He did not mention the Eastern Orthodox branch of Christianity.
67 "In the salient features of their doctrines, the Ebionites, Gnostics, Marcionites, Manichæans, Arians and Nestorians represented Arab Christianity; the Montanists, Donatists and Athanasians represented Western Christianity." Al-Faruqi, *On Arabism*, p.101.
68 Al-Faruqi, 'Islam and Christianity: Diatribe or dialogue', p.49 and reprinted by Siddiqui, (ed.) *Ismail Raji al-Faruqi*, p.244.
69 Esposito, 'Ismail al-Faruqi: Pioneer in Muslim-Christian relations', p.34.
70 Esposito, 'Ismail R. al-Faruqi: Muslim scholar-activist', p.69.
71 See Edward Said, *Orientalism* (New York: Vintage Books, 1979).
72 Al-Faruqi, 'The challenge of western ideas for Islam', pp.39f.
73 Al-Faruqi, 'Is the Muslim definable in terms of his economic pursuits?', p.184.
74 In this case, context is important. Satan tempted Jesus to depend not on God but on himself and hence the reply of Jesus. It does not say man must separate bread (physical need) from the word of God (spiritual need). It only emphasizes that the word of God has priority and in this context it implies obedience to God.
75 John 18: 36 is the only record of these words by Jesus.
76 Jay, 'Review of *Christian Ethics*', pp.288f.
77 Acts 2:45 "And they *began* selling their property and possessions, and were sharing them with all, as anyone might have need." (*NASB*) [Italics mine]. For a similar comment see Cragg, 'Isma'il Al-Faruqi', p.140f.
78 Critiques of varying lengths and detail can be found in Zebiri, *Muslims and Christians Face to Face*, pp.142-145; 149-154; 160-161. Ford, 'Isma'il al-Faruqi on Muslim-Christian dialogue', pp.268-282. Cragg, 'Ismāʿīl al-Fārūqī in the field of dialogue', pp.399-410.
79 Esposito, 'Ismail al-Faruqi: Pioneer in Muslim-Christian relations', p.36.
80 Geisler and Feinberg, *Introduction to Philosophy*, pp.238f.
81 Esposito, 'Ismail al-Faruqi: Pioneer in Muslim-Christian relations', p.34.
82 Al-Faruqi, *Christian Ethics*, p.11.

83   While introducing the six principles in *Christian Ethics* (pp.21-32), he never clarified his ideas. He did mention that he would fully elaborate on these principles in a never published book entitled, *A Perspective of the History of Religion in the Near East*. Al-Faruqi, *Christian Ethics*, p.22. Nevertheless he did apply these in principle in his discussions on dialogue. For example in his 1965 article, 'History of religions: Its nature and significance for Christian education and the Muslim-Christian dialogue', he introduced the ideas of B. E. Meland in support of meta-religion in relation to dialogue. In his 1986 article, 'Meta-Religion: Towards a critical world theology', (p. 29) he states that he would not elaborate on the system of meta-religion. Lastly, he redrafted his principles in his book *Al-Tawḥīd*.

84   Al-Faruqi, *Christian Ethics*, p.31.

85   Al-Faruqi, 'History of religions', pp.178-183.

86   Meland, 'Response', pp.87f.

87   Ibid., p.88.

88   Ibid., pp.88-91.

89   Ibid., p.90.

90   Ibid., p.94.

91   See Chapter Five.

92   Al-Faruqi, 'Meta-Religion: Towards a critical world theology', pp.56f.

93   See Chapter Five.

94   Examples of differences can be found in *Al-Tawḥīd*, (pp.9-15), where the principles become: 1) Duality; 2) Ideationality; 3) Teleology; 4) The capacity of man and the malleability of nature; 5) Responsibility and judgment. See also our discussion in Chapter Five, where al-Faruqi re-casts and applies his meta-religious principles in 'Islam and other faiths', pp.314-18.

95   Al-Faruqi, 'Islam and Christianity: Prospects for dialogue', pp.230f. idem, 'Islam and Christianity: Problems and perspectives', pp.170f. At the heart of *Christian Ethics* is al-Faruqi's attempt to reinterpret the ethics of Jesus. This is considered here as his attempt to re-fiqurize Jesus. *Christian Ethics*, pp.50-135.

96   Al-Faruqi, 'Islam and Christianity: Diatribe or dialogue', pp.53-57, 59-67.

97   Ibid., p.253.

98   Ibid., p.253. He mentions truth, goodness, value, God and the divine will.

99   Ibid., pp.258-267. See above note 94.

100 "Would such a re-presentation or rediscovery necessitate the Christian's and the Muslim's going out, as it were, of their own figurization, out of their 'catholic' truths? Not *simpliciter*. For there is no *a priori* or wholesale condemnation of any figurization. But we should never forget that, as a piece of human work, every figurization is capable of growing dim in its conveyance of the holy, not because the holy has changed, but because man changes perspectives. Truth, goodness and value, God and the divine will, for man as such are always the same. But His will in the changes and flux of individual situations, of the vicissitudes of history – and that is

precisely what the figurization had been relational to – must be changing in order that the divine will for man be always the same. To question the figurization is identically to ask the popular question: What is God's will in the context of our generation, of our historical situation, indeed, in the context of our personal individuation? The dimness of the figurization must be removed at all costs; its meaning must be rediscovered and its relevance recaptured." Ibid., p.253.

101 Al-Faruqi, 'Prospects for dialogue', 32. idem, 'Problems and perspectives', p.173.

102 Esposito, 'Ismail al-Faruqi: Pioneer in Muslim-Christian relations', p.35.

103 Ford, 'Isma'il al-Faruqi on Muslim-Christian dialogue', p.278.

104 Al-Faruqi, 'Problems and perspectives', pp.172-178.

105 Al-Faruqi, 'Rights of non-Muslims under Islam: Social and cultural aspects', pp.90-101.

106 Al-Faruqi, 'Rights of non-Muslims', p.294.

107 Muhammad Shafiq and Mohammed Abu-Nimer, *Interfaith Dialogue: A Guide for Muslims* (Herndon, VA: IIIT, 2007), pp.25f.

108 Al-Faruqi, 'The Muslim-Christian dialogue, a constructionist view', p.16.

109 Ibid., p.14.

110 Ibid., p.17.

111 'Discussion', in Cotter, (ed.) *The Word in the Third World*, p.193. More will be said about this topic later.

112 Andrew Porter in his study of British Protestant missionaries notes that equating mission activity with imperialism is inaccurate. He writes that: "No more were conversion, subjugation and possession necessarily linked in missionary minds and to suggest so is surely to confuse much evangelical thought and motive with entirely different and distinct forms of imperial activity." Andrew Porter, *Religion versus Empire? British Protestant Missionaries and Overseas Expansion, 1700-1914* (Manchester, UK: Manchester University Press, 2004), p.9. Similarly see Norman Etherington, "Introduction," in Norman Etherington, ed. *Missions and Empire.* (Oxford: Oxford University Press, 2005), pp.1-18.

113 Al-Faruqi, 'Meta-Religion: Towards a critical world theology', p.15.

114 Ibid., p.16.

115 Although al-Faruqi could at times sound harsh in his critique, he did value and appreciate dialogical efforts such as those initiated by the Muslim-Jewish-Christian Conference (MJCC). Al-Faruqi, (ed.) *Trialogue*, p.x.

116 One can point to the controversy surrounding Pope Benedict XVI's comments about Islam delivered at the University of Regensburg, Germany on 12 September 2006. The Pope's message originally appeared in translation at <http://www.cwnews.com/news/viewstory.cfm?recnum= 46474> (12 March 2007). Interestingly the same speech appears translated on the official Vatican website with an important modification, which distanced the Pope from his earlier controversial comments. For example,

in the first translation, when the Pope comments on the 14th century Byzantine emperor Manuel II Paleologus' discussion, he says: "he [Manuel II] turns to his interlocutor [unnamed Muslim] *somewhat brusquely* with the central question on the relationship between religion and violence in general...". However, in the version on the Vatican website, this comment becomes: "...he [Manuel II] addresses his interlocutor [unnamed Muslim] *with a startling brusqueness, a brusqueness that we find unacceptable*, on the central question about the relationship between religion and violence in general...". [Italics are mine for emphasis]. (12 March 2007) <http://www.vatican.va/holy_father/benedict_xvi/speeches/2006/september/documents/hf_ben-xvi_spe_20060912_university-regensburg_en.html>.

117 Zebiri, *Muslims and Christians Face to Face*, p.149. See also Cragg, 'Ismāʿīl al-Fārūqī in the field of dialogue', p.399.

118 Al-Faruqi, *Christian Ethics*, p.15f.

119 Cragg went so far as to question the integrity of al-Faruqi's scholarship calling it prejudiced. Cragg, 'Ismaʿil al-Fārūqī in the field of dialogue', p.400.

120 For example in 1967 and 1976, he listed six principles [*Christian Ethics* (1967), pp.21-32; and 'On the nature of Islamic daʿwah' (1976), pp.314-18], in 1980 and 1982, he listed five principles ['The role of Islam in global inter-religious dependence' (1980), p.75 ; and *Al-Tawḥīd* (1982),pp.9-15]; in 1977, these became four principles ['The Muslim-Christian dialogue, a constructionist view' (1977), pp.8-10] and in 1986, he listed eight principles ['Meta-Religion: Towards a critical world theology' (1986), pp.56f].

121 Al-Faruqi, *Christian Ethics*, p.ix-x.

122 Al-Faruqi, 'Islam and Christianity: Problems and perspectives', pp.168f.

123 Cragg, 'Ismāʿīl al-Fārūqī in the field of dialogue', p.399.

124 Ibid.

125 Ibid., p.401.

126 W. C. Smith, 'Comment by Wilfred Cantwell Smith', in Cotter, (ed.) *The Word in the Third World*, p.192.

127 Al-Faruqi, 'Islam and Christianity: Problems and perspectives', p.172.

128 Ibid.

129 Ibid., p.176.

130 Al-Faruqi, 'Common bases between the two religions', pp.224-236.

131 However, he did not entertain the idea that dialogue can be more than verbal conversation. Mutual cooperation for common ethical/moral and religious causes can in themselves be a form of dialogue in action.

132 Frost in his foreword to al-Faruqi's *Christian Ethics*, p.vi. However, depending upon the context, al-Faruqi could also be cordial, engaging and courteous. Rahman found al-Faruqi personally charming and noted that during the three years that he knew al-Faruqi at McGill University, he never quarrelled with anyone. Rahman, 'Palestine and my experiences with the young Fārūqī', p.39.

133 Cragg, 'Ismāʿīl al-Fārūqī in the field of dialogue', p.406.

134 Ibid., p.405.
135 Ibid., p.407.
136 'Discussion', in Cotter, (ed.) *The Word in the Third World*, p.194. See also Ford, 'Isma'il al-Faruqi on Muslim-Christian dialogue', p.275.
137 Al-Faruqi, 'Common bases between the two religions', pp.217f.
138 Yushau Sodiq, 'Teaching Islamic studies at American universities', in *Proceedings of the First Annual Symposium of the Institute of Islamic & Arabic Sciences in America* (Virginia: IIASA, 1993), p.22.
139 Ford, 'Isma'il al-Faruqi on Muslim-Christian dialogue', pp.273, 278; Esposito, 'Ismail al-Faruqi: Pioneer in Muslim-Christian relations', p.36.
140 John Azuma, 'The integrity of interfaith dialogue', *ICMR*, vol. 13, no. 3, (2002), p.273.
141 Al-Faruqi, *Islam*, p.68 and cited by Cragg, 'Ismā'īl al-Fārūqī in the field of dialogue', p.406.
142 Seyyed Hossein Nasr notes that: "Dr. al-Faruqi, who was always attracted to the life of action and wanted to recapture the power and glory of Islam, appeared more as a religious warrior out to defend the citadel of Islam than a detached scholar who would seek to reach mutual religious and intellectual understanding with other religions. Nevertheless, this understanding was also his concern as seen in numerous conferences on religious dialogue in which he was a participant." Nasr, 'The essence of Dr. Faruqi's life work', p.26.

Chapter Seven

1   One must take into account that al-Faruqi was an Arab Muslim who was trained in western philosophy and primarily addressed western audiences. He was not a passive recipient of previous ideas nor was he immune from previous Muslim ideas. To argue that he was a Mu'tazilite would be difficult to maintain because one would need to demonstrate that his thought was either shaped by the Mu'tazilites or that he adopted all their major doctrines. The use of neo-Mu'tazilite to describe him is, therefore, limited to his acceptance of reason as humanity's ability to know what is morally good and evil. See Daniel Gimaret's discussion about the centrality of the justice of God in Mu'tazilite dogma. Since God is just in terms of his fundamental nature, He will always act justly. It is not a question as proposed by the Ash'arites that whatever God does is just. The necessity of God's justice, according to Gimaret, excludes predestination as something unjust and therefore humanity is granted freedom and ability (by way of reason) to obey God. When al-Faruqi's methodology is examined, particularly with his ideas of ethics and the nature of people, one is able to see a parallel with Mu'tazilite ideas. In this way, the term neo-Mu'tazilite can be used when describing al-Faruqi. D. Gimaret, 'Mu'tazila', *Encyclopaedia of Islam*. 2nd edition. Edited by: P. Bearman, Th. Bianquis, C.E. Bosworth, E. van Donzel and W.P. Heinrichs. Brill, 2008. Brill Online. McGill

University. (29 June 2013) <http://referenceworks.brillonline.com/entries /encyclopaedia-of-islam-2/mutazila-COM_0822>.

2   One might see his use of figurization as similar to imagination, but the former is based on rational ideas whereas the latter is free to go beyond the rational. In addition, he did appeal to intuition on the level that all humanity intuitively recognises ethics and value as proposed by Max Scheler. However, knowledge based solely on individual intuition would be rejected.

3   The types and limits of rational thought along with the means to understand and articulate difficult to understand ideas will be explored later when we examine Margaret Somerville's contribution to ethics.

4   One example of al-Faruqi's encouragement to his fellow Muslims to make dialogue a priority is found in a letter dated 12 December 1976 when he writes the following to Reverend Metropolitan Juvenaly of Tula and Belev (Moscow): "At the International Conference on Muslim-Christian Dialogue held at Tripoli, Arab Republic of Libya, 5-12 February 1976, I have expounded the desire of all Muslims to give priority to interreligious cooperation, over theological discussion, with a view to remove the causes of injustice among the nations, especially between Muslims, Christians and Jews. I have repeated the same Muslim determination at the International Islamic Conference organized by the Muslim Council of Europe and held in London in April, 1976, and lately at the Muslim-Christian Dialogue Conference called by the World Council of Churches and held at Geneva in June, 1976." PPBox #3 1977.

5   The attempt to have IIIT endow a Chair of Islamic Studies at Temple University in honour of Professor Isma'il al-Faruqi met some opposition and was declined by the university resulting in IIIT withdrawing their offer. For more information, see the Philadelphia Inquirer online article entitled "Donor cancels Islamic chair for Temple" written by Kathy Boccella on 5 January 2008. (15 March 2008) <http://www.philly.com/ inquirer/home_top_left_story/20080105_Donor_cancels_Islamic_chair_for _Temple.html>. The Temple Association of University Professionals (TAUP) has initiated an investigation into circumstances that led to the withdrawal of the offer. (15 March 2008)   <http:// www.iiit.org/NewsEvents/News/ tabid/62/articleType/ArticleView/articleId/30/Default.aspx>.

6   Jane I. Smith, 'Muslims as partners in interfaith encounter', in Zahid H. Bukhari, Sulayman S. Nyang, Mumtaz Ahmad and John L. Esposito, eds., *Muslims' Place in the American Public Square* (Walnut Creek, CA: AltaMira Press, 2004), p.189. See also Irfan Omar ed., *A Muslim View of Christianity: Essays on Dialogue by Mahmoud Ayoub* (Maryknoll, NY: Orbis Books, 2007).

7   Mahmoud Ayoub, 'Islam and Christianity between tolerance and acceptance', *ICMR*, vol. 2, no. 2, (1991), p.175.

8   Jane Smith, 'Muslims as partners', p.190.

9   Jane Smith, *Challenge of Interfaith Dialogue*, p.70.

10 Mohammed Arkoun, 'New perspectives from Jewish-Christian-Muslim dialogue', reprinted in Leonard Swidler, (ed.) *Muslims in Dialogue: The Evolution of a Dialogue* (Lewiston, NY: The Edwin Mellen Press, 1992), p.347.

11 Ayoub writes: "What we need is more Muslim scholars who can study Christianity as part of man's religiousness with the objectivity and sensitivity that such a study deserves. It is only by this kind of sensitive and objective approach that Muslims can break away from the traditional arguments, the distortions of scriptures by Christians, and Christian polytheism. Such arguments cannot objectively be supported, nor are they helpful to bring about a positive understanding of the two religions by the two peoples, an understanding which our world today needs most." Mahmoud Ayyoub, 'Islam and Christianity: A study of Muhammad Abduh's views of the two religions', p.137.

12 This list is not exhaustive. One can add the contributions made by Hasan Hanafi, *Religious Dialogue and Revolution*. Hanafi was a colleague of al-Faruqi's from 1971-75 at Temple University. See also Khurram Murad, *Da'wah among Non-Muslims in the West: Some Conceptual and Methodological Aspects* (Leicester: The Islamic Foundation, 1986).

13 Jane Smith, 'Muslims as partners', p.191.

14 Seyyed Hossein Nasr, 'Islamic-Christian dialogue: Problems and obstacles to be pondered and overcome', *ICMR*, vol. 11, no. 2, (2000), p.215. See also idem, 'Comments on a few theological issues in the Islamic-Christian dialogue', in Haddad and Haddad, (eds.) *Christian-Muslim Encounters*, pp.457-467.

15 Hasan Askari, 'Within and beyond the experience of religious diversity', in John Hick and Hasan Askari, (eds.) *The Experience of Religious Diversity* (London: Grover, 1985), p.191.

16 Hasan Askari, 'The dialogical relationship between Christianity and Islam', *JES*, vol. 9, no. 3 (1972), p.477. He writes: "To me, personally, Christ as Sign of God liberates man from the dead circle of monological religion and restores unto him his genuine dialogical existence." p.483. Askari sees Jesus as a unique sign of a different realm that of the deep relation between God and man. He does not discuss any impact this position has on the place of Muhammad.

17 Askari says the Qur'ān has two forms of revelation – words and as a 'person'. These are held in tension to avoid either becoming a form of idolatry. "When the Qur'ān rejects the incarnation of God in Christ, it corrects the idolatry of the Person as word of God, and this it does by establishing the supremacy of Speech ("kalām") in revelation." idem, 'Dialogical relationship', p.484.

18 Abdulaziz Sachedina, 'Islamic theology of Christian-Muslim relations', *ICMR*, vol. 8, no. 1, (1997), p.36.

19 Ibid., p.27.

20 Jane I. Smith, 'Muslims as partners in interfaith encounter', p.190. The comment by Sachedina was part of his response to questions Smith asked of him regarding his article 'Islamic theology of Christian-Muslim relations'.

21 Siddiqui, *Christian-Muslim Dialogue*, p.124. For the background of Ahmad in addition to Siddiqui, *Christian-Muslim Dialogue*, pp.123-125, see Esposito and Voll, 'Khurshid Ahmad: Muslim activist-economist', in Esposito and Voll, (eds.) *Makers of Contemporary Islam*, pp.39-53.

22 Esposito and Voll, 'Khurshid Ahmad', p.44.

23 Siddiqui, *Christian-Muslim Dialogue*, p.125.

24 Ibid., pp.125, 128.

25 For a background on his life and discussion of his thought, see Zebiri, *Face to Face*, pp.154-160. Akhtar's books include, *The Final Imperative: An Islamic Theology of Liberation* (London: Bellew, 1991). *A Faith for all Seasons: Islam and Western Modernity* (London: Bellew, 1990). *The Light in the Enlightenment: Christianity and the Secular Heritage* (London: Grey Seal, 1990).

26 Akhtar, *A Faith for all Seasons*, p.182.

27 Ibid., p.38.

28 Ibid.

29 Ibid., pp.11f.

30 For a background on Mohammed Talbi, see Siddiqui, *Christian-Muslim Dialogue*, pp.136f and Zebiri, 'Relations between Muslims', p.267.

31 He was educated in the French system in Tunisia and then completed his Ph.D. at the Sorbonne in 1966. He taught in the Faculty of History at the University of Tunisia until his retirement in 1986.

32 Mohammed Talbi, 'Islam and dialogue: Some reflections on a current topic', in Richard W. Rousseau, (ed.) *Christianity and Islam: The Struggling Dialogue* (Scranton, PA: Ridge Row Press, 1985), p.70.

33 Talbi, 'Islam and dialogue', pp.59-61.

34 Ibid., p.58.

35 Ibid., p.62.

36 Cragg suggests that beneath the assurance of al-Faruqi's pen and practice, there laid a deep concern for the vulnerability of Islam. He wonders if al-Faruqi's outspokenness was a means to counter inner anxiety. Cragg, 'Isma'il Al-Faruqi', pp.129f.

37 Leonard Swidler, 'Interreligious and interdialogical dialogue: The matrix for all systematic reflection today', in idem, (ed.) *Towards a Universal Theology of Religion* (New York: Orbis, 1988), pp.15f.

38 Among those who advance 'respect' as a prerequisite is Abdallah Omar Nasseef, 'Muslim-Christian relations: The Muslim approach', *Journal of Muslim Minority Affairs*, vol. 7, (1986), pp.27-31. He argues equity (*qisṭ*), justice (*'adl*) and kindness (*birr*) are Qur'ānic values on which to base interfaith relations. (p.27) The idea of equality is also promoted by Alwi

Shihab, 'Christian-Muslim relations into the twenty-first century', *ICMR*, vol. 15, no. 1, (2004), p.76.

39   Al-Faruqi, *Islam*, p.68.

40   Sachedina, 'Islamic theology', p.27.

41   Askari, 'Dialogical relationship', p.477.

42   In particular Kenneth Cragg and Stanley Brice.

43   Toshihiko Izutsu, *Ethico-Religious Concepts in the Qur'ān* (Montreal: McGill University Press, 1966), p.252.

44   Sachedina, 'Islamic theology', p.27.

45   Ziaudin Sardar, 'The ethical connection: Christian-Muslim relations in a postmodern age', *ICMR*, vol. 2, no. 1, (1991), pp.56f.

46   Suha Taji-Farouki, 'Muslim-Christian cooperation in the twenty-first century: Some global challenges and strategic responses', *ICMR*, vol. 11, no. 2, (2000), p.182. See Julian L. Smith, 'The politics of population and the Cairo conference', (16 May 2007) <http://www.juliansimon.com/writings/Articles/POPNAM.txt>.

47   Taji-Farouki, 'Muslim-Christian cooperation', p.169.

48   Fazlur Rahman, 'Law and ethics in Islam', in Richard G. Hovannisian, *Ethics in Islam* (Malibu, CA: Undena Publications, 1983), pp.3-15; Muhammad 'Abduh as noted by Mahmudul Haq, *Muḥammad 'Abduh: A Study of a Modern Thinker of Egypt* (Aligarh: Aligarh University, 1970), p.86. Nasseef, 'Islamic-Christian relations', p.27. Nasr, 'Islamic-Christian dialogue', p.213.

49   For example, Charles Taylor's *The Sources of the Self* (Cambridge, MA: Harvard University Press, 1989). Chapter One, in particular, provides a framework for modern identity which includes a detailed discussion about morality and ethics.

50   Margaret Somerville, *The Ethical Imagination: Journeys of the Human Spirit* (Toronto: Anansi Press Inc., 2006), pp.1, 7.

51   Margaret Somerville, *The Ethical Canary: Science, Society, and the Human Spirit* (Toronto: Penguin, 2000). pp.xi-xii.

52   Somerville, *The Ethical Imagination*, pp.7f.

53   Ibid., p.2.

54   Ibid., p.28.

55   Ibid., pp.28-31.

56   Ibid., pp.38f.

57   Shafiq and Abu-Nimer, *Interfaith Dialogue: A Guide for Muslims*, pp.25f.

Appendix

1   This list is not exhaustive and is based on primary research into his personal papers, his publications and secondary sources. One will notice that over the course of four years (1968–1971), al-Faruqi published and presented very little. The main focus of his energy was spent in building the Islamic studies programme at Temple University.

2   'Muḥāḍarāt', pp. 65-74. The exact dates are unclear. The publisher indicates the lectures date from May 1959, but were published in 1963.
3   PPBox 1964.
4   Ibid.
5   Ibid. Al-Faruqi noted that the Arab League offered to publish both lecture series in Arabic.
6   PPBox 1963.
7   PPBox 1964. Three lectures were given as part of the interview process by the Department of Religion at Syracuse University and the Maxwell School of Citizenship, which runs the South Asian programme. Aside from a lecture on comparative religion, he also spoke on Islamic studies and South Asia.
8   Ibid.
9   PPBox 1963.
10   PPBox 1963.
11   'History of religions', pp.35-65, 81-86. Reprinted in Siddiqui, (ed.) *Ismail Raji al-Faruqi*, pp.161-194.
12   PPBox #1 1967.
13   PPBox 1964.
14   PPBox #1 1967.
15   PPBox 1966.
16   Ibid.
17   PPBox #1 1967.
18   PPBox 1966.
19   PPBox #1 1967.
20   PPBox 1981.
21   PPBox 1966. The letter in this file does not offer a specific date for this conference. The exact dates are unknown.
22   'Islam and Christianity: Prospects for dialogue', pp.29-33.
23   PPBox #1 1967.
24   Ibid.
25   Ibid.
26   Ibid.
27   Ibid. The letter dated in 1972 apparently was placed in the wrong file.
28   PPBox #1 1974.
29   PPBox #1 1975.
30   PPBox #1 1967. From an acceptance letter dated 27 January 1975 and apparently was placed in the wrong file.
31   PPBox 1981.
32   'Common bases between the two religions', pp.229-264.
33   PPBox #1 1975.
34   'On the nature of Islamic da'wah', pp.33-42.
35   'Islam and other faiths', pp.153-179.

36 For his own account of the Islamic Studies section of the AAR, see Ismaʿil al-Faruqi, 'Introduction: The Islāmic Studies', pp.1-3. See also PPBox #1 1979 for his papers on various aspects of the AAR.

37 PPBox #3 1977. See also Gremillion, ed., *Food/Energy and the Major Faiths*, pp.viii, 6, 237.

38 PPBox #3 1977.

39 PPBox 1981.

40 PPBox #2 1985.

41 Ibid.

42 PPBox 1978.

43 PPBox #2 1985. The same lecture was given at Harvard on 20 February 1978.

44 PPBox 1978. The lecture was published as 'Rights of non-Muslims under Islam: Social and cultural aspects', pp.90-101.

45 PPBox #2 1977.

46 Ibid.

47 Ibid.

48 PPBox #2 1986.

49 Ibid.

50 PPBox #2 1985.

51 Ibid.

52 Ibid.

53 Ibid.

54 Al-Faruqi, 'The Nation state and social order in the perspective of Islām', pp.49-61.

55 'The role of Islam in global inter-religious dependence', pp.19-38. Reprinted in Siddiqui, (ed.) *Ismail Raji al-Faruqi*, pp.71-108.

56 PPBox #2 1984.

57 PPBox #2 1985.

58 Lewis, (ed.), *Towards a Global Congress of the World's Religions*, pp.xi, 11.

59 PPBox #1 1985.

60 PPBox #2 1985.

61 Ibid.

62 PPBox #2 1984.

63 PPBox #3 1984. Published as 'Daʿwah in the West: Promise and trial', pp.319-351.

64 PPBox #2 1985.

65 Ibid.

66 Ibid.

67 Ibid.

68 PPBox #2 1984.

69 'Divine transcendence and its expression', pp.267-316. Reprinted in Siddiqui, (ed.) *Ismail Raji al-Faruqi*, pp.21-70. Originally given in December 1981 in Maui and titled, 'God: The contemporary discussion'.

70 PPBox #2 1984.

71 PPBox 1967. Letter filed in the wrong box. The lecture was likely *Humanism and the Law: The Case of the Shari'ah* (Lagos, Nigeria: The Nigerian Institute of Advanced Legal Studies, 1983).
72 PPBox 1983.
73 PPBox #2 1984.
74 PPBox #1 1967. The letter dated in 1984 apparently was placed in the wrong file. Al-Faruqi mentions this conference in passing and provides no other details.
75 PPBox #2 1985.
76 PPBox #2 1984.
77 PPBox #2 1985.
78 Ibid.
79 PPBox #3 1985.
80 PPBox #2 1985.
81 'The path of Da'wah in the West', pp.54-62.
82 Staff reporter, 'Christian and Moslem Workshop at Rice/Visionaries look to future of understanding'.
83 PPBox #1 1967. The letter dated in 1986 apparently was placed in the wrong file.

BIBLIOGRAPHY

Primary Sources

Books

Al-Faruqi, Isma'il, Personal Papers collected into 53 boxes of files arranged according to year from 1960-1985 and housed at IIIT.

Al-Faruqi, *On Justifying the Good: Metaphysics and Epistemology of Value* (Unpublished Ph.D. Dissertation), (Bloomington: University of Indiana, 1952)

Al-Faruqi, *On Arabism: 'Urubah and Religion: A Study of the Fundamental Ideals of Arabism and of Islam at Its Highest Moment of Consciousness* (Amsterdam: Djambatan, 1962)

Al-Faruqi, *Uṣūl al-Ṣahyūnīyah fī al-Dīn al-Yahūdī* (The bases of Zionism in the Jewish Religion) (Cairo: Institute of Higher Arabic Studies, 1964)

Al-Faruqi, *Christian Ethics: A Historical and Systematic Analysis of Its Dominant Ideas* (Montreal: McGill University Press, 1967)

Al-Faruqi, *Al-Milal al-Mu'āṣirah fī al-Dīn al-Yahūdī* (Contemporary sects in the Jewish Religion) (Cairo: Institute of Higher Arabic Studies, 1968)

Al-Faruqi, Wing-tsit Chan, Poolla Tirupati Raju and Joseph Kitagawa, *The Great Asian Religions: An Anthology* (New York: Macmillan, 1969)

Al-Faruqi, (ed.), *Historical Atlas of the Religions of the World* (New York: Macmillan, 1974)

Al-Faruqi, *Islam* (Niles, IL: Argus Communications, 1979; Brentwood, MD: International Graphics, 1984, 1979; Beltsville, MD: Amana Publications, 1998, 1995)

Al-Faruqi, *Islam and Culture* (Kuala Lumpur: Angkatan Belia Islam Malaysia, 1980) Reprinted as 'Islam as culture and civilization', in Salem Azzam, (ed.), *Islam and Contemporary Society* (London: Longman, 1982), pp.140-176

Al-Faruqi, *Islam and the Problem of Israel* (London: The Islamic Council of Europe, 1980)

Al-Faruqi and Abdullah Omar Naseef, (eds.), *Social and Natural Sciences: The Islamic Perspective* (Sevenoaks, UK: Hodder and Stoughton, 1981)

Al-Faruqi, (ed.), *Essays in Islamic and Comparative Studies* (Herndon, VA: IIIT, 1982)

Al-Faruqi, (ed.), *Islamic Thought and Culture* (Herndon, VA: IIIT, 1982)

Al-Faruqi, (ed.), *Trialogue of the Abrahamic Faiths* (Herndon, VA: IIIT, 1982)

Al-Faruqi, *The Islamization of Knowledge: The Problem, Principles and the Workplan* (Islamabad, Pakistan: National Hijra Centenary Committee of Pakistan, 1982)

Al-Faruqi, *Humanism and the Law: The Case of the Shari'ah* (Lagos, Nigeria: The Nigerian Institute of Advanced Legal Studies, 1983)

Al-Faruqi, *Al-Tawḥīd: Its Implications for Thought and Life* (Kuala Lumpur: IIIT, 1982; 2nd Ed., Herndon, VA: IIIT, 1992)

Al-Faruqi & Lois Lamya' al-Faruqi, *The Cultural Atlas of Islam* (New York: Macmillan, 1986)

Al-Faruqi, *Islamic Da'wah: Its Nature and Demands* (Indianapolis, IN: America Trust Publishers, 1986)

Al-Faruqi, *Toward Islamic English* (Herndon, VA: IIIT, 1986)

Translations

Ghali, Mirrit Butrus, *The Policy of Tomorrow* (Translated by Isma'il al-Faruqi), (Washington, DC: American Council of Learned Societies, 1953)

Al-Ghazali, Muhammad, *Our Beginning in Wisdom* (Translated by Isma'il al-Faruqi), (Washington, DC: American Council of Learned Societies, 1953)

Haykal, Muhammad Husayn, *The Life of Muhammad* (Translated by Isma'il al-Faruqi), (Indianapolis: North American Islamic Trust, 1976)

Khalid, Khalid Muhammad, *From Here We Start* (Translated by Isma'il al-Faruqi), (Washington, DC: American Council of Learned Societies, 1953)

Al-Wahhab, Muhammad ibn 'Abd, *Sources of Islamic Thought: Three Epistles on Tawḥīd by Muḥammad ibn 'Abd al Wahhāb* (Translated with an introduction by Isma'il al-Faruqi), (Indianapolis: North American Islamic Trust, 1979)

Al-Wahhab, Muhammad ibn 'Abd, *Kitab al-Tawḥīd: Essay on the Unicity of Allah, or, What is Due to Allah from His Creatures* (Translated by Isma'il al-Faruqi), (London: IIFSO, 1980)

Articles

Al-Faruqi, Isma'il, 'Review of Fayez Saygeh's *Arab Unity: Hope and Fulfillment*', *Islamic Literature* (May 1960), pp.197-200

Al-Faruqi, 'Review of Stanley Brice Frost's *The Beginning of the Promise*', *Christian Outlook* vol. 16, no. 1 (November 1960), pp.16-18

Al-Faruqi, 'On the significance of Reinhold Niebuhr', *Canadian Journal of Theology* vol. 7, no. 2 (1961), pp.99-107. Reprinted in *Muslim Life* vol. XI, no. 3 (Summer 1964), pp.5-14

Al-Faruqi and Fazlur Rahman, 'Christliches verständnis des Islam?', *Kairos: Zeitschrift für Religionswissenschaft und Theologie* Jahrang III, (1961), pp.225-233

Al-Faruqi, 'Muḥāḍarāt fī Ta'rīkh al-Adyān', (Lectures on the History of Religions) *Bulletin of the Faculty of Arts* vol. 21, no. 1 (Cairo: Cairo University Press, May 1959, published 1963), pp.65-74

Al-Faruqi, 'Towards a new methodology of Qur'anic exegesis', *Islamic Studies* vol. 1, no. 1 (1962), pp.35-52; Reprinted in *Muslim Life* vol. 11, no. 1 (January-March, 1964), pp.4-18

Al-Faruqi, 'Towards a historiography of pre-Hijrah Islam', *Islamic Studies* vol. 1, no. 2 (1962), pp.65-87

Al-Faruqi, 'On the raison d'être of the Ummah', *Islamic Studies* vol. 2, no. 2 (1963), pp.159-203

Al-Faruqi, 'A comparison of the Islamic and Christian approaches to Hebrew scripture', *Journal of the Bible and Religion* vol. 31 (1963), pp.283-293. Reprinted in Ataullah Siddiqui, (ed.), *Ismail Raji al-Faruqi: Islam and Other Faiths* (Leicester: IIIT, 1998), pp.109-126

Al-Faruqi, 'History of Religions: Its nature and significance for Christian education and the Muslim-Christian dialogue', *Numen* no. 12 (1965), pp.35-65, 81-86. Reprinted in Ataullah Siddiqui, (ed.), *Ismail Raji al-Faruqi: Islam and Other Faiths* (Leicester: IIIT, 1998), pp.161-194

Al-Faruqi, 'The self in Mu'tazilah thought', *International Philosophical Quarterly* vol. CI, no. 3 (September 1966), pp.366-88; also in Poolla Tirupati Raju and Albury Castell, (eds.), *East-West Studies on the Problem of the Self* (The Hague: M. Nijhoff, 1968), pp.87-107

Al-Faruqi, 'Science and traditional values in Islamic society', *Zygon* vol. 2 (1967), pp.231-246

Al-Faruqi, 'Islam and Christianity: Prospects for dialogue', *Sacred Heart Messenger* (September 1967), pp.29-33

Al-Faruqi, 'Science and traditional values in Islamic society', in Ward Morehouse, (ed.), *Science and the Human Condition in India and Pakistan* (Bombay: Popular Prakashan, 1968), pp.12-28

Al-Faruqi, 'Islam and Christianity: Diatribe or dialogue', *JES* vol. 5, no. 1 (1968), pp.45-77; Reprinted in Ataullah Siddiqui, (ed.), *Ismail Raji al-Faruqi: Islam and Other Faiths.* (Leicester: IIIT, 1998), p.241-280 and reprinted in Leonard Swidler, (ed.), *Muslims In Dialogue: The Evolution of a Dialogue* (Lewiston, New York: The Edwin Mellen Press, 1992), pp.1-35

Al-Faruqi, 'The problem of the metaphysical status of values in the Western and Islamic tradition', *Studia Islamica* vol. 28 (1968), pp.38-63

Al-Faruqi, 'Islam and Christianity: Problems and perspectives', in James P. Cotter, (ed.), *The Word in the Third World* (Washington, DC: Corpus Books, 1968), pp.159-181and Discussion, pp.181-220

Al-Faruqi, 'Ideal social order in Arab world', *Journal of Church and State* vol. 11, no. 2 (1969), pp.239-251

Al-Faruqi, 'The challenge of western ideas for Islam', *Islamic Literature* vol. 15, no. 9 (September, 1969), pp.39-44

Al-Faruqi, 'Essence of religious experience in Islam', *Numen* vol. 20, no. 3 (1973), pp.186-201; Reprinted in Ataullah Siddiqui, (ed.), *Ismail Raji al-Faruqi: Islam and Other Faiths* (Leicester: IIIT, 1998), pp.3-20

Al-Faruqi, 'Islam and other faiths', in *Middle East 1* edition Graciela de la Lama (30th International Congress of Human Sciences in Asia & North Africa, 1976), (Mexico: Colegio de México, 1982), pp.153-179; Reprinted as 'Islam and other faiths', in Altaf Gauhar, (ed.), *The Challenge of Islam* (London: Islamic Council of Europe, 1978), pp.82-111; Reprinted in Ataullah Siddiqui, (ed.), *Ismail Raji al-Faruqi: Islam and Other Faiths* (Leicester: IIIT, 1998), pp.129-160

Al-Faruqi, 'On the nature of Islamic da'wah', *International Review of Missions* vol. 65, no. 260 (1976), pp.391-406. See also Emilio Castro, Khurshid Ahmad and David Kerr, (eds.), *Christian Mission and Islamic da'wah: Proceedings of the Chambésy dialogue consultation* (Leicester: The Islamic Foundation, 1982), pp.33-42; Reprinted in Ataullah Siddiqui, (ed.), *Ismail Raji al-Faruqi: Islam and Other Faiths* (Leicester: IIIT, 1998), pp.305-318

Al-Faruqi, 'The Muslim-Christian dialogue, a constructionist view', *Islam and the Modern Age* vol. 8, no. 1 (1977), pp.5-6

Al-Faruqi, 'Adapting the Qu'ran!', *Impact International* vol. 7, no. 4 (February-March 1977), pp.10f

Al-Faruqi, 'Rights of non-Muslims under Islam: Social and cultural aspects', *Journal of Muslim Minority Affairs* no. 1 (1979), pp.90-101; Reprinted in Ataullah Siddiqui, (ed.), *Ismail Raji al-Faruqi: Islam and Other Faiths* (Leicester: IIIT, 1998), pp.281-302

Al-Faruqi, 'Islamizing the social sciences', *Studies in Islam* vol. 16, no. 2 (April 1979), pp.108-121; Reprinted in Isma'il al-Faruqi and Abdullah Omar Naseef, (eds.), *Social and Natural Sciences: The Islamic Perspective* (Sevenoaks UK: Hodder and Stoughton, 1981), pp.8-20

Al-Faruqi, 'Is the Muslim definable in terms of his economic pursuits?', in Kurshid Ahmad and Zafar Ishaq Ansari, (eds.), *Islamic Perspectives: Studies in Honour of Mawlānā Sayyid Abul A'lā Mawdūdī* (Leicester: Islamic Foundation, 1979), pp.183-193

Al-Faruqi, 'On the metaphysics of ethics in Islam', *Listening* no. 14 (1979), pp.25-43

Al-Faruqi, 'Islam and labor', in *Towards Islamic Labour and Unionism* (Cairo and Geneva: The International Islamic Confederation of Labour, 1988), pp.11-58

Al-Faruqi, 'Islamic faith and the problem of Israel and Jerusalem', in Salem Azzam, (ed.), *Jerusalem: The Key to World Peace* (London: Islamic Council of Europe, 1980), pp.77-105

Al-Faruqi, 'The role of Islam in global inter-religious dependence', in Warren Lewis, (ed.), *Towards a Global Congress of the World's Religions* (Barrytown, NY: Unification Theological Seminary, 1980), pp.19-53; Reprinted in Ataullah Siddiqui, (ed.), *Ismail Raji al-Faruqi: Islam and Other Faiths* (Leicester: IIIT, 1998), pp.71-108

Al-Faruqi, 'Common bases between the two religions in regard of convictions and points of agreement in the spheres of life', in *Documents and Researches of Seminary [Seminar] of the Islamic-Christian Dialogue* (Tripoli, Libya: Popular Office of Foreign Relations, Socialist Peoples Libyan Arab Jamahiriya, 1981), pp.229-264; Reprinted in Ataullah Siddiqui, (ed.), *Ismail Raji al-Faruqi: Islam and Other Faiths* (Leicester: IIIT, 1998), pp.211-240

Al-Faruqi, 'Da'wah in the West: Promise and trial', Paper presented at the *International Conference of the 15th Century Hijrah*, held at Kuala Lumpur, Malaysia, (24 November – 4 December 1981); Reprinted in Ataullah Siddiqui, (ed.), *Ismail Raji al-Faruqi: Islam and Other Faiths* (Leicester: IIIT, 1998), pp.319-351

Al-Faruqi, 'Divine transcendence and its expression', in Henry O. Thompson, (ed.), *The Global Congress of the World's Religions, Proceedings of 1980-1982 Conference* (Washington, DC: The Global Congress of the World's Religions, Inc., 1982), pp.267-316; Reprinted in Ataullah Siddiqui, (ed.), *Ismail Raji al-Faruqi: Islam and Other Faiths* (Leicester: IIIT, 1998), pp.21-70

Al-Faruqi, 'The nation state and social order in the perspective of Islām', in Isma'il al-Faruqi, (ed.), *Trialogue of the Abrahamic Faiths* (Herndon, VA: IIIT, 1982), pp.49-61

Al-Faruqi, 'Islam and the theory of nature', *Islamic Quarterly*, vol. 26 (1982), pp.16-26

Al-Faruqi, 'Islamization of knowledge: The general principles and the work plan', *Pakistan Journal of History and Culture*, vol. 3, no. 1 (1982), pp.21-69

Al-Faruqi, 'Islamic ideals in North America', in Earle H. Waugh, Baha Abu-Laban and Regula B. Qureshi, (eds.), *The Muslim Community in North America* (Edmonton: University of Alberta Press, 1983), pp.259-270

Al-Faruqi, 'Islam and human rights', *Islamic Quarterly*, no. 27 (1983), pp.12-30

Al-Faruqi, 'Islam and Zionism', in John. L. Esposito, (ed.), *Voices of Resurgent Islam* (New York: Oxford University Press, 1983), pp.261-267

Al-Faruqi, 'Tawhid: The quintessence of Islam', *Journal of South Asian and Middle Eastern Studies*, vol. 8, no. 4 (1985), pp.9-33

Al-Faruqi, 'Meta-Religion: Towards a critical world theology', *American Journal of Islamic Social Sciences*, vol. 3, no. 1 (1986), pp.13-57

Al-Faruqi, 'Self-portrait', *Impact International*, vol. 16, no. 11 (13-26 June, 1986), p.6

Al-Faruqi, 'First principles in the Islamization of knowledge', in Robert D. Crone, (ed.), *Preparing to Islamize America* (Reston, VA: IIIT, 1987)

Al-Faruqi, 'The path of da'wah in the West', *The Muslim World League Journal*, vol. 14, nos. 7-8 (1987), pp.54-62

Al-Faruqi, 'The Islamic critique of the status quo of Muslim society', in Barbara Freyer Stowasser, (ed.), *The Islamic Impulse* (London: Croom Helm, 1987), pp.226-243

Al-Faruqi, 'Towards a critical world theology', in *Toward Islamization of Disciplines* (Herndon, VA: IIIT, 1989), pp.409-453

Al-Faruqi, 'Islamic ethics', in S. Cromwell Crawford, (ed.), *World Religions and Global Ethics* (New York: Paragon House, 1989), pp.212-237

Al-Faruqi, 'Moments of the religious life', in Roger Eastman, (ed.), *The Ways of Religion: An Introduction to the Major Traditions* (New York: Oxford University Press, 1991), pp.428-435

Al-Faruqi, 'The self-perpetuating core of the malaise of ummah', *Islamic Thought and Scientific Creativity*, vol. 4, no. 3 (1993), pp.71-75

Al-Faruqi, 'On the nature of Islamic da'wah', in Don A. Pittman, Rubert C. Habito and Terry C. Muck, (eds.), *Ministry and Theology in Global Perspective: Contemporary Challenges for the Church* (Grand Rapids: Eerdmans, 1996), pp.283-287

Al-Faruqi, 'Contemporary Islamic renaissance and its historical background', in Muhammad Mumtaz Ali, (ed.), *Modern Muslim Movements: Models, Problems and Prospects* (Kuala Lumpur: A.S. Noordeen, 2000), pp.3-17

Al-Faruqi, 'Why Islam?', Islamabad, Pakistan: text of an unpublished audio recording, (International Islamic University, Islamabad, Pakistan, n.d.)

Secondary Sources

Aasi, Ghulam Haider, *Muslim Understanding of Other Religions: An Analytical Study of Ibn Ḥazm's Kitāb al-Faṣl fī al-Milal wa al-Aḥwā' wa al-Niḥal* (Pakistan: IIIT, 1999)

Abbott, Walter, (ed.), *The Documents of Vatican II* (London: Geoffrey Chapman, 1966)

Abbott, Walter and Joseph Gallagher, *The Documents of Vatican II: With notes and Comments by Catholic, Protestant and Orthodox Authorities* (New York: Guild Press, 1966)

'Abduh, Muhammad, *The Theology of Unity* (Translated by Ishaq Musa'ad and Kenneth Cragg), (London: George Allen & Unwin, 1966)

AbuSulayman, 'AbdulHamid, *The Islamic Theory of International Relations: New Directions for Islamic Methodology and Thought* (Herndon, Va.: IIIT, 1987)

Adang, Camilla, *Muslim Writers on Judaism and the Bible: From Ibn Rabban to Ibn Ḥazm* (Leiden: Brill, 1996)

Adnan, Aslan, 'Islam and religious pluralism', *Islamic Quarterly*, vol. 40, no. 3 (1996), pp.172-187

Ahmad, Khurshid, 'A Muslim response', in Joseph Gremillion and William Ryan, (eds.), *World Faiths and the New World Order: A Muslim-Jewish-Christian Search Begins* (Lisbon: The Interreligious Peace Colloquium, 1978), pp.171-193

Ahmed, Akbar S., *Journey into America: The Challenge of Islam* (Washington, D.C.: Brookings Institution Press, 2010).

Akhtar, Shabbir, *The Final Imperative: An Islamic Theology of Liberation* (London: Bellew, 1991)

Akhtar, Shabbir, *A Faith for all Seasons: Islam and Western Modernity* (London: Bellew, 1990)

Akhtar, Shabbir, *The Light in the Enlightenment: Christianity and the Secular Heritage* (London: Grey Seal, 1990)

Al-Albait Foundation, *Religious Pluralism: The 6th Muslim Christian Consultation* (Amman: Al-Albait Foundation, 1989)

Al-'Ani, Salam, 'Faruqi investigation being undermined?', *Islamic Horizons*, vol. 15 (Special issue August-September, 1986), pp.29-30

ADC [American-Arab Anti-Discrimination Committee] Special Report, *The al-Faruqi Murders* (Washington, DC: ADC Research Institute, 1986)

Amin, Ajmad, *Ḍuḥā al-Islām* (al-Qāhirah: Matba'at Lajnat al-Ta'līf wa-al-Tarjamah wa-al-Nashr, 1952)

Anidjar, Gil, *Semites: Race, Religion, Literature* (Stanford, California: Stanford University Press, 2008)

Ansari, Zafar Ishaq, 'Some reflections on Islamic bases for dialogue with Jews and Christians', *JES*, vol. 14, no. 3 (1977), pp.433-447

Ansari, Zafar Ishaq and John L. Esposito, (eds.), *Muslims and the West: Encounter and Dialogue* (Washington, DC: Georgetown University, Center for Muslim-Christian Relations, 2001)

Arkoun, Mohammed, 'New perspectives from Jewish-Christian-Muslim dialogue', *JES*, vol. 26 (1989), pp.523-529; Reprinted in Leonard Swidler, (ed.), *Muslims in Dialogue: The Evolution of a Dialogue* (Lewiston, NY: The Edwin Mellen Press, 1992), pp.343-352

Arnaldez, R., 'Ibn Ḥazm, Abū Muḥammad 'Alī b. Aḥmad b. Sa'īd', *Encyclopaedia of Islam* 2nd Edition, P. Bearman, Th. Bianquis, C. E. Bosworth, E. van Donzel and W. P. Heinrichs, (eds.),Brill, 2007. Brill Online. McGill University. (28 June 2013) <http://referenceworks. brillonline.com/entries/encyclopaedia-of-islam-2/ibn-hazm-COM_0325>

Askari, Hasan, 'Within and beyond the experience of religious diversity', in John Hickand Hasan Askari, (eds.), *The Experience of Religious Diversity* (London: Grover, 1985), pp.191-218

Askari, Hasan, 'The dialogical relationship between Christianity and Islam', *JES*, vol. 9, no. 3 (1972), pp.477-487; Reprinted in Leonard Swidler, (ed.), *Muslims in Dialogue: The Evolution of a Dialogue* (Lewiston, NY: The Edwin Mellen Press, 1992), pp.37-47

Aydın, Ali Arslan, *İslām - Hristiyan Diyaloğu ve İslām'ın Zaferi*. 3rd Baskı (İstanbul: Kültür Basın Yayın Birliği, 1991)

Ayoub, Mahmoud, 'Islam and Christianity between tolerance and acceptance', *ICMR*, vol.2, no. 2 (1991), pp.171-182

Ayoub, Mahmoud, 'The Islamic context of Muslim-Christian relations', in Michael Gervers and Ramzi Jibran Bikhazi, (eds.), *Conversion and continuity: Indigenous Christian communities in Islamic lands eighth to eighteenth centuries* (Toronto: Pontifical Institute of Medieval Studies, 1990), pp.461-472

Ayoub, Mahmoud, 'Islam and Christianity: A study of Muhammad Abduh's views of the two religions', *Humaniora Islamica*, vol. 2 (1974), pp.121-37

Azuma, John, 'The integrity of interfaith dialogue', *ICMR*, vol. 13, no. 3 (2002), pp.269-280

Ba-Yunus, Ilyas, 'Al-Faruqi and beyond: Future directions in Islamization of knowledge', *AJISS*, vol. 5, no.1 (1988), pp.13-28

Beaver, Pierce R., *Ecumenical Beginnings in Protestant World Mission* (New York: Nelson, 1962)

Behloul, Samuel-Martin, *Ibn Hazms Evangelienkritik: Eine Methodische Untersuchung* (Leiden: Brill, 2002)

Al-Biruni, Abu al-Rayhan, *The Chronology of Ancient Nations: An English Version of the Arabic Text of the Āthār-ul-Bākiya of Albiruni, or "Vestiges of the Past"* (Translated by C. Edward Sachau), (London, 1879; repr. Frankfurt M.: Minerva, 1969)

Borrmans, Maurice, 'Recent history of Christian-Muslim dialogue', *Encounter*, nos. 61-62 (January-February 1980), pp.1-23

Borrmans, Maurice, 'The Muslim-Christian dialogue of the last ten years', *Pro Mundi Vita Bulletin*, no. 74 (Sept-Oct, 1978), pp.1-52

Borrmans, Maurice, *Guidelines for Dialogue between Christians and Muslims* (Interreligious Documents I, Pontifical Council for Interreligious Dialogue), (New York: Paulist Press, 1990)

Brand-Ballard, Jeffery, 'Why one basic principle?', *Utilitas*, vol. 19, no. 2 (June 2007), pp.220-242

Braibanti, Ralph, 'A memorial tribute', *Islamic Horizons*, vol. 15 (Special issue August–September, 1986), pp.76-79

Breiner, Bert, 'Christian-Muslim relations: Some current themes', *ICMR*, vol. 21 (1991), pp.77-94

Brogan, A. P., 'Objective pluralism in the theory of value', *International Journal of Ethics*, vol. 41, no. 3 (April 1931), pp.287-295

Brown, Stuart E., (ed.), *Meeting in Faith: Twenty Years of Christian-Muslim Conversations Sponsored by the World Council of Churches* (Geneva: WCC Publications, 1989)

Bruner, Jerome, *Acts of Meaning* (Cambridge: Cambridge University Press, 1990)

Bryant, Darrol M. and S. A. Ali, (eds.), *Muslim-Christian Dialogue: Promise and Problems* (St. Paul, MN: Paragon House, 1998)

Caspar, Rudi, 'Un aspect de la pensée Musulmane moderne: Le renouveau du Mo'tazilisme', *Mélanges Institut Dominicain d'études Orientales du Caire*, vol. 4 (1957), pp.141-202

Castro, Emilio, Khurshid Ahmad, and David Kerr, (eds.), *Christian Mission and Islamic Da'wah: Proceedings of the Chambésy Dialogue Consultation* Leicester: The Islamic Foundation, 1982); Reprinted as 'Proceedings of the Chambésy dialogue Consultation', *International Review of Mission*, vol. 65 (October, 1976), pp.391-406

Cook, Michael, *Commanding Right and Forbidding Wrong in Islamic Thought* (Cambridge: Cambridge University Press, 2000)

Cotter, James P., (ed.) *The Word in the Third World* (Washington, DC: Corpus Books, 1968)

Cragg, Kenneth, 'Ismā'īl al-Fārūqī in the field of dialogue', in Yvonne Yazbeck Haddad and Wadi Z. Haddad, (eds.), *Christian-Muslim Encounters* (Florida: University Press of Florida, 1995), pp.399-410

Cragg, Kenneth, 'Isma'il al-Faruqi', in *Troubled by Truth: Life-Studies in Inter-Faith Concern* (Edinburgh: The Pentland Press Ltd., 1992), pp.127-146 and 290-292

Cragg, Kenneth, 'A lantern on the stern', in *Troubled by Truth: Life-Studies in Inter-Faith Concern* (Edinburgh: The Pentland Press Ltd., 1992), pp.262-277, 304f

Crone, Patricia, 'Post-Colonialism in tenth-century Islam', *Der Islam*, vol. 83, no. 1 (2006), pp.2-38

Curry, Oliver, 'Who's afraid of the naturalistic fallacy?', *Evolutionary Psychology*, vol. 4 (2006), pp.234-247

Dennett, Daniel, *Elbow Room: Varieties of Free Will worth Wanting* (Cambridge: MIT Press, 1990), pp.74-100

Dio, Abdur Rahman, *Non-Muslims under Shariah* (London: Taha Publishers, 1983)

Duran, Khalid, 'Muslims and non-Muslims', in Leonard Swidler, (ed.), *Muslims in Dialogue: The Evolution of a Dialogue* (Lewiston, NY: The Edwin Mellen Press, 1992), pp.87-109

Dye, Eric R., *The Apologetic Methods of Isma'il al-Faruqi and Cornelius van Til* (Unpublished M.A. Thesis), (School of Oriental and African Studies, University of London, 2000)

Eck, Diana, 'What do we mean by dialogue?', *Current Dialogue*, vol. 11 (1986), pp.5-15

Ekkehard, Rudolph, 'Muslim approaches towards Islamic-Christian dialogue: Three decades in retrospect', in Lutz Edzard and Christian Szyska, (eds.), *Encounters of Words and Texts: Intercultural Studies in Honor of Stefan Wild* (Hildesheim: Georg Olms, 1997), pp.149-158

Ellis, Kail C., (ed.) *The Vatican, Islam, and the Middle East* (Syracuse, NY: Syracuse University Press, 1987)

Esposito, John L., 'Ismail al-Faruqi: Pioneer in Muslim-Christian relations', in John L. Esposito and John O. Voll, (eds.), *Makers of Contemporary Islam* (New York: Oxford, 2001), pp.23-38

Esposito, John L. and John O. Voll, 'Khurshid Ahmad: Muslim activist-economist', in John L. Esposito and John O. Voll, (eds.) *Makers of Contemporary Islam* (New York: Oxford, 2001), pp.39-53

Esposito, John L., S.v. 'Fārūqī, Ismāʿīl Rājī al', *Oxford Encyclopedia of the Modern Islamic World* (John L. Esposito editor in Chief) (New York and Oxford: Oxford University Press, 1995)

Esposito, John L., 'Ismail R. al-Faruqi: Muslim scholar-activist', in Yvonne Yazbeck Haddad, (ed.), *The Muslims of America* (New York: Oxford University Press, 1991), pp.65-79

Esposito, John L., 'Teaching Islam the old fashioned way-living it!', *Islamic Horizons*, vol. 15 (Special issue August-September, 1986), pp.49-51

Esposito, John L., *Islam and Development: Religion and Socio-Political Change* Syracuse, (New York: Syracuse University Press, 1980)

Esposito, John L. and Haddad Yvonne Yazbeck, (eds.), *Muslims on the Americanization Path?* (New York: Oxford University Press, 2000)

Etherington, Norman, 'Introduction', in Norman Etherington, (ed.), *Missions and Empire* (Oxford: Oxford University Press, 2005), pp.1-18

al-Faruqi, Maysam, 'Tawhid: The measure of a life', *Islamic Horizons*, vol. 15 (Special issue August–September, 1986), p.47

Fitzgerald, M.L., 'Muslim-Christian consultation (July 1972)', *Encounters*, no. 1 (January 1974), pp.1-16

Fitzmaurice, Redmond, 'The Roman Catholic Church and inter-religious dialogue: Implications for Christian-Muslim relations', *ICMR*, vol. 3, no. 1 (1992), pp.83-107

Fitzmaurice, Redmond, 'Twenty-five years of dialogue: The Pontifical council for inter-religious Dialogue', *Islamochristiana*, vol. 15 (1989), pp.109-120

Fletcher, Charles, *The Methodology of Abdolkarim Soroush: A preliminary study* (Islamic Research Institute, Islamabad. Occasional Papers, no. 70), 2006; Originally published in *Islamic Studies* vol. 44, no. 4, (2005), pp.527-552

Ford, F. Peter, 'Isma'il al-Faruqi on Muslim-Christian dialogue: An analysis from a Christian perspective', *ICMR*, vol. 4, no. 2 (1993), pp.268-282

Frankena, William K., 'The naturalistic fallacy', *Mind*, New Series, vol. 48, no. 192 (October, 1939), pp.464-477

Frankfurt, Harry, 'Identification and externality', in Amélie Rorty, (ed.), *The Identities of Persons* (Berkley and Los Angeles: University of California Press, 1976), pp.239-252

Freeman, Mark, *Rewriting the Self: History, Memory, Narrative* (London: Routledge, 1993)

Freidmann, Yohanan, *Tolerance and Coercion in Islam: Interfaith Relations in the Muslim Tradition* (Cambridge, UK: Cambridge University Press, 2003)

Gaudeul, Jean-Marie, *Encounters and Clashes: Islam and Christianity in History*, 2 Vols. (Rome: Pontifical Institute for Arabic and Islamic Studies, 1984)

Gauhar, Altaf, *The Challenge of Islam* (London: The Islamic Council of Europe, 1978)

Geisler, Norman L., *Christian Apologetics* (Grand Rapids, MI: Baker, 1976)

Geisler, Norman L. and Paul D. Feinberg, *Introduction to Philosophy* (Grand Rapids, MI: Baker, 1980)

Ghamari-Tabrizi, Behrooz, 'Loving America and longing for home: Ismail al-Faruqi and the emergence of the Muslim diaspora in North America', *International Migration*, vol. 42, no. 2 (2004), pp.61-86

Gillet, Grant, 'Schechtman's narrative account of identity', *Philosophy, Psychiatry and Psychology*, vol. 12, no.1 (2005), pp.23-24

Gimaret, D., 'Mu'tazila', *Encyclopaedia of Islam*. 2nd edition. P. Bearman, Th. Bianquis, C. E. Bosworth, E. van Donzel and W. P. Heinrichs, (eds.), (Brill, 2008) Brill Online. McGill University. (28 June 2013) <http://referenceworks.brillonline.com/entries/encyclopaedia-of-islam-2/mutazila-COM_0822>

Goddard, Hugh, 'Christian-Muslim relations: A look backwards and a look forward', *ICMR*, vol. 11, no. 2 (July 2000), pp.195-212

Goddard, Hugh, *A History of Christian-Muslim Relations* (Edinburgh: Edinburgh University Press, 2000)

Goddard, Hugh, *Muslim Perceptions of Christianity* (London: Grey Seal, 1996)

Gremillion, Joseph, (ed.), *Food/Energy and the Major Faiths* (Maryknoll, NY: Orbis Books, 1978)

Gremillion, Joseph and William F. Ryan, (eds.), *World Faiths and the New World Order: A Muslim-Jewish-Christian Search Begins* (Washington: Interreligious Peace Colloquium, 1978)

Haddad, Yvonne Yazbeck, 'The dynamics of identity in North America', in John L. Esposito and Yvonne Yazbeck Haddad, (eds.), *Muslims on the Americanization Path?* (New York: Oxford University Press, 2000), pp.19-46

Haddad, Yvonne Yazbeck and I. Qurqmaz, 'Muslims in the West: A select bibliography', *ICMR,* vol. 11, no.1 (2000), pp.5-49

Haddad, Yvonne Yazbeck, 'Islamist depictions of Christianity in the twentieth century: The pluralism debate and the depiction of the other', *ICMR*, vol. 7, no. 1 (1996), pp.75-93

Haddad, Yvonne Yazbeck, 'A tenth-century speculative theologian's refutation of the basic doctrines of Christianity: Al-Bāqillānī (d. A.D. 1013)', in Yvonne Yazbeck Haddad & Wadi Z. Haddad, (eds.), *Christian-Muslim Encounters* (Florida: University Press of Florida, 1995), pp.82-94

Haddad, Yvonne Yazbeck, 'Muhammad Abduh: Pioneer of Islamic reform', in Ali Rahnema, (ed.), *Pioneers of Islamic Revival* (London: Zed Books, 1994, 2005), pp.30-63

Haddad, Yvonne Yazbeck and A. Lummis, *Islamic values in the US* (New York: Oxford, 1987)

Haddad, Yvonne Yazbeck, 'Muslims in America: A select bibliography', *Muslim World*, vol. 76 (1986), pp.93-122

Haines, Byron L. and Frank L. Cooley, (eds.), *Christians and Muslims Together: An Exploration by Presbyterians* (Philadelphia: Geneva Press, 1987)

Haleem, Amer A., 'Muslim America–on the threshold', *Islamic Horizons*, vol. 15 (Special issue August-September, 1986), pp.52-54

Hammad, Ahmad Zaki, 'The seeds of violence', *Islamic Horizons*, vol. 15 (Special issue August–September, 1986), p.84

Hanafi, Hasan, *Religious Dialogue and Revolution: Essays on Judaism, Christianity and Islam* (Cairo: Anglo Egyptian Bookshop, 1977)

Hartmann, Nicolai, *Ethics*. 3 vols. (Translated by Stanton Loit), (London: Allen, 1932)

Hartmann, Nicolai, *New Ways of Ontology* (Translated by Reinhard C. Kuhn), (Chicago: Henry Regency, 1952)

Heinimaa, Markus L.A., 'Past personal identity', *Philosophy, Psychiatry and Psychology*, vol. 12, no.1 (2005), pp.25-26

Huda, Qamar-ul, 'The 40th anniversary of Vatican II: Examining *Dominus Iesus*, and contemporary issues for inter-religious dialogue between Muslims and Catholics', *ICMR*, vol. 15, no. 3 (2004), pp.331-347

Hume, David, *A Treatise of Human Nature* (Edited with an introduction by Ernest C. Mossner), (New York: Penguin Books, 1985, c1969)

Impact International, 'Prof. and Mrs. Ismail Faruqi–first degree premeditated Murders', *Impact International*, vol. 16, no. 11 (13-26 June, 1986), pp.5-6

Islamic Horizons, 'The Faruqis' assassination, what does it mean for Muslim America?', *Islamic Horizons*, vol. 15 (Special issue August-September, 1986), pp.13-18

Islamic Horizons, 'Dr. Lamya' al-Faruqi: The woman behind the man (1926-1986)', *Islamic Horizons*, vol. 15 (Special issue August-September, 1986), p.19

Islamic Horizons, 'A Glance at the life of Isma'il R. al-Faruqi (1921-1986)', *Islamic Horizons*, vol. 15 (Special issue August-September, 1986), p.21

Islamic Horizons, 'Faruqi killings spark response', *Islamic Horizons*, vol. 15 (Special issue August–September, 1986), pp.22-23

ISNA, 'Memorial convocation: Isma'il Raji al Faruqi, Lois Lamya' al Faruqi', (Washington: ISNA, September 26, 1986)

Izutsu, Toshihiko, *Ethico-Religious Concepts in the Qur'ān* (Montreal: McGill University Press, 1966)

Jay, Douglas C., 'Review of *Christian Ethics*', in *Canadian Journal of Theology*, vol. 14 (1968), pp.287-290

Johnson, Steve, 'On justifying the good, a glimpse at Isma'il al-Faruqi's doctoral dissertation', *Islamic Horizons*, vol. 15 (Special issue August-September, 1986), pp.69-71

Johnstone, Penelope, 'An Islamic perspective on dialogue: Articles from Islamic Journals', *Islamochristiana*, vol. 13 (1987), pp.131-171

Kashif, G. N., 'Al-Faruqi's memorial: A tribute', *Islamic Horizons*, vol. 16 (November 1986), p.5

Kateregga, Badru D. and David W. Shenk, *A Muslim and a Christian in Dialogue* (Scottdale, PA: Herald Press, 1997)

Kerr, David A., 'Islamic da'wa and Christian mission: Towards a comparative analysis', *International Review of Mission*, vol. 89, no. 353 (2000), pp.150-171

Khalid, Detlev, 'Some aspects of neo-Mu'tazilism', *Islamic Studies*, vol. 8, no. 4 (December, 1969), pp.319-348

Khan, Mohommed A. Muqtedar, 'Constructing the American Muslim community', in Yvonne Yazbeck Haddad, Jane I. Smith, and John L. Esposito, (eds.), *Religion and Immigration: Christian, Jewish, and Muslim Experience* (New York: Altamida Press, 2003), pp.175-198

Khan, Mohommed A. Muqtedar, 'Muslim and identity politics in America', in John L. Esposito and Yvonne Yazbeck Haddad, (eds.), *Muslims on the Americanization Path?* (New York: Oxford University Press, 2000), pp.87-101

Kiekegaard, Søren, *Fear and Trembling* (Translated by Walter Lowrie), (Princeton: Princeton University Press, 1968)

Kimball, Charles, *Striving Together: A Way Forward in Christian-Muslim Relations* (Maryknoll, New York: Orbis Books, 1991)

Köylü, Mustafa, 'A common human agenda for Christians and Muslims', in Mustafa Köylü, J. Dudley Woodberry and Osman Zümmit, (eds.), *Muslim and Christian Reflections on Peace: Divine and Human Dimensions* (Lanham: University of America Press, 2005), pp.102-115

Lazarus-Yafeh, Hava, 'Taḥrīf', *Encyclopaedia of Islam.* 2nd edition. P. Bearman, Th. Bianquis, C. E. Bosworth, E. van Donzel and W. P. Heinrichs, (eds.), (Brill, 2008). Brill Online. McGill University. (29 June 2013) <http://referenceworks.brillonline.com/entries/encyclopaedia-of-islam-2/tahrif-SIM_7317>

Lewis, Warren, (ed.), *Towards a Global Congress of World's Religions: Conference Proceedings at San Francisco, Barrytown, Bristol* (Barrytown, NY: Unification Theological Seminary, 1978)

Lewis, Warren, (ed.), *Towards a Global Congress of the World's Religions: Conference Proceedings at Boston* (Barrytown, NY: Unification Theological Seminary, 1979)

Lewis, Warren, (ed.), *Towards a Global Congress of the World's Religions: Conference Proceedings at Los Angeles* (Barrytown, NY: Unification Theological Seminary, 1980)

Locke, John, *An Essay Concerning Human Understanding* (Edited by Peter H. Nidditch), (Oxford: Clarendon Press, 1979, first published in 1690)

Malik, Hafez, 'Review of *On Arabism*', *The Muslim World*, vol. 53 (1963), pp.337-338

MacIntyre, Alasdair, 'The virtues, the unity of a human life, and the concept of a tradition', in Stanley Hauerwas and L. Gregory Jones, (eds.), *Why Narrative* (Grand Rapids, MI: Eerdmans, 1989), pp.89-111

Marshall, D., *Isma'īl Faruqi and Christianity* (Unpublished MA Thesis), (University of Birmingham, 1988)

Martin, Richard C., Mark R. Woodward and Dwi S. Atmaja, *Defenders of Reason in Islam* (Oxford: Oneworld, 1997)

McAuliffe, Jane Dammen, *Qur'anic Christians: An Analysis of Classical and Modern Exegesis* (Cambridge: Cambridge University Press, 1991)

Meland, Bernard E., 'In response to Dr. Faruqi', *Numen*, no. 12 (1965), pp.87-95

Michel, Thomas, 'Social and religious factors affecting Muslim-Christian relations', *ICMR*, vol. 8, no. 1 (1995), pp.53-66

Mohammed, O. N., *Muslim-Christian Relations: Past, Present, Future* (Maryknoll, NY: Orbis, 1999)

Moore, G. E., *Principia Ethica* Rev. ed., (Edited and with an introduction by Thomas Baldwin), (Cambridge: Cambridge University Press, 1993)

Mooreland, J. P. and William Lane Craig, *Philosophical Foundations for a Christian Worldview* (Downers Grove, IL: IVP, 2003)

Mulder, Dick, 'Developments in dialogue with Muslims: World Council of Churches', in G. Speelman, J. van Lin and D. Mulder, (eds.), *Muslims and Christians in Europe: Breaking New Ground* (Kampen: Uitgeverij Kok, 1993), pp.153-161

Murad, Khurram, *Da'wah among Non-Muslims in the West: Some Conceptual and Methodological Aspects* (Leicester: The Islamic Foundation, 1986)

Murad, Khurram, *Islamic Movement in the West* (London: The Islamic Foundation, 1981)

Muroeh, Husayn, *Al-Naza'āt al-Māddiyya fī al-Falsafa al-'Arabiyya al-Islāmiyya* (Material Tendencies in Arab-Islamic Philosophy) 2 vols. (Beirut: Dār al-Fārābī, 1988)

Nasseef, Abdallah Omar, 'Muslim-Christian relations: The Muslim approach', *Journal of Muslim Minority Affairs*, vol. 7 (1986), pp.27-31

Nasr, Seyyed Hossein, 'Intellectual autobiography of Seyyed Hossein Nasr', in Lewis Edwin Hahn, Randall E. Auxier and Lucien W. Stone, (eds.), *The Philosophy of Seyyed Hossein Nasr* (Chicago and La Salle, IL: OpenCourt, 2001), pp.3-85

Nasr, Seyyed Hossein, 'Reply to Enes Karić', in Lewis Edwin Hahn, Randall E. Auxier and Lucien W. Stone, (eds.), *The Philosophy of Seyyed Hossein Nasr* (Chicago and La Salle, IL: OpenCourt, 2001), pp.792-797

Nasr, Seyyed Hossein, 'Islamic-Christian dialogue: Problems and obstacles to be pondered and Overcome', *ICMR*, vol. 11, no. 2 (2000), pp.213-227

Nasr, Seyyed Hossein, 'Comments on a few theological issues in the Islamic-Christian dialogue', in Yvonne Yazbeck Haddad and Wadi Z. Haddad, (eds.), *Christian-Muslim Encounters* (Florida: University Press of Florida, 1995), pp.457-467

Nasr, Seyyed Hossein, 'The essence of Dr. Faruqi's life work', *Islamic Horizons*, vol. 15 (Special issue August–September, 1986), p.26

Nasr, Seyyed Hossein, 'Response to Hans Jung's paper on Christian Muslim dialogue', *Muslim World*, vol. 77 (1987), p.105

Nasr, Seyyed Hossein, *Traditional Islam in the Modern World* (London: Routledge, 1981)

Nasr, V. R., *Islamization of Knowledge: A Critical Review* (Islamabad, Pakistan: IIIT, 1992)

National Council of Churches, *Newsletter of the task force on Christian-Muslim relations*, no. 2 (March 1978), pp.1-2

Nawwab, Isma'il Ibrahim, 'Muslims and the West in history', in Zafar Ishaq Ansari and John L. Esposito, (eds.), *Muslims and the West: Encounter and Dialogue* (Washington, DC: Georgetown University, Center for Muslim-Christian Relations, 2001), pp.1-51

New International Version of the Bible, (*NIV*) (Grand Rapids, MI: Zondervan, 1973, 1978, 1984)

Newman, N. A., (ed.), *Early Christian-Muslim Dialogue* (Hatfield, PA: Interdisciplinary Biblical Research Institute, 1993)

Nielsen, Jorgen S., (ed.), *The Christian-Muslim Frontier: Chaos, Clash or Dialogue?* (London:I.B.Tauris Publishers, 1988)

Noonan, Harold, *Personal Identity* (London: Routledge, 1991)

Olender, Maurice, *The Languages of Paradise: Race, Religion and Philology in the Nineteenth Century* (Translated by Arthur Goldhammer), (Cambridge, MA: Harvard University Press, 1992); Originally published as *Les langues du paradis: Aryens et Sémites, un couple providentiel* (Paris: Gallimard le Seuil, 1989)

Omar, Irfan, (ed.), *A Muslim View of Christianity: Essays on Dialogue by Mahmoud Ayoub* (Maryknoll, NY: Orbis Books, 2007)

Parfit, Derek, *Reasons and Persons* (Oxford: Clarendon Press, 1984)

Perry, John, 'The Importance of being identical', in Amélie Rorty, (ed.), *The Identities of Persons* (Berkley and Los Angeles: University of California Press, 1976), pp.67-90

Perry, John, 'Can the self divide?', *The Journal of Philosophy*, vol. 69, no. 16 (September 7, 1972), pp.463-488

Perry, John, 'The problem of personal identity', in John Perry, (ed.), *Personal Identity* (Berkley and Los Angeles: University of California Press, 1975), pp.3-12

Plato and Aristophanes, *Four texts on Socrates: Plato's Euthyphro, Apology, and Crito, and Aristophanes' Clouds* (Translated with notes by Thomas G. West and Grace Starry West), (Introduction by Thomas G. West), (Ithaca, NY: Cornell University Press, 1998)

Porter, Andrew, *Religion versus Empire? British Protestant Missionaries and Overseas Expansion, 1700-1914* (Manchester, UK: Manchester University Press, 2004)

Poston, Larry, *Islamic Da'wah in the West* (New York: Oxford University Press, 1992)

Pratt, Douglas, *The Challenge of Islam: Encounter in Interfaith Dialogue* (Burlington, VT: Ashgate, 2005)

Pratt, Douglas, 'Phenomenology and dialogue: A methodological consideration', *ICMR*, vol. 5, no. 1 (1994), pp.5-13

Proceedings Tripoli Seminar, *Seminar of the Islamic-Christian Dialogue, Tripolis 1-5 February 1976* (Tripolis: Libyan Popular Office of Foreign Relations, 1981)

Quraishi, M. Tariq, *Ismail al-Faruqi: An Enduring Legacy* (Plainfield, IN: The Muslim Students Association, 1987)

Quraishi, M. Tariq, 'The legacy of Isma'il al-Faruqi', *Islamic Horizons*, vol. 15 (Special issue August–September, 1986), pp.32-34

Qureshi, R.B., 'In memorium: Lois Lamya Ibsen al-Faruqi (1927-1986)', *Ethnomusicology*, vol. 32, no. 2 (1988), pp.93-96

Rahman, Fazlur, 'Palestine and my experiences with the young Fārūqī, 1958-1963', *Islamic Horizons*, vol. 15 (Special issue August-September, 1986), pp.39-42

Rahman, Fazlur, 'Law and ethics in Islam', in Richard G. Hovannisian *Ethics in Islam* (Malibu, CA: Undena Publications, 1983), pp.3-15

Ramadan, Tariq, *Western Muslims and the future of Islam* (Oxford; New York: Oxford University Press, 2004)

Recognize the Spiritual Bonds which Unite Us: 16 Years of Christian-Muslim Dialogue (Vatican City: Pontifical Council for Interreligious Dialogue, 1994)

Renan, Ernest, *Studies in Religious History: History of the People of Israel and Religions of Antiquity* (London: Mathieson & Co., 1895)

Renan, Ernest, 'Nouvelles considérations sur le caractère general des peoples sémitiques, et en particulier sur leur tendance au monothéisme', *Journal Asiatique* (1859), pp. 214-282 and 417-450

Renan, Ernest, *Histoire générale et system comparé des langages sémitiques* (Paris: Calmann-Lévy, 1877)

Renan, Ernest, *Oeuvres complètes* 10 vols., H. Psichari, (ed.), (Paris: Calmann-Lévy, 1947-1961)

Sachedina, Abdulaziz, 'Islamic theology of Christian-Muslim relations', *ICMR*, vol. 8, no. 1 (1997), pp.27-38

Safi, L., 'The quest for Islamic methodology: The Islamization of knowledge project in its second decade', *AJISS*, vol. 10, no. 1 (1993), pp.23-48

Sailhamer, John L., *Genesis* in *The Expositor's Bible Commentary* vol. 2, (general editor Frank E. Gaebelein), (Grand Rapids, MI: Zondervan, 1990)

Salam, Halide, 'Lamya': A tribute to a friend', *Islamic Horizons*, vol. 15 (Special issue August–September, 1986), pp.45-46

Samartha, Stanley J., (ed.) *Christian-Muslim Dialogue, Papers from Broumanna, 1972* (Geneva: WCC, 1973)

Sardar, Ziaudin, 'The ethical connection: Christian-Muslim relations in a post modern age', *ICMR*, vol. 2, no. 1 (1991), pp.56-76

Sartre, John-Paul, *Being and Nothingness* (New York: Washington Square Press, 1956)

Schechtman, Marya, 'Personal identity and the past', *Philosophy, Psychiatry and Psychology*, vol. 12, no.1 (2005), pp.9-22

Schechtman, Marya, *The Constitution of Selves* (Ithaca, NY: Cornell University Press, 1996)

Scheler, Max, *On the Eternal Man* (Translated by Bernard Noble), (London: SCM Press, 1960)

Scheler, Max, *Man's Place in Nature* (Translated and introduction by Hans Meyerhoff), (Boston: Beacon Press, 1961)

Scheler, Max, *Formalism in Ethics and non-Formal Ethics of Value: A New Attempt Toward the Foundation of an Ethical Personalism* 5th revised edition (Translated by Manfred S. Frings and Roger L. Funk), (Evanston: Northwestern University Press, 1973)

Schoun, F., *Christianity/Islam – Essays on Esoteric Ecumenism* (Translated by G. Polit), (Bloomington, IN: World Wisdom Books, 1989)

Seminary [Seminar] of the Islamic-Christian Dialogue, [Documents and Researches of] (Tripoli, Libya: Popular Office of Foreign Relations, Socialist Peoples Libyan Arab Jamahiriya, 1981)

Seminar of the Islamic-Christian Dialogue (Tripoli, Libya: 1976). *Buhūth wa-wathi'iq Nadwat al-Hiwār al-Islāmī al-Masīhī*, [Tripoli], (al-Jamāhīriyyah al-ʿArabiyyah al-Lībiyyah al-Shaʿbiyyah al-Ishtirākiyyah: Maktab Ittiṣāl al-Khārijī li-Muʾtamar al-Shaʿb al-ʿĀmm, 1991)

Seminar of the Islamic-Christian Dialogue (Tripoli, Libya: 1976). *İslâm-Hristiyan diyaloğu ve İslâm'ın Zaferi* 3rd baskı (Translated by Ali Arslan Aydın), (İstanbul: Kültür Basın Yayın Birliği, 1991)

Shafiq, Muhammad, 'Islamization of knowledge: Philosophy and methodology and analysis of the view and ideas of Isma'il al-Faruqi, Seyyed Hossein Nasr and Fazlur Rahman', *Hamdard Islamicus*, vol.18, no.3 (1995), pp.63-75

Shafiq, Muhammad, *Growth of Islamic Thought in North America: Focus on Isma'il Raji al Faruqi* (Brentwood, MD: Amana Publications, 1994)

Shafiq, Muhammad, 'Trilogue of the Abrahamic faiths - guidelines for Jewish, Christian and Muslim Dialogue: Analysis of the views of Isma'il R. al-Faruqi', *Hamdard Islamicus*, vol. 15 (1992), pp.59-74

Shafiq, Muhammad and Mohammed Abu-Nimer, *Interfaith Dialogue: A Guide for Muslims'* (Herndon, VA: IIIT, 2007)

Sharon, Moshe, *Judaism, Christianity and Islam: Interaction and Conflict* (Johannesburg: Sacks, 1989)

Shihab, Alwi, 'Christian-Muslim relations into the twenty-first century', *ICMR*, vol. 15, no. 1 (2004), pp.65-77

Siddiqui, Ataullah, *Christian-Muslim Dialogue in the Twentieth Century* (New York: Palgrave Macmillan, 1997)

Siddiqui, Ataullah, 'Ismail R. al-Faruqi: From 'Urubah to Ummatic concerns', *AJISS*, vol. 16, no. 3 (1999), pp.1-26

Siddiqui, Ataullah, (ed.) *Ismail Raji al-Faruqi: Islam and Other Faiths* (Leicester: International Institute of Islamic Thought, 1998)

Siddiqui, Muzammil H., 'Isma'il al-Fārūqī's methodology in comparative religion', *Islamic Horizons*, vol. 15 (Special issue August-September, 1986), pp.81-82

Smith, Jane I., *Muslims, Christians and the Challenge of Interfaith Dialogue* (New York: Oxford University Press, 2007)

Smith, Jane I., 'Muslims as partners in interfaith encounter', in Zahid H. Bukhari, Sulayman S. Nyang, Mumtaz Ahmad and John L. Esposito, (eds.), *Muslims' Place in the American Public Square* (Walnut Creek, CA: AltaMira Press, 2004), pp.165-197

Smith, Wilfred Cantwell, *The Meaning and End of Religion: A New Approach to the Religious Traditions of Mankind* (New York: Macmillan Company, 1963)

Smith, Wilfred Cantwell, 'Comparative religion: Whither - and why?', in Willard G. Oxtoby, (ed.), *Religious Diversity: Essays by Wilfred Cantwell Smith* (New York: Harper and Row Publishers, 1976), pp.138-157

Smith, Wilfred Cantwell, *On Understanding Islam* (The Hague: Mouton, 1981)

Smith, Wilfred Cantwell, 'Some similarities and some differences between Christianity and Islām', in Wilfred Cantwell Smith, *On Understanding Islam* (The Hague: Mouton, 1981), pp.233-246

Sodiq, Yushau, 'Teaching Islamic studies at American universities', in *Proceedings of the First Annual Symposium of the Institute of Islamic & Arabic Sciences in America* (Virginia: IIASA, 1993), pp.21-24

Somerville, Margaret, *The Ethical Imagination: Journeys of the Human Spirit* (Toronto: Anansi Press Inc., 2006)

Somerville, Margaret, *The Ethical Canary: Science, Society, and the Human Spirit* (Toronto: Penguin, 2000)

Sperber, Jutta, *Christians and Muslims: The Dialogue Activities of World Council of Churches and their Theological Foundation* (Berlin and New York: Walter de Gruyter, 2000)

Stenberg, Leif, *The Islamization of Science* (Lund: Lunds Universitet, 1996)

Swidler, Leonard, (ed.), *Muslims in Dialogue: The Evolution of a Dialogue* (Lewiston, NY: The Edwin Mellen Press, 1992)

Taji-Farouki, Suha, 'Muslim-Christian cooperation in the twenty-first century: Some global challenges and strategic responses', *ICMR*, vol. 11, no. 2 (2000), pp.167-193

Talbi, Mohammed, 'Possibilities and conditions for a better understanding between Islam and the West', in Leonard Swidler, (ed.), *Muslims in Dialogue: The Evolution of a Dialogue* (Lewiston, NY: The Edwin Mellen Press, 1992), pp.111-153

Talbi, Mohammed, 'A community of communities: The right to be different and the ways of harmony', in John Hick and Hasan Askari, (eds.), *The Experience of Religious Diversity* (London: Grover, 1985), pp.66-90

Talbi, Mohammed, 'Islam and dialogue: Some reflections on a current topic', *Encounter*, no. 11-12 (January-February, 1975), pp.1-19; Reprinted in Richard W. Rousseau, (ed.), *Christianity and Islam: The Struggling Dialogue* (Scranton, PA: Ridge Row Press, 1985), pp.53-73

Talbi, Mohammed, 'Islam-Christian encounter today: Some principles', *MECC Perspectives*, no. 4-5 (July/August, 1985), pp.7-11

Taylor, Charles, *The Sources of the Self* (Cambridge, MA: Harvard University Press, 1989)

Taylor, Charles, 'Responsibility for the self', in Amélie Rorty, (ed.), *The Identities of Persons* (Berkley and Los Angeles: University of California Press, 1976), pp.281-324

Troll, Christian W., 'Catholic teachings on interreligious dialogue: Analysis of some recent official documents, with special reference to Christian-Muslim relations', in Jacques Waardenburg, (ed.), *Muslim-Christian Perceptions of Dialogue Today.* (Leuven: Peeters, 2000), pp.233-275

Ushenko, Andrew Paul, *The Field Theory of Meaning* (Ann Arbor: University of Michigan, 1958)

Von Denfler, Ahmad, *Some Reflections on Dialogue between Christians and Muslims* (Leicester: The Islamic Foundation, 1989)

Von Denfler, Ahmad, *Dialogue between Christians and Muslims* 3 vols. (Leicester: The Islamic Foundation, 1980-84)

Waardenburg, Jacques, *Muslim and Others: Relations and Context* (Berlin and New York: Walter de Gruyter, 2003)

Waardenburg, Jacques, (ed.) *Muslim-Christian Perceptions of Dialogue Today* (Leuven: Peeters, 2000)

Waardenburg, Jacques, 'Muslims and Christians: Changing identities', *ICMR*, vol. 11, no. 2 (2000), pp. 149-162

Waardenburg, Jacques, (ed.), *Islam and Christianity: Mutual Perceptions since the mid-20th Century* (Leuven: Peeters, 1998)

Waardenburg, Jacques, 'Critical issues in Muslim-Christian relations', *ICMR*, vol. 8, no. 1 (1997), pp.9-26

Waardenburg, Jacques, 'Migrants and minorities: Religion as a factor in identity', in *Specificities and Universality: Problems of Identities. Report of the seminar held in Klingenthal (France), June 23-25, 1994.* Driss Dadsi. (Strasbourg: Council of Europe Press, 1995), pp.47-56

Waardenburg, Jacques, (ed.), *Classical Approaches to the Study of Religion* 2 vols. (The Hague: Mouton, 1973)

Waugh, Earle, Baha Abu-Laban and Regula B. Qureshi, (eds.), *The Muslim Community in North America* (Edmonton: Alberta University Press, 1983)

World Council of Churches Office on Interreligious Relations, 'Documentation: Striving together in dialogue: A Muslim-Christian call to reflection and action', *ICMR*, vol. 12, no. 4 (2001), pp.481-488

World Council of Churches, *Guidelines on Dialogue between Muslims and Christians* (Rome: Liberia Editrice Ancora, 1969)

World Council of Churches, *Christians Meeting Muslims: WCC papers on 10 Years of Christian-Muslim dialogue* (Geneva: WCC, 1977)

World Council of Churches, *Guidelines on Dialogue with People of Living Faiths and Ideologies* (Geneva: WCC, 1979)

Zebiri, Kate, *Muslims and Christians Face to Face* (Oxford: Oneworld, 1997)

Zebiri, Kate, 'Relations between Muslims and non-Muslims in the thought of western-educated Muslim intellectuals', *ICMR*, vol. 6, no. 2 (1995), pp.255-277

INDEX